Enter The Open Door

One Year of Brief Devotions,
each readable in about ten minutes
as part of a closer walk with our Lord and Savior Jesus Christ

Ann Conner

xulon PRESS

Enter The Open Door
One Year of Brief Devotions, each readable in about ten minutes
as part of a closer walk with our Lord and Savior Jesus Christ
by Ann Conner

Printed in the United States of America

ISBN 978-1-60647-803-5

www.xulonpress.com

Dedicated to
our Lord and Savior, Jesus Christ

ACKNOWLEDGMENTS

Many thanks to the Lord for providing all that was needed for this book with joy. Thanks also to my family for their support; to my sisters in Christ, Ginny and Jo, for their prayers and suggestions over the years; and to the others who read portions of the completed text, including Janet, Shirley, Bea, Marie, and Patricia. Many thanks as well to those who helped me learn the ways of the Lord by example as well as by teaching, including my pastors over sixty years (too many to list), and Louise and Daisy, whose prayers and wisdom go ahead of me. Also, many thanks to those whose advice for the project helped the editing and production process go smoothly. May the result be more praise to God for what He is doing.

"Oh, give thanks to the Lord, for He is good! For His mercy endures forever."

Ps. 118:1

INTRODUCTION

By the grace of God, these devotions are offered as reflections of how the Lord leads through times of trial and blessing. (Amazing how those go together!) These lessons are from the battle zone of ordinary life with some extraordinary circumstances. The victory belongs to God. Since I'm still learning many of the lessons and joys, they are intended not as preaching but as insights from someone with much to change, sharing gifts with others also learning much. Many readers will have walked through greater struggles and learned greater lessons, the most important simply to love God and walk humbly with Him, but not all had the time or opportunity to write. Whatever your challenge, may these devotions confirm what the Shepherd is already teaching you and increase your faith to follow Him.

Each devotion can be read in about ten minutes or less, but who can watch the clock and really seek His face? Hopefully, the reader will take more time first to be with the Lord and to rest in Him. There will be times when you can't read, but you can pray from a heart already full of His life, and this is the key to the devotional life—knowing God on a daily basis and drinking the living water of Jesus Christ, ready to overflow at the right time. Through God's Word, He reveals what we cannot know any other way so that in the middle of trouble He is already in the middle of us.

When this book was written, my battle zone included surviving a major car crash followed by months of physical therapy; recovery from cancer and surgery; coping with other family health problems, including Alzheimer's; and major career changes. Most of the second part of the book was completed during six weeks away from home for radiation therapy for cancer, which also provided time to write. No descriptions of the specific problems appear in these pages, but the answers from the Healer apply to all of life. Some of the verses are repeated, but so is truth in daily life. With grateful hearts, our strength is to count it all joy in the Lord who brings us through what gives Him glory!

May God bless you as you seek Him first each day, especially when the impossible is facing you. Rain or shine, seek His face. Follow His Son.

OPEN DOOR

January 1

"If anyone loves Me, he will keep My word; and My Father will love him, and We will come to him and make Our home with him."

John 14:23

If we love someone, it is easy to obey. We will rush to do something to please those we love, and even the most difficult job seems easy if we share it with them. So Christ said those who love Him are able to keep His Word. If we pursue obedience without love first, we miss the mark, even if we obey. How could we follow Christ without love first? We might say, "I must do this. It is expected; it is God's commandment." Yet mental agreement is not the same as love. Without love, our obedience eventually will fall short. Good intentions will not move through the door only love can open. How much of what we do is motivated by pride or hard-bound duty? Yes, discipline is required, but the big changes and the best fruit come from faith that works by love (Gal. 5:6). Love is real work. Love is real warfare and victory. Love is real faith that forms a foundation for every solid gain in Christ.

Nothing can be built to last without love forming the frame for every window and door. It would be possible to know the right design and to assemble all the right materials, but they will never hold together without love that accepts the nails. It is possible to identify the right door and understand how it opens, but we will never go through unless we are filled with the love that obeys and eagerly runs to the Father's heart. By grace, His love draws us through the gift of His Son.

Trust and obedience come through divine love that moves us through the door that only Christ's sacrifice has opened. There is a two-way movement, as we come into the kingdom of His love, and He comes through the Holy Spirit to dwell with us. On the cross, God reached out to us, and through Christ's love, we come to Him. We are moving through that door. Without love-directed obedience, we try to crash through some way on our own, or in our blindness we miss and hit the wall. Only the love that says, "Yes, Lord!" moves through the door in perfect harmony with the love of the Father and the Son that opened the door in the first place and still reaches out to us. Moving in that same stream of Christ's sacrifice, we walk steadily into the heart of our Father's joy.

Father, I want to live with You in Your love. In obedience, bring me through the door of the cross of Jesus Christ, opened in love. In Jesus' name, amen.

John 10:9   John 3:14-17   John 14:15-17

January 2

MAKE US YOUR NEW CREATION

Move us, O Lord God, from who we were into who we are becoming in Jesus Christ. Please make us Your creation and not our own. Change us to live in the future You have planned, not in our past sin and dead ends. Through the Holy Spirit, open us to amazing grace in Christ. Even now, help us to see Your new creation and to walk in it, a little closer to You each day. In Jesus' name, amen.

But God forbid that I should boast except in the cross of our Lord Jesus Christ, by whom the world has been crucified to me, and I to the world. For in Christ Jesus neither circumcision nor uncircumcision avails anything, but a new creation.

Gal. 6:14-15

Col. 3:1-11

PRAY IN ACTION   January 3

"But what do you think? A man had two sons, and he came to the first and said, 'Son, go, work today in my vineyard.' He answered and said, 'I will not,' but afterward he regretted it and went. Then he came to the second and said likewise. And he answered and said, 'I go, sir,' but he did not go. Which of the two did the will of his father?"

Matt. 21:28-31

As much as our words, our actions are prayers. May our entire lives become prayers to the Creator, who is still making us new in Jesus Christ, making us more like His Son. If we pray only in words and never put that faith into action, our prayers are incomplete. The work of our faith life completes the prayers and brings glory to God. What Jesus did on the cross completed His great prayer of John 17, asking for God's glory and His love to be revealed in us in unity with Him, both in this world and the next. Without Jesus' action through the cross and resurrection, praying in His name would be useless. His entire life was a prayer like no other, manifested in teaching and in touching, in healing and in feeding. We are to be like Him, drawing others to Him as much by our daily actions as by our prayers.

Even the best prayers we say are only partial. The Father is listening and looking to see if our actions will complete our words. Whatever we have prayed today, may our lives complete and confirm each prayer. If we went through the entire day praying only in action, without words, what would that prayer say? If our lives years later, minus the words, were to be read as a prayer, what would they say? Humbly, gratefully, we can let simple action complete every prayer. Before you start the words, what is the prayer of your life today?

Father, turn me from my will to Yours, from my plans to the full joy of living for Your glory. May Your love in Jesus Christ be revealed in my actions. In Jesus' name, amen.

John 17:10-23   Matt. 7:21-23   John 15:5-8

THE SHARPENED AX   January 4

Shall the ax boast itself against him who chops with it?

Isa. 10:15

Most of us do not want to live on the edge, particularly a sharp edge. As axes in the Master's hand, we would prefer no grinding, no sharpening. It's safer to be dull, even if the work is a struggle in our own strength and seems to take forever. Yes, we know sharpening would make the work easier and faster, but sharpening also means a decrease in our personal desires and the weight of selfish will. There is a struggle in our own will where we contact the world. At that point of impact, we need a sharp edge to move through the world in Christ's work. We must decrease so the sharpness of His work can increase through the Holy Spirit. This work begins on the ax itself, slowly and carefully, before it's ever applied to anything in the world.

As long as the ax remains in the Master's hand, it will be formed to a readiness that shines more than the most attractive dull ax in the best of circumstances. To be sharp, an ax must lose a lot of its original form to acquire that thin, gleaming blade. In surrender, it submits to gradual grinding and filing to create a really clean edge that can penetrate the thick bark of the world. Our Master will not let the ax be ground away so thin that the work would destroy it, but only to the point where the blade can move through cleanly to penetrate whatever obstacle is ahead.

If it kept most of its old form, your life would be so dull it could not go through the future God has planned. When you experience a decrease in your own form and will, if your life seems to be grinding away, it can also acquire that sharp edge for the work God wants you to do. At the very point of the greatest loss, the ax becomes sharpest. Will you let Him use you to move on through, to cut through the outer layers and get to the heart of His work?

Lord God, use my loss to sharpen me for Your purpose. I surrender my will to Your life and power. In Jesus' name, amen.

Heb. 4:12-16   Rom. 6:11-14   Rom. 5:3-10

January 5

ALWAYS BETTER

The best thing about living in Your will, O God, is that whatever happens, You are always better than any answer or event. You are far more to us than the total of all our hopes and prayers. Your presence is true life. May we seek Your face above all and follow Your heart forever through Your Son. In pure joy, You, Yourself, are our supply and the only source of life. In Jesus' name, amen.

How precious is Your lovingkindness, O God! Therefore the children of men put their trust under the shadow of Your wings. They are abundantly satisfied with the fullness of Your house, and You give them drink from the river of Your pleasures. For with You is the fountain of life; in Your light we see light.

Ps. 36:7-9

John 6:5-14, 28-40

ACCOUNTABLE TO THE BLOOD   January 6

For you were bought at a price; therefore glorify God in your body and in your spirit, which are God's.

1 Cor. 6:20

It is true that our salvation is free, but we are accountable to use that freedom given us in Christ's blood. He saved us from sin, something we cannot do ourselves. He paid the price in full, but we are accountable to His blood to receive that gift and to put it into action in this world. If we receive our freedom and say, "Thank You very much," but then continue to sit in the jail cell and groan, He has opened the door in vain for us. We must get up and praise Him and walk out in the liberty of the new covenant in His blood. That covenant is for this life as well as heaven. A covenant requires the cooperation of both parties. One cannot agree for another, even though He may provide the sacrifice for both. Both must accept the sacrifice and the sealing with blood. In our case, we had no sacrifice acceptable to offer, so Christ became a living sacrifice for us. Now we must live in that sacrifice today, agreeing with God's gift. Will you live accountable to the blood of Christ shed for you personally? Does your life follow His?

If Christ redeems your debts and infuses your bank account with a million dollars, and then you say, "Thank You; I believe it's in there," but never use or claim the treasure, what value is the redemption? When we finally stand before Christ to give account for the abundant salvation He gave us, will we say, "It's still in the bank, still buried, hidden; I just never had time to put it into action"? Free grace is not passive, but active on both sides of the transaction. True freedom works with accountability.

In this case, we are accountable both in action, to follow the way of the cross, and in attitude, to let it change our hearts. Are we accountable to His blood in the thoughts and desires of our hearts? To offer public service is easier than to offer the quiet submission of a joyful heart. It would be better to stay home and rake leaves with joy and a heart inclined to hear the Father than to work hours on some big project for God without any joy in His presence. Because the joy that led Christ to the cross is humanly impossible, it is a mystery of God's grace and power working in us (Heb.12:1-2).

Are we accountable to that mystery that led Christ to the cross and to the fountain that flows from His sacrifice beyond measure? Are we drinking from the cup that He has given us? As stewards of the mysteries of God, we already participate in Christ's riches. Stewards are definitely held accountable. How does your life reveal the power of His blood?

O Lord God, make me accountable to the blood of Your Son, given for me so that I can drink fully of Your cup of salvation with joy. In Jesus' name, amen.

John 15:10-11   1 Cor. 4:1-2   Ps. 116:1-14

ACTION IS THE BEST THEOLOGY   January 7

He answered them, "He who made me well said to me, 'Take up your bed and walk.'"

John 5:11

Action is the best theology. Words and worry can paralyze us. For thirty-eight years, the man at the pool of Bethesda waited for a better opportunity and someone to help him. Jesus told him to put his theology into action now. An explanation is good, but it can get in the way of a living testimony. Instead of sharpening our own intellectual interpretation of the Bible for the sake of human control, we should let the Living Word sharpen our lives, piercing every area like a two-edged sword.

Action comes out of what that sword pierces. While the religious experts discussed the law, Jesus revealed its fullness in all of life. Piercing joints and marrow and the thoughts and intents of the heart, He asked the man at the pool, "Do you want to be made well?" The man offered an explanation. Jesus offered action. It is one thing to study religion, history, or the local customs for healing, but another thing to take up one's bed and walk.

The sick man had waited for someone else to take him to a certain place, while the kingdom of heaven was ready, waiting to be released in faith. What are we waiting for today? If we wait for the right time, the right place, the right understanding, and someone to help us, we wait lamely for the kingdom that could be released in us if we simply obey what Jesus calls us to do now. Listen for His voice. Ask for more faith to do what He tells you. At the moment this man's heart turned to obedience, his healing was complete, his response revealed the power of God, and his action gave glory to the One who makes us all new.

No analysis of the Bible is more important than putting it into action to reveal its true meaning. At first, there may be a quiet wait to hear God's word through the Holy Spirit, but when His word becomes clear to us, we must move. Then God's creative power is revealed beyond any debate or theory. To fully understand and to communicate that understanding to others, we must take up our crosses, take up our beds and walk. We can be in the right place with the right teaching but miss God's power in our lives unless we release ourselves to Him in complete obedience. Whatever He says to you, do it. Rise, take up your bed, and walk!

Father, forgive me for waiting for something or someone else when Your Son has already come to save me. Help me to hear His voice and then rise up to walk now in His power in the place where I am today. In Jesus' name, amen.

John 14:15-17   John 5:1-17   James 2:14-20

January 8

~~~~~~

BEAUTY MORE THAN BEAUTY

Lord God, Your beauty is more than beauty, Your love is more than love, and Your purity is more than purity. Cleanse me so that I can see You above all and follow Your will. Your Son is my only path, my only true wealth and wisdom. May I see Your light and life in Him changing me into His image. In Jesus' name, amen.

"Blessed are the pure in heart, for they shall see God."

Matt. 5:8

Rom. 8:29   Matt. 13:15-23

~~~~~~

ANOINTING OF CHRIST ALONE
January 9

"The Spirit of the Lord is upon Me, because He has anointed Me to preach the gospel to the poor; He has sent Me to heal the brokenhearted."

Luke 4:18

Christ, the Anointed One, comes into our lives to give us the riches of His oil, which surpasses any other. We may try to cover ourselves with an anointing of human goodness and effort, but only the anointing of the King of Kings who died for all and rose again has the power to change us. As Christ, His resurrection light is rubbed into our souls. We need the anointing of Him alone. If we seek the anointing of other things and activities for the approval of men, we won't receive the anointing from God that makes us alive in Him. As oil will not combine with other liquids, His pure anointing won't mix with any other anointing. No dilution of it with other things will allow His love to heal broken hearts and proclaim liberty to the captives and recovery of sight to the blind.

1. **The anointing of Christ alone breaks the power of sin.** As His blood flowed freely for us on the cross, so the anointing of the resurrected Christ flows freely for us now to release us into His life. The anointing of Christ alone, administered by the Holy Spirit, applies the power of His blood directly to our lives. In unity with Him, His life poured out will work in our hearts to bring us to freedom and joy. Whatever is captive in us and around us is released into a sweet, ongoing liberty—the deep peace that passes understanding. Human effort may give an outward image of false peace, but the inner life is hollow, restless, and still subject to evil. The anointing of Christ alone fills every crevice that sin might occupy. Even in suffering, the power that sin holds over us is broken as Christ's anointing covers us, soaks in, and shines out (John 8:12).
2. **The anointing of Christ alone burns with His fire.** Some other anointing will not produce the steady flame of pure love that is ignited in hearts covered with the anointing of Jesus Christ alone. When other things are mixed in, the flame does not burn cleanly and brightly, but if the pure oil of Christ's life is poured on us and we soak in it, there will be enough of Him in us to burn brightly in the fire of His Spirit. This burning of the Holy Spirit brings light, revelation of God's Word, change, and healing to purify His people. His life in us becomes a sweetly burning sacrifice to God (Eph. 5:1-2).
3. **The anointing of Christ alone reflects the glory of God.** The anointing of Christ makes our faces shine, as skin shines when anointed with olive oil to reflect the light that falls upon it. So those who are saturated inwardly can reflect outwardly the glory poured upon us and in us as a witness. Only the anointing of the Light of the World can in turn reflect the holy light of God's glory (2 Cor.3:18—4:6; Matt. 3:11).

Father, cover me in the anointing of Christ alone and light Your fire. In His name, amen.

John 8:36   1 John 2:27   2 Cor. 1:19-22

AT HIS FEET

January 10

And one of them, when he saw that he was healed, returned, and with a loud voice glorified God, and fell down on his face at His feet, giving Him thanks. And he was a Samaritan. So Jesus answered and said, "Were there not ten cleansed? But where are the nine? Were there not any found who returned to give glory to God except this foreigner?" And He said to him, "Arise, go your way. Your faith has made you well."

Luke 17:15-19

At Jesus' feet is the place of worship and surrender to God's power. When we bow down at His feet, we are no longer on our own feet. We are not going anywhere on our own power. It is the only position from which we cannot step away from Him or distance ourselves from His love. Thus it is the only place of complete healing. All ten lepers were healed physically, but perhaps only one received complete healing of mind and spirit with gratitude to our Lord, the shalom of eternity. Many today pray for what they need and call Jesus their Lord and Master, but few take time to fall in gratitude at His feet, giving glory to God for His complete victory in their lives.

At the Lord's feet, all enemies are conquered, even the old enemies of selfishness, death, and doubt. He steps on stiff necks and conquers completely for all to see, as ancient kings did when clear victory was won. It is not enough for our King to hear of His enemies' demise and His victories in us at a distance. He wants them at His feet, as all will ultimately be under His feet in final judgment and glory. Perfection and judgment arrive together in the treading out of the grapes, for the new covenant is sealed in Christ, our Vine. At His feet is the place for pressing out the grapes from the harvest. It is the place of judgment and crushing, separation, and the beginning of new wine, that good wine saved until last. Have you fallen at His feet to drink in His mercy and healing, His judgment and peace, poured out as new wine for you today?

At Your feet, Lord, may I worship You in spirit and in truth, in the purity of Your holiness, and in the pressing out of Your new wine in my life. In Jesus' name, amen.

John 12:3   1 Cor. 15:25-28   John 2:5-10

January 11

~~~~~~

APPROACH ME, DRAW NEAR

Lord God, thank You for loving us enough to call us to draw near. Even today, cause those who are called by Your name, all who will come through the blood of Your Son, to approach You, as we pledge our hearts—not only our minds and the work of our hands but also our hearts—to You. You are our defense and shield. Your Word is our judge and deliverer. Your mercy is our only hope. So we approach You, Father of nations, Ruler of all, as Your humble servants, as the children by adoption through Your Holy Child, Jesus, the only begotten of the Father. We come, draw near, and approach in the love that You gave Him for us.

By His blood, wash our sin away. Heal us and change us into the family You want. We have no other inheritance. We seek no other God but You. Make us the people You have wanted for Your own. For this, we pledge to You our hearts through the cross and our lives through the power of the resurrection of Your Son. You are our God. Make us Your people. In Jesus' name, amen.

"'Then I will cause him to draw near, and he shall approach Me; for who is this who pledged his heart to approach Me?' says the Lord. 'You shall be My people, and I will be your God.'"

Jer. 30:21-22

Heb. 10:19-39

~~~~~~

ABUNDANT LIFE   January 12

"I have come that they may have life, and that they may have it more abundantly."

John 10:10

For any newborn, life comes through a painful gate. For us now, abundant life requires suffering with grace, the grace of Christ. And out of that experience, we find a life more beautiful than if we had never suffered. Though the gate is narrow, living in the way of the cross opens us to sacrifice and unseen pleasures. Yet many of us hide, still floating dead in the womb of our own desires, our own routine, and our own control, not wanting to go through the birth process of a changed life into the expansive love of God.

Abundant life is not found in abundant things, wonderful people, a "nice" life, or a big bank account, but in receiving Christ and suffering for righteousness as His life moves through us. Through that opening, we enter into the overflowing life of God. It's astounding! That's where true joy grows. His Son calls us first to the cross to find Him. We want to look everywhere else for Him, but that's where He still calls on a daily basis to live in communion with His suffering and so enter the power of the resurrection.

The sacrificial love of our Creator lived out through His Son is the only way to abundant life, because it joins us with His life through the cross. Then, in resurrection power, He can transform us into His likeness. The significance of a burnt offering is that the "owner" sacrifices his right to whatever is being offered (Rom. 12:1-2). On a daily basis, do we live mainly for ourselves or for God? In the fire, a sacrifice loses its original identity as it is transformed and ascends into the will of God. By sacrificing in our hearts what we want for the Father's will and living in His love, we will be changed to receive more than if we had our own way.

Such a beautiful paradox does not come naturally from a human source. It is generated from the divine Lover who offered Himself sacrificially for us. This kind of love carries us beyond ourselves to focus on the desires of the Beloved and through Him to reach the Creator's heart, our source of abundant life. Whatever our need is today, if we offer it to Him, it will lead us straight into God's heart. Our sacrifice goes through the door His sacrifice opened. Then our cups, even worn and empty, will overflow at a table reached only through suffering and prepared in the presence of our enemies. Daily, the feast that begins to feed us in the wilderness with the Shepherd will grow more abundant until we feast in the house of the King. At His table, we become more than ourselves. We are transformed in His eyes and made new in His power.

Father, lead me and feed me by the waters, through the valleys, and in the presence of my enemies. Even in suffering, I want to taste Your life in Jesus now. In His name, amen.

Ps. 23   2 Cor. 4:16-18   1 Pet. 2:21-25

A BANQUET BEFORE YOU   January 13

You prepare a table before me in the presence of my enemies; You anoint my head with oil; my cup runs over.

Ps. 23:5

Even in the presence of our enemies, God prepares a feast for us. This is what the Good Shepherd does when He gives His life for the sheep. He not only leads us to fresh pastures and water in this world, but He also gives eternal life with rivers of living water flowing from our innermost being even now.

We are brought into communion with our Lord when we dine with Him, when we become one with the Vine. The table God prepares for us is the living sacrifice of His Son, made life for us through His death and resurrection. In fellowship with Him, we receive the bread of life broken, given, and multiplied beyond understanding. To forgive our sin, He offered His blood as atonement and a covering for all who receive Him. This is the banquet set before us now that leads to the heavenly marriage supper of the Lamb. Notice that even in this world, the table is prepared before us, not behind us. Go forward in faith. Do not look back. The burdens of the past are not our banquet. Our future in the Lord is a banquet we enjoy now by inviting Him into our lives to be head of the table.

We might expect a banquet in the presence of friends, or in honor of great achievements, or in a season of fruitful harvest. However, our banquet appears after a walk through the valley of the shadow of death, where the Lord's rod and staff comfort us in discipline and protection. Often, at the worst possible time in our lives, our Shepherd comes in a new way to refresh us. We find ourselves at His table in unlikely places—battle zones. There is the table spread before us, and God protects us while we eat what He provides. In His presence is fullness of joy and strength. Enemies threaten, but at His table, protection and victory are sure. In our imperfection, He sets a perfect table. When enemies come, they stumble and fall (Ps. 27:2) as we sit down with the Master in peace, satisfied in His goodness. For by His stripes we are healed, and by His faith at work in us, by the power that raised Jesus from the dead, our weakness is changed into His strength (Eph. 1:19-23).

Our emptiness only makes room for His fullness, and because we have nothing of our own, He can give us everything. He can prepare beauty in a barren place. If we try to set the table and provide the food, or if the table is already full of our own works, we cannot receive His food. What we might expect to keep us away from the table—loss or risk—are often what God uses to get us there. Then He can feed us, anoint us with the oil of His Son, and fill us with His Spirit so that our cups run over. Come and dine.

Father, bring me to the table You have prepared. In Jesus' name, amen.

Isa. 25:6-9   Matt. 22:1-14   Matt. 26:26-29

January 14

~~~~~~

WHEN I AWAKE

Father, when I awake, I am still with You. When the slumber of my own life and the numbing pace of the world's demands are over, You will still be my Keeper. Even now, when I awake out of myself, I will move in the love You share with others. When I awake from the fears of my past and the shadows of despair, today I will walk in Your light that overcomes the darkness. When the night of my sin is over, I will arise in the power of Jesus Christ, who still comes. When everything else is said and done, shaken and gone, all folded into eternity and laid aside, I am still with You forever. Wake me up now to see where I really am in Christ through His cross. In His name, amen.

When I awake, I am still with You.

Ps. 139:18

Ps. 17:15   Eph. 5:13-21

~~~~~~

BEGOTTEN OF THE LIVING WORD   January 15

Of His own will He brought us forth by the word of truth, that we might be a kind of firstfruits of His creatures.

James 1:18

In Christ we are born of truth, and in that truth, we are free to live. When we pass through death, we can go into the life He purchased through His cross and confirmed through His resurrection. He purchased it for us here, for right now as well as for heaven. This is possible because the Son of God became fully human. In love, He entered our world and took our sinful life away through His death on the cross to bring us into His new life. To be born again is more than a process of following instructions or reading what is written, even if the book is the Holy Bible. We must receive Christ. The Bible alone will not save us. It can lead us to let Christ save us, but it is the person of Christ sent by the Father, working in us by the Holy Spirit, who brings us into His new creation. There is no other way to get there (John 14:6; John 6:44-68). We cannot study it out or work it out without Him living in us. We cannot do it or buy it or sell it or make it or dream it, because the life required is divine, the blood of the Creator Himself.

We have the wrong DNA, which has accepted a thread of the lie that we can live our way without God. Therefore our hearts lean toward death. The scales have already tipped against us. We are weighed in the measure and found wanting, but we cannot move the scales because they are weighed in the balance of all creation. We are too weak, too little, and too late. Only the Creator can move them. So He came into our human lives and moved the scales for us. If we try to do it, we claim to be our creator.

The Potter started over with a new Adam, who was stronger than death and yet went through the worst of death for us all. Jesus was not a clay vessel shaped into a likeness of God. He was the Potter Himself with enough clay on His hands and enough humility to become a servant shrunk to a size that we could recognize Him—and to a size that we could kill Him, if He was willing. Jesus came forth directly from the Father, of the same nature, the same blood or life stream, and the same heritage. The Creator offered Himself in a recognizable human package, which He completely transformed by raising Jesus from the dead. God does the same today. He wants us to be children who receive His life—not statues of clay (John 1:12-13; Rom. 8:29). Let His truth come alive in you as a new creation, formed according to the life of Christ.

Father, I receive Your Living Word into my heart that by Your Spirit I can be born of the truth and life in the blood of Jesus Christ. In Jesus' name, amen.

1 Pet. 1:3-5   John 3:5-8   John 5:39-40

January 16

BOTH KNOWN AND UNKNOWN

Thank You, Father, for saving me from all sin, both known and unknown, by the gift of Your Son's life. When I cannot see clearly what is happening, still I rest like a child in Your protection, trusting You to cleanse completely what is seen and unseen. Nothing is hidden from Your eyes. Keep me in Your purity and power in Jesus Christ, who is Lord of all in the past, present, and future. In Jesus' name, amen.

In Him we have redemption through His blood, the forgiveness of sins, according to the riches of His grace which He made to abound toward us in all wisdom and prudence, having made known to us the mystery of His will, according to His good pleasure which He purposed in Himself, that in the dispensation of the fullness of the times He might gather together in one all things in Christ, both which are in heaven and which are on earth—in Him.

Eph. 1:7-10

Pss. 130-131

ALL TOGETHER

January 17

"But the fruit of the Spirit is love, joy, peace, . . ."

Gal. 5:22

The fruit of the Spirit is one fruit, whole and complete in God's Word. Love, joy, peace, and the other fruit of the Spirit are all together in one complete fruit of new life. Can you taste them all together? When you eat a fruit, you eat all of its chemical components together for nourishment. The life of the fruit goes on in you, and the seed remains. In Christ, we taste life everlasting and grow as His life is revealed in us by the fruit of the Spirit. The whole seed of Christ's new life always remains. Thinking of love, joy, and peace each individually, we might learn something, but we do not taste the life, the full flavor that comes from taking them all together. If someone studied the chemical components of fruit and isolated them for research, this might educate us about fruit, but it would not give us the sweet taste or the energy to live and move in God.

In asking for love each day, in seeking joy each day, and in knocking on the door of peace each day, are you ready to receive them all together to fully experience each one? Ask God to produce His fruit in you. Consider the movement of your spirit in asking, seeking, and knocking as a reflection of God's life seeking you, and the unity of His Spirit will produce more fruit than words can say.

All the fruit of the Spirit flows through us in one stream, as out of love, joy, and peace arise the others. Always love is first. It is the closest connection to the Vine, and without it, the others will dry up and wither away. Let everything that happens to you today, even the bad things, become fertilizer for more fruit. Ask, seek, and knock, so you will find the whole fruit of the love of Christ growing in you. Then other fruit will follow. Abide in the Vine, feed on Him, and let His fruit multiply.

You can see this fruit, smell it, taste it, and give it away, but you cannot sell it or buy it. Through Christ, God has already paid for it all together, as whole fruit, intending for it to grow through you and come back to Him in praise. With the taste of that whole fruit in you, bring an offering of praise to the Creator today, and more will grow.

O Lord God, in the unity of Your Spirit, do whatever is necessary to produce Your fruit in me, all together, for Your glory. In Jesus' name, amen.

Heb. 13:15   Matt. 7:15-20   John 15:1-4, 16-17

BE STILL AND KNOW   January 18

Be still, and know that I am God; I will be exalted among the nations, I will be exalted in the earth!

Ps. 46:10

To be still is to know God more deeply than we can know Him in any other way, even by working for Him or studying about Him. If we are still, He can be heard. If we wait, He can move. When we love someone, we let that person go first. Loving and listening are keys to the same door of intimacy. When we wait for God and focus on Him, then God can reveal Himself to a heart with room to receive Him. When we lay down our ability, our thoughts and words, then He can fully reveal His. Otherwise, we're only catching little glimpses of Him between the big blocks of time we have invested in ourselves. Inspiration does not come from within us, but from our Creator.

There is a silence in our will as well as our words. In our lives the cross actively works death to self and more life in God. Without the cross, we often strive as hard for our own desires as for His. Even in worship, we may praise Him for our own advantage. Much of our prayer life consists of talking about ourselves, making requests, and expecting God to reveal Himself in the box we have built. Our prayers often focus on our work instead of His. What about our Creator Himself and His work? If we're occupied with this world, we will miss Him. The answer to prayer, the real solution comes when we seek God for who He is more than for what He does. He provides when we make room to receive Him.

When we are still, there is a place for Him alone to come in, unpolluted by our suggestions. If we are still, God can empower us to do mighty acts only He can do. If we are still, He alone will be exalted among the nations and in our little part of the earth. Then our words and actions will take on holiness and power that come only from Him.

There will be time to speak and things to do, but first immerse your life in His and soak in His everlasting Word. Focus on God, simply rest in Him, as you open His Word. The inspiration to understand and apply His truth comes not from within you, but from God by the Holy Spirit. These are your most productive minutes of the day. Before you run the race ahead, be still and let Him fill you with the breath of His life, breath to run.

Father, I come to You, I wait for You, and I love You through the love of Your Son. Teach me how to live in Your Word and move in Your love. In Jesus' name, amen.

Ps. 37:3-11   Mark 12:28-34   Ps. 81:8-16

THE BEST YOU   January 19

And He said to me, "My grace is sufficient for you, for My strength is made perfect in weakness." Therefore most gladly I will rather boast in my infirmities, that the power of Christ may rest upon me.

2 Cor. 12:9

The worst you with Christ is better than the best you without Him. Whatever you plan to do today, the stronger you are in yourself, the less there will be of Him in the work. It will all taste like you. He will not come in and flavor the stew you are in with a taste of heaven unless your door is open and your heart is ready. Then He will take out the old and put in the new and stir you up.

What is your idea of the best you? There is nothing more productive you can do than to let Christ reveal Himself through your weakness today. In His hands, everything is flavored with amazing grace. On your own, a busy day with huge accomplishments in the world's eyes really means nothing for eternity. It tastes flat. No matter what projects are planned, how hard the work is, or whom you must reach, the best you is the least you and the most of Him. Then the full light and energy of His love can permeate all the planning and the doing. On your own power on your best day, you are much less than Jesus with you on your worst day. Each day, He brings us the same question: Are we willing to let Him produce our righteousness, or do we want to provide it ourselves?

Since our strongest work can never be enough, we are lost without Christ's help, without His very being living in us now. Even with the best intentions, nothing you do without Him will bear any eternal fruit (John 15:5). All the ability of human life eventually shrivels in the traffic of this world. A lot of busy leaves, a lot of growth, a lot of stretching, are pointless without the fruit of that one Seed of life rising up in the Vine. Joined to Him, we let Christ produce His life in us, flowing out of His side into our open hearts. He can produce new growth even when it seems impossible because He created us in the first place. With the Lord all things are possible. Whatever your assignment today, wait for Him. Let Him lead you and break your bread. Live in Him. Rejoice with Him. Eat with Him. Love Him. In that active communion, He will reveal the best you.

Father, I give up my own way and ask for Your way in Jesus Christ. Reveal Your love in me as I receive Him. Change me, even in weakness, to share His joy and strength now and forever. In Jesus' name, amen.

John 15:5   Heb. 9:14   1 Cor. 2:9-14

January 20

BREATHE IN ME THE BREATH OF LIFE

Lord God, breathe in me the breath of life. Form my faith in the wounded hands of Your Son. Free me from the tomb of my own will. In Your Living Word, wash me and lead me in the paths of righteousness for Your name's sake through the power of Jesus Christ who died for me and rose to bring me to You forever. In Jesus' name, amen.

. . . that you may know what is the hope of His calling, what are the riches of the glory of His inheritance in the saints, and what is the exceeding greatness of His power toward us who believe, according to the working of His mighty power which He worked in Christ when He raised Him from the dead and seated Him at His right hand in the heavenly places, far above all principality and power and might and dominion, and every name that is named, not only in this age but also in that which is to come.

Eph. 1:18-21

John 20:19-29

ALL IN ALL
January 21

"for in Him we live and move and have our being."

Acts 17:28

Some people try to keep God in a small box. They allow Him to be all in all within familiar boundaries that they control. Others put Him in a very big box, but they still keep the key. In reality there is no box, and He has the key! When we receive Christ, our lives become new as we receive Him all in all. In His holiness, our fragile, broken lives, once easily shaken, become whole. In totality, His life, which cannot be shaken, fills us with eternal glue. Infused in us and through us, His power holds everything together (Col. 1:16-17; Heb. 12:25-29). As we let Him be Lord in the little things, the big things begin to fit in His will. Steep mountains melt in His love.

God's creative power burns through all humanly controlled boundaries. In essence, we are living within Him, and He alone sets the boundaries and moves beyond them. In whose will do you live and move and have your being? If it depends on us to keep it all ticking, even with the best human effort, it's a struggle as one piece falls off here, and cracks appear there as we try to make everything fit.

Only in union with Christ's life, can we build a house that will not fall to the storms that come. He fits it all together, not with some formula, but with Himself. Our all in all is a Person, not a concept or a narrative. As our Creator, He incorporates us through Christ into His love and eternal stability. A life built in and on the One who fills all creation grows forever in Him. Since Christ already conquered death, we rise above human limitations as we live daily with God in the sacrifice and resurrection of His Son. To abide in Him is to let Him fill all the cracks and recreate us in His image, all in all, each one individually and each one joined to others who live in His love.

In divine mercy, we walk by faith, not by sight, moving in supernatural power each day. God's power acts as a kind of eternal, transparent, moving glue that holds everything together, not in our individual wills, but in our Creator. Since He created us for life in the grace of His Son, if we're in His will, that's what we have! If we're still acting in our own desires, we get only ourselves and the death that drags behind us. Today, is there something that, if it were removed from your life, would cause everything to fall apart? Human love, career, money, work for God, fame, talent, health—these are all candidates for our glue, but none will hold. At some point, they will all fall apart. However, the love of God Himself in Jesus and the power of His blood given for us never fail to hold. From today, they will carry us through eternity.

Father, I don't know how to live in You or to let You be all in all. Show me, teach me, carry me in Your love. Bring me into the life of Jesus Christ. In His name, amen.

John 17:20-23   Col. 3:9-11   Matt. 7:24-27

BIG AND LITTLE   January 22

"In My Father's house are many mansions."

John 14:2

Our idea of the One to whom we pray and the answers we expect are much smaller than the reality of our Father and the answers He has planned. Jesus said His Father's house contains many mansions. I thought the "many" had to do with many people, each having a different mansion, which it may, but now I begin to see there is also more. Our idea of a house cannot describe the dwelling place that He is preparing. We are going into many rooms of unknown dimensions. So in this life, we are often looking for a little answer when He is preparing a big one. We are so pinned on our views of life that we can hardly stretch to receive the abundance that is going to flow out of our Father's love for us. Are your prayers built on your dimensions or His?

The most direct demonstration of the difference in God's scale and our smaller human scale is the life of Christ. The King of Glory came to earth and had to fit into a tiny human body with tiny human desires. He stretched the boundaries of what is called human to a greatness no one has seen before or since. Yet He was willing to be confined within a fragile human frame to die to save us (John 1:29). As He still does, Jesus showed a tenderness and intimate concern for the details and needs of human life. He noticed a widow's small gift and pointed to the larger dimension of her faith. Impossibly, He healed those whom no one else would touch. He saw the lilies' beauty as more than royalty. He even entered the supreme limitation of death and then stepped out of the tomb, expanding the horizon of our lives to the size of eternity. That is life abundant!

Whatever you want to enjoy on earth, multiply it by 100,000 times, and you have not yet scratched the surface of the dimensions of heavenly joy. What we know here in Christ is only a miniature replica of reality in heaven. Just as the tabernacle in Moses' time was a copy of a heavenly pattern, so our knowledge here of love, joy, and peace are miniatures and partial copies, even in our best experience, of what it really means to be alive. The bigger version is what we inherit when we pass through the little version on earth by living in Christ who brings us into the dimensions of the Father's house. Even here, our little versions must fit the guidelines given by Christ to match up with the big pattern that is coming. In His love, Christ will enlarge our hearts in His to match what He is preparing for eternity.

Father, teach me to live now in the pattern of Your Son's life so that I can live with You forever in the abundant life of Your kingdom. In Jesus' name, amen.

John 10:10, 30   Ps. 36:5-9   Matt. 3:11-17

BRING US THROUGH

Lord God, bring us through the door that You create. Through the blood of the Lamb Jesus who came in human flesh to conquer the world, the flesh, and the devil, change us and bring us to You in the purity of Your Son. We trust only in His living sacrifice to make us clean and new now, even here. Thank You that He is the way, the truth, and the life for all who will receive Him. In Jesus' name, amen.

"And I, if I am lifted up from the earth, will draw all peoples to Myself."

John 12:32

Heb. 10:1-23

THE CARPENTER AND THE FISHERMEN January 24

Then He said to them, "Follow Me, and I will make you fishers of men."

Matt. 4:19

Jesus was not a fisherman. He was a carpenter. Without a carpenter, there would be no boat for the fishermen to ride out to the depths. A carpenter works with wood to produce what can float out to deep water for a larger catch than any fisherman can find walking along the shore. If we are to follow Jesus Christ and become fishers of people, we must use the boat He has made from the wood of the cross. Otherwise, we go only where we can walk on our own to catch fish in shallow water.

In Luke 5 and John 21, the Carpenter instructed experienced fishermen on how to fish, on the very thing they thought they knew best, and their catch was surprising. The first catch came after Jesus got into their boat to teach. They put out a little from the shore, and He spoke to the people. Then it was time to fish. Why listen to a carpenter about where to fish? Wouldn't these fishermen have more skill than a young carpenter from Nazareth? Hadn't they already tried everything the best fishermen with years of experience could do? Yes, but the Carpenter has worked with the wood of the cross. He has made the boat, and He can walk on the water. With whom are you fishing today?

Through the wood of the cross, Jesus has purchased and shaped everything needed to build the boat of your life. He wants it out on the water as He directs, not parked along the shore. He measured your boat and nailed it together with the faith that took Him through the dark night of Gethsemane to Calvary and into the resurrection. So don't worry; this boat will hold together through any storm and move wherever He directs you to go. The Carpenter is doing everything necessary to equip you for deeper water.

On your own, the best thinking and human strength will only become weaker as the night grows longer. Where do you think the Master directs you now through the wood of the cross? Wherever you are, listen for the Morning Star to call you with His resurrection voice. He will tell you where to throw your nets for many fish that He already sees. There is no use trying to do it your own way. When your catch is full according to His plan, you will see Him preparing breakfast for you on the shore with heavenly fire. Come and dine with the Carpenter. Bring the fish He told you to catch!

Father, teach me how to fish and to reach out to others in Jesus' name by following His direction. Only He can supply all I need and bring the catch at the right time. In Your kingdom, I won't try to fish any other way. In Jesus' name, amen.

John 21:3-15   Luke 5:1-11   Matt. 19:26

CERTAINTY
January 25

"Greater love has no one than this, than to lay down one's life for his friends."

John 15:13

The certainty of God's love is indisputable and incorruptible. Even if you don't trust yourself or someone else in any other relationship, you can trust your Creator, who is completely who He is and never changes. In mercy, He comes for you in Jesus Christ. From the beginning of time, He has worked out the answer to your questions and already has the end in His sight. With certainty, God sees more than you see. As Alpha and Omega, He moves where you cannot go to change everything in the path of His will. In that path, life will grow.

Whatever circumstances challenge you now, whether a health problem, job situation, or family crisis, face the problem honestly. Look at it head-on. Then place all of it into the path of God's love, into the certainty of His will moving inside, over, and around it. With God's power now fully on it, you will have to take your hands off so that He can work. In holiness, He will move clear through what you could never reach and restore life to the very root. His love is big enough to cover anything as the living stream of His purity changes it and you in the process. As your perspective changes, tone of voice, rush of thought, and stiffness of will all begin to melt in the furnace of His love, which makes all things new.

When we try to fix something, it's from a shallow level underneath, and our view is cold and limited. We hunker down and tinker around with it, worried as much about how we look as how it gets fixed. God works from above in eternity's fire, penetrating deeply to the core of any false appearances and rearranging every part to fit His view and plan. What was partial looks different when it is made whole. As the certainty of holy power flows into what seemed impossible, our uncertain world is turned upside down. Truth fills in the gaps our doubts left for dead, and we have a sure foundation for life that is free and stable. Where are you standing today? Build on the certainty of His presence with you. In that love, begin to place those around you on the same foundation.

Father, forgive my hurry and worry. Slow me down so I can taste the truth of Your love.
Bring me to the sure foundation of Your life in Jesus Christ. In Jesus' name, amen.

Matt. 21:20-22, 42 John 8:28-36 1 Cor. 3:11-13

January 26

CHANGE ME

To change these circumstances, Lord, change me. Have your way completely. Nothing else will move until my heart moves in Your direction. Make me obedient to Your creative power. Today, Lord, increase my faith. I surrender; I open my heart to Your Holy Spirit so You can make all things new and work them together for good, according to Your purpose. Help me to love You enough to let You do all of Your will in my life and to praise You now for what You are creating in Your time. Thank You for filling me with new life. In Jesus' name, amen.

He went a little farther, and fell on the ground, and prayed that if it were possible, the hour might pass from Him. And He said, "Abba, Father, all things are possible for You. Take this cup away from Me; nevertheless, not what I will, but what You will."

Mark 14:35-36

Gal. 2:20—3:14

CARRY THE LIGHT   January 27

For it is the God who commanded light to shine out of darkness, who has shone in our hearts to give the light of the knowledge of the glory of God in the face of Jesus Christ. But we have this treasure in earthen vessels, that the excellence of the power may be of God and not of us.

2 Cor. 4:6-7

On its own, a lamp cannot produce light but only serves to hold the light and let it pass through. A lamp does not light itself or move itself but waits for one who is stronger to fill it, light it, and then carry it in his hands to the place he wants it to shine. As clay vessels, we carry the light of God by grace. In reality, God carries us and fills us to shine out where He chooses. Our responsibility is to be available, clean, and ready to move. The positioning, lighting, and uncovering is all in God's power and timing. We may have to stay hidden until He turns on the lights.

If we look only at the container and outer situation to judge the value of a lamp, we can miss the beauty the Master will cause to shine out when darkness comes. There are many who appear strong and ready who later prove empty when darkness arrives. Others who appear weak suddenly glow with the power of the true light that overcomes the darkness. To let God shine in and through us, we must let Him uncover us and reveal deep truth. Just as oil or electricity moves through the core of a lamp, we can't expect only a touch on the outside to produce any light. We need to be filled and changed within. Only then can God heal us, fill us with the oil of Christ who redeems us, and ignite us in our very depths by the Holy Spirit through the power of Christ's resurrection.

In Him, the flame never goes out. In the anointing of Christ, the light of life shines not only in temporary clay packages but also through all eternity. The light of heaven runs through us here on earth. Even if our vessel is cracked and weak, His light does not change. The brightness of a lamp depends not on the lamp's beauty but on the beauty and clarity of the light. It is the light that overcomes the darkness, not the lamp.

Just as Gideon carried the pitchers with torches inside into battle, at the right time God will carry us, as clay vessels bearing torches of His love, into victory. Even if we're outnumbered, when the trumpet blows for God's timing and the clay pitchers are broken, His holy light will shine through, defeating any enemies (Judg. 7:16-21). At the right time, our outer shell is broken and falls away to reveal only God's light and victory. It is one thing to have His light burning in us; it is a far greater thing to be carried into battle as He breaks the will of the flesh to reveal His Spirit shining in victory here.

Turn us, O God, to Your living light. Cause Your face to shine, and we shall be saved. Break in us whatever hides Your light so that the power of Your life will overcome our darkness. In Jesus' name, amen.

Ps. 80:3   Matt. 5:14-16   1 John 1:5-7

A CLEAN CUP
January 28

"Woe to you, scribes and Pharisees, hypocrites! For you cleanse the outside of the cup and dish, but inside they are full of extortion and selfish indulgence. Blind Pharisee, first cleanse the inside of the cup and dish, that the outside of them may be clean also."

Matt. 23:25-26

To be clean, the inside of a cup must be emptied. It is possible to clean the outside while the cup is full; but for the inside, the cup must be empty, ready to be filled with clean water. When we think of cleansing, we think of washing and wiping, but emptying is the first step that permits all the others. Sometimes we hang onto the old sludge in the bottom of our cup while asking Jesus to change us. When we say we want our lives to be clean, do we want only the outside cleaned up so the appearance is acceptable to the world?

To be emptied means to let go of deep things, to go to the cross and take ours up daily, leaving behind the filthy rags of our old ways. Once empty, we can receive much more from God. By His Word, in Jesus' blood, and through the Holy Spirit, we are washed and made completely clean (John 15:3; Rev. 1:5; Titus 3:5-6). What He is cleansing may be hidden for a time, as if under a living stream, where it remains invisible to the world but visible to God. The blood of the Lamb Jesus takes away all our sin.

As we follow Him on the road and get our feet dirty, Jesus continually washes us and keeps us moving forward. Some prefer to sit safely on the shelf with a good exterior, but a shiny exterior can camouflage a filthy interior. The glow of life that truly makes us shine comes only from God's light released within a pure heart, a quiet heart washed in the water of His Word. There is no duplicating that divine shine in the life of someone who walks and breathes the life of Jesus.

Even if such a cup, filled with His forgiveness and love, has a chip or a crack somewhere, it is still more beautiful than an otherwise perfect piece of china with stains hidden inside. Have you ever picked up a nice cup only to be surprised by some piece of dirt or a bug in the bottom? You can shake it out and put it down, but even the sight of that unexpected dirt ruins the taste of everything else you're eating. It has to be washed on the inside before anything will taste right again.

Viewing your life today as a cup, consider for a moment where the dirt may be, inside or outside, a spot here or there, or perhaps years of buildup in the deepest part. When people touch your life and ask for a drink, what will they find?

O King, wash me completely and use me as a clean cup to give a cool drink to others. Empty me, change me, and fill me with Your life and love. In Jesus' name, amen.

Ps. 51:1-12   Ezek. 36:25-27   1 John 1:8-9

COME SIMPLY

January 29

"Assuredly, I say to you, unless you are converted and become as little children, you will by no means enter the kingdom of heaven. Therefore whoever humbles himself as this little child is the greatest in the kingdom of heaven."

Matt. 18:3-4

Come simply. Don't try to come to the Lord complicatedly. He calls children to come, not champions and captains, not experts and executives. Come simply. With humble honesty, simplicity walks in unseen power. Children are willing to receive what their Father gives them, while adults think they must do for themselves. Jesus looked for tired fishermen and shunned tax collectors, not popular heroes with important agendas. In a busy world, He wanted people empty enough of themselves to receive all that He had to give them for eternity.

Whatever problems or assets and human accomplishments are clinging to you now and ruling your time, drop them off like old garments so He can clothe you with His purity. Whatever you are willing to let go of, the Lord can use creatively or remove promptly. Let your best and your worst alike disappear in the brightness of His coming with mercy and power. Let Him gather you under His wings. There's room there only for the person you really are. In humility, worship God now in spirit and in truth. Come forward in faith, and you will arrive at a new place, clean and simple.

Lord, You came simply to us as a baby. Now as a child, I come to You. Make me clean in the power of Your sacrifice, free in the blood of the Lamb. In Jesus' name, amen.

Matt. 19:13-26   Mark 12:28-34   1 Cor. 1:20—2:5

CROSS OVER

Lord God, help me to cross over, out of myself and into Your kingdom. I lay down my old life to receive the life of Your Son. In humility, bring me in Jesus Christ on the bridge of the cross to higher ground by Your Holy Spirit. Let the resurrection power that raised Jesus from the dead work in me now for new life in this world and the next. In Jesus' name, amen.

On the same day, when evening had come, He said to them, "Let us cross over to the other side."

Mark 4:35

Mark 5:1-15, 25-43

CHILDREN OF THE KING   January 31

For we are members of His body, of His flesh and of His bones. "For this reason a man shall leave his father and mother and be joined to his wife, and the two shall become one flesh." This is a great mystery, but I speak concerning Christ and the church.

Eph. 5:30-32

In Christ's death and resurrection, the way is opened for us to become God's children by adoption through unity with Christ. As Christ's bride, the church becomes the daughter-in-law of the King and His child by relationship, brought into His family by Christ. Only the Son is the begotten of the Father, of the same essence as the Father, very God and very Man. Since Christ became completely human, though without sin, He is the bridge to bring us into relationship with the Father, even as children made worthy of an inheritance. Whether male or female, we are one in Christ as His bride. In that sense, Christ fulfilled all the law and paid the penalty of sin so we could come to the Father.

Just as a Jewish bride takes the bridegroom's name after he pays a price for her and brings her into his family, we claim the family name and divine inheritance of Christ, who gave Himself for us. Although the bride is not of the same essence as the Father, through her relationship with the Son, she shares in His inheritance and is adopted into the family. Fruit produced through her union with the Son bears His nature and power.

A bride's name change indicates she has entered a relationship beyond herself that can produce life beyond herself. Though not of the same nature as God, through our union with Jesus Christ, we become partakers of the divine nature so that He can produce holy fruit through us, fruit beyond human limitations, in union with the Son and His inheritance. To redeem us from sin, the Creator sent His Son here, to our dark depths, and raised Him up to bring us with Him into the light of the Father's house.

A bride must leave her own house. Putting childish things aside, she must prepare for a new life. Becoming a "bride" implies preparation, change, surrender, union, and new life. We who are now in Christ are no longer children of this world but maturing citizens of the next, and not just citizens, but maturing children of the King, whom He blesses in union with Jesus Christ to produce fruit in His name. We enter this world as children of Adam. When we become Christ's bride, we become children of the Father, learning the ways of the next world, the new creation of God. Have you received the Bridegroom's gift? Live in His name now and into eternity. No other name goes there.

Father, bring me into Your house in unity with Your Son, Jesus. In His name, amen.

John 1:12-14   Rev. 19:6-9   Matt. 25:6

COME THROUGH THE DOOR   February 1

"And you will seek Me and find Me, when you search for Me with all your heart."

Jer. 29:13

To come through a door, you can't carry the whole room with you or have so much in your hands you can't reach the handle. Only what is in your heart can go through the door of the cross. Seek the simple way, building beauty each day, even in suffering. The beauty is in passing through, not in claiming and counting, or in trying to squeeze everything we can control through the door of life in Christ. Many of us are busy counting our human treasure in this world and trying to stamp Christ's name on it, but it won't fit through the door of eternity.

In our effort, it is even possible to point others to the door and never go through ourselves. If we wait for the quiet treasure that is only in Christ, then the liquid gold of His purity will carry us through in truth by the refining fire of the Holy Spirit. His life lived in us will bring us through the door. It is one thing to sit and look at the door, sing songs to the door, learn all about the door, and talk about the door, but it is another thing entirely to go through the door and live where it opens now.

Consider for a moment only what is in your heart. Is there enough treasure there in Christ to carry you through the door with nothing else in your hand? With His treasure burning in your heart, can you count all else as loss to win Him and press forward in the upward call of God that draws you to Him alone? Once your heart is firmly fixed on the treasure of Christ, it will not be hard to decide what to let go of and what to pick up for the journey. Our Savior has purchased the treasure that runs all the way from here to heaven. He has waited a long time to see your heart move freely in His love.

Father, help me to let go of whatever does not move through Your door of life in Jesus Christ. Bring me through that door with Your pure treasure in my heart, so I can live in the power of His cross and resurrection. In Jesus' name, amen.

John 10:9   Phil. 3:7-14   Matt. 6:19-21

COME AND SEE
February 2

Then Jesus turned, and seeing them following, said to them, "What do you seek?"
They said to Him, "Rabbi . . . where are You staying?" He said to them, "Come and see."

John 1:38-39

Just as today, Jesus comes to where the disciples are so the disciples can go where He lives. The disciples heard John the Baptist say of Jesus, "Behold the Lamb of God," and they decided to go see for themselves. After they heard, they began to follow Him. As we hear that Jesus is the Lamb of God, we must follow. It is one thing to accept the concept but another to follow the person and His lifestyle. There is that moment when He turns to each of us personally and asks, "What do you seek?" He does not ask, "Whom do you seek?" because we have already met the Lamb of God. The question now is whether we will walk with Him daily. What kind of life do we want? What about our priorities and schedules? The question is startling to those who follow only concepts and debates of doctrine. Do we want to study with the scribes and discuss God's ways, or do we want to actually follow His ways, to personally walk with our Savior and live where He lives?

We can follow curiously from a distance and then retire safely to our own home, or we can go where Jesus lives and spend time getting to know Him and those He serves. Just listening to John the Baptist, the disciples could learn about Jesus and receive instruction from John on the way of repentance. But what they learned by going home with Jesus and remaining with Him was something more. Jesus could have just told them where he was staying so they could come later on their own, at a convenient time. Instead, He invited them as He does each one of us to come and see now, to walk with Him now. Let Him show you where and how He lives today through the Holy Spirit.

This means to get up and out of a comfortable place in this world and come to His place. It's not our place. There will be a cross. First we come; then we'll see. Otherwise, no matter how much we study or read or discuss, we are blind. And without the cross, we are powerless. What are you seeking? In your heart, come. By the Holy Spirit, you will see Jesus as He really lives. Things in your world that were invisible will become visible through His eyes, and you will see clearly. But first, come without knowing all that is ahead. If we could have gone with Jesus that day to see where He lived, by comparison to our lives now, we would be surprised at the simplicity, meager circumstances, perhaps poverty where He stayed by choice. The richest King did not live in a palace. He doesn't today either. Come and see!

My Father, may I follow Jesus to the place where He lives today and take the time to stay, learning to live as He does in this world by the Holy Spirit. In Jesus' name, amen.

Luke 9:23   Mark 1:17-18   John 14:15-17

February 3

~~~~~~

CHANGE ME IN THE HEART OF CHRIST

Father, change my heart in the heart of Christ. Heal me by His wounds. Wash me clean today. Finally, I've given up trying to change myself or those around me. Instead, I place everything in Your hands. Turn me completely in Your justice and love that never end. Surprise me with the revelation of Your Son in me and in others. Only then will I be a new creation. In the name of Jesus Christ, amen.

"At that day you will know that I am in My Father, and you in Me, and I in you. He who has My commandments and keeps them, it is he who loves Me. And he who loves Me will be loved by My Father, and I will love him and manifest Myself to him."

John 14:20-21

Luke 7:44-50

~~~~~~

COMMUNION WITH HIM
February 4

"Behold, I stand at the door and knock. If anyone hears My voice and opens the door, I will come in to him and dine with him, and he with Me."

Rev. 3:20

Jesus knocks on the doors of our lives because He wants to come in and dine with us. Notice, He did not say He wants to enter to teach us or to work with us but to change us through intimate communion with Him. After a long walk and talk, Jesus was revealed to the disciples at Emmaus only when they asked him to come in, to stay and eat with them. It's the same today. We often focus on hearing His Word and obeying His teaching, which is good, but the purpose of opening our lives to Him is fellowship with Him, to receive Him in direct communion. The Vine knows that if the branches abide in Him, fruit will come.

There is nothing we can discover in the Bible that is more important than the truth of Christ's presence with us. His Word, His call is represented by the knock, and we hear its meaning in the wood of the cross as His hand touches our door. Many Christians are content just to hear that knock and know He's out there. They focus on His teaching separate from His presence and enjoy having Jesus on their doorstep. As long as He is recognized outside, there is a comfortable knowledge of both His Word and His work. Yet they are still in control. They have Jesus where they want Him, just outside in case He's needed. These believers have the Word and a distant knowledge of His action on the cross, but they do not have His intimate presence inside their lives, reigning with love.

Unless we take hold of the door, the cross, and open it in our lives by receiving Jesus and breaking bread with Him, the power of His Word does not truly enter us and live in us (John 6:53-58, 63; 17:20-23). Correct doctrine and a lifestyle of service to others without a hunger for His presence are not enough. Ask Martha. Her sister, Mary, knew Jesus came for fellowship, for intimate communion that empowers service to others and an understanding of His Word, which only His presence can give. When Jesus comes to knock on your door, He comes mainly to change you, to share your life, and to bring you into communion with God through the Holy Spirit. Then you will be ready to serve.

When Jesus called the twelve disciples, their first purpose was simply to be with Him (Mark 3:13-15). Then they were sent out. The whole point of the cross is to bring us to His table, to restore our broken fellowship with God. All people are invited to the King's banquet table, but they won't all come. Often, we are eager to work for Jesus but not to eat with Him or His humble friends. As in Emmaus, Jesus pauses today to see who will invite Him to come in and dine in unhurried love. He won't force His way in if all we really want are just the words and the works. Are we hungry for His presence?

Father, feed me with the life of Jesus. May He come in and stay. In Jesus' name, amen.

Luke 22:14-20   Matt. 22:1-9, 15-21   Luke 24:28-36

February 5

COMING SOON

Heavenly Father, thank You for Your Son coming here, knowing exactly where we are and loving us out of this world. Thank You for making us new through Him who brings us to You. Help us to receive Him and to abide in Your Son now through the Holy Spirit, who makes us fruitful witnesses of Your mercy and power in Jesus Christ, who is coming soon. In His name, amen.

"And this is eternal life, that they may know You, the only true God, and Jesus Christ whom You have sent. . . . I do not pray for these alone, but also for those who will believe in Me through their word; . . . I in them, and You in Me; that they may be made perfect in one, and that the world may know that You have sent Me, and have loved them as You have loved Me. Father, I desire that they also whom You gave Me may be with Me where I am, that they may behold My glory which You have given Me; for You loved Me before the foundation of the world. O righteous Father! The world has not known You, but I have known You; and these have known that You sent me."

John 17:3, 20, 23-25

1 John 4:9-19

COOK US UP   February 6

"I came to send fire on the earth, and how I wish it were already kindled!"

Luke 12:49

Even if all the ingredients are in place, our food is not yet cooked and ready to eat until fire is applied. Fire softens and transforms each ingredient, blending the flavors and releasing a sweet aroma. Sufficient heat is required to purify the food and make it consumable. In some individual lives and churches, all the ingredients are in place, but there is no fire of the Holy Spirit to make the food digestible, transforming it into practical results in God's kingdom. When people come into our lives and our churches, we can't offer them frozen words and lukewarm programs. They can only digest what is heated in holy fire, ready to be transformed into energy for His work.

We must ask God to cook us up in His holy fire, to bend us and mold us to His will so we fulfill our purpose for His glory. It's possible to have correct doctrine and still be cold or lukewarm in the kingdom. Also, we can be hot but rotten at the core and a stench to all around until that fire eventually burns out all the impurities, lifting us out of ourselves. The best combination is both good ingredients and holy fire. Do you have both? Perhaps the ingredients are in place, but there is no fire. Ask God for the real fire, not the physical fire of human effort but the spiritual fire of His holiness active in you.

In Psalm 51, David found the answer as he poured out his heart to God in repentance and humility. David wanted to make a clean offering, not just outwardly but inwardly as well. From a broken, humble heart, sacrifices of righteousness are acceptable to God. His fire will consume them and lift a sweet aroma to heaven in Christ's name and His righteousness, not our own. Only in His fire, will a whole burnt offering rise to heaven, as the bulls of earthly gain are slaughtered and surrendered to God (Ps. 51:15-19).

After His resurrection, Christ prepared breakfast on coals of fire for his disciples (John 21:1-17). They had fished on their own with no result, but Christ brought them a harvest when they humbly obeyed Him. Then, after they ate what Jesus had cooked on the fire, He had a question for Peter: "Do you love Me more than these?" Each of us must answer this question. Full of His forgiveness, the fire and the food of the Lord's making will help us answer, "Yes, Lord; You know that I love You." Then we can feed His sheep with the same forgiveness, the same food, and the same fire.

Father, take my frozen life and cook it up in Your kingdom. I want to love and serve You in the purity and love of Jesus Christ by the fire of the Holy Spirit. In Jesus' name, amen.

Matt. 4:17   Acts 1:4-8, 14; 2:1-11   Matt. 3:11-12

THE COST AND THE VALUE February 7

"Most assuredly, I say to you, unless a grain of wheat falls into the ground and dies, it remains alone; but if it dies, it produces much grain."

John 12:24

To produce fruit, the dying grain lets go of whatever it was holding and surrenders all to God. The cost is everything one grain of wheat can give. "But if it dies, it produces much grain." The end provides a beginning. Personally, the cost is very great, but the value of that turning over and letting go increases far beyond the value of what might have been kept. One grain dies, but many more are produced. Looking at the future generations of grain coming from that one, we see hundreds upon hundreds of grains coming out of one sacrifice. Jesus was speaking of His own sacrifice and the new life He would purchase for us and all the generations to come. He was also speaking of a principle that increases the value of our daily lives now when given over to His purpose, even in suffering. The cost is painful, but the coming value is greater.

In His love, the value multiplies quietly beyond human terms and human pain into a total sweetness that remains. Somewhere in the darkest depths, a root stirs. A full shoot springs up to the light. Some fruit appears as a definite, shining treasure that lasts forever. When a grain is truly lost and let go—down-in-the-earth dead and given to God—then a sweetness pours in and surrounds the dying seed. You can feel it even in the depths of winter. Gradually, the cost of the pain is converted into a higher value that moves up and out of the heart. What once held only grief is sprouting wings, like leaves growing on a vine with fruit ripening.

The loss has to be complete. Otherwise, bitterness creeps in. There is no halfway letting go that will produce life. A seed that is half in and half out of the ground will not grow. Only as we completely surrender do we grow each day. The weight of suffering begins to leave, and the weight of Christ's life fills in all wounds like ointment. This filling is startling. We are familiar with pain, but joy surprises us. Like fire on the altar, God's mercy lifts the sacrifice and multiplies its value in an upward form. Even in daily life, we can smell the fragrance of this transformation. His presence burns steadily right there in the place of the loss and gradually shines up and out beyond all boundaries. It is the oil of Christ's anointing, His joy on fire. It multiplies in value even in loss. As we experience loss, we also feel the lift of His joy burning on the altar of sacrifice. What can replace our lost treasures? Ask the One who gives beauty for ashes.

Father, light Your fire in the place of my loss and illumine my life to bear fruit that grows into a treasure in Your kingdom. In Jesus' name, amen.

Luke 9:23-25   Isa. 61:1-3   Rom. 12:1-2

February 8

CUT TO THE HEART

In Your Living Word, Lord, I feel You cutting on my heart where the powerful slice of Your holiness meets flesh that wants its own way. There has been a scraping away of other things, and now we come to this gentle but piercing cutting that slices through my strength and will, piercing them with Your truth. First, the outer edges are cut, and then we get to the inner, throbbing life. Finish Your work as You will. Perform Your perfect surgery on this child who needs to walk in tune with Your saving heartbeat. Circumcise my heart to produce the new life purchased with Christ's blood. If You have to make me weaker to undergo this surgery, I give You my permission to do a complete work of cutting and healing. I will let go of everything and fall into Your arms. Then You can place me on the open table of Your will. Cut through whatever holds me back and release me into the life flow of Your kingdom. Thank You for the clean blade that separates me from my own death and frees me into the life to come. I see the cutting edge is purified with holy fire, and my Surgeon has hands that are scarred yet living, moving in Your love. In Jesus' name, amen.

For the Word of God is living and powerful, and sharper than any two-edged sword, piercing even to the division of soul and spirit, and of joints and marrow, and is a discerner of the thoughts and intents of the heart.

Heb. 4:12

Rom. 2:28-29

DO YOU LOVE ME?   February 9

So when they had eaten breakfast, Jesus said to Simon Peter, "Simon, son of Jonah, do you love Me more than these?" He said to Him, "Yes, Lord; You know that I love you." He said to him, "Feed My lambs."

John 21:15

When Jesus asked Peter whether he loved Him, Peter answered three times, relating to the three times he had denied Jesus. Most of us have denied our Lord more than three times, either by word or by actions. Today, if Jesus came to you and asked the same question, how would you answer? The questions to Peter were followed by Jesus' commandment, "Follow Me" (John 21:19). Have we answered His love, not only with words, but also with the action that proves the words are true, that follows through in obedience? Beyond words, what is there in your life today that shows in action and attitude that you love the Lord? List below some attitudes, relationships, and work that reveal the depth of your love for Him and how that love is growing. Even without words, true joy is a good sign. What is your love in action?

_____

_____

_____

_____

_____

Whether or not any of the blanks are filled in now, at the completion of our lives, this is perhaps the only list that will be considered when we present our works to the Lord and cast our crowns before Him, the One in whom we live and move and have our being. Whatever else we are doing or saying will not count that much. Trust Him in love and let Him complete what He has planned for this day and forever. Follow the Lamb.

O Lord God, show me today what I can do to actively reveal my love for You in a way that satisfies Your heart and feeds Your sheep. In the name of the Lamb, Jesus, through Your Holy Spirit, breathe Your love into each moment I live. Amen.

1 Cor. 8:1-3   Matt. 5:42-48   1 John 4:20—5:5

EACH DAY AN OFFERING
February 10

A woman of Samaria came to draw water. Jesus said to her, "Give Me a drink."

John 4:7

In the middle of a dusty and busy day, the woman of Samaria had just another demand. The impact is nearly the same today when in the middle of a busy day, we are asked to give an offering to God—in fact to make each day a complete offering to Him. Give Him a drink? Well, we may think we have nothing in our lives for Him to drink. What could God possibly want out of my life that would be satisfying to a divine thirst? And do I really have time for it?

After the Samaritan woman questioned Jesus about why He was talking to her, He made a surprising suggestion: "If you knew the gift of God, and who it is who says to you, 'Give Me a drink,' you would have asked Him, and He would have given you living water" (John 4:10). We give Him a drink only out of what He has given us.

Every day, we could just do good things and try to offer them to God. That would be "nice" but not as satisfying to Him as a drink from the spring of love He wants to open in our hearts. Out of this spring, the water that flows from His love wells up to produce many deeds, thoughts, songs, and wordless leaps of faith with joy that truly will give Him a drink. He is not satisfied with offerings that are man-made. This is true even when we help those who thirst physically as Jesus did that day. He said, "'Inasmuch as you did it to one of the least of these My brethren, you did it to Me'" (Matt. 25:40). As important as the drink is the love that pours it. The drink is needed, but the love even more so.

When given with divine love, the drink completely satisfies. The stream of joy that He gives will multiply from a divine source and carry an eternal sparkle, a true flavor. Other waters of merely human intentions will eventually taste flat or dry up in the heat. To offer each day to God, we must first ask Him for a cool drink of His love today, the day that He has made, that flows into His purpose and comes only from Him. Then we can rejoice in what He is doing and with joy offer what He has given back to Him.

Our Creator would like a drink of His creation in us, moving through us to others, singing in the earth, humming through the tough places, and finally rising in praise. It is possible to offer a complete day to God and never leave your house, or to offer Him a busy day in the world. The offering is in the living water that flows through your heart.

Lord God, make this day an offering in my heart to You. Please give me a drink of Your living water, and I will offer it to You first, then to others. In Jesus' name, amen.

Ps. 51:15-17   Isa. 43:19   John 7:37-39

DO WHAT IS NEW   February 11

And so we have the prophetic word confirmed, which you do well to heed as a light that shines in a dark place, until the day dawns and the morning star rises in your hearts.

2 Pet. 1:19

Do what is new. If things are not going well, it may be that you are trying to do what is old. Now God is doing in you and around you a new thing that is not operating in the same gear as the old. If you are still in the same old mode headed the same direction, it may be time to make a turn toward God and shift your heart and hands into a new gear to follow His plan. Or if you are already in a new situation headed in a different direction, you must also let Him change your heart completely to match His purpose. Either way, don't do the old things forever. Don't grind up the engine trying to reach tomorrow in yesterday's gear. Do what is new that is born of God's love and purpose.

Let Him do a new thing in you first and then through you in His timing. Each day turn, reach forward from what is only a beginning, and take hold of His full promise. Otherwise, you are stuck with endless beginnings and no completion in God's power. Although you can remember your roots, tomorrow cannot come to completion in them. From the root, there must be a shoot, then branches and fruit. This is only possible in the Creator, who brings each new season, starting with a new day in His power (2 Cor. 5:15-18). Grow into the time He has planned forever.

The purpose of the old was to prepare you for the new, not to keep you on the old treadmill. Your best tribute to yesterday is to walk forward into tomorrow in the resurrection power of Jesus Christ, who is the same yesterday, today, and forever. He will lead you all the way by grace. How can you take a step today into what is new?

Father, I wanted to keep the old for me, but now I ask You to make me new for You. In its time, I agreed with the old. Now, I agree with Your plan and walk into Your new creation, according to Your power. In Jesus' name, amen.

Jer. 18:1-6   Mark 3:3   Matt. 9:16-17

February 12

~~~~~~

ONGOING CREATION

I praise You, Father, for the creation You called good following the pattern of Your purity. Forgive me for missing the mark of Your truth. Today, create in me a clean heart to match Your design and to reflect the heart of Jesus Christ. In Him, bring me into Your new creation that moves from here into eternity, beginning where I am now. In Jesus' name, amen.

For we ourselves were also once foolish, disobedient, deceived, serving various lusts and pleasures, living in malice and envy, hateful and hating one another. But when the kindness and the love of God our Savior toward man appeared, not by works of righteousness which we have done, but according to His mercy He saved us, through the washing of regeneration and renewing of the Holy Spirit, whom He poured out on us abundantly through Jesus Christ our Savior, that having been justified by His grace we should become heirs according to the hope of eternal life.

Titus 3:3-7

Ps. 19

~~~~~~

COUNSELOR   February 13

And His name will be called Wonderful, Counselor, Mighty God, Everlasting Father, Prince of Peace.

Isa. 9:6

How are knowledge, wisdom, and counsel different? Knowledge, we could say, is the accumulation of facts. Wisdom is a deeper understanding that grasps how to apply those facts. Counsel implies all of the above, but something more: the presence of the one who counsels. To acquire knowledge, we can read a book. Experience teaches us wisdom. For counseling, we must go to a counselor, or he must come to us.

It is that personal contact that makes it so effective. We can sense emotion and emphasis, tone of voice, and commitment that reveal more than words alone can convey. For example, we might acquire some famous evangelist's knowledge from his books and perhaps even gain wisdom by applying what he teaches, but to have his counsel, we must meet with him in person and share our heart with him. Then he could pray with us and take a walk with us. His presence would communicate more than words on paper. The Holy Spirit, our heavenly Counselor is made available to us through the gift of the Father in Christ who said, "It is to your advantage that I go away; for if I do not go away, the Helper will not come to you; but if I depart, I will send Him to you" (John 16:7).

The word for "Helper" or "Comforter" is also translated "Counselor." God sent His personal counsel to us in Christ and then in the Holy Spirit, who comes alongside us now and walks our road, as Jesus did with the disciples. He does not just leave us with a book of instructions but comes to us personally to give comfort and to live out those instructions with us in the details of our lives. The author of a book may never know who reads it. A counselor, on the other hand, gets to know the one he advises. Our Counselor wants to know us so closely He can breathe God's Word into our lives, step by step. Since a good counselor listens as well as speaks, we can depend on the Holy Spirit to take the time and walk the miles to engage us in an active exchange with the Father in prayer.

If our Counselor comes but we ignore Him for our own reading, talking, and working for God in human power, how can we truly know God and His power? When we invite the Lord into our lives, He will come to live with us so that we can know Him in reality through the Holy Spirit. This is more than instruction. As with the disciples walking to Emmaus, He wants us to encounter the fulfillment of God's Word with us now (Luke 24). Hopefully, we'll want more than analysis and ask Him to come in and stay with us, to reveal God's truth each day as our personal Counselor.

Father, let Your counsel flow through my life in Your Holy Spirit so I can truly follow Your Son and love You more. In Jesus' name, amen.

1 John 5:11-12   John 16:12-15   John 14:23-27

CRACKING THE SHELL   February 14

"No one can serve two masters; for either he will hate the one and love the other, or else he will be loyal to the one and despise the other. You cannot serve God and mammon."

Matt. 6:24

Mammon, or desire for worldly gain, has wrapped us in a tight shell. The love of this world and its riches, its activities and its shiny things, can trap us in a hard shell of self-concern. Sometimes our own wills have a hold over any new spiritual life that tries to move in our hearts. This thin shell of self-focus must break away if we are to grow into the life that God has planned. Christ broke the shell. To be born again in God, we receive Christ and break out of this shell through grace into the freedom of our Creator. The life of God stirs within, but what about a calcified ceiling of human will that does not bend? Breaking through the shell of self may take exercise in His Living Word and spiritual heat shining from above. Only God's truth can crack our shell of sin.

In a paradox of truth, the narrow way, the crack through the shell that leads to God opens up more possibilities for life than the well-paved, blind way of the world, which despite its attractions still holds us in a prison of self-centeredness. Even the good that mammon would do, such as helping others, is motivated by the need for self-approval in doing good and the approval of others who might say, "What a generous person to give to others, and what a help to our community!" What mammon gives stays always within the shell of self-focus, even if it benefits others.

In the light of Jesus' life, we can work for God's kingdom, not our own, by helping others to see not our effort but the magnificent greatness of the Father, revealed in the sacrificial love of His Son. The focus is on God more than on what people can do or what people want. He is the Giver of life. The baby chick that breaks out of the shell is looking beyond itself. Having incubated in the heat of the Holy Spirit, the life within breaks out to meet the life from above.

Incubating in the power of the Holy Spirit, we wait for maturity to meet that life from above and to move in the wider world of God's will. Once the shell is cracked, there is no going back. At first, the chipping out is a very narrow way with only a little hole to peek through. Eventually, we're able to see more and to go places we never knew while still inside ourselves. Where is your old shell cracking to release new life today? Live there.

Lord God, bring me out of my shell into the fullness of new life in the cross of Jesus Christ. Crack open any limitations my will puts on Your amazing grace. Let the wings of prayer unfold, bringing me closer to You each day. In Jesus' name, amen.

Matt. 23:37-39   John 8:28-32   Matt. 16:24-17:7

DON'T LOOK BACK   February 15

But Jesus said to him, "No one, having put his hand to the plow, and looking back, is fit for the kingdom of God."

Luke 9:62

Don't look back. If you don't look back, you won't go back. The importance of the direction of your gaze right now is crucial because it determines where you will be tomorrow. First, your eyes travel to where your mind will soon arrive; then your heart unloads its luggage, and actions soon follow. What you are looking at now is where you will live and work in the future. The things you consider and hold fondly in your mind as the focus of your intent will guide your feet and form your path. So what will that path be: past problems, present worries, or God's eternal promise? It's an important choice.

Some necks have grown stiff from the stress of twisting to see what should be left behind while trying to go forward. Many have stumbled, looking at what God told them to forget and pass by. Where are the eyes of your heart leading you today? God is moving ahead of you, not toward the past. No matter what has happened before, He has something good planned for all who receive the gift of Jesus Christ. Look for Him, not for you.

In God's will, the past is sealed like a letter addressed only to Him. He will take care of it and finish it. The future is also addressed and delivered only to Him. It doesn't belong to us. Already, He has cleansed the road behind you and in front of you. He has prepared a new path for your future. Look and see where the Lord is shining ahead of you today. Then in the glow of that light, you can see clearly those who walk with you. Walk forward in the light that goes all the way into eternity, and never look back. By faith, begin to see clearly today where you're going in your Savior's steps.

Father, I want to move in Your light in Christ that heals my life and leads me forward into what only You can do. By grace, give me faith to receive Your Son, who conquers my darkness. In Jesus' name, amen.

John 8:10-12   Ps. 37:3-6   2 Cor. 5:7

DIVIDE THE SACRIFICE February 16

Then he [Abraham] brought all these [sacrifices] to Him and cut them in two, down the middle, and placed each piece opposite the other; but he did not cut the birds in two . . . And it came to pass, when the sun went down and it was dark, that behold, there appeared a smoking oven and a burning torch that passed between those pieces.

Gen. 15:10, 17

Covenants were sealed with sacrifice and the pouring out of blood. The main sacrifice was divided, and in this case the presence of God passed between the pieces. It would seem enough simply to kill an animal and lay it before God as a sacrifice, but the divided pieces allowed those making the covenant to pass through them, sealing their unity. This division shows the sacrifice was completely surrendered to God, and there was room for Him to walk inside of it. Whatever was offered had no more life or cohesion in itself, but the Creator moved through its core and claimed it for His own.

Unlike us, God cannot be divided. He is the One who is who He is. His name is "I am." He is completely, eternally one. Everything that is created can be divided—people, animals, plants, rocks. All are compositions of molecules that can be divided or split apart at various points. Only an eternal Creator can create and perform an eternal covenant by bringing us through a divided sacrifice that is completely His.

When His physical body died and was pierced, Christ was divided from His Father. This was the only time He ever experienced division because He was dying in our place for our sin. The miracle of the resurrection is that the Eternal One passed through and beyond this division in His divine integrity and brought all together in the perfect unity of His resurrection. This power is the new covenant in His blood. He healed us from the division of death once for all. Yet we must each pass through it in Christ. Even in our prayers now, we are to offer to Him a divided, surrendered sacrifice, knowing that in the power of His covenant, all can be made whole.

But first, He must pass between the pieces and move through the core of our lives. If we let the sword of His truth divide us, His power will resurrect us. Think of anything you are praying for now, and offer it up to God as a sacrifice split right down the middle, divided at the core, and laid out before Him. In this, your will is broken and dies. In that place of division and surrender, let His light pass through the center of your life in resurrection power. Healing begins, and unity is possible. It is the early morning rays of the sun coming into the open tomb. It is the Son living in you!

Father, receive my life and my will as a sacrifice divided and laid out before You. Walk between the pieces, claim me, and make me whole in Your power. In Jesus' name, amen.

Heb. 4:12-13 John 19:17-19, 30 Rom. 12:1-2

~~~~~~

FEED ME YOUR BREAD OF LIFE

Lord God, feed me Your bread of life in Jesus Christ so I no longer starve with the stones of man. Without Your Son, I hunger for life and wait for death, apart from You. Fill me up with Christ's life that never ends, bringing me into unity with Your will, close to Your heart. Thank You for the bread of heaven, broken for me and multiplied into eternity, complete in You. In Jesus' name, amen.

"Most assuredly, I say to you, he who believes in Me has everlasting life. I am the bread of life. Your fathers ate the manna in the wilderness, and are dead. This is the bread which comes down from heaven, that one may eat of it and not die. I am the living bread which came down from heaven. If anyone eats of this bread, he will live forever; and the bread that I shall give is My flesh, which I shall give for the life of the world."

John 6:47-51

John 6:52-63

~~~~~~

AT WHAT DISTANCE? February 18

Draw near to God and He will draw near to you. Cleanse your hands, you sinners; and purify your hearts, you double-minded.

James 4:8

At what distance are you looking for Jesus? When He draws near, do you back up to keep a safe distance between your life and the life that went to the cross? I have asked for healing from a distance, wisdom from a distance, and even His presence from a distance, and received whatever I could at that distance. But there is more, much more, in coming closer to kneel at His feet. There is no distance in His love. We are the ones who move away. Often we call out from an interested but safe distance to Christ to please do something for us here today. Words alone cannot open the door of prayer. Do we keep Him locked away in the past or in heaven, or do we look into the face of someone across the table, along the street, even in the eyes of our biggest problem, and see Jesus?

His first message was "Repent, for the kingdom of heaven is at hand." Right here! Even near you and in you! That close. Slow down, turn around, and receive Him. There is no distance Jesus Christ has not already covered, whether of time or location or life or death. He has covered the distance in love for us. He has spoken peace in unspeakable conditions. We don't have to go anywhere else or become anything different to step into peace and newness of life. But we do have to allow Him to come closer and touch us. The power of that touch changes us and others. For some, this seems more frightening than whatever the problem is, so they prefer to struggle with the problem at a distance, not close enough to sit down and eat with the Healer.

Preoccupation with old wounds will hold us back to a safe distance. Too many words will keep Him away. Constant work and activity, even good projects, will increase the distance. We can make another person whom we try to control our god instead of Him. Religious activities done for their own sake also can maintain the distance.

Of course, sin would be what we expect to keep Him away, but that is why He came and comes today. He can come closer to a sinner who seeks Him than to a religious person who is too busy. A casual attitude toward His holiness will safely increase the distance. Human preconditions and manipulation will keep Him still farther away. Only humility and unconditional surrender will shrink the distance to the point of contact. For some, the distance shrinks instantly in one moment of conversion. For others, it comes closer day by day until, amazingly, we find ourselves standing in His presence on holy ground, receiving His transforming touch and His Word in our hearts.

O God, draw me to You so I can truly know You. In the name of Jesus, who comes as close as the breath of the Spirit, may I now be still enough to know You here. Amen.

Luke 7:36-50 John 5:39-40 Luke 10:38-42

EAT THE WORD   February 19

But He answered and said, "It is written, 'Man shall not live by bread alone, but by every word that proceeds from the mouth of God.'"

Matt. 4:4

As food for true life, Scripture comes to us from our Creator. Others may convey it to our table, but they are not the source of the food. We are to eat God's Word and digest it for both spiritual and physical action, not merely dissect and rearrange it on our plates for discussion or decoration. Who would know most about this food—those who have eaten it, digested it, and moved in its energy, or those who are still dissecting what is on their plates? Only by receiving the Author, the Creator, can we receive and live what is written. It is good to study food, but if we do only this, we will die.

The time for analysis is after we have eaten enough to stay alive and are filled with energy to complete the work at hand. We can explore, but this should be after we have tasted and eaten the food of faith, absorbing its truth, to know the life and power it can give in order to know the Source. If our food merely stays on the plate, any illumination we bring to the discussion is limited by an empty perspective. Only those who digest spiritual truth and live in the spiritual energy of the gospel will be able to explain its depth and reveal its ongoing life, because the Author is living in them.

Food that is left too long on the plate becomes spoiled and unappetizing. In this atmosphere, will newcomers to our table be eager to eat the food they need to survive? Will there be any real food left to serve them? After lengthy dissection and debate, we may know the chemical composition of the food, as well as its history of production and processing before it got to the plate. But we will not know its life—what it can produce in us, what action and changes might result from letting it burn at the core of our lives.

At some point, the morsels of speculation we are toying with become inedible and lose nutritional value. We should eat our daily bread hot out of the oven as it is served to us by the Holy Spirit! Then the exploration of its meaning will be full of the energy and personality of the Author. It is first His life we are seeking and eating, not an explanation of nutritional theory. If you knew people who needed this food to survive, would you encourage them to analyze it or to eat it? Would you have anything to feed them?

Father, fill me with the power of Your Living Word today. Let its love flow through me in action. Open my heart to receive Your truth and then to do it and fully understand. In Jesus' name, amen.

John 6:63   James 1:17-25   John 13:17

February 20

~~~~~~

DO GOD'S LOVE

Father, make me do what You love. Make my heart right with Yours, no matter how everything else turns out. For years, I've asked You to make me obedient to what You require. I have prayed for You to help me to do what is right and to finish everything that is needed. Now, I simply ask that You make me do what You love, for walking in Your love fulfills all requirements and finishes the work Your way. You are more pleased with the inner degree of my love for You and others than with the outer perfection of the work. In fact, love is the true perfection. Even if the requirements seem to be unmet or the work unfinished in human eyes, this imperfect work in love is more pleasing to You than anything else done without love. Living in Your heart changes mine. Your love completes everything in due season. Please bring me out of my works and into Your love so that Your fruit will grow in this place for Your kingdom. In Jesus' name, amen.

And above all things have fervent love for one another, for "love will cover a multitude of sins."

1 Pet. 4:8

John 14:21

~~~~~~

CUT CLEAR THROUGH   February 21

"I am the true vine, and my Father is the vinedresser. Every branch in Me that does not bear fruit He takes away; and every branch that bears fruit He prunes, that it may bear more fruit."

John 15:1-2

At some point, most of us are bogged down in problems that only God's truth can penetrate and solve. Each hindrance must be cut through completely by His Word. In trying to untangle things, human solutions only weigh us down further as we struggle in a growing thicket of complications. Today, simply lay your life before God and allow Him to cut through to the core of the situation. Something will have to go. It might surprise you what stays and what goes. Then you can see clearly once the unnecessary debris is cleared away. The first step in removing an unfruitful branch is to penetrate it. Once the clear, clean truth of His life has penetrated your situation, change can begin.

A surface poke or a little scratch does not reach the core. Some of us try to remove what is wrong without letting God cut clear through it first. We try to manipulate it in our power or to change the appearance of it with our words, but only God's Word can cut to the core and render it lifeless, even though the outer shell of the problem may still be visible. Once it is cut through, any bondage, a past failure, or even a human strength that holds you back, will become a husk of its former power which can be safely removed in God's time. He will take it away to make room for good fruit.

Whatever concerns you today, whatever keeps you from going forward in faith, lay it out and expose it to the Creator's sharp sword of truth. This you can do now, no matter how bad things are. Pray on the basis of some Scripture that directly affects your problem, or if you don't know any, apply the gospel of John or the book of Romans, a few verses at a time. All day, let the situation rest against that Word of God, while morning and evening you thank Him in the midst of the problem. During this time, watch what you say during the day and your tone of voice so there is plenty of room for His Word to penetrate deeply.

Listen for His voice while you are surrendered, and keep your eyes on the glistening edge of His truth working below the surface. Continue to press the situation against His Word. Focus on the point where truth touches and begins to sink in. Once the situation is penetrated, God can easily remove any dead wood as you release it to Him. (It may be something good in the world's eyes, even your old means of survival.) Once the wood is dead in your mind, it can be removed with much less pain than a branch still green with human desire. Let Him cut clear through to victory.

Lord, cut through the mess in my life. Cut through to the core. Let Your truth make me free in Jesus Christ to walk in new life in Your power. In Jesus' name, amen.

Heb. 4:12-16   Heb. 9:14   Rev. 1:12-18

AT THE END OF THE DAY   February 22

"Simon, son of Jonah, do you love Me more than these?"

John 21:15

At the end of the day, after we've talked and taught about Jesus, unless we love Him first, it doesn't matter. All the hopes and projects in the world are lifeless without His loving presence active now in us and moving through us to others. We can work hard for Him, do devotions, and attend church regularly, but unless we love Him more than these, it won't matter. If we have a degree in theology and all the knowledge books can give or a busy ministry but have no love, it doesn't matter. If we are the most concerned parents in the world, striving to do everything for our children and loving them with every ounce of human love we can muster but don't have the love of Jesus, it doesn't matter. Only when we are rooted first in His love can we love them enough.

We can be the worst of sinners, reformed and converted with powerful testimonies and the ability to help others, but if we don't love Him more than our testimony and reaching others, it doesn't matter. At the end of the day, who we are, what we have done in the past, or what we're doing now counts as nothing compared to whether we love Him as He loves us. Out of that love, real fruit grows, and we can love others more deeply.

Some of His servants may accomplish only one visible act of service for the Lord, but it might be done with more love for Him in that one simple act than you or I will offer Him in a lifetime. He sees the love and knows those who offer it. Our love for Him opens our lives completely to His power. If you had a great inheritance to offer your children, would you give the most to those who were hardworking and stable, those who were extremely talented and educated, or those who loved you the most, although they had faults? Love is the key. To love Jesus "more than these" could mean to love Him more than others do, or to love Him more than we love other people. Either way, it is the same. Love is the key that opens the door. No amount of pounding or knowledge of locks and hinges will work without the key that turns the lock.

When faith works through God's love (Gal. 5:6), then it is matched and multiplied into eternity. Human love falls short. Its fruit looks good, but it dies early and leaves little behind. Divine love, agape love, comes from above and produces fruit that lasts, flowing from and returning to God's heart. What do others hear in your voice and work: earthly urgency, worldly love for people, worry, good intentions, knowledge? Do you love Him more than these?

Father, open me to love You first with all of my heart, soul, mind, and strength, and then my neighbor as myself. Put my life in order according to the power of Your love that alone can transform and draw us to You. In Jesus' name, amen.

John 13:35   Mark 12:28-31   1 Cor. 13:1-10

February 23

~~~~~~

FIND ME

Find me, Lord God, where I am. Carry me home in Your strength on Your Son's shoulders, which carried the cross. Until now, I didn't let you carry me, preferring to come in my own strength, my way. Now I ask: Please, carry me wherever You want to go, Your way. I will let You move me instead of my trying to move You. Find me here, carry me where You will, and bring me home. In Jesus' name, amen.

"What man of you, having a hundred sheep, if he loses one of them, does not leave the ninety-nine in the wilderness, and go after the one which is lost until he finds it? And when he has found it, he lays it on his shoulders, rejoicing. And when he comes home, he calls together his friends and neighbors, saying to them, 'Rejoice with me, for I have found my sheep which was lost!'"

Luke 15:4-6

Phil. 3:7-12

~~~~~~

DONE WITH THE DIRT
February 24

"He who believes in Me, as the Scripture has said, out of his heart will flow rivers of living water."

John 7:38

Belief in Jesus leads to action. When rivers of living water start to flow through our hearts, they bring a cleansing that changes everything. On the inside, sin and sorrow are washed away. On the outside, our lives shed the worldly habits and caked-on dirt that keep the light of God from shining clearly into us and through us. When the waters flow, the dirt has to go. As the new comes in, we begin to be done with the dirt. The process takes a while, but the results are startling. Subtle webs and unseen dust suddenly become obvious when we begin to see our lives through the mind of Christ. His eyes can spot camouflaged filth, and His power can wash it out if we let Him do a complete job. Both spiritually and physically, our Lord can clean like no other. As our Bridegroom, He washes and changes us through His blood and His Living Word to be His spotless bride. These cleaning tips let us cooperate with Him to remove the dirt.

Don't just move the filth to another place. Get it clear out. What's true for cleaning your house or your car is the same for your life. What if each time you vacuumed the car, you emptied the dirt into your trunk? You can try cleaning your house by moving the mess to another room, but eventually it will creep out. End it and reject it.

Realize there is always spiritual dirt you can't see. Clean regularly with the washing of the water of God's Word and the washing of regeneration and renewing of the Holy Spirit. Even when you think you don't need it, in reality, you do. Continuously, the branch must be joined to the Vine. Our physical bodies require regular food and cleansing, just as a fruitful plant needs regular sunshine. To be done with the dirt, allow the Living Word to wash you regularly through the Holy Spirit and remove unseen stains before they are firmly set in your soul.

Follow the directions completely. It does no good to get out the cleaning supplies each week, read the directions to one another, make a symbolic swipe here and there, and then put it away until next week. Apply the directions now. Don't stop half way through or omit the steps that are inconvenient. Once the process starts, let it come to completion. If you clean all the floor except one corner, is it clean? If you wash the windows but leave one section dirty, what will you see? For a moment, look at your life through that window. The section left unclean is your blind spot. Everyone has one. Only Jesus Christ can make us whole, open to His light. Ask Him to wash everything and wipe your life clean. Be done with the dirt.

Father, cover me in the blood of the Lamb, Jesus. Wash me in Your Word today. Make my heart clean and pure so I can see Your life growing in me. In Jesus' name, amen.

Titus 3:3-7   John 15:3-4   Eph. 5:25-27

EAT WHAT IS GOOD   February 25

"It is the Spirit who gives life; the flesh profits nothing. The words that I speak to you are spirit, and they are life."

John 6:63

To grow, we must eat what is good. Appealing poison, even if self-chosen and preferred by multitudes, will kill us in the end. Consider your menu for today, your activities and priorities. There are probably a few "specials" highly promoted by the world, things you must do now to get the best deal and the most satisfaction for yourself. Yet, if you are eating only what human ability offers, you will die. There are also healthy choices, probably simpler and not as appealing, but sure to give you energy for what you really need to do. Spiritually, are the choices you make today causing you to grow or to die? There is food that the world does not understand. Have you ever tasted anything totally beyond what the world has packaged and promoted?

Jesus offers a meal that will satisfy all who come to Him and receive His life, transformed into action. In His body and blood given for us on the cross, we find the secret to what is good for us both spiritually and physically. The resurrection proved the effectiveness of this meal, still eaten by servants, sinners, fishermen, doubters, and tax collectors, each fed by a Master who first washes their feet. Much more than food is included in our meal with Him. Our Provider wants our fellowship at the table. Most of all, He wants to eat with us, sharing His life with us completely. Imagine eating food that someone prepared and left for you on a table, but both of you never took the time to sit down and share a meal together. Would you know the provider? In the breaking of the bread of life, Jesus Christ reveals Himself personally to us, and we enter a relationship of selfless love that nourishes us day by day into eternity. What are you eating today? More importantly, with whom are you eating?

Father, feed me with the pure life of Jesus Christ. Let Your Living Word move through me in action to bring others to the feast of Your love. In Jesus' name, amen.

Ps. 81:10-16   Rev. 3:20   John 6:26-40, 51-54

EVERY MOLECULE   February 26

All things were made through Him, and without Him nothing was made that was made. In Him was life, and the life was the light of men.

                                                              John 1:3-4

Without God, we have no life. Every molecule in intricate detail was created by God through His breath and spoken power. Even parts of the universe that are not aware of Him are still spoken and formed by the same life that goes on forever (Acts 17:24-28; Col. 1:16-17). From the beginning, each of our lives was formed by Him for a holy purpose, whether or not we acknowledge it or even try to follow the plan. The purpose remains unchanged and fulfilled only in God. Without our Source, we are only partially fulfilled in this life and ultimately changeable into death. Since God does not change, He transforms us through His Son so we are not consumed (Mal. 3:6).

No matter what we do, our spirits are a gift from the Creator. Through free will, we are able to work with Him eternally or against Him briefly. As each molecule in our bodies was originally created by God for His purpose, in a sense we are only borrowing them to use for a short while. Daily, He is watching to see what we will do with them. Everything—the minerals and proteins, the electricity that charges through us, and all the networking of nerves and brain cells that makes the body work—is a gift we use on borrowed time. Even the time is not ours and flows quickly beyond us. No matter how our schedules are packed, since we certainly did not create the time, we cannot control it by adding or subtracting even one second.

Freely, we are simply passing through, walking into what our Creator has already planned. As we go along, our eyes are either closed spiritually or open to see the big picture of what is developing around us and in us through His eternal power and amazing grace. Today, consider that every atom you're using and every moment you walk through is borrowed for a short time. You can do whatever you want with them for now, but ultimately they belong to the Originator. He has a plan. What will you do with this unique gift already on its way back to Him?

Father, create in me what pleases You and fits with the beauty of Your creation. Redeem me in the blood of Your Son so I am completely Yours. In Jesus' name, amen.

Ps. 139   Eph. 2:4-10   Luke 19:11-27

ENVELOPE OF FIRE   February 27

For with You is the fountain of life; in Your light we see light.

Ps. 36:9

Living and growing in Christ, we are covered in His life and light. His light burns within us as "this little light of mine," but we also have His light burning around us in a living envelope of spiritual fire. Just as a seed that is encased in a covering of layers, once the chaff falls away, we are awakened in the envelope of His life to slowly produce visible fruit. The closer we are to Him, the more His energy will burn in us as well as around us. In this living, moving, breathing envelope of pure fire, we can move through the world and not be of the world. The Lord's presence around us protects the living flame within us. God brought His people into the Promised Land to settle after He had built His tabernacle with them. It held a flame within and followed a pillar of fire.

God doesn't ask us to burn alone for Him in our world today. As we are drawn into the fire of His love, we come to the altar and burn in Him as one in the fire of Christ's sacrifice. We don't burn alone, but as one in the living sacrifice of Jesus Christ that burns forever (Eph. 5:2). Enveloped and aflame with that love, we are covered within and without in the power of His resurrection. When we ask Christ's presence to go with us, we are moving into the envelope of eternity. Whatever does not fit into that envelope of living fire cannot be in our lives now. Our focus must be on Christ's life.

As a symphony keeps all eyes on the conductor to make beautiful music, so we let Christ lead us in the music of life that surrounds us and fills us with that singing fire. We are fully alive when enveloped as a living flame in that sound. The heat of this living envelope, burning with one purpose, fits us together with the pattern of heaven. If we are content to let our single flame burn alone for God, unaware of the enveloping symphony of His beauty, we miss the composition of the ages that burns far wider than any one flame alone. There are solo seasons, but they will merge again into His larger pattern. Like God's tabernacle in the wilderness, the covering of His life protects and purifies us, leads us, and envelopes every holy thing dedicated to Him. As with the cloud by day and the pillar of fire by night, His people do not move until the covering moves. What is inside does not move until what is outside, what is higher and holier, moves first. Each one in his own tent moves with the larger covering to reach God's destination.

In Christ, God has finished His tabernacle with men, and He is completing it in and around each one of us now, burning truth in us. Each day, He moves us in the living envelope of His light. Sealed in the living flame of God's love, we can move in unity with the tabernacle of heaven (Heb. 8:1-5; Rev. 15:5).

Father, let me live always in the fire of Your love in Jesus Christ. In Jesus' name, amen.

1 John 1:7   Gal. 3:26-29   Ps. 97:3-5

February 28

EVERYTHING

Father, I want to know Your fullness in Christ. Help me to let go of everything I'm trying to do for You and instead let You do everything in me so I become complete in Your will. With no preconditions, I surrender my entire life to You, not just a piece here or there. Everything is Yours. How can the Holy Spirit fill me with the fullness of Your Son, and how can I be part of His body when I am so full of myself? Empty me of my own will so You can be all and all in me for Your purpose alone. My selfishness blocks not only my filling with Your Spirit but also the connection to the growing body of Christ in Your kingdom. Before, You were an important part of my life, but now I give You full reign. Make me part of Your kingdom. Bring me into steady alignment so pure light shines through, and You're seen as You really are: Master and Sustainer, All in All, Redeemer, Lord of everything. Make me one with Your truth in Christ with nothing between His righteousness and my life enveloped in the flame of Your love. It's all Yours, and everything rests under His feet. In Jesus' name, amen.

And He put all things under His feet, and gave Him to be head over all things to the church, which is His body, the fullness of Him who fills all in all.

Eph. 1:22-23

Luke 12:27-40

FAITH TO BUILD ON   February 29

By faith Abraham obeyed when he was called to go out to the place which he would receive as an inheritance. And he went out, not knowing where he was going. By faith he dwelt in the land of promise as in a foreign country, dwelling in tents with Isaac and Jacob, the heirs with him of the same promise; for he waited for the city which has foundations, whose builder and maker is God.

                                                          Heb. 11:8-10

Faith is the only sure foundation for the future that will pass the test of time. Everything else is sand. Even the best plans can sift through the hourglass very quickly. If we seek something real, we will find it, as Abraham did, in obedience to God. When we go out, not knowing where we are going and still living in tents, we are waiting for the same foundation as Abraham received. Tents are temporary, but God's promise is eternal. Whatever He is building, laying the foundations while we wait, it will stand complete and last forever (1 Cor. 3:11). Since we walk by faith and not by sight, our eyes are on the city of God, even while we're in the shaky tents.

The world, which is busy building its sand castles, thinks tents are very foolish. Some say we should join them on the beach and have something to show for ourselves. Abraham left all he had to show for himself and went out to see what God would show him. He answered the call. He left it all to let God build him, his family, all those with him, and even future generations in faith a house much bigger than what he could see with his eyes.

The architect sees not what is there, but what will be. He draws out walls, doors, and rooms, and allows plenty of space for the people to live. The builder follows the plan. The owner pays the price and then moves in. God is supreme architect, builder, and owner. Seen with the eyes of faith, His earliest promise contains the complete result so we can know that what He has planned will appear. Whatever is in the seed blooms out later, even as a mustard seed becomes a tree large enough for birds to nest in.

When Jesus heals our blindness, we can see not only with our faith but also with His faith that carries us through to the complete result. Faith to build on is a gift from God that lays the foundation for the future. We really have no future without it, but only sand that washes away. Our Creator may let us play in a sandbox until we're ready to let Him build something that will last (Gal. 3:14, 23-25). Upon what is your future built today?

Father, You know I've been busy with this sandy mess for a long time. The best I can do keeps crumbling. Please help me to grow up and get out of the sandbox. Build my future on Your foundation in Jesus Christ. Give me His faith. Call me out, and I will come to the city You are building in love. In Jesus' name, amen.

Heb. 3:3-6   Heb. 12:22-27   Acts. 3:1-16

PASSOVER — DELIVERANCE, RESURRECTION

Enter the season of passing out of our captivity and into the kingdom of God through His Son's death and resurrection to restore all things according to God's eternal plan.

Exod. 12:1-17; 14:9-15:2

John 1:29; 19:17-37

John 20:11-31

Acts 3:19-21

Col. 1:1-20

THE PASSOVER DOOR   March 1

"And they shall take some of the blood [of the Passover lamb] and put it on the two doorposts and on the lintel of the houses where they eat it."

Exod. 12:7

In receiving Christ, we receive complete deliverance from the bondage of old ways and move into full covenant life with God in the way and the place He chooses. As it was for the Jews coming out of captivity in Egypt, it is the same for us now. We must not only realize the Lamb has been slain for us but also receive Him and apply His blood to our lives. The blood of the Lamb Jesus must be placed directly on the door where we actively share His life. We must not hide it but instead ask God to apply His Son's life visibly to the outward side of our service in this world, as well as to the inner sanctum of our hearts. On the way to freedom, we touch the wood of the cross on the door posts of our lives, covered in the blood of the Lamb.

Knowing about the power of the blood of the Lamb is not enough. Only those who applied it that night in Egypt were saved. His protection and deliverance require a visible sign with specific action. We can't just agree with it and sit there. To be free, God's people in Egypt had to apply the blood, leave the past behind, and go through that door of deliverance that led to a future full of the promises of God.

Have you not only eaten the Lamb and applied His blood, but also come through the doorway that He covers? This door is the place of coming in and going out, a gate of transformation covered in the righteousness of Christ. Feast on Him and walk through His life wherever He leads, confidently satisfied in God's power to deliver you into complete freedom and to bring you to the place in His kingdom where He wants you to be for His glory.

Father, thank You for complete deliverance in Jesus Christ through His blood given for me, the same life that rose from the dead. He came into my heart to bring me out of myself and into Him with joy. Make me free to live in Your Son. In Jesus' name, amen.

John 1:29   John 8:31-36   Luke 22:14-20

FIND US

Father, find us where we are now. Even in a storm, the Shepherd goes out to look for lost sheep. In love, Your Son brings us home because You long for us and You send Him to search for us even now. Find us in this rocky place. Forgive us for hiding in our own plans, our own wounds, and human solutions. When we call out wherever we are, Your Son seeks and saves the lost. In the Holy Spirit, He finds us, blessing us with the peace that passes understanding. Through the cross, You work wonders even in weakness. We've fallen over the cliff of our own desires with lame excuses, slipping under the pressure of the world. We've wasted time trying to please people and fix everything ourselves. O Father, heal us now. We turn and call out like lost lambs. Old burdens have broken us, but now we give them to You. Find us, Father. Bring us home in the new light of Your Son. In Jesus' name, amen.

"For the Son of Man has come to save that which was lost. What do you think? If a man has a hundred sheep, and one of them goes astray, does he not leave the ninety-nine and go to the mountains to seek the one that is straying? And if he should find it, assuredly, I say to you, he rejoices more over that sheep than over the ninety-nine that did not go astray."

Matt. 18:11-13

John 10:1-11, 30

DO SOMETHING   March 3

Finally, my brethren, be strong in the Lord and in the power of His might.

Eph. 6:10

If we want to do something for the Lord, we must be willing to be weak. Then He can make us strong. To really do something, we must let God do it. "Be strong in the Lord," says Paul, not "with" the Lord or "for" the Lord. Only His power fills us to overflowing. Otherwise, the more we try to do on our own, the more exhausted we become until there is a fainting in our spirits, and the work is left undone. When we come to the King to receive what He can do, it will be at His command, not ours, and by His Spirit alone (Zech. 4:6). First, He works in us and then through us with the result of praise rising to Him from those who see what He can do. They are not going to praise Him for what we can do. If the people are to see Jesus as He really is and come to know the Father, they must see Him at work.

As we get out of the way, they will see Him as He is, far better than if we simply tell them what He is like. In order for God to be glorified, it must be clear that the works are His, not ours. That is why many people leave a church—because it is doing its own works for human goals. It tastes artificial. People know when it is not really of God. He has built into us all a capacity for truth, and we are hungry for it. Since anything that really works and lives is for His satisfaction, we will be blessed and most satisfied when He is satisfied and His will is done. "O taste and see that the Lord is good!" (Ps. 34:8)

We're not supposed to just keep reading the menu on our own. As we turn to receive Christ, we discover that whatever God provides is pure and wholly satisfying. To our hunger, it tastes really good. There can be no improvement on it with human energy or knowledge. God has created us to let Him work but He has also given us a free will to try to do our own things without Him. Who is doing something in your life? And how does it taste?

Father, I give up and let go of all I have tried to do on my own. I bow before You alone who changes everything and works through me what only Your power can create. In Jesus' name, amen.

Phil. 4:13   John 15:5   Ps. 84

HOLY FIRE BURNING

March 4

So he looked, and behold, the bush was burning with fire, but the bush was not consumed. Then Moses said, "I will now turn aside and see this great sight, why the bush does not burn." So when the Lord saw that he turned aside to look, God called to him from the midst of the bush and said, "Moses, Moses!" And he said, "Here I am."

Exod. 3:2-4

God's holy fire draws people to Him. Sometimes it burns quietly for years, softening the edges of unbelief before breaking through to shine clearly in the mind and will. In others, it shines so intensely there is a sudden melting and turning to God. Christ said, "No one can come to Me unless the Father who sent Me draws him; and I will raise him up at the last day" (John 6:44). By the Holy Spirit, God draws us with the fire of His love, even if we struggle in a wilderness or tend to business in some desert. His fire claims our attention without destroying what will burn for Him and let His truth speak.

If something stands against Him, God's holy fire burns it up; but He will not destroy what stands for Him and what He can speak through to deliver His people and glorify His name. In the early church, it was not large buildings with impressive rituals or fun programs that attracted new believers. It was the fire of God burning in the hearts of His children, shining on their faces and bringing glory to His name even in the worst persecution. People with questions saw the answer burning in the faces of Christians who not only preached His Word but also lived it. Would I be willing to die for a discussion or a building or a ritual? Not likely. But I would die for the love of One who died for me when His flame is shining in the face of a brother or sister living in His truth and that fire touches my heart. Where do you see His love burning today?

You will never see anything more beautiful. It will turn your head and change your mind. I have seen faces even in great hardship shining with the love of Jesus, and that silent, burning witness still changes my heart. More than anything we can do or say for God, He wants us to burn with His love here, releasing a heavenly stream of transforming fire. The bush was not consumed but simply provided a framework in which the fire could speak. This is what the wood of the cross does in us. Never destroyed, it becomes a living, burning framework of sacrificial love in our lives that allows God to speak through us and shine into other hearts. He is the only source.

If we live in the cross, His love will burn in us and His love will speak louder than words. Then people will come to see holy fire, not a church building or activities, but His love in your face, your words, and your life. By the Holy Spirit, this fire speaks now.

Father, let the fire of Your love burn in me and speak life. In Jesus' name, amen.

Matt. 3:11   Matt. 5:16   2 Cor. 3:2-6

March 5

~~~~~~

THE EXTRA LOAD OFF

Father, I understand that Christ spoke to Peter about how Peter would eventually die for Him, and told Peter to follow Him anyway. I don't really want to be a martyr; I've just wanted to do everything expected by the world and also whatever You ask me to do. This is what is killing me—trying to do both. In trying to save it all, I am losing it all. Help me to do what You want first. Make me like Peter, the strong one who had denied Christ and yet was forgiven, so that after my mistakes I can still love You enough to follow Your way. I have been carrying the extra load of worldly mammon. I have been carrying the extra load of trying to meet human expectations that distract me from You. Now I want only Your way. Free me to follow the cross of Christ that carries me into new life. My freedom comes in laying down my old life so the load will be lighter. If I listen to You, there will be less material gain, but life will be richer and deeper. You can make the bitter taste sweet with honey from the Rock. When difficulties come, Christ lifts the load with me. In the past, present, and future, He is the same. Help me to listen to You and do just what You ask, and nothing more than what I see You doing in love. I lay down the extra load of mammon and ask for the manna, the living bread of Jesus Christ. In total forgiveness, place His yoke upon me so I can fly to You as if that wood were wings, lifting up the power of the cross in my life. In Jesus' name, amen.

This He spoke, signifying by what death he would glorify God. And when He had spoken this, He said to him, "Follow Me."

John 21:19

Luke 9:12-29

~~~~~~

FAITHFUL IN LITTLE
March 6

"And he said to him, 'Well done, good servant; because you were faithful in a very little, have authority over ten cities.'"

Luke 19:17

Little things are the secret roots of big things. Spiritual riches and power come through being faithful in what is little in the world's eyes. In fact, all of our things are little in God's eyes. Compared to His kingdom, the finest human accomplishment seems very small. On the other hand, all of God's things are very big, though at first they may seem little and weak to us in this world. One simple act of kindness can be the key that unlocks huge benefits and eternal spiritual reward (Matt. 10:42). A small seed of faith can move mountains. As we are faithful in very little, God weaves a multitude of tiny, beautiful acts of kindness into a much larger plan. Our Creator is an expert at fitting small things together to make something greater than we can see if we will give Him control of the masterpiece taking shape in us and around us.

Give Him all the details, and the overall project will succeed. If you give Him just the tall things in your plans, eventually the foundation will begin to crumble. The little, low things are the key. What seems important in worldly eyes may be of slight consequence for the future. Give the Master Potter everything so He can wash it in the blood of His Son, turn it together on the wheel of His will, and bring forth beauty in the fire of His love, more beauty than we can handle.

On the other hand, if we think something is too important in the world's eyes to surrender to Him, it becomes a stiff lump on the wheel and has to be crushed before it can merge into God's plan. Once given to Him, humble things, whatever their size, will fit in well. They blend in smoothly, move easily with the water of life, bow to the curve of the Master Potter's hand, and finally reflect the shining image of His touch. By faith, they become the basis and sustaining structure for all the big things yet to come.

Lord, teach me the importance of little things. Make me faithful in whatever You put in my hand to do. Humbly, I place it all in Your hand to form beauty out of my life, a beauty turning beyond me into the fullness of Your kingdom. In Jesus' name, amen.

Matt. 17:18-21   Zech. 4:6-10   Luke 16:10-13

FOCUS ON THE LIGHT   March 7

In Him was life, and the life was the light of men.

John 1:4

We may try to view many things through our darkness—entertainment, work, family, the past, present, and future—but we can truly see them only if we look at them through the light of Christ's truth. Focus on that light and what it shows you. All around you and in you there may be darkness and some false lights that glitter only with a surface sheen but have no real light living in them. Focus on the real light of God. Like a beacon for a ship in a dark night, His light will guide you as you focus on it, not on the waves and the rocks or the shadowy line of the shore.

There is a type of beacon that guides ships from one point to another. The pilot focuses on a large light ahead and lines it up with another smaller light below it. These lights shine steadily even through a storm. When the lights are lined up, he is right on course. If they begin to separate, the pilot knows he is veering off to the side and needs to make a correction. When we line up with Christ, so that the lower light of our lives is not separate from Him but is in complete alignment, then the two lights burn as one. When our eye is single to Him to receive the life-giving flow of His faith and truth, we will not only move toward His light but also grow in that light of life. We will go straight into His kingdom without wavering.

It is the light of His love that draws us to God, for out of the bosom of Christ, He has shined on the nations and has lit a fire in our hearts that lines up perfectly with His purpose and truth. Focus on the true light, wherever it shines in your life. Fix your eyes and heart on the Living Word and follow Him. Don't focus on the shifting darkness all around and its deceptively flashy signs. Line up with the Giver of life and let His pure, steady light bring you through to glory!

Father, when I keep my eyes on You in Jesus, all the darkness around me dissolves in Your presence. Shine in me now and bring me through the cross into Your glory. In Jesus' name, amen.

Ps. 43:3-4   Matt. 6:21-23   1 John 1:6-9

FIRE CONSUMES UPWARD

March 8

For our God is a consuming fire.

Heb. 12:29

In worship and obedience, our lives become one with Christ, a living sacrifice to be consumed upward in God's holy fire. Our willingness to come to the altar is not enough to lift us. It's the heat of the fire that raises us as an offering into God's realm. The sacrifice does not light the fire. Through the Holy Spirit, God sends His fire to purify and transform what is offered, to change it completely from what it was before to what it is becoming in His power. As Jesus, though sinless, was offered on the cross and then raised in the pure fire of the resurrection, in Him we are changed by the same process (Matt. 3:11). When we ask for the fire of the Holy Spirit to come, we are asking not only for Him to ignite us for worship and work on the earth now, but we are also asking to be transformed and consumed upward into the reality of God's power for all time.

When we are willing to be consumed, His fire will come. That purifying fire prepares us for heavenly as well as earthly things. In the Old Testament, burnt offerings fulfilled God's law on earth and also prefigured the coming transformation of all creation in Jesus' sacrifice and in the power of His resurrection with a new heaven and a new earth. His fire is already burning in obedient hearts even today. It burns with a song of grace and regeneration, mercy and truth, loss and gain. An offering consumed by fire loses its old shape and function. It collapses in the fire to become a sweet-smelling savor that moves up and out, traveling heavenward and yet filling more space on earth with its pleasant odor of sacrifice than its earthly shape could occupy.

Only ashes are left behind to be exchanged for His beauty and purity. Are we willing to leave behind old structures that enabled us to move on our own power? In His fire, they will collapse and become a sacrifice in Christ, producing a sweet aroma. The offering of your life in Jesus Christ will spread farther in His love than if you kept it and worked for Him in your own power. It is not enough just to put it on the altar. You must also let Him light the fire.

Like incense ignited in the temple, your life will become an expanding prayer in His presence. Often we expect His fire to improve some human ability to serve God. Instead, it is the end of reliance on our ability and the beginning of His burning in us to bring us completely into the reality of His life. As we surrender in prayer and obedience, our High Priest lights the fire. He stands before you now with living fire in His hands, and the flame of His eyes sees what you have placed on the altar.

Father, light your fire in me so my life will burn as one with the sacrifice and resurrection of Jesus Christ. I place everything on Your altar. In Jesus' name, amen.

Rev. 1:12-18   Luke 12:49   Rom. 12:1-3

~~~~~~

EMPTIED TO BE FULL

O Lord God, only when I'm emptied, can I be filled with Your life through Your Son. Forgive me for trying to be so full of myself and others that there is no room for You to truly dwell here, to come in to stay. In the humility of Jesus, empty me to hold Your living sacrifice as true beauty. Let Your refining fire cleanse me to receive more of Your Son's life now so my cup overflows in the joy of Your presence. In the name of Jesus Christ who gave Himself for me, amen.

Then He said to them all, "If anyone desires to come after Me, let him deny himself, and take up his cross daily, and follow Me. For whoever desires to save his life will lose it, but whoever loses his life for My sake will save it."

<div align="right">Luke 9:23-24</div>

Matt. 5:1-12

~~~~~~

THE FRUIT OF PRAYER   March 10

"Abide in Me, and I in you. As the branch cannot bear fruit of itself, unless it abides in the vine, neither can you, unless you abide in Me."

John 15:4

Prayer produces more fruit than work or knowledge. By the Holy Spirit, God reveals His glory, the outer edges of His presence, to empower us to do what He would do here and now. It may seem a waste of time to pray when so much needs to be done, but from time in prayer and abiding in the Vine comes the only power for life, not dead works. Coming through light-filled, honest prayer, this power reveals the life flow of Jesus Christ, the Vine, active in our world now (Rom. 8:26-32).

If we go ahead to work and then pray depending on how things turn out, the unconnected branch will strain to produce something, often a flat mirror image of itself, but not the full life of the Vine. Then the prayers become more anguished because we sense there is no life, just lots of action and earnest attempts to do good, but no living fruit. The smell of death is on the things we plan for ourselves. The fruit that remains and lives and grows will come only from the Spirit of God. People and programs can't produce it.

The living seed and flowing sap of full-dimensional fruit remains and reproduces from God's Word and the intents of His heart communicated to us in prayer by the Holy Spirit. A man-made replica of a seed will not grow. On our own, we can praise the planting process and sing as loud as we want, but nothing will come up!

Time in prayer opens us to receive the real seed of God's creative Word. Its fruit is so vast, we may never see it all, but in our nearness to Him in prayer, we can sense the fire of His purpose working, even in a tiny seed, a holy remnant, perhaps something almost unnoticeable, something in faraway places or in hardened hearts that as yet reveal no glimmer of hope. Meanwhile, His fire burns wider and deeper than we can fully understand, and we feel its heat in drawing near to God in fruitful prayer.

Unseen, the Creator's shining life still moves through the Vine into the branches. Where is the fruit revealed? It is revealed in His presence and in unexpected places where grace alone grows. God has already created all our works in Jesus Christ. He is only waiting for us to come and kneel before Him to find out what they are and how to move in His power!

Father, breathe Your life in me so that my prayers produce fruit in Your kingdom. Open my heart completely to Your power. In Jesus' name, amen.

Eph. 2:10-13   Matt. 8:1-17   1 Cor. 2:1-12

FOLLOW HIM March 11

Then He said to them, "Follow Me, and I will make you fishers of men." They immediately left their nets and followed Him.

Matt. 4:19-20

Jesus said to follow Him. He will not follow us. Often we try to go first, leaving Jesus in second place in case we need help. Wouldn't we rather just study Him and give directions based on what we think is best? Even religious people may try to keep Jesus in line behind them or their plans. "Aren't we working for Him? Why doesn't He help us?" they ask. In the flesh, it's easy to think of what should be done, but the Holy Spirit does not follow flesh. Instead, in the fire of God, our ways melt. When we read His Word, we wait on Him and listen for His voice. He may have something more productive in mind that requires the renewing of our minds and, above all, the surrender of our wills. Perhaps He is changing us more than those we try to serve.

Through the Holy Spirit, our carnal minds and wills must be conformed to the mind and will of Christ, who made Himself a servant and followed His Father's will, not His own (Phil 2:5-9). If we lead, we will avoid the cross. With us in charge, there is no dying to our self-focus and our flesh, and so there is no resurrection power to bring in the harvest or draw in the fish. If your boat is empty or headed the wrong direction, take a look at who is in the lead. Get behind Jesus. Be sure He goes first. Then you will have the authority to tell the enemy to get behind you. When you are following Jesus, He will say to all around you, "Peace, be still." That does not mean there will not be a storm, but that the storm will be conquered (Matt. 8:23-27). In safety, you will cross over to where the harvest is waiting in God's power alone.

Father, change me to let Your Son lead and bring many to You. Help me to follow Him humbly so others can hear His voice and respond to Your Spirit's work. In Jesus' name, amen.

John 10:3-11 John 21:3-14 Isa. 55:6-11

THE FULLNESS OF SILENCE   March 12

"Listen carefully to Me, and eat what is good, and let your soul delight itself in abundance. Incline your ear, and come to Me. Hear, and your soul shall live."

Isa. 55:2-3

Humble silence helps us to hear clearly and to receive the truth of God's word from above, implanted in us through Scripture, not from within us. Holy silence reveals our true identity and uncovers our motives. It allows us to receive the Father's revelation of Himself to us, without the interference of human static. Then when we do speak, the life of that revelation will carry more truth than human understanding and effort can produce. The Living Word, born in purity and humility can speak to us and through us if we will listen in that same humility. In a quiet heart, His Word speaks most loudly.

We have the written Word of God today because someone was willing to be silent and hear what God had to say. The Bible is not what human knowledge wanted or said. As God's Word, it reveals not just a story or a reason or "a narrative," but His divine essence. The character of the voice presents the character of the invisible personality, and since He is all in all, a clear revelation comes in our humble silence and obedience.

It's hard to hear when you're always talking. When you love people and truly know them, you can sit quietly with them, enjoying their presence. On the other hand, a relationship based on illusion must continually justify and promote itself loudly, holding up false props and facades. In silence, there is a humble rest that lovingly joins our communication with God to the center of His will. In that rest, we can receive His Word.

A relationship based on truth is secure in silence. More clarity and power is projected through pure silence than a false project can generate with multiple layers of words and images. Smoke and mirrors will need a lot of talk to keep the illusion going. Truth presents itself humbly and only grows greater in the piercing light of silence.

Then our words spoken later will carry the weight of that truth. All our fruitful words flow from God's Word from above in freedom from human chatter and our hasty "improvements" on the simple majesty of divine design. In this freedom, we can move with the right words to produce fruit rooted in the fertile silence woven through God's creation, speaking ever more loudly of His power alone. Vibrating with unspeakable love, the mystery of that silence amplifies the certainty of our faith. Lay your problems at His feet today. Apply His Word. Wait on the Lord and hear what He has to say.

Father, speak to me in the depths of Your beautiful presence in Your Word. Humbly, I wait for You first, and then my knowledge or answers will come. I will listen more than speak so that You can speak Your life in me through Jesus Christ. In His name, amen.

John 8:42-43   Isa. 53:6-9   John 7:44-46

March 13

〰〰〰〰〰〰〰〰〰〰〰〰〰〰〰〰〰〰〰〰〰〰〰〰〰〰

THROUGH THE EYE OF A NEEDLE

Father, only You can bring us into Your kingdom as through the eye of a needle. One thing goes through that eye, and it is a scarlet thread as Your Son was pierced—a sacrificial thread carrying us through the eye of truth into Your kingdom. The scarlet thread of the blood of Your covenant reaches through all time, even to this day. Bring me into the power of Your covenant through Jesus' blood poured out to save many. Draw Your people through the narrow gate into a wider reward than anything the world has to offer. Forgive us for attaching ourselves to things and desires that will not pass through that eye of sacrificial truth. Whatever would hold me back, I release it, lay it down, and leave it behind. Let nothing else try to squeeze into my thoughts or attach to my will or ride upon my heart that will not go through, covered in the blood of Your Son. In Him alone, I come, offering all my life to You as a living sacrifice. Your love in Christ will go through. Your mercy goes through. Your beauty goes through in holiness, humility, and the power of Jesus Christ living in me now. Nothing else I was counting on in this world will fit through that eye into eternity. Wash me in His blood, change me, and bring me through to You. In Jesus' name, amen.

"For it is easier for a camel to go through the eye of a needle than for a rich man to enter the kingdom of God."

Luke 18:25

Heb. 9:14

〰〰〰〰〰〰〰〰〰〰〰〰〰〰〰〰〰〰〰〰〰〰〰〰〰〰

FOLLOWING THE RULES March 14

"And the tax collector, standing afar off, would not so much as raise his eyes to heaven, but beat his breast, saying, 'God, be merciful to me a sinner!'"

Luke 18:13

God's rules are clear in His Word. Often we piece together additional rules to please ourselves and to make us think we are pleasing God. Many religious systems are constructed on the foundation of our need to build. We want to do it by human design; we want to make a tower to heaven. Yet God is our Maker. He is the only Builder, and our efforts are like sand. Jesus said the tax collector's justification was in confessing his sin, not in trying to follow all the rules the Pharisees were wearing proudly like rich robes. Often, we make up difficult rules so that in keeping them, or some of them, we can be rewarded or justified in letting ourselves off the hook for something else we want to do.

"I have kept these rules," I've said. "Surely I deserve a reward or an excuse or some time off." We deserve nothing, even if we kept all the rules. Although the kingdom of God is very near, it is so far beyond us that we will never walk there on human power. May the Lord have mercy on us all, especially those of us who think we might deserve it. May He also have mercy on those of us who think we don't deserve heaven and thus cannot go there. We go there only because Jesus Christ deserves heaven, He is already there, and the power of His cross and resurrection can bring us there.

With their eyes on themselves, the Pharisees had chipped the law of God down into little pieces of sand, little human-sized rules to be manipulated. But if we walk in these rules, we soon find that no sooner does one foot go forward than the other sinks in deeper. When rules are the foundation, pride creeps in, accompanied by the fear of man. This cycle of fear and pride fuels the engine of religiosity. Jesus replaces that grinding, clanking machine sinking in sand with a living faith and a relationship of grace and freedom rising in a daily cross that lifts up our Savior instead of ourselves.

Jesus' rules are simple. We must have a love of God that lifts up our eyes to Him, and a love that reaches our neighbor. When we follow these rules, all the others will fall into place, as Jesus on the cross is lifted up. Human-made rules tend to construct little rooms of pride and fear. In God's love, His dwelling place grows openly into the measure of the stature of the fullness of Christ. If we have our eyes on Him, we won't be looking to measure and mark our neighbor's faults or achievements, or our own. We'll see Jesus.

Father, let Your love rule in my heart so I can follow Your rules simply through the cross and not my own design. In Jesus' name, amen.

Mic.6:6-8 Luke 15:18-24 Mark 12:28-44

WHEN THE FRUIT IS RIPE   March 15

"But he answered and said to him, 'Sir, let it [the fig tree] alone this year also, until I dig around it and fertilize it. And if it bears fruit, well. But if not, after that you can cut it down.'"

                                                                Luke 13:8-9

Only our Father knows when His fruit is ripe, and He knows when it is not. In our lives and in the lives of others, He cultivates and watches for buds, blossoms, and fruit ripening on the branches. Even when it appears to us that nothing is happening, fruit may be coming that we do not see. At the right time, He will check it carefully. The Master Gardener knows how much pressure will reveal the condition of the fruit. He knows the aroma of readiness and sacrificial love. He knows the feel of fruit that is firm to do His will. Even now, His hands press gently on the body of Christ's church, to see where more time is needed or where a change of direction would allow more light.

We cannot rush the season or try to tie artificial fruit onto the branches to look good. He wants the real thing the real way. In the church, we must not shake the branches, wanting something to ripen and fall into our hands, until first the Father has tested it with His hands. He will pick it at the right time and provide for His people so all can be nourished for His glory. The Master Gardener knows the times and has seen each season come and go from the very beginning to the end. He also knows the feel and smell of rotten fruit that is too old for this time of new wine. In order to eat well and be satisfied abundantly, we must let the Master Gardner choose and pick the fruit when it is ripe for His purpose, ready to please Him.

Father, forgive me for reaching for the fruit before its time. Feed me as you will and make me grow in Your kingdom in the sweet aroma of Jesus Christ. In His name, amen.

John 15:1-2, 16-17   1 Pet. 1:22-25   James 3:17-18

GET DRESSED

March 16

"Consider the lilies of the field, how they grow: they neither toil nor spin; and yet I say to you that even Solomon in all his glory was not arrayed like one of these."

Matt. 6:28-29

The simplicity of trusting God is more beautiful than anything you could do to dress up your life yourself. There is nothing you can do that is more powerful or more beautiful than the anointing of Christ that covers you now. So why do people put on so many other things? Some dress for the world and insist that others do the same, so everyone will look good in their human mirror of success. Others wait for the Master's touch and let Him arrange their lives for eternity. Even Solomon in all his glory, impressive for his time, could not compete with the simple beauty of a lily.

If Jesus considered your life today, what would He insist that you put on? What things or activities would He lay aside? As the bride of Christ, each one in the church should be dressed for Him, clothed in what God alone can provide. Focused and intense, the beauty of simplicity flows through a singleness of purpose that makes each part complete. In unity with Him, simplicity keeps us close to Him like a child to a father. His garments of pure holiness are our protection and perfection, both internal and external.

If we accept them, these garments will change us. Without them, no matter how richly we dress, our complexities and iniquities mask the true beauty of Christ in us. Take off your mask and false clothes of heaviness. Put on the Lord Jesus Christ in repentance, receiving His life of joy and strength. Focus on the Savior's beauty, and He will cover you with it, washing away any trace of your old costume (Gal. 3:27). In truth, He will clothe you with a light-filled life made in heaven to wear on earth. Get dressed today in His reality.

Father, clothe me in the purity of Jesus Christ and help me to trust You. I lay aside my old ways and accept the simplicity of a child of God. Cleanse me so I can live in true beauty today. In Jesus' name, amen.

Matt. 18:1-4   Rom. 13:11-14   Rev. 3:17-20

FILL ME WITH YOUR TRUTH

Father God, fill me with Your truth. I know that my lies and sin are related, so when you take away my sin, I must also let You take away the subtle lies I've been living with everyday. Forgive me for clothing myself with old illusions and hidden excuses. Now it's time to stand free on a clean foundation. Wash me in the blood of the Lamb Jesus and cover me with His purity. With the sword of Your Living Word, release me from the past and fill me with Your truth, placing my life openly on the rock of Jesus Christ. Please overflow me now with Your Holy Spirit to follow Your will and to worship You in spirit and in truth. In Jesus' name, amen.

Then Jesus said to those Jews who believed in Him, "If you abide in My word, you are My disciples indeed. And you shall know the truth, and the truth shall make you free."

John 8:31-32

Rom. 6:4-14

FUEL FOR LIFE

March 18

And the Lord God formed man of the dust of the ground, and breathed into his nostrils the breath of life; and man became a living being.

Gen. 2:7

Our lives are running on some kind of fuel. Often, it's the fuel of society and secular success. We pull up to the pump and pay the price for worldly fuel that soon runs out and ruins our spiritual engines. Grinding and chugging, we produce a lot of smoke and noise trying to refill and fulfill conflicting directions for ourselves and others. Keeping our lives fueled by the stuff of this world to meet the drives of our own internal combustion is a full-time occupation.

Most of us try to fit God in somewhere, usually to help us accomplish what we already think we have to do, or we look to other people as our refueling station, expecting them to satisfy us. If our only pleasure in life is pleasing others whom we cannot satisfy, happiness is always deferred until some human expectation is fulfilled. God created us to be full of Him and fulfilled in Him, to live from the life He breathed into us and still breathes today through the Holy Spirit. We're designed to run on Him. Other things make us sick. God did not create us to please the world or other people or to be conformed to their image. In His own image, He created us, and we are never complete until we move into that pattern and match the deep call of His will for our lives.

In His shining love, God was our original source and requirement for life. At the very core of our being, He poured in Himself so we could live without dying. In the garden, He provided all that Adam and Eve needed, including His presence. Each day He was there with them, breathing and speaking the knowledge of whole, pure life. We are designed to live out of Him and His pattern of creation. When we seek Him first, everything we need follows in that eternal relationship outlasting all earthly desires.

Adam and Eve simply decided, as we often do, to try something else besides God for their fuel. They turned from the fountain of life and decided to fill up at the pump of their own self-will. Instead of God as the source of their lives, with His knowledge and provision flowing through them, they chose self-ruled lives and ate self-directed knowledge, which brought evil and death. God sent His Son to break us out of our death and to restore us to His life-giving presence. That's why Christ asks us to feed on Him and receive the gift of eternal life. What fuel is your life running on? Let God pour into you the pure fuel of life in Jesus Christ. At the cross, open yourself to the fullness of His truth. Then you can run on resurrection power. Even here, you'll be close to paradise.

Father, empty me of the dead fuel of this world and fill me with Your life in Christ.
Let His love burn in me as my main source of supply and joy. In Jesus' name, amen.

Rom. 12:1-2   John 6:33-44   Eph. 3:16-19

FIRING THE BULLET   March 19

"If you keep My commandments, you will abide in My love, just as I have kept My Father's commandments and abide in His love."

John 15:10

Like a rifle barrel, a narrow road to light will take you farther than a wider way wandering into darkness. On the narrow road of life, you will know where you are going, as God's power propels you straight into the light at the center of His will. There are no detours and side exits, just one way leading directly to the mark. Since none of us really wants to choose anything narrow that might appear to be less, God often brings us into this narrow road through hardship or whatever it takes to block every detour. Suddenly, we find ourselves on a road of humility and loss, but also of beauty beyond compare. The way is hard, but it leads upward, ever higher in the light of His love. Which road are you on today? Is it broad and easy but going nowhere? Or is it hard and still going nowhere?

If you get on the narrow road with Jesus, you will go in His power to the city of the King, a city not made with hands and beyond every visible limitation. As you go, even the road will change so that you begin to see it not as rocky and hard but instead as impossibly beautiful with water from the Rock, flowing with power beyond this world. Yes, it is a narrow way, but the power that moves along it is like the power that moves a bullet to the center of the target. Firing that bullet through a broad tube would only make it bounce off the sides, losing power and direction. There is no way to aim it accurately unless the path is limited, focused right down to the pinpoint accuracy of a cross within a circle.

A rifle barrel is long and narrow in order to deliver its charge accurately. When the bullet's route is limited and guided, it hits the mark. When you let God load you into His plan and slip you into His inner chamber, then His fire will personally charge you, ignite you, and send you on a narrow journey right through the center of His will to the goal, much farther than you could possibly propel yourself. This journey, this trajectory, is invisible to earthly eyes, but the results are clear when it hits the target. A sign of impact appears. Your destination is determined by the cross and planned from eternity to enter the circle of God's love. The time is now. Lay aside everything else and enter the narrow way of life that takes you the full distance into the center of God's will and the impact of His power.

Father, turn me from my ways to Your straight way so I can live in the center of Your love. Burn in me the fire of Your will and complete Your purpose in my life. Make an impact. In Jesus' name, amen.

John 14:6   Matt. 7:13-23   Phil. 3:7-14

March 20

~~~~~~

REST FROM ABOVE

Father, I come to You as Your child, willing to grow in faith and to live in Your strength. Help me to lay down old weapons and broken toys and to accept the victory of forgiveness. Cleanse my will to rest in Yours. Increase my faith, lift up my head, and open my eyes. Today, give me the hope of Your light, which shines in the darkness, and the darkness does not overcome it. Heal my wounds, some self-inflicted and some caused by others. In mercy, shine the light of Your Son in me and take the weariness of this world away as I rest safely in Your arms. Let Your presence be my hope and shield. In Your truth I stand, no more in the trap of lies and lingering worry, but in the living truth that runs the race with joy. Lead me in Your living way, and let me see with eyes of faith the rest from above that lifts me forever in Your love. In the name of Jesus, who comes, amen.

Lord, my heart is not haughty, nor my eyes lofty. Neither do I concern myself with great matters, nor with things too profound for me. Surely I have calmed and quieted my soul, like a weaned child with his mother; like a weaned child is my soul within me. O Israel, hope in the Lord from this time forth and forever.

Ps. 131

Heb. 12:11-24

~~~~~~

THE HARVEST IN YOU   March 21

"Behold, I say to you, lift up your eyes and look at the fields, for they are already white for harvest!"

John 4:35

Eagerly, we look outward to the fields of the Lord's harvest, ready to go wherever He sends us. But first, the Lord has a harvest to do within each of His workers. Before we can cut and thresh the wheat, He must cut and thresh within us to separate the chaff from the grain of spiritual life. Chaff cannot winnow out chaff; neither can immature grain fuel a full harvest of fields white enough to feed multitudes. When we have ripened and the Lord has brought us to His threshing floor, then we'll be made ready to go out and bring in the other wheat. He will put His sharp sickle to our wills. He checks for fruits of repentance and humility within us and the aroma of His Son's love moving through our lives (Matt. 3:8-12; Eph. 5:1-2).

In His workers, the Lord of the harvest looks for the pure grain willing to lay down its life to multiply in new life through the cross. Otherwise, there is no real sharing in the body of Christ. The workers must become as one loaf together in the Lord of the harvest. The harvest within must be farther along than the harvest without. Some grain has to be processed and refined so there will be unity before the laborers can go out to the fields today. The Lord of the harvest has work for you to do and work to do in you. How far along is His harvest in your life?

Lord of the harvest, bring me to maturity, thresh me, and send me out wherever You choose. I can only work in Your harvest as You harvest me. In Jesus' name, amen.

Isa. 55:6-11   Matt. 9:35—10:1   1 Cor. 10:1-17

GREATEST DESTINY   March 22

"For what will it profit a man if he gains the whole world, and loses his own soul?"

Mark 8:36

Even most non-Christians would agree that it is hard to find a better example of a human life than that of Jesus Christ. Our greatest freedom is to know the truth, and the truth is a Person. No One has been more truly human and also truly God. How can some say that following the Son of Man might lead to less human achievement? To follow Him is freedom to grow beyond ourselves, to reach the highest completion of humanity in surrendering to the Creator of the universe. By infusing humanity with divine grace through His sacrifice, Jesus brings us into the resurrection power of His life. He is widely known as the finest, most effective human being who ever walked the earth. People of all cultures can agree about His goodness, but when it comes to following His teachings and the laws of God that He affirmed, we often disagree.

Instead, like spoiled children, we want what we want when we want it. Obstinate two-year-olds think they understand the immediate situation, and they know what they want. Therefore, they must have it. Today, our culture promotes self-gratification whenever and however we want it. We want all the so-called benefits, actually poisons, of self-directed gain without being accountable for their long-term effects. We want our thoughts and desires to be the basis of reality, not knowing there is much more to reality than we can know or want and more joy in a higher dimension of God's knowledge revealed in humility than in our narrow vision of power and wealth.

We insist on arguing about tricycles when the spiritual equivalent of a new car and a space shuttle await us. If we keep whining in a universe that far exceeds our ability to grasp it, what do you think our Parent should do? Discipline us, destroy us, or divinely save us? Lovingly, He divinely saves us and also disciplines us so that we can mature and walk in the life of His Son, who gave Himself to keep us from destruction. He made a way for us to walk out of our human limitations into His limitless love. We can choose to follow His way or to die in our own. We can choose to walk in relationship with Him. It is the greatest destiny we will ever have. Are you there or still on your own?

Father, I put my old desires aside so You can fulfill in me the destiny I have been given in Jesus Christ. Bring me forward in faith in Your eternal plan. In Jesus' name, amen.

John 14:5-6   Matt. 26:39-46   Titus 2:11-15

March 23

~~~~~~

FIRE OF HEAVEN

Father God, in the fire of heaven, You come to earth for a sacrifice. Make my life one that lives through the cross of Christ on the altar of Your will and rises in Your love. Help me to live now to the praise of Your glory. Make me new in Your love so that I fear nothing but only You alone in awesome reverence and unspeakable joy. In Jesus' name, amen.

Now this, "Yet once more," indicates the removal of those things that are being shaken, as of things that are made, that the things which cannot be shaken may remain. Therefore, since we are receiving a kingdom which cannot be shaken, let us have grace, by which we may serve God acceptably with reverence and godly fear. For our God is a consuming fire.

Heb. 12:27-29

Rom. 12:1-21

~~~~~~

THE GARDENER   March 24

"I am the true vine, and My Father is the vinedresser. Every branch in Me that does not bear fruit He takes away; and every branch that bears fruit He prunes, that it may bear more fruit."

John 15:1-2

The Master Gardener is in His garden. He comes to you, O tender plant, and digs all around to soften your patch of earth and loosen it so that moisture can reach your roots. Carefully, He examines every leaf and new shoot, turning them one by one. His hand removes any parasites or adhesions. He smoothes out any edges curled the wrong direction. With a smile, He lightly touches the bright tips of new growth and feels each green stem for flexibility and moisture. Some dead branches the Gardener prunes away, but His touch, even in cutting, is firm and gentle. The Gardener breathes His pleasure on every side of this plant and speaks peace to your heart. You reach higher in the strength of the vine into the fragrance of His breath.

As time goes by, and you reach higher still, He brings a wooden frame, placing it against the center of your best growth. At first, you will think it is too hard against you and blocks the way, but then you will lean on it when the wind blows and cling to it in every storm. On its outstretched arms, your branches will grow in the right direction and your leaves will stay open to air and light, not turning inward as those without this cross of wood. When bud and blossoms appear and the fragrance of your worship rises to Him, the Gardener is pleased. Entering His house, the sweet aroma of praise fills the air.

When the blossoms go and the fruit is coming, you feel an urgent pressure in your branches that could only be supported by the cross the Master has given you. At first you thought it was only for the storms, but now you lean all your fruit-bearing weight on this structure like a woman about to give birth. When the fruit comes, you bear down hard, giving all the weight to the cross, becoming so one with the weathered wood that it is hard to tell where your branches end and it begins.

When harvest season arrives, the Gardener takes great care to check each piece of new fruit individually by pressing on it to test for maturity. He turns each piece fully in His gaze and holds it to the light. When completely ripe, the Gardener will bring it into His house, not just to look at, but for the nourishment of His household and to share His life. In every season, the Master Gardener sees the potential for fruit, and each season is necessary in its timing. He cares as much for the silent plants in winter as for the sprouting shoots in spring. In resurrection power, He will meet you in your season.

Father, make me grow into the likeness of Your Son, bearing fruit that remains. Thank You for His life flowing through me. In Jesus' name, amen.

Phil. 1:9-11   John 15:8-17   Gal. 5:16-26

HEALING THE BLIND   March 25

"As long as I am in the world, I am the light of the world." When He had said these things, He spat on the ground and made clay with the saliva; and He anointed the eyes of the blind man with the clay. And He said to him, "Go, wash in the pool of Siloam" (which is translated, Sent). So he went and washed, and came back seeing.

John 9:5-7

As Christ healed the blind man with clay wet with the life of His mouth, so He can heal our blindness today by becoming one with our clay and changing us through the application of His Word. That Word will wash us when we go where we are sent. But first, we must receive an application of the Master's life directly to our need, touching us with His life. Yes, He can heal by speaking from a distance, but in this example, Jesus shows us the importance of direct contact, even in using what is earthly. When consecrated with His life, clay can carry healing. Only then can we see what has been invisible in our darkness from birth.

Are we willing to have clay applied to our eyes, wet with what comes from His mouth? Isn't that too messy? The Pharisees did not want a clay Messiah. They wanted a king who did not associate with sinners, let alone touch them. The Pharisees wanted a king worthy of their own pride. Dirt with spittle on it would not have been acceptable to them. They were looking for royal power, not a touch of humble earth wet with new life for the lost.

Will we allow clay to be applied to our eyes with the humility of His incarnate life, or do we prefer our usual blindness? Healing may bring difficult questions and even persecution. Our routine will be ruined. We may be thrown out of the synagogue, but we will see the One we worship and know His touch. Jesus is coming our way now. And He may use something we least expect, something the world rejects, to heal us. He is taking some of our earth and spitting on it, moistening it to a consistency He can use to apply it to our blind spots and our pride. He wants to make it stick. The Lord makes His healing stay in our clay, right where He places it for God's glory. Will you let Him touch you and open your eyes today?

Father, touch me with the life of Jesus and heal me in Your way. Through Him, I want to see and know Your new life walking here. In Jesus' name, amen.

John 9:29-41   Luke 4:16-30   John 12:20-21

March 26

~~~~~~

FORGIVE ME FOR HIDING

Forgive me for hiding, Lord God. Take away my old cover, my excuses, and my restlessness, and find me in Your peace. The life of Your Son is the light of my life and the broken bread that satisfies. Shine in me so I can see clearly that blessing waiting in the assignments You give, which I've been trying to avoid. Now I accept them in Your power. Make me able to do Your will and to come out of the cave of self-concern and the blindness of doubt and fear. Lead me in Your living light. In the name of Jesus Christ, amen.

"Nor do they light a lamp and put it under a basket, but on a lampstand, and it gives light to all who are in the house. Let your light so shine before men, that they may see your good works and glorify your Father in heaven. . . . Therefore if you bring your gift to the altar, and there remember that your brother has something against you, leave your gift there before the altar, and go your way. First be reconciled to your brother, and then come and offer your gift."

Matt. 5:15-16, 23-24

1 John 1:4-7

~~~~~~

THERE IS A HIGHWAY   March 27

"Prepare the way of the Lord; make straight in the desert a highway for our God."

Isa. 40:3

There is a highway shining in the King's light. It is the holy way He comes and the way His love brings us to Him. In the distance, we sometimes see a highway shining with reflections on its surface as heat rises from the pavement. That is the way we are going in Christ—straight on into the kingdom on a highway He has already purified with fire. As light comes down from above, it reflects back in its own heat. So the fire in our hearts answers the love that comes down from the Father of lights, and as we follow His Word, the way ahead is illuminated in clear, shining truth.

This highway is built in mercy by the One who creates it—even through a wilderness. No matter what rocky ground it goes through, the highway runs straight to the planned destination. In fact, God's highway is an extension of the destination, a direct connection reaching out to us, like a narrow path to heaven marked out here on earth. Once we get on that highway and follow the direction of His Word, we are guaranteed to arrive. The way itself is completely linked to the kingdom we enter, so that both the journey and the destination become one in Christ. He said, "I am the way, the truth, and the life. No one comes to the Father except through Me" (John 14:6).

It is not as if we are on a path down here and hope to see Him someday up there, if we finally make it. By the Holy Spirit, we are brought into Christ now to share in a foretaste of the life we will live with Him eternally. Even on this earth, we are walking in a living way that is already joined to its destination as a branch is joined to the Vine. The same shining sap flows through both the way and us to reveal Christ.

As we go along the way He has marked out, the signs are clear: eternal love and the humble power of the cross. It's all very simple, but staying on the road requires discipline. There are so many inviting detours. Stay on the road! Go straight! Live in His pure Word. If we get off for a detour, even for what seems a good reason, we can be lost forever (Matt. 7:13-14).

God's design governs every turn, and He has planned each day's journey. Like the moving conveyor belts in airports, if we get on God's highway, it will carry us to His house. Highways are literally higher than other ways, and if we go up in His will, we are moving above the rush and the doubts, above the constant starting and stopping of local traffic. Get on the King's highway! Turn up the ramp of obedience. Let go of all else to go forward in faith. Each day, ask directions and look up. Your journey is in the Son.

Father, straighten out my life by grace; bring me home Your way. In Jesus' name, amen.

Matt. 9:9   John 8:4-12   Prov. 4:14-19

March 28

HEALED BY HIS WOUNDS

Father, thank You for the blood of Jesus Christ that heals us completely. In His wounds, He joins us in our humanity, even our death, and raises us beyond it. You did not send Christ just to heal our sickness and change us from a distance but to join us in it and go through it with us. In His blood, You overcame all destruction, disease, and everything in us, blotting out our sin and making us new. We come humbly, asking You to apply the blood of Jesus directly to our wounds, even those unknown to us, and to the root cause of our diseases, both physical and spiritual, so that we can become whole in the power of Your Son, who emptied Himself for us. We receive Him today in His fullness, as He really is, not as we have imagined Him to be, but in the fullness of life in His blood, which works in us, through us, and with us in resurrection power even now. Fill us with His life. To receive that life, we do not have to be perfect, because He is. We do not have to be strong, because He is. We do not have to be able, because He is. Yes, we do have to ask and open ourselves to the power of His blood by acknowledging that He is our Savior, and we do this now, because He is. In Jesus' name, amen.

"For as the Father has life in Himself, so He has granted the Son to have life in Himself."

John 5:26

1 Pet. 2:21-25

JUST ONE GLANCE   March 29

"But blessed are your eyes for they see."

Matt. 13:16

Whatever our situation, just one glance at Christ can change everything. One day when working in a corner cleaning the floor, I thought I didn't have the supplies needed to finish the job. It was impossible. The whole day had been difficult. Frustrated and struggling, I kept up the losing battle for a while, and then turning at an angle, I suddenly saw on the table behind me just what I needed. It had been set out earlier but was invisible from my position in the corner. All my attention had been poured into the problem while I complained with my back to the available supply. Finally, I turned and reached for it. There was just enough to finish the job.

In the same way, Christ is waiting for us to turn and take just one glance at what He can provide. We can't solve our problems by looking constantly at them and trying harder. Wounds are not healed by looking always into the wounds. With a true glance from the heart, we need to turn to the One with clean hands who will wash everything completely, even the hard corners, remove any old dirt, cleanse the situation, and cover it with the truth and healing power of His blood. It is the only way out of our unclean corner.

One glance to Him is much more practical than to continue working in human power. One look away from our human effort to the "useless" beauty of His presence will change everything around us. He is the only One who can make something out of nothing. The humble Servant we often ignore will surprise us with His power. The One we fear to approach will come gently to the least and to the lost. He is already looking for us more than any of us ever look for Him. He is watching to see where we will turn for help. And now, all He asks is just one glance, deep from the heart.

Turn and look for Him. Whatever He shows you today, reach for it in His grace, in His timing. Take hold of what He offers. Just one glance can let Him finish the job.

O Lord God, I turn now and look for Your Son. First, open my heart to see Him, and then give me grace to reach out and accept His hand. In Jesus' name, amen.

John 20:11-21   Titus 2:13—3:6   John 19:5

March 30

A FULL DAY

Father, if I do nothing else today, let me first love you with my whole heart as You love me. This is the most important thing, the only activity to truly fill the day. No matter how hard I work, everything else will leave some empty space. Only love overflows each cup. Then Your full love and pure joy will flow out to others through open vessels dedicated to You. This is the fruit of Your kingdom, which tastes sweet in both worlds, the harvest that fills Your heart, and the feast that never ends. Fill Your people with Your presence and peace. In Jesus' name, amen.

He brought me to the banqueting house, and his banner over me was love.

Song of Sol. 2:4

John 16:31 — 17:23

HUMAN IMPERFECTION   March 31

So then it is not of him who wills, nor of him who runs, but of God who shows mercy.

Rom. 9:16

Improvements to humanity will not save us. We can run faster, but we have no destination without God. Without His mercy, we run nowhere. Our best efforts and highest achievements can bring temporary relief from the ongoing symptoms of selfishness, but the underlying disease still remains. It is fatal. Only an immense selflessness can cure us. God gave Himself to us in Christ completely, not in partial revelation or in a sign of heavenly things far away, but in a complete revelation of Himself in humanity, right in the middle of our imperfection. Only His perfection can redeem us.

Unlike anyone else, Jesus Christ did not have to die. All the human heroes who ever gave their lives were going to die anyway eventually; they just offered themselves a little sooner. Such sacrifice is still hard, but not nearly so hard as offering yourself if you don't have to die at all, if you are in fact the Creator of the very lives that are nailing you to the cross. The cross offers a complete revelation, not only of God's love but also of our humanity drowning in self-will (1 Cor. 15:21-23). He reaches us in our own flesh, in the very place where we are weakest (Isa. 53:4-5). He reaches us at the core, even in that subtle death of depending on human control and effort, which leads only to the grave.

Christ embraces our humanity and voluntarily accepts our death so that we can voluntarily accept His life. Voluntarily. When Christ stepped out of the tomb, He stepped beyond us and took us with Him, if we want to come. Even through death, His perfection in us carries us past imperfection. He steps through our humanity into eternal life. Human frailty cannot be improved to that point of perfection. Instead, it is nailed to the cross, and God's life in His Son in us is revealed. This truth shines within our lives now to transform us and those around us far more than any human achievement.

If we focus on our humanity to save us, then we miss His divinity, which makes our humanity glorious in following Him. In Christ, we are transformed and refined into a brighter light than we can generate, a brighter humanity than we can design. To settle for anything less is to deny the best that we can become. All human effort falls short of what humanity can be in Christ's sacrifice. Many try to improve themselves by following steps and paths and methods. But eternal dimensions are not scaled with a human ladder. Instead, eternity has poured itself into human dimensions. In Bethlehem's stable, God offered us His perfection humbly as a child. We can only accept it the same way.

Father, my imperfection is in Your hands. I let go of my life, of trying to improve it, and ask You to change me. Make me new through Jesus Christ alone. In His name, amen.

2 Cor. 5:17-18   Phil. 1:6   Matt. 11:27-30

IN HIS HOUSE

April 1

"'Compel them to come in, that my house may be filled.'"

Luke 14:23

To live is to dwell in the Lord's house, full of His life. We can dwell in our own partial houses, which will soon be gone, or we can dwell in His house to truly live right now through the Holy Spirit. Ask, seek, and knock in order to dwell in His presence today as well as later in heaven. Only in God's house can we live with joy in this world. His house is big enough and clean enough for all the changes. There we and those with us can grow to the utmost and also find a place of rest. If we try to solve problems while living in our own houses and the little rooms that define our way of doing things, there won't be room for abundant life to develop. Not only are our houses and our ways too small for us, they are too small for those who are growing with us. The rooms are too small, and the ceilings are too low.

If we try to make someone or something else the focus of our lives, then they or that thing will become our house. And it is still too small. We can add on rooms and activities, but ultimately the foundation won't support them. Each day, our goals and limitations are the walls of the house where we choose to live. If we cannot see the kingdom of God, we're living in ours. In our house, we are always in charge, sometimes doing things for others, including God, but still frustrated and unsatisfied. The house is too small. When we live in His house, He is in charge and provides for us and others as His children. There's plenty of room for all. It's His house forever.

If we're not at peace and everything around us is crumbling, it's a human house. The walls and decor soon wear thin and fade away. In God's house, His character and love stand forever. He decorates His house to please His infinite beauty and fortifies its walls with salvation. The rooms are full of light. There is a flowing peace, God's peace, and it is found only in His house, in His design. If we think we're living in His house but have no peace, we're actually living somewhere else. In His house is infinite rest, good food, deep joy, and a cool drink of water. To step into this divine house is to live each day more in His presence than in anyone else's presence, more at peace within His walls than within any other walls, more aware of His beauty than any other beauty or attraction.

Those who dwell in His house are satisfied. Their foundations run deep. Some seekers come to His house briefly, look around, and then hurry back to their own places and ways. It's visible on their faces, where the addresses of hearts are written. To dwell in God's house is to have beauty shining out through your life as light shines out from windows in the night. There will be trouble and storms, but His love is brighter, and His peace shelters you. The door is already open. Have you entered intending to stay?

Father, I have come home to Your house and I plan to stay. In Jesus' name, amen.

Ps. 27   Heb. 3:4-14   Eph. 2:19-22

April 2

~~~~~~

HIDE ME IN HUMILITY

My Father, hide me in humility from the desires of the world so I can see Your majesty and move in the power of Your love out of the prison of my will and into the fullness of Yours. Change my heart to dwell in Your house forever. In Jesus' name, amen.

Then Jesus called a little child to Him, set him in the midst of them, and said, "Assuredly, I say to you, unless you are converted and become as little children, you will by no means enter the kingdom of heaven. Therefore whoever humbles himself as this little child is the greatest in the kingdom of heaven."

Matt. 18:2-4

Ps. 25:4-15

~~~~~~

HOLY FIRE   April 3

"I came to send fire on the earth, and how I wish it were already kindled!"

Luke 12:49

Jesus describes His purpose as sending fire on the earth, a holy fire that changes us from the image of man into the image of God's Son. As our hearts and wills melt in that fire and receive His life, we can be born anew as God's children. Fire is unique, a moving, changing process made visible by its very working. So God's transforming power is made visible as the fire of His Spirit moves in us today through His Son's sacrifice and resurrection. He is the perfect sacrifice, and it becomes a burning one, a burnt offering within His people.

When fire touches a substance, drastic change takes place. Some things are changed a little by water, others by wind, but everything is transformed by fire. Even "fireproof" materials are not completely fireproof, only to a certain degree. Beyond that, in the intensity of maximum fire, everything will be changed.

Perhaps we have never seen fire like this in a physical sense, but Jesus Christ has already brought maximum fire into the spiritual dimension of human life. The purity of His holiness and righteous sacrifice melt everything in their path. The flame of His love melts the hardest of hearts. The only way for these to stay intact and hardened is to stay away from the fire, to keep a safe distance. All the mountains in our lives will melt like wax at the presence of God (Ps. 97:5). The only thing that fire does not change is fire. Therefore, to survive the coming wrath of God, we must be already in the fire of His love. In His mercy, living in His fire, we can become one with Him in Christ.

If you come close, that fire will melt you and change you into His everlasting life. There is no going back with fire. What it purifies is clean to the depths. There is no hiding from fire. It does not wash the surface or blow against the outside edges. Fire transforms to the core, melting every layer into a new creation that is whole, completely merged with pure life, and no longer divided by darkness. In this light, what was hidden is revealed (1 Cor. 3:13-15). As fire consumes a sacrifice, it reveals its true nature, reducing it to the basic elements left behind as ashes and releasing a complete surrender of life to God, ascending as smoke to heaven.

His fire releases the Holy Spirit in resurrection power, rising and purifying all who receive the sacrifice of Jesus Christ. Nothing else has that much fire. Even now, we're going up as His love burns in us.

Father, consume my death in Your living fire and make me one with You, transformed in Jesus Christ. In His name, amen.

1 Kings 18:22-39   Luke 24:32-36   Rev. 1:12-18

April 4

I KNOW WHO

Father God, I have no idea what is coming in the future, but I know who is coming to complete all things according to Your will. Forever, O Lord, Your Word is settled in heaven. May it also be settled in my heart. Make me ready for whatever comes by fully trusting You now. Help me first to seek Your face and then to let You mold me each day into the life of Your Son. In Jesus' name, amen.

But Jesus kept silent. And the high priest answered and said to Him, "I put You under oath by the living God: Tell us if You are the Christ, the Son of God!" Jesus said to him, "It is as you said. Nevertheless, I say to you, hereafter you will see the Son of Man sitting at the right hand of the Power, and coming on the clouds of heaven."

Matt. 26:63-64

1 John 5:10-21

JACOB'S LADDER   April 5

Then he dreamed, and behold, a ladder was set up on the earth, and its top reached to heaven; and there the angels of God were ascending and descending on it. And behold, the Lord stood above it and said: "I am the Lord God of Abraham your father and the God of Isaac; the land on which you lie I will give to you and your descendants. . . . and in you and in your seed all the families of the earth shall be blessed. Behold, I am with you and will keep you wherever you go, and will bring you back to this land; for I will not leave you until I have done what I have spoken to you." Then Jacob awoke from his sleep and said, "Surely the Lord is in this place, and I did not know it." And he was afraid and said, "How awesome is this place! This is none other than the house of God, and this is the gate of heaven!"

Gen. 28:12-17

You may have sung the song, but have you ever climbed the ladder in Jesus Christ one day at a time, one step at a time, standing on the promises and the cleansing power of His cross? Take the first step higher today. Jesus said He is the ladder, and as you come into His life one day at a time, you will go higher, growing steadily closer to God right in the place where you are now. You don't have to go to some other place. In Christ, the place where you are now is the gate of heaven as you follow Him who is the same yesterday, today, and forever (Heb. 13:8).

As Jesus was lifted up on the cross for you, as you walk in His life, you can take hold of the wood of the cross and step up through faith into sacrificial love, the narrow way that leads to life more abundantly, even in a desert place. When you feel you have not yet reached your destination and are unsure which way to go, God is there, preparing a way for the future. He has made the gate of heaven and opened it in Jesus Christ. Step up now in faith in the place where you are. Then you can move forward in love.

Father, may I see Your open door to heaven in this place as I see the ladder of the cross and take hold of it in Christ. Whatever I have to do, help me to take the first step in faith today. I worship You and praise Your mercy in setting up this ladder on earth that reaches from here to heaven through Your Son. Thank You for fulfilling Your promises and for the awesome wonder of Your power to love. In Jesus' name, amen.

John 1:51   John 12:32   Gal. 5:5-6

HUMILITY'S COVERING   April 6

"Blessed are the meek, for they shall inherit the earth."

Matt. 5:5

As children of the King, humility is our only strength as we enter His house through Jesus Christ. Knowing that it is not our house and we can do nothing in our own strength to open the door, we are totally surrendered to His power. On the other hand, if we claim this life is ours and we are humanly capable of doing God's work, there is no entrance. The gate is made to fit a humbler heart and a smaller head.

First, humility protects us from our own egos, which slide toward sinning. Even if we think we can recognize the difference between right and wrong and make allowances, our own understanding will not lead us into God's kingdom. Only the life of Christ will. Second, humility protects us from others who would rule us through flattery or fear. Both grow out of the same need for control and are rejected by a heart immune to such lies.

Third, humility keeps us from the lust of the world, which easily seduces the proud. Even wanting to do what is wrong, a child who accepts parental authority will be restrained by the parent's command to take only one cookie. However, if the child thinks he himself is the final authority, all the cookies are easily devoured, and sickness follows. Fourth, humility protects us from the enemy searching for a foothold in our lust for illusion and self-centeredness. Deception is easy in overbooked adults who expertly rationalize their gratification, but try explaining their excuse to a child, and you will get a look that stops you in your tracks. Children know instinctively the truth of simplicity.

Pride exposes us to many unknown dangers. A quiet and humble spirit hides safely under the wings of the Almighty, who gathers His children, those not too high-minded to be drawn closer to Him than they can bring themselves. God dwells with them and enjoys their company (Is. 57:15). The humble heart makes divine discoveries never revealed to those wise in their own eyes. With intimate knowledge of God, humble hearts move unafraid of what terrifies the world. Be safe today. Be bold by staying small, so God can move powerfully in your life and bring you where your pride cannot go.

Father, make me small enough to see You and follow Your Son in humility through the narrow way into the fullness of Your kingdom. In Jesus' name, amen.

James 4:3-6   Prov. 3:5-12   Ps. 9:11-14

IMPOSSIBLE
April 7

But Jesus looked at them and said to them, "With men this is impossible, but with God all things are possible."

Matt. 19:26

If the impossible is impossible, why do we have a word for it? Something truly impossible would not require a description because it would never occur. However, built into our concept of reality is the concept of the impossible, which does happen when an eternal cause meets our finite expectations. Unlike politicians who follow opinion polls, our unlimited Creator has not planned the universe according to our expectations but according to His reality. We can all be glad, because He plans to make us more than we even want to be, certainly more than we are capable of being on our own. He wants to make us like His Son, who said, "Father, forgive them for they know not what they do."

Infinite generosity lifts us out of our self-centered tombs into a new creation. We receive life beyond our own through the death of the only Man who never had to die but did so out of love for those who couldn't fully understand or love Him. Impossible! Though Jesus' friends left Him, He still saved them and returned to them again, even through closed doors (John 20:24-29). Then He caused a small bunch of scared people to become brave enough to turn their world upside down. Do you think your problem is too hard for Jesus? Impossible? Even when fear closes your doors, He still comes.

Father, I give up saying what You can and cannot do. Have Your way. Please do it for eternity. Make me a new creation in Jesus Christ, and live in me now through Your Holy Spirit. In Jesus' name, amen.

Luke 1:34-38, 46-55   Gen. 18:11-14   Matt. 9:28-29

April 8

I APPROVE OF YOUR WAYS, O LORD

I approve of Your ways, O Lord. For my own life and all those around me, I agree with Your will and accept Your power, which is marvelous in our eyes! Do whatever pleases You here today, as Your ways are higher than our ways. Lead me in the straight path of life, and never let me go back to the crooked ways that kept me from a closer walk with You. I know that what You have promised, You are able also to perform. In Jesus' name, amen.

"Enter by the narrow gate; for wide is the gate and broad is the way that leads to destruction, and there are many who go in by it. Because narrow is the gate and difficult is the way which leads to life, and there are few who find it."

Matt. 7:13-14

Rom. 4:16-25

HOLY

April 9

"Holy, holy, holy is the Lord of hosts; the whole earth is full of His glory!"

Isa. 6:3

Holiness is pure wholeness that reveals God's glory. It is totally different from our divided, self-focused lives and fractured ideas of religion. So overwhelming is this divine holiness that it will fill the earth and everything beyond it. Even though we cannot grasp it, our lives are being swallowed up in the holiness of God like a purifying flame of love, changing us into the image of His Son. Eventually, God's holiness contains us. We do not contain it. Wonderfully, it is more than we can be or do. Holiness is often described as being set apart for God, and this is true, for holiness separates us from our divisions, our conflicted interests, and brings us into unity with God's creative power in Christ.

In the dissolution of physical death, molecules and cells fall apart, but He rescues us in a living unity that is entirely new. So when the angel said to Mary that the Holy Spirit would come upon her, something new began to unite all of us in the wholeness and the holiness of God, leading to the cross and resurrection. Though it was more than she could understand, Mary was completely filled with His life. God said, "I Am Who I Am," and He alone is perfectly holy. Thus, He is the only One who can make us whole, fully integrated with Christ's holiness, complete in His life.

This unity with Christ is the key. We cannot become holy on our own, regardless of our religious rituals or good deeds. The Holy Spirit must come upon us to heal and renew us. We cannot glue ourselves together, spiritually or physically, because everything human is only partial. Check out human history. At the core, our lives are fractured by selfishness and sin, even to the point of death. We are a mixture of truth and lies, a shaky combination of good tries and false starts, of mutual illusions and tragic beauty that easily fall apart. We can't fill our own gaps with us.

Only the One who created us is big enough to fill us and make us completely new, integrating our lives into eternity. God pours the offering of His Son into us and releases the Holy Spirit to heal the fractures and conform us in love to His will. To be holy, our heart must melt into union with His, and only He can do the melting. Holiness is that inward flow into God through Christ, not through us or our offerings. Some religions try to attain this unity through human effort or special knowledge. But only the Creator, who is bigger than the separate pieces, can bring them all together. In Christ, God pours Himself directly into our brokenness through the cross. Then He seals us with the Holy Spirit through the power of the resurrection to bring us wholly into Himself.

O Lord God, lead me into the purity and power of Your holiness. In Jesus' name, amen.

John 5:19-24   Acts 3:1-16   1 Pet. 1:15-23

~~~~~~

HELPLESS PRAYER

Father, even my best strength is weak to You. My attempts at control only get in the way. If I try to do it all, there is no room for Your glory to shine through, even in a good thing. So now I will get out of the way and let You work in and through me. Help me to realize Your power and surrender to it by letting You be who You are now in this world, as well as in the world to come. To line up with the truth, I must fall at Your feet. When I seek You first, when You are more real to me than my own weakness or whatever the need is for others, when You are more real to me in prayer than what I am asking for, then the answer will come because I have given You room to move and change things, including my heart. Even when I've forgotten You, still You have not forgotten me. I need Your touch now. Move me into Your plan, and line me up with the order of Your beauty. I could not receive it before because I was too busy talking and trying to be strong in my own will. Now helpless, I wait and bow to receive strength in Your hand. You are the Potter, and I am the clay. Turn me as only You can do in Your living water. In Jesus' name, amen.

And He said to me, "My grace is sufficient for you, for My strength is made perfect in weakness." Therefore most gladly I will rather boast in my infirmities, that the power of Christ may rest upon me.

2 Cor. 12:9

Matt. 4:17—5:12

~~~~~~

IT'S TIME

April 11

From that time Jesus began to preach and to say, "Repent, for the kingdom of heaven is at hand."

Matt. 4:17

When it's time to do God's will, it's time. We cannot move the hands on the clock forward or backward, according to our understanding. Time moves to the rhythm of His plan, which works all things together for good to those who love Him, who are the called according to His purpose, not their own will. If you were living completely for God today, what would be different in your schedule? Surrendered to His time and His strength, you can do it now. As Creator, He can make time where we think there is none, and He can expand our hearts to follow the rhythm of His action and rest.

There is a direct relationship between action and time. Certain actions are for certain times, and when that time comes, we must move into the action that matches that time to see real fruit grow in God's plan for each individual life. In the aroma of new growth, the beauty of His mercy precedes the fruit. From a single incorruptible seed of faith, complex and beautiful blossoms of action begin to unfold. The faith of Christ, the Vine, the Living Word, moves in us to cause fruit to appear where at first we saw only branches and leaves. Unable to know it all, the branch simply stays in the Vine.

Often, we find coincidences in our world that are not coincidences. Many deep stirrings of the soul are not coincidences either, but signals to move out in what God has already started in line with His Word. He still tends this garden and sets up situations for maximum fruit. Timing is important, and so is our action that matches it, as the grace for each day unfolds. Both go together in a beauty that transcends any calendar or human agenda. What does God have time for you to do today?

The love that moved Jesus Christ to give His life for you is ready to move you now in His direction. When His time had come, He went to the cross; and in His resurrection, He moved through time and beyond it to complete all things, even God's purpose in you today.

My Lord and Creator, create in me a clean heart so I can move in Your will for this time, this place, and this life You have given me through Your Son. My time is Yours. Move me in Your life in Jesus to produce much fruit. In Jesus' name, amen.

John 9:4-5   Eph. 2:8-10   Phil. 1:6-20

April 12

~~~~~~

HEAL MY BLINDNESS

Lord God, thank You for sending Your Son, the Bright and Morning Star, to interrupt my blindness. Please give me sight in Your pure light and heal me entirely. Make me see where and how to walk, but first let me see how to worship You in spirit and in truth. Then the way will be clear, and my steps will be sure. In the name of Jesus, amen.

The people who walked in darkness have seen a great light; those who dwelt in the land of the shadow of death, upon them a light has shined. . . . For unto us a Child is born, unto us a Son is given; and the government will be upon His shoulder. And His name will be called Wonderful, Counselor, Mighty God, Everlasting Father, Prince of Peace.

Isa. 9:2, 6

Mark 10:46-52

~~~~~~

DEEP JOY   April 13

"Ask, and it will be given to you; seek, and you will find; knock, and it will be opened to you."

Matt. 7:7

Joy often appears through the cracks of whatever else we are busily doing and seeking. To find joy, we may think of something uplifting and beautiful: a surprise party, a visit with a loved one, or winning a fortune! But that may not be God's joy. He wants to give us a deeper drink of joy than we expect. Today, ask this one thing of our Father: that He would show you His joy and perfection (Ps. 119:92-112).

A child may want something that looks good but does not satisfy. The joy of the Lord, His joy, gives us strength (Neh. 8:10). In thinking of my own limited joy, I realized I was missing more—that deep joy of the Lord, that swift strength from on high, that refreshing drink of pure beauty, that unexpected view of the riches of the heart even in what the world considers poverty. His joy runs in unusual circles, ever expanding like the ripples on a pond penetrated by one surrendered stone, a simple leap of faith.

One day when I tried to seek His joy, I had several possibilities in mind, but it was none of these. He showed me an impossibility, and there was the first glimpse of His joy, emerging in what I would never try. Of course, I thought it would not work, but it did. I gave away my safe opportunity and saw His impossible joy in the face of another, as together we risked what He really wanted done to help someone else. This was the joy of the Lord. It was His joy, not mine, but it truly became mine. By stepping aside, getting out of the way, I saw what He could do, and His joy was revealed. How very different. How very refreshing! It is His joy that gives us everlasting strength, not our joy.

Look for His joy today, even in one small thing. It may not be your idea of joy. Roll down the windows of your life a little, and breathe in some fresh air. In humble service, step out of the way, and watch for His joy on the face of another. In unexpected places, it still shines brightly, warming your heart even in suffering or in giving away what you thought was yours. The Creator gives you what is forever new. Watch for Him in the turns and colors of nature, in the delight of His creation. At the end of the day, seek the Lord in pure worship, at the altar of His sacrifice. There joy shines brightest, and there His joy will find you and overflow.

Father, anoint me with the oil of gladness in Jesus Christ so I can reflect Your joy in the love light of His face shining in a dark world. In Jesus' name, amen.

Zeph. 3:12-17   John 15:9-13   Ps. 16:8-11

FOUR SIDES OF HUMILITY   April 14

Humble yourselves in the sight of the Lord, and He will lift you up.

James 4:10

Humility, like faith, brings great potential to small things. When you begin to build according to God's plumb line of righteousness, do not despise the day of small things, for small things will grow according to His complete power (Zech. 4:6-10). In humility, we grow as a mustard seed. If we are puffed up, there is no life in us.

B - Beauty of the Lord. It is impossible to be humble by thinking we should be. That only makes us proud for trying to do it. But when we see the beauty of our Lord and bow before Him, His beauty makes us humble. When we give Him time to reveal Himself to us, and as His beauty quietly enfolds us, then we see truly how small we are and shrink by comparison. As we think on His ways and words, we let go of whatever puffs us up, so we can go through the cross into His kingdom. In His presence, old wounds heal. Pride is much like the swollen area surrounding a wound. When the wound is healed, the pride subsides so we can see Him (2 Cor. 3:16-18).

O - Open to surprises. When we are surprised by God's ways, our reaction reveals either pride or humility. Being open to our Creator's surprises in daily life makes our lives flexible, allowing more of His life and blessings to flow. Our schedules are not our own. As we look for Him and what He can do, we enter the center "o" of His joy. In His humility, we become humble to receive what God can give us. The bondage of the human will is released by the cross of Christ, who, for the joy set before Him, endured the cross to bring us to victory. Is your heart open to His joy (Heb.12:1-2)?

W - Washed in the Lord. We are the Lord's laundry project. First, He buys the clothes, and then He keeps washing us so that His Holy Spirit can come into us and wear us around to do His work. When we are soiled in the world, back into the washing machine we go, and He cleans us up again. To deny by pride that we are soiled and demand that He use us just as we are would require the Lord to walk around in dirty clothes to do His work. He loves us as we are, but He will wash us up to be like Him. Without humility, we are unwashable. As clothes lie limp on the floor, so are we until the Master picks us up and cleans us up. Are you washable (Titus 3:5; John 13:6-8)?

S - Serving the Lord with gladness. Pride can serve and get something done, but only humility can serve and touch the Father's heart. Pride carries a heavy heart that prefers to do its own things and be with "better" people. We can serve people, even touch human hearts, but we cannot touch our Creator's heart until He creates the work in us for the least of these. Whose heart do you want to touch? Serve Him and see (Matt. 5:7).

Father, give me the mind of Christ instead of my own way. In His name, amen.

Matt. 25:37-40   Phil 2:1-13   Rom. 12:9-21

April 15

I SEEK YOUR FACE

Father, I seek Your face, not just Your words and works. I want to live in Your Son, not just learn about Him and work for Him. Lead me into Your heart. Reveal Yourself through the Holy Spirit, making my life a reflection of Your life in Christ, conforming me to His image for Your pleasure and purpose alone. In Jesus' name, amen.

When You said, "Seek My face," my heart said to You, "Your face, Lord, I will seek."
Ps. 27:8

2 Cor. 3:18—4:18

KEPT IN GRACE   April 16

"My sheep hear My voice, and I know them, and they follow Me. And I give them eternal life, and they shall never perish; neither shall anyone snatch them out of My hand. My Father, who has given them to Me, is greater than all; and no one is able to snatch them out of My Father's hand. I and My Father are one."

                                                         John 10:27-30

We cannot keep ourselves in God's grace, but we can hear the voice of the Shepherd who keeps us. Because He knows us and reveals Himself to us, we can follow Him—if we keep our eyes on Him. When our eyes wander to trouble or even to the other sheep who would lead us in circles, He calls us back to Him. Only our Shepherd will lead us to real life, not plastic grass and mirages of water.

His keeping power is eternal and leads us even through the valley of the shadow of death. No one else can lead us through there, and no one can snatch us out of His hand. When we see the dangers ahead, we cry, "I can't do it. It's too much for me!" But it's not too much for Him. He is not leading us through what we can handle but through what only He can handle. Both the route and the destination have divine dimensions. Did we expect to get there on human power? Are we trying to manufacture our own grace when our lives are already kept in grace by God?

Our keeper is the Lord of all, the Creator of the universe, the gentle Shepherd who carries lambs struggling to walk. He knows our struggle and will carry us on shoulders that felt the sting of a whip, the weight of a cross, and then left the cold of a tomb behind. There is the fragrance of lilies on those shoulders. He carries us on shoulders clothed in resurrection majesty. To keep us, He conquers everything, but He also allows us our own free will to reject Him or to receive Him. That is the choice of grace.

We are free to live in His keeping or die in our own. To die, we must believe a lie as old as the Garden of Eden: that we can be like God. However, He has already chosen to become like us in His Son and so bring us through the cross into His life by grace. The true Owner has the keeping power, and His life is truth. He who is the First and the Last, the Alpha and the Omega, will keep His flock today and bring us home.

Father, help us to hear the Gentle Shepherd's call that leads us in the truth of Your grace. He will carry us in His arms that were spread out on the cross for all people. Speak life to us now and guide us in Your love. In our Savior's name, Jesus, amen.

1 Thess. 5:23-24   John 6:28-35   Eph. 1:3-10

LIVING THE LAST DAY

April 17

"Which of you by worrying can add one cubit to his stature? So why do you worry about clothing? Consider the lilies of the field, how they grow: they neither toil nor spin; . . . But seek first the kingdom of God and His righteousness, and all these things shall be added to you."

Matt. 6:27-28, 33

If you knew this was the last day of your life, how would you live it? Would you live any differently than your usual routine? The answer to this question is the key to living fully every day. Of course, we can't leave all work behind and go off to hide on some tranquil beach, but the deeper things that draw our attention when time is short are the very things we need to focus on when there seems to be plenty of time. If you knew this day would be your last, would there be disappointment in something left undone or words left unsaid? These are the things you need to do now and the words you need to say now.

Under pressure, limited time squeezes out all but the most essential things, things that often were buried in levels of empty activity. Look closely at your life today, and pose this question through each part of your schedule: Is this something I would do on my last day? Of course, your last day here could overlap with your first day in heaven, which is a wider perspective and all the more reason to look into and live fully the life of Christ available today, especially in the words you speak, which will echo into the future. Consider the following questions as if this were your last day.

Is what I'm doing here fruitful in God's kingdom and a pleasure to Him?
Is what I have said today what I want to be remembered by?
Is there anything left undone or compromised that should be fully committed?

The answers to these questions are the starting points for real change. Growth is a series of gradual changes that lead to enduring fruit. For a long time, you may have been carrying the seeds around, doing nothing with them. But now it's time to sow what will last. God's love prepares good ground—broken, rich, and deep, ready for the Son to shine into every part. Now consider the three questions again. Do you think Jesus would look at your life today and answer them in the same way? Let Him make the changes.

Father, I want to live completely for You. Change me in the light of Your Son to make each day count for eternity. In Jesus' name, amen.

Matt. 6:9-13, 24   Ps. 84:10-12   Luke 19:10-27

April 18

LET ME HIDE

Life flows from my Savior's side. There, O God, let me hide. In the life of Your Son, in the reality of His sacrifice, I run into Your mercy and power through the Holy Spirit. Cover me completely and protect me now from enemies within and without. Wash away my sin in the blood of Your Son, and make me new in His resurrection power to live in Your will today. In Jesus' name, amen.

Then the soldiers came and broke the legs of the first and of the other who was crucified with Him. But when they came to Jesus and saw that He was already dead, they did not break His legs. But one of the soldiers pierced His side with a spear, and immediately blood and water came out.

John 19:32-34

Col. 3:1-17

KNOW TO LOVE   April 19

"I am the good shepherd; and I know my sheep, and am known by my own."

John 10:14

Sometimes we prefer to read about Jesus instead of actually living with Him. Often, I've tried to follow Him from a safe distance. "I'm studying His directions to learn what I can do to please Him," I have insisted, not realizing that the close, living presence of Christ is the direction I need, and spending time with Him alone is the key to action. Time spent in worship as well as God's Word connects us to the source of power. Otherwise, our effort is like studying a letter about someone instead of meeting that person and sharing his life. If a friend wrote and came to visit us, would we stay home studying his message instead of going to the airport to pick him up? This is what we do with Jesus, read and talk about Him but never actually welcome Him into our lives.

The Living Word calls you to a personal relationship. He wants you to take time out of your schedule to meet Him and enjoy all of life together. It's good to study His Word, but it's also necessary to spend time with the Author, who alone can work its truth in and through us by the Holy Spirit. In love, He wants us to fully listen before we rush ahead to do what we think is needed. Out of that love comes the power to do the work His way and to see the needs He sees. Only then can we fully understand His Word. Our main purpose is not to do His work but to be with Him so He can do His work through us.

The Pharisees and scribes knew all about God and all about the Messiah. They just didn't know Him personally. Their lives were closed to His immediate presence, His amazing love. So they killed Him. So will we, if we do not truly know Him now. On our own, we will quench the Holy Spirit and drive God's love away.

Without a direct, personal knowledge of Christ, we make Him into our own image as an abstract power for human use or a mere sentimental token, and we miss a full relationship of divine love and life (John 5:39-40). He wants to make us into His image with pure love and intimate communion. In loving someone, you understand his heart's desire, and he understands yours. You've taken time to listen as well as talk. You put his hopes and plans first. On a moment's notice, you would change your schedule for him. You anticipate his preferences and the particular way he would solve a problem. There is nothing you delight in more than just being with him. You can count on the One you know and depend on him based on your past experience together. In love, God wants you to know His Son so well that you will count on Him and not on yourself. Take time to love Him first, and the rest will follow (John 1:11-13).

Father, open the eyes of my heart to know Your Son living in me. In His name, amen.

John 14:3-6   Ps. 63:1-5   John 21:3-15

LEADERSHIP: TURNING AND BURNING   April 20

Then Moses said, "I will now turn aside and see this great sight, why the bush does not burn." So when the Lord saw that he turned aside to look, God called to him from the midst of the bush and said, "Moses, Moses!" And he said, "Here I am."

Exod. 3:3-4

True leaders turn aside to seek God alone and to be led by His purpose. They listen to His counsel before doing any work or leading anyone anywhere. God did not speak to Moses until Moses had turned toward Him. This priority continues throughout our journey as the Shepherd of our souls leads all, leader and follower alike. In fact, the leader must first be a good follower of the Shepherd. For any given job, there may be many people humanly qualified to lead, but God is looking for the one who will turn aside from any human agenda to follow Him and to seek His face.

In Christ, we find the power of humility that enables us to leave our usual work, take off our shoes, and listen to the voice of God speaking in holy fire that illumines and does not consume. True leaders live with the burning bush, the tree of the cross, aflame inside their lives to illumine all who come near. Before directing the people, a leader after God's heart will first ask who is doing the sending and ultimately doing all of the work. Otherwise, there is no point in going.

There is nothing we can do that God is not already doing. In the cross of Christ, He still leads us now. For deliverance, God gave Moses a staff of wood and made it alive with divine power, just as the bush burned with the power of God. The staff in Moses' hand produced miracles in a worldly kingdom and brought deliverance to many people as Moses obeyed the voice of God he had heard alone in the desert.

The one whom God calls to leadership, God first moves to a humble place and then calls aside to see His power revealed. The shoes of our own ways must come off. This is the scope of our training: laying down our methods, turning aside from the world, seeing God's power, and hearing His voice. Will we take off our shoes and draw near? Without this vision of our true Leader, the people will perish. In the cross, His power still burns for deliverance and revelation in the light of His Word, calling us forward in faith. Turn and see; then let His truth burn in you.

Lord, turn me aside from my world to see Your power and to hear Your Word today. Make me obedient to what You say when I seek You alone. In Jesus' name, amen.

Ps. 119:57-60   2 Cor. 4:5-7   Matt. 10:6-8

April 21

~~~~~~

LIKE THE DEW

Lord God, come and water us here like the dew in Your presence. In the moisture of the Holy Spirit, wash us as a new day dawns even in the desert. Move upon us with Your footsteps, leaving the imprint of Your love in every place, according to Your will. Let our lives be changed by the footsteps of Your will to bring all things into conformity with eternity. When we can't yet see clearly because of the recent darkness, open the eyes of our hearts to see You living here with power. Even before the sun rises, the dew already appears to glisten at the first move of dawn. Thank You for Your Son's resurrection. Because of that kiss of life, we welcome even through the night Your presence, bringing all things into submission under the feet of our Savior, Jesus Christ. Renew us in the perfect unity that receives the life of our High Priest who comes. We live under His feet in the dew of the morning. Bring us out of darkness through Your cleansing power so we can see clearly this new day as You create it. In Jesus' name, amen.

"I will be like the dew to Israel. He shall grow like the lily, and lengthen his roots like Lebanon."

Hos. 14:5

Num. 11:7-9   Luke 24:1-2

~~~~~~

THE LILIES   April 22

"Consider the lilies, how they grow: they neither toil nor spin; and yet I say to you, even Solomon in all his glory was not arrayed like one of these."

                                                                Luke 12:27

In the beauty of the lilies, there is something we cannot produce. "Eye has not seen, nor ear heard, nor have entered into the heart of man the things which God has prepared for those who love Him" (1 Cor. 2:9). The lilies are clothed in more than chemical compounds and sunlight. They are clothed in the iridescent beauty of God's holiness, in the silent wakefulness of His creation, which is involved in His purpose and visible even to those who reject it. Solomon had beautiful robes, but they were man-made. In wisdom, he had the interior beauty of God, but his exterior was clothed in human skill.

What the lilies wear is woven by light inside and out, shaped by the breath of God. It is His pure intention, touched by no other hand. All our wisdom and talent, even as inspired by God, can never match the transcendent colors of the living design of God's heart. Yet He has given us free will either to prefer our own clothes or to choose His. If we choose His, our free will adds a beauty beyond the lilies as He clothes us in His Son.

What are you wearing today? No matter how good it looks, it is beautiful only if it's made new in His love and humility. The lilies not only look good, but they are good, as God created them, the same inside and outside. The presence of His beauty is the core of their being, and it shines through without interference. They are not trying to do anything else or wear anything else other than what He intended.

In our toiling and spinning, we put on layer after layer of our own making, attitudes and facades for admiration by other people; or we try to appear to be something we are not. Then His beauty cannot shine through. Of course, we need regular clothes, but deeper, we need to shed our layers of protective deception and be spiritually clothed in God's grace. Before saying, "Clothe me," we must repent and remove what is not His.

Humility is the only thing we can wear before God. Reality leads to humility, and when we are dressed in only that, our Creator can wash us in the blood of the Lamb. Come just as you are. He will wash you with the dew of the morning in Jesus Christ and clothe you daily on holy ground. His garments carry the aroma of life and are woven so strong that even death cannot unravel them. As in baptism, the flow of His holiness will surround and protect. Even now, live in the liquid light of His power as a covering. To walk in that kind of beauty is to walk in the trust of those who neither toil nor spin. They still do daily work, but not as toil, for His yoke is easy, and His burden is light.

Father, I repent of my sin. Please remove it, wash me, and clothe me in the beautiful garments of Your life in Jesus Christ. In Jesus' name, amen.

Gal. 3:27   Isa. 61:1-3   Matt. 6:30-33

LOVE LISTENS   April 23

So then, my beloved brethren, let every man be swift to hear, slow to speak, slow to wrath; for the wrath of man does not produce the righteousness of God.

James 1:19-20

Listening is a channel of love that leads to change. Together, listening and love go farther than either can alone. Trying to change something or someone in love without first taking time to listen will produce barriers and bitterness. Being right doesn't produce change. Gathering arguments doesn't produce change. Listening in love does. Likewise, listening without love will only dig the well of anger deeper. When you meet with a friend, are you as ready to listen as you are to talk? When you meet with God, is it to listen to Him? Our prayers will be answered when we are as willing to wait and listen for His direction, as we are to ask.

True listening requires more than open ears; it requires an open heart that trusts God first to let Him do what is needed without our talking about it or giving directions. Listening is resting in His power to move hearts, including ours, in His direction and to give us the right words to say. Try the challenge of listening before speaking for just one day, and see what happens. The results may surprise you. Waiting to speak changes you as well as others, allowing them slowly to expose hidden wounds for healing or the motivation for their blunders that angered you. God allows the secrets of hearts to be exposed to those who love enough to listen.

Jesus said His disciples would be known by their love, not by their words or their ability to debate or to please people. To hear someone's heart, your mouth must be quiet and your hands still long enough to show others they are more important to you than whatever you wanted to say or do. Yes, people need words; they need helping hands, but more importantly, they need your love revealed in the silence of a mind tuned to them. Then you will be able to hear something new and act on what you could not know before. People will realize you are more interested in them than in what you are going to say. That gives the words you do speak the full power of honest love to bring true change. Listen in God's love, and healing will come, producing more than words can say.

Lord, lead me to love as You love, to listen as You listen, and to care for others as You care for Your sheep, including me. Put a guard on my lips, and open my heart. In the name of our Shepherd, Jesus, who leads His flock by still waters, amen.

Isa. 55:1-3   James 1:26-27   Luke 10:38-42

April 24

JEWELS

Thank You, Father, that You see the end from the beginning. Time is a tool in Your hand to fashion jewels we cannot see. We will let You do the cutting and polishing, but first comes separation from the dark earth, then complete cleansing, exposure to the light, and the first hint of sparkle. Finish the work in Your order and power so that Your love will shine through each life surrendered to You. In Jesus' name, amen.

Then those who feared the Lord spoke to one another, and the Lord listened and heard them; so a book of remembrance was written before Him for those who fear the Lord and who meditate on His name. "They shall be Mine," says the Lord of hosts, "on the day that I make them My jewels. And I will spare them as a man spares his own son who serves him."

Mal. 3:17

Heb. 12:7-25

A LITTLE DEEPER   April 25

"For whoever desires to save his life will lose it, but whoever loses his life for My sake will save it."

Luke 9:24

The repentance Jesus invites us to experience is more than a surface adjustment. Instead of merely rearranging our current lives, He calls us to radical change, like that of a baby being born (John 3:3-17). Undoubtedly, a baby thinks he is dying while on the way to new life. Coming out, the baby is still a baby but must go through a tremendous transition that separates him from the source of his past life. The umbilical cord to the fetal existence is cut, and we don't like cuts. Our idea of repentance often suggests a minor pull or tug, as we would adjust our clothes in a mirror with a little brushing off at the shoulders or a pull to straighten out a few wrinkles. This is not real change.

To bring us to real life, Jesus asks us to lay aside our past garments and cut the cord to our old life completely. Then He offers us new garments, clean in the blood of His sacrifice and woven with the pure thread of His covenant love. There is no match in this world for what He offers, so we must begin as newborns. Unable to take care of ourselves, we can't clean up our old clothes to His degree of holiness or mend our ways to fit His ways. To be reborn spiritually from within, there must be a cutting away of the old. Some things we did before may be transformed in God's purpose by being surrendered to Him, but they no longer belong to us.

Instead of carnal power, we let Christ infuse us with resurrection power, transforming both the inside and the outside of our lives through the cross. Some try to take up the new without laying aside the old, but this is impossible, resulting in extra burdens that leave us exhausted, because there is no new birth within to change us from the inside out. It's not just a change of lifestyle but a change of life at the core, which then affects everything else. We step into a pattern that leads us beyond ourselves into the life of Christ.

Whatever He is calling us to change today, let's go a little deeper. Instead of sporadic efforts in human strength, move deeper into the power of the cross. With love, our Savior waits for us to accept His power, to let go of surface things, to lay them down completely, and to walk into a new creation. Go a little deeper, and cut the cord.

Lord, lead me out of my old ways and into Your new ways through the cross. In laying down my old wardrobe and weapons of this world, I accept Your beautiful garments of peace and the power of Your Word alive in me now. In Jesus' name, amen.

Luke 10:30-37   Matt. 7:21-29   2 Cor. 5:14-18

THE LION AND THE LAMB April 26

"Do not weep. Behold, the Lion of the tribe of Judah, the Root of David, has prevailed to open the scroll and to loose its seven seals." And I looked, and behold, in the midst of the throne and of the four living creatures, and in the midst of the elders, stood a Lamb as though it had been slain, . . . Then He came and took the scroll out of the right hand of Him who sat on the throne.

Rev. 5:5-7

The Lion of the tribe of Judah was found able to open the seals of judgment, but as the opening occurs, it is the Lamb who stands before us, takes the scroll, and finishes the work. In all of creation, Christ is both. His lineage and position as Messiah authorized the Lion to open the process, but the actual execution of the judgment and purging of the earth is carried out through the sufferings of the Lamb slain from before the foundation of the world. So for us, the Lion we want to reign must first go to the cross as the Lamb to emerge victorious in resurrection power. He will not conquer without the Lamb's humility. In prayer, we often call on our Lord as the Lion to save us by changing our circumstances, but the actual victory and purging of our situation may come only as we humbly recognize and join the suffering of the Lamb for us right where we are now.

Without the sacrificial love of the cross, the Lion of Judah would not be able to open the seals of Revelation or the seals of our own lives, even though He is ready and He is powerful to perform God's will. In the completion of all things, those who were enemies will lie down together, and a little child shall lead them (Isa. 11:1-10). This is not how we usually seek to solve our problems. We want the Lion of Judah to come roaring in on our behalf and clean up the whole mess immediately, destroying enemies right and left (Luke 9:51-56). Yet the true conqueror is the One who submitted quietly to His enemies in order to save them, and who forgave, healed, blessed, and transformed the whole world to reveal the true strength of the Lion. He will come again as the Lion with the purity of the Lamb. Without the Lamb's sacrifice, the Lion is powerless to complete His mission. And without the Lion, the Lamb has no boldness or strength for the task.

In our lives, may the Lion and the Lamb lie down together. May the Christ Child lead us where neither power nor humility can go alone. Each needs the other to complete its purpose in God's kingdom. May we see more of the Lion and Lamb together to make us strong in humility and pure in the power of Christ. Are your prayers inviting both into your situation? In humility, they are willing to be led by a little Child. Are you?

Lord God, reign in me through Your Son, the Lion and the Lamb. Lead me in the grace of Your Child, Jesus. In His name, amen.

Matt. 18:1-4 Matt. 16:21-27 John 1:29-34

April 27

LET MY CUP OVERFLOW

Father, what You have poured out in Jesus, help me to receive and release, letting Your life flow beyond earthly cups and what we try to keep in them. Free my heart to hold more than I can know and to overflow in Your grace to give You glory and to help others. In humility and power, fill me with the life of Your Son in His cross and resurrection. In Jesus' name, amen.

"Whoever drinks of the water that I shall give him will never thirst. But the water that I shall give him will become in him a fountain of water springing up into everlasting life." The woman said to Him, "Sir, give me this water, that I may not thirst, nor come here to draw." Jesus said to her, "Go, call your husband, and come here."

John 4:14-16

Deut. 8:2-16   Mark 9:41

THE LINCHPIN April 28

"I have been crucified with Christ; it is no longer I who live, but Christ lives in me; and the life which I now live in the flesh I live by faith in the Son of God, who loved me and gave Himself for me."

Gal. 2:20

A linchpin is the essential link between moving parts, such as a wheel and axle. If the linchpin for our lives is faulty, the ride will be bumpy every day, because the essential connecting element is crooked. No matter how well we smooth over the other parts, if the inner linchpin is out of place, nothing works right. To know Jesus Christ is to let His cross remove the old linchpin of sin and put in the straight truth of His love with the oil of the Holy Spirit. Then our lives can turn fully and completely in His will. Christ removed sin for all people, and if we follow Him in the way of the cross, the core of our lives will run clean.

We might prefer to change the other parts, get a new wheel or a better axle, but the deep cycles of our lives turn upon the thoughts and intents of our hearts. Everything else is just surface paint, lots of moving parts and a tooting horn. Many are trying to go on the highway to heaven in elaborate vehicles that look good but revolve on an inner linchpin of selfishness. Their journey lurches in ragged circles around self-focus.

When the cross is inserted and turning at the core of life, we can move straight on the highway to heaven. Only the cross can knock the old linchpin of sin out of its socket so that the whole structure of self-centered lives comes crashing down. When the linchpin of selfishness is removed, then everything will fall at Jesus' feet to be transformed. The cross pulls the underpinnings out from all the various sins piled on our lives. There may be a huge, complicated network of them, but underneath somewhere is one tiny central pin of self on which everything else is turning.

With self-help methods, we could try to correct all the things piled on top one by one, but we would just end up loading on more. Or we could just go right to the core, give it to Christ, and let Him pull out the central linchpin of sin. When the old things come crashing down, His cross can be lifted up, uniting our hearts with His and turning us forever in His life and power.

Father, turn me in Your will. Take out the old and put in the new power of Christ's cross and resurrection. In the oil of Your Spirit, turn my heart to You. In Jesus' name, amen.

2 Cor. 1:19-22 Mark 7:6-8, 15-23   Gal. 6:14-15

LIKE NO OTHER
April 29

Among the gods there is none like You, O Lord; nor are there any works like Your works. . . . For You are great, and do wondrous things; You alone are God. Teach me Your way, O Lord; I will walk in Your truth; unite my heart to fear Your name. I will praise You, O Lord my God, with all my heart, and I will glorify Your name forevermore.

Ps. 86:8, 10-12

We often try to make ourselves more comfortable with God by making Him more like us so we can safely please Him. But God is like no other; He is not a super human. He is more than we can know, yet knowable as He reveals Himself to us through His Son Jesus, crucified and raised. Some people have their own routine or project to please God, but they don't want Him actually to come into their lives in power—especially through a cross. God reveals Himself as a personal Father yet Creator of all, who gave His Son for us in love. Shouldn't we follow His directions about how to know Him?

God is untouched, unmeasured Divinity, burning with a purity we can never grasp or contain; He is totally other than humanity. Yet in His Son He became like us to bring us to Himself. In essence, He is not like us, yet He loves us and wants us to live with Him. And what does He require? Justice, mercy, humility, and a simple love deeper than polite ritual (Mic. 6:6-8). Yet for our pleasure and comfort, we often insist on treating Him like an earthly king we can appease by bringing earthly offerings as pagans would: money, food, promises, magnificent works, material monuments, complicated programs.

However, from His perspective, all these things in themselves are as nothing. So what shall we bring then? His request is for love, childlike trust, obedience, and a humble heart (1 Sam. 15:22-23). How do you please God? The amount of work you do for Him will never please Him as much as the love with which you do it and your quickness to obey. In Psalm 51:16-17, David, a king with all the power and wealth of a nation at his disposal, sang to God, "For You do not desire sacrifice, or else I would give it; You do not delight in burnt offering. The sacrifices of God are a broken spirit, a broken and a contrite heart—these, O God, You will not despise." When David did offer material sacrifices to God, they came after the main offering of his heart each day.

What do you bring to God today? Are you more interested in what you plan to do for Him than in the love He has already planned for you?

Father, teach me to love you like the child You have created, not a worker You have hired. In Jesus' name, amen.

Mark 12:28-34   Rom. 10:2-3, 8-13   Heb. 10:8-14

~~~~~~

A ROOT OUT OF DRY GROUND

Father, send Your Holy Spirit to reveal Your Son, springing up in my heart like a root out of dry ground. Let there be fruit to please You right where I am now, even in a desert. When I seek Your face to know You first, then the healing rain will come. In Jesus' name, amen.

For He shall grow up before Him as a tender plant, and as a root out of dry ground. He has no form or comeliness; and when we see Him, there is no beauty that we should desire Him. He is despised and rejected by men, a Man of sorrows and acquainted with grief. And we hid, as it were, our faces from Him; He was despised, and we did not esteem Him. Surely He has borne our griefs and carried our sorrows; yet we esteemed Him stricken, smitten by God, and afflicted. But He was wounded for our transgressions, He was bruised for our iniquities; the chastisement for our peace was upon Him, and by His stripes we are healed.

Isa. 53:2-5

Gen. 18:1-4, 10-19

~~~~~~

TO KNOW HIM   May 1

And we know that the Son of God has come and has given us an understanding, that we may know Him who is true; and we are in Him who is true, in His Son Jesus Christ. This is the true God and eternal life.

1 John 5:20

To know God through the Son is eternal life, which begins already in this world when we walk through the door of Christ's love. To know Him is more than to know about Him or to try to live a nice life based on His instructions. God did not save us so that we could do something for Him. He saved us to know Him and to live with Him now in love. In salvation, He desires fellowship with His creation. Adam and Eve stepped outside of His will, blocking that fellowship with their decision to seek knowledge for themselves. They wanted their knowledge more than they wanted Him.

God prefers the fellowship of obedience. Then He can work through us to draw us and others closer to Him. To restore that fellowship, God sent us His Son, not just to give us instructions but to give us Himself. Our salvation is in relationship to God through the Son, in becoming part of His life as He becomes the center of our lives.

It's the same with people. To really know them, you must do more than read about them or try to imitate their lifestyle. You spend time with them in person, get to know the rest of their family, become genuinely interested in pleasing them from the heart, and generally enjoy their company. Often, you spend time just listening to them. You must be more interested in their presence than in what they can do for you, or they will sense you don't really care about them personally. In Matthew 7:21-23, Jesus makes it clear that not everyone who calls Him "Lord" is someone He recognizes as enjoying His presence through obedience more than he or she enjoys His power.

The greatest commandment focuses on relationship as the foundation of all action (Mark 12:28-34). The second commandment flows out of the first, just as obedience to God flows out of our love for Him. It is impossible to fully obey God without loving Him, even if we try to do everything else right. So the rich young ruler went away sorrowful (Matt. 19:16-22). He did not love God enough to recognize the treasure of divine love standing before him and the riches of His Creator's presence. Do we?

Is our treasure to work a lot for the Lord or to know Him and the beauty of His work in love, even though we never accomplish anything the world can see? In focusing on God, we allow Him to do more for others through us. Why did God save us? To love Him in Christ, with cups overflowing. They are never thirsty who know Him now.

Father, draw me near to You, close enough to hear Your heart. Then everything else will fall into place, and others will benefit as I live at one with Your will. In Jesus' name, amen.

John 5:39-40   John 17:1-3   John 6:37-38

LOOK FOR HIM   May 2

"And you will seek Me and find Me, when you search for Me with all your heart."

Jer. 29:13

Look for the Lord now with all your heart. Nothing else matters
until you do. You can look for healing or
knowledge or deliverance
or riches or peace,
but you will find none
of these until you look for Him
above all
and let Him find you.

O King, now I look for You—not for me, but for You. When I find You, let me be completely alive with the joy of a child arriving home, welcomed to a feast, and made free in the blood of the Lamb, Jesus. In Jesus' name, amen.

Ps. 27:7-8   John 8:12, 28-32   Phil. 3:12

A LIVING LETTER   May 3

Clearly you are an epistle of Christ, ministered by us, written not with ink but by the Spirit of the living God, not on tablets of stone but on tablets of flesh, that is, of the heart.

                                                                2 Cor. 3:3

It is possible to carve words in stone, but love cannot be written there. As living letters, our hearts are open to be read by all, to reveal the One who was crucified and rose again, living here now by the Holy Spirit. When the Spirit writes in us the active love of God, the letter is composed not only of words but also of thoughts, actions, love and laughter, tears and trials.

To become a living letter of God, we must let His love write in us more than words can say. A look, a tone of voice, an offer to help, a reach toward the unreachable, a humility that reveals the Prince of Peace in a listening heart—all of these compose the letter God writes. He comes with healing in His wings and gives wisdom in an instant that is more effective than hundreds of books. How? First, we allow His written Word to write itself deeply in our hearts as well as our minds. If we ask, God will help us. On our own, we may try to put His Word into our minds, but only the Holy Spirit can write it in our hearts and so renew our minds after the mind of Christ (Titus 3:4-7; John 15:26).

By the Spirit, God's Word is ignited in us, engraved by holy fire even deeper than mind and will, carved into the core of our being (Acts 1:8). In that fire of life, the Bible becomes a living seed in us that produces more than minds can learn. At the right season, the meaning comes out in visible action as fruit alive with the love of God. From the fuel of the Living Word in us, the Holy Spirit can start a pure fire that is contagious.

A living letter is written in the power of God's life that came out of the grave. Its Author is not dead. We may look for His Word in the place where men have put Him, but He is not there. The stone is rolled away. The Vine is growing. The cold tablets have been replaced by a living body that increases daily in love as each part works together, as every joint supplies, and the Holy Spirit cleanses us to be one in Christ. To be part of that letter, we join others in His body who live His Word as well as read it.

Our lives overlap and combine to record in action and love a truly living letter. Covered with Christ's blood, it speaks truth and mercy. What He writes breaks the power of sin. Other people are not the only ones who read this letter. The Lord Himself will read us all. He may do some editing. Then He signs His name. The living letter that we are is not delivered over our signatures, but with the name that is above all names signed in the blood of the cross. Let Him write as He will and deliver what He has finished!

Father, write Your truth in my heart as an open letter of love. In Jesus' name, amen.

John 14:15-17, 22-27   Ezek. 36:25-27   Luke 24:30-32

LOVE THAT PREVAILS
May 4

"I in them, and You in Me; that they may be made perfect in one, and that the world may know that You have sent Me, and have loved them as You have loved Me."

John 17:23

At some point, human love will fail. It means well, but it falters or flickers out somewhere along the way. Sometimes in our own power, we keep pushing an empty wagon when our Creator is ready to carry us by grace. God's heart burns the same for His people now as in the days of Abraham, or Noah, or Adam, or Jesus, for you, for me, for the child next door. Even His judgment flows out of love to preserve a holy relationship with His people, whom He died to save. There is a love that prevails, and it is the Genesis-creating, Vine-abiding life and stone-moving resurrection love that will bring us home (John 3:14-17).

God's love prevails over sin through Christ's blood on the cross. It prevails over doubt and death by the power of His resurrection and the truth of His Living Word active in us today. It prevails over the world by the power of the Holy Spirit and the purging of holy judgment. His love prevails over time by the ongoing heartbeat of the Father's covenant with His people. It prevails over the narrow pit of human pride and fear by lifting us in Christ through the freedom of the cross. It prevails in you by penetrating the hard ground of self-focus and disappointment to bring forth fruit that remains to the praise of His glory. Forever, His Word is settled in heaven. Even now, God's love conquers the farthest reaches of our hearts and renews our minds in peace that passes understanding. Like prodigal children, we turn toward home and are received into our Father's house with His embrace and His love that prevails.

Lord, reign over and conquer all in me that questions Your love. In Jesus' name, amen.

Jer. 31:3   Luke 15:18-24   Rom. 5:5-10

~~~~~~

LET US SEE YOU, LORD, MORE THAN US

Let us see You, Lord, more than we focus on ourselves. Let us pray what You see so the answers will be Yours and not ours. Even when we can see no clear way, increase our faith to match the future You have planned and to trust You for the answers, according to Your will. We know Your plans are more amazing than what we can comprehend. Let us see You first, Lord, in this place too full of us. In Jesus' name, amen.

"I speak what I have seen with My Father, and you do what you have seen with your father." They answered and said to Him, "Abraham is our father." Jesus said to them, "If you were Abraham's children, you would do the works of Abraham. But now you seek to kill Me, a Man who has told you the truth which I heard from God. Abraham did not do this."

John 8:38-40

John 5:17-23, 30

~~~~~~

MAKE ROOM   May 6

"the Spirit of truth, whom the world cannot receive, because it neither sees Him nor knows Him; but you know Him, for He dwells with you and will be in you."

John 14:17

If someone took inventory of your life and your house today, would it be obvious that your first priority is Jesus Christ? Look at what fills and surrounds your space today at home and at work. Are other things in your life crowding out the full light of Christ shining now? After pondering these questions, I recently gave away books, clothes, magazines, and CD's, none of which were actually bad. They were just not as good as He is in Person. I had to make room for the Holy Spirit to live and move in every area, shelf, and corner of my life. We can let go of some good things to make way for what is finer, more beautiful by far, simpler and holier, as the new life of the Creator's love moves in us. What could be more important?

Our old stuff not only takes up physical room, but it also occupies spiritual room, weaves emotional ties, and takes up valuable time that could be invested in new life in Christ. Was I the one who said I didn't have time to help the poor because I was studying about Jesus in all these books? His presence in action was crowded out by piles of books about Him, references and articles, clothes, gadgets, souvenirs of past events, and tips on how to serve Him—whenever the opportunity arose that didn't interfere with my schedule of maintaining all this stuff.

Patiently, He waits for us to want Him more. So, out went the books to make room for the Author and Finisher of our faith. The clothes and other stuff went to someone who would use them more than once a year, and the result was breathing room for the Holy Spirit. Old ties and fears, as well as things, can block the free flow of His living presence in us and around us. In Christ alone, we are free. Through the Holy Spirit, He wants to dwell in us and move openly through our lives.

Now is the time to make room for the Living Word to change us beyond words on paper, beyond past mistakes, and to stretch us to reach out to those who need Him today. Jesus is much more powerful in person, touching others in our world, than He is in any book or memory. Even "good" activities that omit Christ can stand in the way. Yes, activities can help people, but if the activities keep us from knowing the One who ultimately solves problems, brings salvation, and gives new life, then they are dead ends that block us from serving Him first on His schedule.

Father, remove anything in my life today that blocks the life of Your Son from growing in me and reaching out to others. Make Your love my first priority. In Jesus' name, amen.

Matt. 6:19-24   Heb. 12:1-2   Matt. 13:22-23

LOVE SPEAKS

May 7

"By this all will know that you are My disciples, if you have love for one another."

John 13:35

Most people already have heard enough words, but very few have heard enough love. Love preaches what words cannot and reveals more than volumes of explanations and well-crafted arguments. Let God speak deeply into all the hearts around you today through your love for Him and His love revealed in your actions. It is the most important thing you could ever do or say.

The fruit that your quiet love produces will outlast all the words you ever speak. Part of God's refining process is to separate in us what is simply true and quietly beautiful from the loud and flashy labels we try to pin on ourselves and others with too many words. Today, simply listen to His love and move in it. Let God's presence shine clearly in you, often without words. In His peace, this love will produce change that lasts, far more than anyone can say.

Father, teach me how to love as You love and to simply live that love each day. Make me ready with an answer that comes in action as well as words. In Jesus' name, amen.

1 John 4:9-21   John 13:3-17   1 Cor. 13:1-7

GOD WILL MAKE A WAY   May 8

And the Lord said to Moses, "Why do you cry to Me? Tell the children of Israel to go forward. But lift up your rod, and stretch out your hand over the sea and divide it. And the children of Israel shall go on dry ground through the midst of the sea."

Exod. 14:15-16

God can make a way where there is no human way. In His way, His name is glorified. In our way, there is no glory for His name alone and no fruit that remains for eternity. His way moves forward—no going back. God makes a way for us now, just as He did to bring the Israelites out of bondage. In making a way for us, He has three goals.

1. **Freedom.** God freed the Israelites in His power, taking them through the Red Sea and destroying their enemies, a human impossibility. He does the same for us today through the blood of Jesus Christ. When God makes a way, it is by His power. By His hand and through His Son, He delivers us from enemies and ourselves. Yet we may foolishly prefer to stay in familiar Egypt. Even today, slavery can be managed to the point that we fool ourselves into thinking we're in control. Are we praying for God to have His way in our lives now, for His kingdom to come, or for our old ways and false kingdoms to prosper?

2. **Fruit.** God's way moves us much farther ahead than we can see, toward real fruit. He didn't bring the Israelites through the Red Sea just to get them to some dry ground. He wanted fruit. All along, He was aiming at the Promised Land while they were anxious to save themselves. They couldn't see that far. They were not delivered from Egypt simply to arrive in the wilderness, nor were they brought through the wilderness just to cross the Jordan, nor did they cross the Jordan just to bring down Jericho. All along, they were going forward to build the walls of God's temple and to produce fruit in good ground. With each step, they went forward in faith to much more than they could see. He makes a way for us now, not just to get us past each problem, but also to make us fruitful and to build our lives into a beautiful temple of His praise.

3. **Fellowship.** God makes a way mainly to draw us closer to Him, not to make us closer to other people or worldly dreams. These may happen in the fullness of His love, but His purpose in deliverance is first to bring us closer to Himself. There is no other destination to which He will pave the way for us. If prayers go unanswered, check the destination. Would the answer we want bring us closer to Him? He will not solve problems to get us anywhere else but resting quietly at His feet. We are to stand still from running after old desires and let God's power work (Exod. 14:13-14).

Father, bring me closer to You in Jesus Christ. I turn from my own way to go forward by Your power and truth. Fight for me now and deliver me. In Jesus' name, amen.

John 14:6   Job 23:10-14   Isa. 51:9-16

May 9

~~~~~~

LIVING IN HOLINESS

Father, may we live in Your holiness, which breathes life through Your name. Our old ways are dusty and dead. Through Your Holy Spirit, breathe in us. Cause our dry bones to stand up transformed and move in Your will for the praise of Your glory. Cover us and keep us. Make us alive now in Your Son, and lead us out of any bondage, known or unknown. In Jesus' name, amen.

And He said to me, "Son of man, can these bones live?" So I answered, "O Lord God, You know." Again He said to me, "Prophesy to these bones, and say to them, 'O dry bones, hear the word of the Lord! Thus says the Lord God to these bones: "Surely I will cause breath to enter into you, and you shall live.""'

Ezek. 37:3-5

Eph. 4:4-24

~~~~~~

NEW CREATION   May 10

Then He who sat on the throne said, "Behold, I make all things new."

Rev. 21:5

God is in the business of making a new creation. Are you still investing in the old one? Everything we do or say is directed to either our old life or our new life in Jesus Christ. It is impossible to face two directions at once, just as it is impossible to serve both God and mammon. Much of our distress and disease are the result of trying to go two directions at the same time. Our minds are split with the ultimate headache of serving two masters. To be made whole and have an eye of single purpose, we must turn all of our hearts and lives into the new order of God's life as He sends it to us in His Son (Matt. 4:16-17). The time is at hand. Are we working in the old pattern or the new?

In Christ's life, death, and resurrection, He not only paid the old debts but also opened the door to a new way of life. In all we do, that gift must be revealed. By becoming one with Christ, we enter new life now, refreshing us and recreating us in the Holy Spirit to produce fruit that lasts (John 15:16; Titus 3:5-6). His new creation is both finished and arriving, as God operates outside of time, yet reveals His purpose to us one day at a time. He has formed the old creation to be part of producing the new one, and He has already paid for our new birth through the gift of His Son. Whatever is not in Him is passing away. Yet He is never old. Jesus passed completely through our old life into new life and promises to carry us with Him, if we let go of our worldly anchors (1 John 2:15-17).

When Jesus said, "It is finished," the old order of the natural realm was redeemed and set in order for the birth of a new kingdom, beginning first in the spiritual realm and then revealed eventually in our natural world. In His resurrection, the compass of time turned from past to future. One day, we will put on what is incorruptible, inconceivable, and unspeakable. Yet today, we live already in its light. Does that light shine now through you, or are you still living in the shadows of the past? Some of us busily try to form our own world rather than allowing Christ to transform us in His. Live new.

Lord, forgive me for asking for an old creation when You want to give me a new one. In Your power, change me and all those around me to receive the power of the living Christ. In Jesus' name, amen.

Col. 3:2-11   2 Cor. 5:17-21   John 3:3-8

MORE THAN EVERYTHING   May 11

"The thief does not come except to steal, and to kill, and to destroy. I have come that they may have life, and that they may have it more abundantly."

John 10:10

"Abundantly" here in Greek is *perissos*, meaning superabundant, overflowing, profuse, extraordinary. Actually, the Son of God offers more than what words can describe. Often we want something right now, right here, when He wants to give us more than everything a step later. More than everything should be enough, but we prefer what we can see now. In His wisdom, God may withhold a few things now in order to give us everything—more than enough! His life is more than we can understand, but sometimes we don't want more than we can understand.

Naturally, we want everything to be exact, obvious, and immediate for our own survival, but our Savior has more than just our survival in mind as He leads us along unknown paths to higher ground. We may not be going where we have planned, but His plan will be more than anything we thought we wanted—or anything we thought we could control.

Waiting for something at the end of our rope, we often wail, "Please, just show me what to do, and I'll do it!" The Lord may answer with something like, "Hang on and let Me do it and hold you. Let Me take you past the top of the rope, to the top of the mountain, and beyond. Take hold of Me, and the answer will come. I'm here with you now. Let Me lift you up into more than you can see." Even through the valley of the shadow of death, He will walk with us and carry us to a divine feast.

When the Shepherd goes out to find a lost sheep, He doesn't go just to wait there beside the sheep, offering encouragement while the poor sheep clings to the side of the cliff. The good Shepherd goes to pick up the sheep and bring him home. That is why Jesus gave His life instead of some good advice on how to save ourselves. Only His blood can bring us home. Are you waiting around, hanging on until you figure it out or something comes along to help you solve it all? It won't be enough if it's anything less than a full relationship with the Son of God and complete surrender to Him. Ask Him to help you receive more than everything.

Father, I've been asking for a human answer, but now I say, "Have Your way." I want You more than my answer. Do what only You can do in Your love and power in Jesus Christ. Change me to accept more than I can understand in Him. In Jesus' name, amen.

Luke 15:1-7   Matt. 19:26   Eph. 3:14-21

May 12

~~~~~~

NOTHING TO SAY

Father, I come to You now with nothing to say. I want to be with You and rest in Your love, quietly loving You in return. I look for You. I wait for You, looking not for what is within me, but for the new life in Your Son, the Living Word, that comes from You by the Holy Spirit into me and beyond me. This waiting for Your presence brings hope, joy, and praise beyond words—even this waiting is beautiful! Prepare me to live as well as to read Your Word. In the time I would have spent talking, I simply come now and listen. I watch, knowing that more will be produced in loving and listening to Your Holy Spirit than in anything I could say or do on my own. Then in Your will, the right action will follow. Truly, You are my only source. Come, O Lord. There is room for You to dwell first in my heart. In Jesus' name, amen.

But seek first the kingdom of God and His righteousness, and all these things shall be added to you."

Matt. 6:33

Song of Sol. 6:3

~~~~~~

ONE CHOICE   May 13

So when the woman saw that the tree was good for food, that it was pleasant to the eyes, and a tree desirable to make one wise, she took of its fruit and ate. She also gave to her husband with her, and he ate.

Gen. 3:6

In a nutshell, Eve's mistake was to choose something other than a relationship with God, something instead of a full commitment to Him with life-giving intimacy and security. And we can't blame her, because it is often our mistake too. Just as Eve, we think we will benefit from knowledge gained or additional activity, when we would benefit more from quietly knowing God in person and spending time with Him. We never hear of anything Adam and Eve gained from their newly digested knowledge, but we do understand what was lost—their lives in Paradise came to an end, and their, and our, separation from God began. In our world today, what have we really chosen?

Eve's mistake was to choose knowledge over a close relationship with God. Adam's mistake was the same but also included wanting to please a human companion more than his Creator.

Judas chose to get immediate results for the changes he wanted, instead of waiting to know Christ and the changes He wanted in His time.

Peter chose the safety of a warm fire and useful lies.

Pilate and Herod chose power and successful careers.

The rich young ruler chose what he could see and touch instead of eternal wealth.

The Pharisees and leaders chose religious ritual and secure social position.

Martha chose service because her need for approval from Christ and others seemed greater than her need to simply listen and enjoy His presence.

Mary chose the best part, which the rest of us often cast aside: She took time to focus on God more than her work, time for a treasure of love in her Savior.

Father, help me to know You in Jesus Christ and to feed on Him alone. In Jesus' name, amen.

John 6:35-38   Rev. 3:20   John 14:19-24

May 14

~~~~~~

MY DELIGHT

O Lord God, You are my delight in the pure power of Your presence, in the hope of Your Word and in Your shining truth that makes a way where there is no way. You are my joy when the way is dark and the future is dim, as Your pure fire burns clear through from beginning to end. Alpha and Omega, You are my delight because You are more than enough. In Your presence there is fullness of joy. In Your Word, there is a living way in Christ, who fulfills the law and saves my soul. For the joy set before Him, He went to the cross, and I delight to follow Him, not because the way is easy, but because Your light has overcome all darkness through His cross and resurrection. My delight is to live in the light of Your countenance as You see Your people made new in Him. You delight most of all in Him, and that is why I want to see Jesus, the One in whom You delight, and be found in Him, not having my own righteousness but the righteousness that is from You without end. O Shepherd of my soul, You became like us that we might become like You, being partakers of the divine nature and entering a delight that only heaven knows. My delight is in You, even while I am still here below, in this heavy clay that is transformable into the light image of Your perfect joy. I see Your delight in me as a child living free, adopted by the gift of Your joy, Your Son, hanging nailed to a tree and then risen forever. I delight in Your terrible simplicity, Your awesome purity, and Your unspoken majesty. Any other delight is partial. You, O Lord, are all in all, my whole delight. In Jesus' name, amen.

Delight yourself also in the Lord, and He shall give you the desires of your heart. Commit your way to the Lord, trust also in Him, and He shall bring it to pass.

Ps. 37:4-5

Ps. 103

~~~~~~

REACH HERE

May 15

Then He said to Thomas, "Reach your finger here, and look at My hands; and reach your hand here, and put it into My side. Do not be unbelieving, but believing."

John 20:27

It is one thing to study Jesus and another to touch His wounds. Thomas was struggling with a question, and he was given a sure answer from others. Yet he still had to respond to the invitation to reach out his finger and touch his Lord's wounds to recognize Him. By faith, Thomas had to place his hand directly into the side of His Savior, where blood and water had poured out for him on the cross before he could reach the eternal hope that blood had purchased.

When we struggle with a decision or a problem, even at the root of our faith, we must do more than listen to the observations of others or study about Jesus from a distance. By faith, we must reach out for ourselves to touch the Savior who was pierced for us. In His wounds, we are made whole, and everything around us suddenly becomes eternally clear in His living presence. Reach out in prayer. Ask, seek, and knock. Through the Holy Spirit, He comes to us now. Just as then, no wall can stop Him.

In honest prayer, submit whatever trouble or question you have to this test: Place your heart at Jesus' feet and your problems on Jesus' wounds. Reach into His side. Let your troubles be completely immersed in His love and mercy. Explore the edges of those wounds and their depth. Whatever you do in the future must be compatible with that touch and the depth of those wounds. The power of His living sacrifice will wash your heart and turn your mind around to match the purity of His power. His presence can unlock the most stubborn heart. Then we can cry out, "My Lord and my God!" wherever we are right now. Our recognition brings a promised blessing, and He wants to hear us say it in action as well as in words. He wants to feel your touch of faith on His wounds today so you will know who He is forever.

Father, let me see Your Son's wounds and touch them through the Holy Spirit. Wash me and cleanse me in the depth of Your mercy. In prayer, I reach out to touch His open hand and let You draw my heart completely inside Your love. My Lord and my God, I believe; please help my unbelief. Increase my faith to receive Your new life. In Jesus' name, amen.

John 20:24-31   John 14:21   Rom. 6:4-14

PRESSED DOWN, SHAKEN TOGETHER   May 16

"Give, and it will be given to you: good measure, pressed down, shaken together, and running over will be put into your bosom. For with the same measure that you use, it will be measured back to you."

Luke 6:38

The measure you give will be the measure you get. That seems simple enough, but there is something more in this process of giving and receiving. The measure we receive is "pressed down, shaken together, and running over," in other words, a good measure stacked in and running over what is expected at the level we would give. In our Father's hands, He presses down and packs more into the same measure. He shakes it up and presses down again to be sure it will hold the most. Then He fills it up past the rim, until it runs over, which we humanly could not do in handing out our measure to others.

Wouldn't that be a little messy, all that packing and shaking and then letting it spill over? Yes, but it produces more than we had to start with because He gives us life abundantly in the process, more than we expect, more than we can give. We will never be able to contain the width and length and depth and height of that love of Christ that passes knowledge as He fills us with all the fullness of God (Eph. 3:17-19).

Notice how He does it. The good measure is pressed down. This is not comfortable. There is not a lot of fluff and room to delay or stray around in this container. It is pressed down, meaning under God's touch we are humbled, perhaps broken to make room for more, for a greater love than we had before. We are disciplined and precisely shaped so no corner is left untouched. We are also shaken. Every particle in our lives may seem stirred and changed, but when the situation settles down, when He presses us into the image of His Son, we can hold more than before. We contain more of His love and power in our lives when pressed and shaken to align perfectly with the cup He has chosen, the measure of grace that Christ purchased for us.

Everyone's container is slightly different, but God knows how to measure and shake, pressing into every angle until the contents exactly conform to the shape of His design. As He fills us, we will hold more than if we tried to pour it in ourselves and fill up our own measure with human effort. If we are too full of ourselves or our own agenda, He cannot fill us—until we are empty, clean, and ready to allow what He pours in to be pressed down, shaken together, and overflowing for His glory. This is the measure that never runs dry and never fails to satisfy.

Father, fill me as You will, not as I will. Conform me to the image of Your Son, Jesus Christ, and overflow me with Your grace. In Jesus' name, amen.

John 4:7-14   Mark 10:17-31   Matt. 10:8

May 17

~~~~~~

LISTEN IN LOVE

Father, teach me to listen in love. Make my prayers less of me and more of You. I've been doing a lot of talking here, trying to help myself and to reach others. First, make me able to hear Your voice clearly and the voices of those around me in Your wisdom and will. Then, later I will be able to speak the truth in love as I hear from You. To set the captives free, only Your love, justice, truth, and mercy completely meet the needs of all from now into eternity. In what I hear deeply from You, I will follow Your Son, as You make the answers to prayer come alive. In Jesus' name, amen.

"He must increase, but I must decrease."

John 3:30

Matt. 11:2-6, 15-30

~~~~~~

PRAISE FIRST

May 18

"Whoever offers praise glorifies Me."

Ps. 50:23

Praise born of love is the very first thing we can and should do. None of our works or words compare to His. None of our sacrifices compare to His. In Hebrews 13:15, our sacrifice of praise is to be offered to God through Christ, by Him. In the cross, Christ purchases us as God's children and in resurrection power enables us to live to the praise of God's glory now, wherever we are, even if still babes in the faith.

"Out of the mouth of babes and nursing infants You have perfected praise," was Jesus' answer to the Pharisees' complaint about the children praising His entrance into Jerusalem (Matt. 21:15-16). When the King comes into our lives, we may think we must do something complicated to please Him. Coming to where we are, He would simply like to hear our praise from sincere hearts, as children with hands raised to honor Him while we place our hearts and actions at His feet each day, like garments and palm branches. Praise gives His love an opening in us to truly welcome Him in trust and obedience.

In Christ, the purpose of our lives is not just to go somewhere or to finish some great work, but simply to "be to the praise of His glory" (Eph. 1:12). Then He can give us more to do that will be fruitful. To those wanting to accomplish something first, time to praise God may seem like a waste, but in praise we actually move forward in faith to focus on what He can do.

Praise gives glory to God and confirms our healing (Luke 17:11-19).

The desire to praise opens our eyes to see the King (John 9:11, 35-39; Ps. 22:2-4).

Praise opens us to God's power to win the battle (2 Chron. 20:15-22).

Praise gives us entrance to the presence of God (Ps. 100:4).

Praise gives God entrance to our lives (Ps. 24:7; Matt. 21:6-11).

Praise is something we do in this world that lasts forever (Ps. 111:10).

Praise is something we can pass on to our children that lasts forever (Ps. 145:1-4).

Praise edifies and builds up God's people (Ps. 89:15-18).

Praise is the purpose of spiritual fruit (Phil. 1:9-11).

Father, fill me with Your praise so my life is all to Your glory. In Jesus' name, amen.

PEACE NOW

May 19

"Peace I leave with you, My peace I give to you; not as the world gives do I give to you. Let not your heart be troubled, neither let it be afraid."

John 14:27

The peace of Christ is for us now. His peace comes after our minds release everything to the Creator to do as He pleases. Where the King reigns, there is peace. Where there is rebellion, there is daily war within us and in the world around us. This peace comes in with a whispered plea, not an order. Peace may pray for an enemy or appear to let him win a skirmish on the outskirts, and so by the humility of Christ win the greater war within that captures our souls.

To experience the King's peace is to lay down our human weapons and to let Him overcome not only the enemy, but us as well. His spiritual weapons work not only on the world and everyone else, but also on us. The victory, the final peace agreement that solves all our problems here, will require our total surrender here to Him. Only then can we pick up all the weapons God has chosen and fight to win. Sometimes the victory is unseen to us but is seen only by God while we look to Him by faith; so even when we can't yet see the victory complete, we can see Him in Christ fighting for us now.

When we give way to the Victor, Jesus Christ wins and works through the battles one at a time, even the battles within us. To share in His victory, we must surrender our wills to the One who gave up His will for us. Then, we will live and move and have our being in the One who is peace. This is the joy that surpasses all the world has to give. His peace is a foretaste of heaven, even in the heat of battle. There is a leap of victory now even in the wounded who rise up freely in the Holy Spirit to proclaim through love in action, "Hallelujah, our Lord reigns!"

Father, I lay down my weapons at Your feet. You fight. I'll stand and praise You for the victory in Your Son that is coming in me and around me and belongs to You alone. Then the warfare is waged according to Your will. In Jesus' name, amen.

Isa. 9:6-7   John 18:37   Col. 3:12-17

May 20

~~~~~~

LORD OF ALL

Father, forgive me for making You Lord of a few things and Lord of other people's things but not Lord of all and Lord of my life, just as it is. Then I wonder where Your full power is in each situation. Change me and cleanse my heart. Come and reign! Take the key to my life, as a car that is now Yours, and drive wherever You will. I'll be the passenger and let You choose the way. Show me what You want me to see in Your power and vision through the life of Your Son. Instead of struggling to control the wheel, I'm going to enjoy the ride in Your grace. In Your mercy, with the world's radio finally turned off, I'll sing Your songs, hear Your Word, and do Your will. In Jesus' name, amen.

"But why do you call Me 'Lord, Lord,' and not do the things which I say?"

Luke 6:46

Acts 10:36-43

~~~~~~

GIVE TO THE LORD   May 21

Give unto the Lord, O you mighty ones, give unto the Lord glory and strength.

Ps. 29:1

Each day, we often think first of what the Lord can do for us. Is there anything we can do for Him? Jesus taught us to pray by beginning, "Our Father in heaven, hallowed be Your name. Your kingdom come. Your will be done on earth as it is in heaven" (Matt. 6:9-10). That's a fertile beginning, rooted in the reality of God's majesty, whether to start a routine morning or to solve an impossible problem. Why? Because even though we can't see it, our Creator's power and glory are the most important things happening here today. These are bigger than any problem and the only true solution. The same power that raised Christ from the dead He causes to work in us even now (Rom. 8:5-11). Nothing we will do or suffer or need or wonder comes even close. Indeed, all of Psalm 29 reveals an earthshaking experience of the Lord's strength and creative power. Have you seen any of it around here?

We can realize that angels give God glory, but how could we weak people have anything with which to give Him strength or glory when we can hardly make it through the day? We have access to the strength and glory He has already given us through Christ, even though we may not acknowledge it. Many of us miss it, because we are searching for human glory and power. At some time, each of us tries to appear mighty in something, even if that human ability proves hollow. But God knows what He can place within us in Christ, and He calls it out of us in worship to return to Him so that the flow of spiritual power will continue from heaven to earth and back to heaven. True life grows only in that flow.

The more glory and strength we give to Him, the more open we are to receive according to His will. Whatever strength you have now, you are giving it to someone or to something—career, family, recreation, perhaps human-focused ministry. Whatever the delight of your heart is will receive your glory and strength for today. Only God can give you more than you will ever give Him. Check for a moment. Where is your greatest delight? Is it in the Creator or the created? The answer is either the root of your problem or the fruit of His grace.

Father, forgive me for looking for human glory and strength. Let Your power in Jesus Christ transform me and move me into the glory of Your life in Him. In Jesus' name, amen.

Eph. 2:1-10   Luke 12:8-15   Rom. 8:16-18, 26-30

BEAUTY OF HOLINESS   May 22

Give unto the Lord the glory due to His name; worship the Lord in the beauty of holiness.

Ps. 29:2

We give the Lord the glory due to His name only when we live each day in the holiness of His nature in Jesus Christ. The simple life of Jesus within us gives glory to the Father far surpassing any human accomplishment or elaborate prayer. If we present ourselves as a living sacrifice to God by denying our selfish desires, the glory is all His. This lines us up with the reality of our Creator. Worship is not an activity of human design, and our good intentions are not enough to take up a cross. Shouldering the weight of sacrifice is possible only when Jesus lifts it with us to bring us into His holiness. Then the sacrifice is a sweet-smelling aroma to God (Eph. 5:2), mingling with the glory He sent down to earth in our Immanuel and poured into us through the Holy Spirit. In Him, our entire lives become worship in the sacrifice of obedience.

If there's no holiness, or dedication to God alone, there is no lasting beauty and no true worship. Humanly, we can never reach that beauty of holiness, but if we ask God to change us, He can do the impossible. Our worship is a gift from God, passing through us and back to Him. When Jesus said the Father was seeking those who would worship Him in spirit and in truth, he pointed us to the entrance to new life in His power. He desires us to realize there is no beauty without His truth and no holiness without His Spirit. Human efforts at self-improvement are wasted, except to reveal their weakness.

Our most difficult problems could be solved today by simply giving glory to God in the middle of them and inviting His Spirit to change us. Since Jesus came to earth and walked among us, suffered with us, and rose again, our chaos is subject to transformation, our unholiness to holiness, our flesh to the Holy Spirit. We are designed for God to make us holy. When we allow the Holy Spirit to put our lives into gear and shift us out of self-focus into the full power of those two verbs, "*Give* unto the Lord . . . *worship* the Lord," then the beauty of His holiness carries us beyond human boundaries. He seeks living worship in the beauty of His holiness.

Father, I want to worship You with my whole heart. Empty me today of any false beauty, any secret sin, and fill me with the glory of Your Son, with His beauty and His holiness working in me. In His sacrifice and resurrection, change me to worship You alone. In Jesus' name, amen.

John 4:13-26   Rom. 11:33 — 12:2   Rom. 5:1-5, 20

OVER THE WATERS

May 23

The voice of the Lord is over the waters; the God of glory thunders; the Lord is over many waters.

Ps. 29:3

The voice of the Lord is not in the waters or of the waters, but over the waters. The King James Version says "upon" the waters, as when the Spirit of God hovered over the beginning of creation. Our Creator, then as now, comes over and above the raging seas of our world and creates new order, a new harmony of purpose, even over many waters. In His Son, He touches and saves us. Some of us have conflicting currents in our lives and many seas of troubles to deal with, but the Lord reigns over them all.

He comes not only over, but also upon them, touching us directly through the life of Christ to rule and help us through the Holy Spirit. God's creative Word brings life where there is no life now and hope where there is no hope visible. Upon the waters, out of nothing, His voice can create something we have never seen before. In every situation, He is not only with us and knows our sorrows as Jesus did, but He is above and beyond, full of supreme authority and creative power to change any situation.

God alone is the only One who can make something out of nothing, because He is uncreated and eternal. It is His very being that fills every void and forms the inner workings of our lives, whether we recognize Him or not. Even though many will not hear, still His voice speaks life today over the seas of our world. People struggle through the waters, both physical and spiritual, but He governs all, and only He can transform for eternity. Those who hear His voice will know which way to go and how to get there. Don't follow the noise of the waters, or the false gods who dwell only in the waters. Follow the Lord who is over many waters and rules them all.

When you go through whatever storm comes up, He will call you at some point to get out of your man-made boat to walk with Him upon the sea, which only He can rule. Keep your eyes on the One who is over and upon many waters. Come when He calls.

Father, bring me to You upon the waters. Even in stormy places, make me a new creation. Help me hear Your voice as Your power transforms me to come farther than I've ever walked before in Your Son. In Jesus' name, amen.

Gen. 1:1-3, 26-27   Matt. 14:22-33   2 Cor. 5:15-17

THE POWERFUL VOICE   May 24

The voice of the Lord is powerful; the voice of the Lord is full of majesty.

Ps. 29:4

The voice of the Lord is not just interesting or awesome; it is full of power. The same creative voice that spoke light and life to create the world can be heard in our hearts, moving us to new life. God doesn't speak to entertain us or to impress us, but to change us. He is still actively creating new life through His Son. How much power you hear is revealed by how much your life changes in response to the sound of His voice.

Those who have not changed have not heard enough to move them, because their hearts were hardened, or God's Word was scarce and muffled by man-made things, or because the first hint of His voice so frightened them that they ran away from its power and stayed in sin. Yet we will all hear God's voice in His Son at least one more time (John 5:28-29). When His Son, who came first as a suffering servant, comes again in majesty, the earth will be shaken by the Living Word of the Lord. The mountains of our own understanding and accomplishment will melt like wax at the presence of the Lord (Ps. 97:5).

When we stand before Him, what will we hear? It is better to seek Him now and listen to the Living Word already implanted in our lives, letting its power transform us into what is in line with His majesty. In our hearts, He can still speak power to heal and forgive through the sovereignty of eternal love in the Lamb's blood. His Word produces fruit that lasts. To hear that voice, our wills must be weak enough to welcome His power and meek enough to recognize His majesty. Listen to the Lamb, the Living Word, the Lion of Judah, the Bright and Morning Star, the Wonderful Counselor, the Mighty God, the Prince of Peace. Open your heart to hear, for He is near, and His voice is powerful.

O King, speak Your true life in me so that I can receive what grows into eternity. Forgive me for listening to the voices of the world that weaken my spirit and leave me lifeless. Work in me now to produce new life in Your power. In Jesus' name, amen.

Matt. 13:16-23   John 6:63   Rom. 10:8-17

BREAKING THE CEDARS   May 25

The voice of the Lord breaks the cedars, yes, the Lord splinters the cedars of Lebanon.

Ps. 29:5

Whatever is strong and beautiful in this world, the Lord can break with His Word, according to His purpose. Notice that the strongest tree that grows out of the earth is not broken by a human tool or weapon but by the voice of the Lord who created it, giving form and life to His will. God's Word, which created all things, can also destroy anything that stands against Him. God's creative power includes destruction of evil and any high thing that exalts itself against His truth. Yes, the Lord not only breaks these strong, beautiful, fragrant cedars, but also splinters them, utterly taking away their ability to be productive. No one can build with these trees.

In our lives, there are cedars already growing. Some are beautiful, planted in the Lord's will to grow even taller. Others are beautiful but not in His will, and they must go. Will we let the Word of His truth break them, even splinter them so that they are no good for any human use? Even the good things growing up in us in His will, when they finally reach full height and stretch out their branches, will we still give Him full control or name them after ourselves? In Psalm 29, the trees that His voice breaks carry the name of the earthly place where they grow. Even though the cedars of Lebanon have good durability and aroma and appear evergreen, as a Christian should, they are not immune to God's judgment, for they are named after their own country. Eventually, God will break what is not in His name, under divine ownership.

If something is not in God's will, His truth will separate it. Many of us want to follow the Lord but still stay in the shade of worldly things that carry our name, the things that make us feel good, give an aroma of success, and produce something to build with for the admiration of others. Listen to the Lord's voice. His Word may break some of our strength, even splinter it, so that nothing will stand against what He plans to do in us, carrying only the aroma of the sacrifice of His Son.

Lord, the One who breaks the cedars, I come humbly and ask You to break anything in my life that stands against You. Free me to do Your will and to grow in Your Spirit. In Jesus' name, amen.

Ps. 51:15-17   Matt. 15:7-14   Ps. 127:1-2

SKIP LIKE A CALF   May 26

He makes them also skip like a calf, Lebanon and Sirion like a young wild ox.

Ps. 29:6

Even the cedars of Lebanon and the mountain of Sirion skip like a calf at the voice of the Lord. Whatever is rooted solidly in this world, seemingly unmovable, can be moved by our Creator, who makes all things new. If we have problems bigger than a mountain or more firmly rooted in our clay than a huge cedar, He can pull them up, break them into a new arrangement, and turn them around.

We've seen young calves skipping in the springtime with the energy and pure joy of new life. In our spirits, though broken, the new life of Christ can lift us out of the past and turn us around to move freely. Even more vigorous, the skipping of a young, wild ox never tamed by people makes our hearts leap for joy, knowing that God reigns even in the wilderness. Whether we're safe with the herd or alone on the mountain, truth will find us in the sound of His voice and fill us with joy, even in testing.

In the previous verse, the Lord's voice broke the cedars that He now makes to skip with new life. Until they were broken, they could not skip. In fact, they had to be transformed into a new kind of life that has legs to skip and can move freely. In our lives, what seemed strong but had to be broken will be transformed in His mercy to move forward with divine energy in the next season. Helpless at first, new birth will begin to skip sometime after the umbilical cord is cut. Old cows and oxen don't skip. Calves still attached to the old version don't skip. Only what's new and ready in God's timing, even emerging out of what was fallen, will move to the sound of His creative voice. If you won't skip, especially after being broken, don't expect to grow. Let the deep promises and fresh truths of His voice carry you where you have never been before. Free in Him, you can skip.

Father, thank You for breaking what held me back and for bringing me forward, lifting me in the new life of Your Son. In Jesus' name, amen.

John 5:5-9   Ps. 126   Phil. 2:8-14

FLAMES OF FIRE
May 27

The voice of the Lord divides the flames of fire.

Ps. 29:7

In the sound of His will through the purity of His being, the voice of the Lord divides the flames of spiritual fire that transform everything. Since this psalm was traditionally read in the synagogues at Pentecost, its reference to flames of fire matches the experience of the apostles in the upper room, when divided tongues as of fire rested upon them, giving the promise of the Father for power to witness (Acts 2:1-4). Holy fire revealed God's presence in the burning bush, in the consuming of sacrifices, and in the golden candlestick in the tabernacle. John the Baptist described Jesus as the One who would baptize His followers with the Holy Spirit and fire (Matt. 3:11).

This spiritual fire includes the flame of His eternal love and the consuming reality of His purity. There is nothing you or I can say that will affect the fire of holiness, but God's voice divides the flames of spiritual fire, shapes them to His will and sends them where He directs. The word translated "divides" literally means to hew out, to separate and form for a purpose. Even spiritual fire is shaped and ordered by God to confirm His covenant.

In the sound of His Word, His power alone, the Lord hews out flames of fire so that their presence becomes manifest in our lives. Just as the pillar of fire and the cloud of His presence led the Israelites, protecting them and making a way where there was no way, even today God's voice divides spiritual flames of fire, seen and unseen, to shape our path forward into His true life.

Lighting the way, these flames also burn in the hearts of those open to the Holy Spirit of truth, who separates light from darkness and discerns the thoughts and intents of hearts by the Living Word, bringing repentance (Heb. 4:12). May our hearts burn in us as the Lord speaks life beyond this life and truth beyond knowledge. In times of trouble, hear Him divide the flames of fire and shape the path of your life, moving you forward in faith to do His will.

Father, let Your Holy Spirit pierce me with the fiery truth of Your creative Word, separating light from darkness in my life. Fill me with the flame of Your love in the sacrifice and resurrection of Jesus Christ. In Jesus' name, amen.

Gen. 15:5-10, 17-18   John 16:7-15   Luke 24:28-32

HE SHAKES THE WILDERNESS   May 28

The voice of the Lord shakes the wilderness; the Lord shakes the Wilderness of Kadesh.

Ps. 29:8

In our time of testing in the wilderness, the voice of the Lord not only speaks but also shakes everything around us. His power removes the things that can be shaken to establish what cannot be shaken. Since Israel doubted, those who carried that doubt were shaken off until only a new generation remained to enter the Promised Land. When he struck the rock instead of speaking to it, Moses also fell short of what God directed, so even this great leader was shaken in the wilderness and never entered the fruitful land.

Kadesh, meaning holy, signifies a place in Barnea, the desert of wandering. At some point, each of us reaches such a holy place. On the way, we may fall short, we may grumble, we may fail to follow directions and consider going back, but the waters of God's mercy still spring out from the place where we meet the Rock of our salvation, which cannot be shaken. Without that Rock and its precious water, we will die.

The place of that Rock is also called the fountain of judgment, because of the sin of the people and God's provision for life. Here the people also received the report of those who spied out the Promised Land and brought fruit and warned of giants, thus forcing a decision. Here, they hesitated. They could either believe the report of the promised fruit and go forward or wander for another generation. Today, we can also see miracles and experience deliverance, but sooner or later there comes a point of shaking, judgment, and decision in the middle of a desert.

Even today, He shakes our wilderness with His judgment, He shakes it with His mercy, He shakes it with His power, He shakes it with His promise, and He shakes it with His presence and His Word. Do you believe God's promise for today? Are you following His direction? Samples of the fruit that is ahead are available to taste. There are also hints of battles coming. Will you follow Him even when those around you are doubting and delaying? When the voice of the Lord shakes the wilderness, take hold of His Word, drink living water from the Rock, and move forward in God's power. You are receiving a kingdom that cannot be shaken.

Father, thank You for shaking my wilderness so I can know what will fall and what will stand. Help me to hear Your voice. Move me forward in Your promises and the strength of Your Son. In Jesus' name, amen.

Heb. 12:7-15, 25-29   Num. 13:26—14:11   Acts 4:29-32

GLORY IN HIS TEMPLE   May 29

The voice of the Lord makes the deer give birth, and strips the forests bare; and in His temple everyone says, "Glory!"

Ps. 29:9

The voice of the Lord brings new life when He speaks to His creation, all of which is groaning and waiting with expectation for the revelation of the sons of God, the children of His promise (Rom. 8:19). As with birth pangs, we are coming today to that new life He has planned from before the foundation of the world. In the new birth, everything that was our old security is stripped bare and bows before the Lord of all. And when finally we come into that temple the Lord has created to fulfill His promises and His desire to live with us, we will say, "Glory!" for its beauty transcends anything of human design. No debates, no delays, no doubts, just "Glory!" all around. Then our speech will reflect what our Creator has spoken.

The voice of the Lord exposes His master plan, both for His children who receive Christ (John 1:12-13) and for all of His creation, which will be delivered from corruption (Rom. 8:18-25). From our Creator, nothing is now hidden that shall not be revealed. Even the forests, our secret places, are stripped bare, as our souls are open before Him in the light of His glory. To truly come into His temple, we must be born again so that our hearts become His dwelling place. We must come out of the forests of this world. Our earthly places and protection, whatever kept our sins hidden, even the place of new birth, must be stripped bare and opened to the presence of the Lord.

When we come out of that forest, we'll be transformed by the light of Christ and give God all the glory. If we're not willing to do that now in this world—to go through the birth process, to see our forests stripped bare, and to be transformed into a new creation as children who glorify God—why would He think we will want to dwell with Him in the age to come? With unveiled hearts, we can give God glory now. Only new life says, "Glory!" without looking back. Through the Holy Spirit, the Creator's temple in us will be filled with glory as everything hidden is revealed.

Father, forgive me for forgetting to worship You now in this world. Open my heart completely to Your power, and make me a new creation in Your Son for Your glory alone. In Jesus' name, amen.

Col. 1:13-20   John 2:18—3:6   2 Cor. 3:18

SITTING UPON THE FLOOD   May 30

The Lord sat enthroned at the Flood, and the Lord sits as King forever.

Ps. 29:10

The Lord sat in victory over His enemies as the flood washed them away and carried Noah to a new place. In the ark, those who obeyed God were safe. They were lifted upon and above the flood. In the King James Version, this verse says, "The Lord sitteth upon the flood; yea, the Lord sitteth King for ever." When we pray, we must pray to the One who sits upon the flood, not in the flood or under the flood. He is not surprised by any wave that slaps this world or pulls at our lives. No matter what seems to overwhelm us, it is already under His feet, and as we stand in faith in Him, we will rise through obedience to that higher position our faith can see.

Don't look for Him in the flood or see yourself under the mess. See Him where He really is—upon the flood—and yourself safe with Him. The Lord reigns over all circumstances and works creatively from the top down, filling us with supernatural strength. The flood also can represent the tossing and turning of this world with its people caught in the churning struggle of self-centered existence. The Lord is not rising and falling with every wave that comes by and will not leave us there either, because His Son went to the cross and rose again to conquer sin and to bring us up out of the flood. He works from the top down to rescue us. As we cry out, He lifts us up with Him.

In the same way, God created the world by the Word of His mouth, cleansing and infusing the world with the unique energy of His power (Gen. 1:1-3). New life appeared in what was once a chaotic flood void of life and light. When He rescues us, we are not the same; He lifts us to a new place in His kingdom. So today, as we pray to the Lord who sits upon the flood, He can infuse our situation with His pure life, taking us far beyond any human solution or ability. By faith, we who are drowning can take hold of the Master's hand and be transformed to walk with Him upon the sea. One day, we will walk with Him in a new creation upon a sea like glass, like gold refined by His very being to reflect the beauty of His glory. Until then, the One who sits upon the flood still shines upon the waters of this world to create new life and bring us to Him. When you call, He will lift you up to where He stays enthroned upon the flood.

Father, rescue me and transform me through the cross of Jesus Christ. In Him, lift me above the flood, cleanse me, and bring me to You forever. In Jesus' name, amen.

Heb. 6:11-15, 19-20   Gen. 7:1-5, 15-24   Ps. 30:1-3

STRENGTH AND PEACE   May 31

The Lord will give strength to His people; the Lord will bless His people with peace.

Ps. 29:11

We can give to God only the strength and peace He first has given us to worship (Ps. 29:1). I used to wonder how weak people could give strength or glory to God, or even be able to see the beauty of His majesty. The opening of this psalm commands, "Give unto the Lord, O you mighty ones, give unto the Lord glory and strength." Who are these mighty ones? Angels? Even they are created beings who return to God only what He has given them. In this verse, we see how this is possible for us. When strength comes from the Lord, it can be returned to Him; then more will come, and as it is returned in worship, the cycle continues. More will come than what we can return. We're created to live in daily communication with heaven, growing in grace, even as we walk imperfectly here.

A higher destination of glory and strength, a beauty of holiness beyond anything we can see here, is what we begin to taste now through the peace of the cross of Jesus Christ and the power of His resurrection. The whole peace that He gives, a multidimensional shalom, brings us a step closer each day and enables us to digest some of the divine beauty that is coming. Even on earth, we can touch the fringe of our Redeemer's garment, which one day will enfold us. In this process, we are transformed into the likeness of the Son of God, who came from heaven to earth, returned there, and will come again for us (Rom. 8:16-17, 28-34). In His peace, there is an exchange going on, a huge eternal exchange that already begins to transform us, as we worship God while in this world, not worshiping this world instead.

What if we do not feel strong or holy or able to render to God any of the glory He is refining in us? We are to worship anyway. It's the Lord's joy that is our strength in Him. His strength enables the weak ones to become mighty in worship, flowing into the beauty of His new creation. Lift up your problems, your hands, your head and will, and the gates of your life to Him, and let them be changed in the joy of the cross. If you don't lift them up, you'll have to carry them alone. In worship, He will carry them, giving you peace to unlock the full strength of His joy.

O King, help me to receive the strength and peace only You can give. Then I will return them to You in worship, in the beauty of Your holiness. In Jesus' name, amen.

Ps. 24   John 6:33-38   2 Cor. 4:16-18

PENTECOST — POWER AND PURITY TO WITNESS

Walk in the Holy Spirit in the narrow path that leads to life beyond this life, power beyond the present world, and purity to present yourself a living sacrifice to God even now, pleasing in His eyes, just as His Son, the Lamb of God, offered Himself once for us, an offering to God and a sacrifice for a sweet-smelling aroma*.

Gen. 2:7-9; 3:1-24

John 3:13-21

John 14:6-27; 20:21-22

Acts 1:1-8; 2:1-24, 36-39

Rom. 12:1-2

Eph. 1:10—2:10; 5:1-2*

FAITH THAT ENTERS THE DOOR   June 1

For we walk by faith, not by sight.

2 Cor. 5:7

To walk in the power of God is to walk in His sight, illuminating us with the light of Jesus Christ through faith. As we sense, but rarely acknowledge, there are two realities: physical and spiritual. God sees both together since He has created both for His glory. We tend to separate them and to focus only on the physical. Our human lives dwell in the physical so much that the two dimensions have become compartmentalized. In the Garden of Eden, Adam's race chose disobedience, which separated the two realities, and so we became subject to blindness and death.

In Christ, our faith brings the physical and spiritual together so that we can see both realities in the unity of God's transforming power. That is why Jesus sometimes said: "Your faith has made you whole" (Luke 17:19 KJV). Faith enters the door between the physical and the spiritual so that Christ's life can redeem and change us. When you pray, is the door open? Is the focus on both the physical and spiritual together?

The same mystery applies to the Lord's Table. When we receive Holy Communion, by faith through the Holy Spirit the bread and wine become one with the unseen body and blood of Christ, as His life comes into our lives both physically and spiritually for action and obedience now, as well as for abstract spiritual remembrance. Some may drink only physical food or only spiritual food, not realizing the fullness of both dimensions in Christ. Just as it was impossible to separate the two natures in Christ in the incarnation, it is impossible to separate the two natures today in His church. We are called to do more than remember Christ only in the past, but also to receive the present reality of His sacrifice and resurrection. Through the Holy Spirit, His life calls us forward in His kingdom in the physical and spiritual together. By faith, we receive the transformed substance of His resurrection life now in His church (Heb. 11:1; John 6:54).

We are eating and drinking through the wine and bread, taking in the actual presence of the living Christ, forever new by the Holy Spirit! He asked us to do this. In communion with our Savior, we receive both the physical and spiritual realities of His life, just as the disciples ate in His presence. Can you receive both realities in faith? His answers to prayer come in both physical and spiritual dimensions. Will you pray in faith that focuses both dimensions together in the unity of Christ? To do so is to walk through the living door of His new covenant, which is active in every area of your life. That is why Christ came as both the Son of God and the Son of Man, totally one for you.

Father, increase my faith so that I can walk as Jesus walked and see what You see. Help me to receive Your Son in the way You gave Him for us. In His name, amen.

John 6:51-67   Matt. 26:26-29   Gal. 2:20

June 2

~~~~~~

LOOKING FOR YOU, LORD

I'm looking for You, Lord. Let the door of freedom swing open as You lead me in Your Son, who is the way, the truth, and the life. Today, I'm searching for You with all my heart, as You have searched for me. Just as You called me to come to You through the wood of the cross, now I ask, seek, knock, and press toward Your calling for my life wherever You lead. Humbly, I'm leaning on Your truth, knocking at the door of the cross, and longing to hear Your voice. Bring me through, new in You today. In Jesus' name, amen.

And you will seek Me and find Me, when you search for Me with all your heart.

Jer. 29:13

John 10:1-4, 11-30

~~~~~~

ONE THING   June 3

One thing I have desired of the Lord, that will I seek: that I may dwell in the house of the Lord all the days of my life, to behold the beauty of the Lord, and to inquire in His temple.

Ps. 27:4

Are you having a day where there just isn't enough time to do it all? We know we should trust God, the Creator who made time, to make everything happen on time, but we wonder, "How will we get it done? There isn't time for everything!" Perhaps He doesn't want us to do everything we have in mind or that others have thrust upon us to meet their expectations. What about God's expectations for this day? As our Creator, it's all His.

There is not time for everything. But there is time for one thing. If we do that one thing, it will cause other things to happen on time and results to multiply. Jesus took a few loaves and fishes, looked to heaven, and blessed them. Then there was enough for a multitude. When that one thing, loving God, is firmly fixed, then our work is truly productive as other projects find their place. Some may drop off the screen entirely and never be done. Suddenly, new assignments may appear. However, if we are primarily occupied with letting God occupy our lives, an amazing calendar will develop, including results we never dreamed would happen.

Who better than our Creator to match the time with the job or the person with the task? Some of the things I worry about doing are supposed to be done by someone else. Some of the problems I have ignored should be faced and handled by me without delay in God's strength. This will change my schedule and my heart.

The simple truth is that in loving God, every part of each day is melted by His presence until our time allotments begin to change shape under His gaze. In the end, He is the only One who really produces anything lasting. If we spend time in prayer and worship, our day will be fruitful on many levels. Even the worst day is not wasted if it is given to God. Will you let His love bend your schedule to produce His fruit?

In the surface rush of daily work, He provides direct answers and energy. In the interior life of our souls, He washes us in grace by the Holy Spirit and refreshes weary hearts with new possibilities. On the eternal scale, even simple tasks have long-term results in God's plan. How is your schedule today? Are you trying to do everything or just the one thing that generates all the others?

Father, come in Your Holy Spirit to work in every part of my life. Make me whole in Your purpose to produce fruit in Your kingdom right where I am. In Jesus' name, amen.

Matt. 6:19-21, 31-33   John 15:4-8   Isa. 26:12

June 4

~~~~~~

REST A WHILE

Father, draw me to come to You and rest a while today. Even if I am working or my mind is clamoring, help me to lay down my concerns at the place of Your peace in Your authority and love, the only place of power. As Jesus called the disciples to separate themselves for time to focus on You, so let me put aside the expectations of the world and be separated to the path that leads to the center of Your will. Forgive me for worrying and straying along the margins when there is rest in the depth of Your presence. Bring me to You, where there is fullness of joy and the light of life. No matter how many worldly candles I try to light, none compares to the shining reality of Your love and the light of the peace of Your countenance. Just gazing into Your holiness brings me closer to holiness. To depend completely on Your peace wins my battle. To turn from the world's goods to Your storehouse makes me rich. To lift before You a little song of joy in the midst of trouble raises me up from the death grip of self-concern. Your power multiplies what little I have and produces more than enough to give to others. I love You, Father, whose Spirit whispers in me the longing of Your heart. Humbly, I come and cast all my cares upon You, the One who cares for me forever. In the quietness of that surrender, Your truth will make me free. Carry me to finish the race in Your power alone. In Jesus' name, amen.

And He said to them, "Come aside by yourselves to a deserted place and rest a while."

Mark 6:31

Pss. 62—63

~~~~~~

PRAISE TO PRAISE

June 5

"He who believes in Me, as the Scripture has said, out of his heart will flow rivers of living water."

John 7:38

Would you be eager to give to someone who asks often but never bothers to thank you? To receive answers to prayer, we must begin in praise and end in praise, which flows into another beginning. So the cycle continues: praise offered to God, our requests made known, our hearts open to receive, and praise back to God for the answer, whether yes or no. A river of living water runs from His throne through Christ into our lives and back again to God by the Holy Spirit. In order to receive from God, the flow must run unbroken in the river of God's life, which never ends. From Him, we receive the ongoing praise and joy that we return to Him (John 4:7-14). As we come to Jesus Christ and drink, we will praise the Lord forever, which is the real answer to every prayer. Those things we think are the answers are only by-products of living to the praise of His glory (Eph. 1:11-13; Col. 3:17).

If we focus only on requests, forgetting to begin with praise and to end with thanks to God, there is no flow, and the stream of His power in our lives soon runs dry. The river goes from praise to praise, making us able to receive as much if not more than what we ask. We think that if we ask well, the answer will come. But do we spend as much time receiving well and praising God well? A thankful heart, even in the worst circumstances, is ready to receive. Open hands, not cluttered with worldly things, human bondage, or self-focus can receive what God gives.

Taking time to listen, obey, and wait will move us into the cycle of prayer that produces results. God can't put straight answers into a crooked life or open blessings into a closed heart. To be immersed in His river, we must step out in faith, get wet, and put the flesh under repentance and grace. Our wills must be wet enough to bend to His. Start with praise now, even in a desert, and you'll be surprised as rivers begin to appear in unlikely places.

Father, help me to praise You with my whole heart. I will drink deeply of Christ's love through the cross and return praise to You in His resurrection power even now. In Jesus' name, amen.

Ps. 86:6-17   John 11:40-44   John 6:10-11

June 6

REST AND REVELATION

Father, call me to rest so I can receive the revelation, the cool drink, the rich nourishment that comes to those who trust in You. Make me obedient simply and completely as a child takes the hand of the Father, the One who knows where we are going. Lead me in Your paths of righteousness. Forgive me for seeking knowledge and revelation without living in the trust and obedience that reveals truth and makes room for You to complete Your work in me. Every time I turn my own way, I close the door on what You want to show me. As my mind fills up with worry, my heart is shut off from the revelation of what You can do now, right here. When my eyes close to the needs of those around me, I miss seeing my Savior's face. Let me finally come to sit in Your lap and let You comfort me, strengthen me, and teach me true life, deep peace, the beautiful rest of the righteous who know Your power and listen to Your heart. This time, I will not run away and hide in other activities. I'm here to listen now, not just to what You will say but to who Your love says You are. Speak, Lord. I rest completely in You. In Jesus' name, amen.

My beloved spoke, and said to me: "Rise up, my love, my fair one, and come away. For lo, the winter is past, the rain is over and gone. The flowers appear on the earth; the time of singing has come, and the voice of the turtledove is heard in our land. The fig tree puts forth her green figs, and the vines with the tender grapes give a good smell. Rise up, my love, my fair one, and come away!"

Song of Sol. 2:10-13

Luke 10:40—11:13

LOOKING INTO JESUS June 7

But we all, with unveiled face, beholding as in a mirror the glory of the Lord, are being transformed into the same image from glory to glory, just as by the Spirit of the Lord.

2 Cor. 3:18

Are we looking at Jesus? Martha looked at Jesus. Mary looked into Jesus. From His words and His eyes, she received everything necessary to live out His teaching in the world. If we take time to gaze deeply into His nature through His Word and put that Word into action, the essence of divine love will transform us to serve Him better than anything we could do on our own for Him. That is why Mary chose the best part. By communing with Him, she was transformed and shared the thoughts of His heart. From this relationship, more fruit was produced for God's kingdom than from human effort.

No matter what good intentions we have, they are not as powerful as the intentions of God's own heart working in the world. Out of worship, the best work flows, even if time is limited. At some point, we must focus on the Source and trust Him to do the work through us. How does your schedule reflect that choice? Are you looking into Jesus or only at Him? When working for God according to what we see in the world, we produce only what our hearts and our vision can contain. When we work for God according to what He reveals to us, there will be abundant and lasting fruit.

Look into Jesus in your life now. There won't be a better time or a better place. Jesus Christ is the same yesterday, today, and forever. We know Him by watching in prayer and waiting to see how He would act in our situation. We watch to see where He is going today and follow Him into surprising places. Jesus is as active now as He was 2000 years ago, or 20 years ago, or will be 20 years in the future. Follow Him.

Look into Jesus through His Word. When we eat food, we do more than look at it, or we will die. We have to dig into it and get it into us. It is possible to study the Bible as an interesting document, but if we begin to gaze deeply into its teaching and take those teachings to heart by listening for how His love would act now, we will do more than study. We will live His Word daily as the Bread of Life energizes us for change.

Look into Jesus in His people. Jesus said, "Inasmuch as you did it to one of the least of these My brethren, you did it to Me" (Matt. 25:40). Go to those in need, and take the time to look into their eyes. Besides sending food or money, take time to look into the faces of those who need someone, and listen for the Master's heart. You will be surprised. Also let those in need look into you and see your need for Christ. He comes!

Father, open my eyes to look into Your Son now and live in His life. Change my heart to welcome His. In Jesus' name, amen.

Mic. 6:6-8 James 1:22-25 John 12:20-32

June 8

~~~~~~

RECREATE ME

Father, recreate me according to Your will by the Holy Spirit. Mold me and move me after Your heart. Bring me through the cross into the life of Christ. Earlier, I asked You to rearrange my priorities, revise my thoughts, and restore my strength, but now I know these must die, not just be rearranged. The old has to go for the new to come. No longer do I ask You to revise the old or to mask it. Now, I ask You to cover it completely in the blood of Jesus, take it away, and make me new, wholly Yours. Instead of rearranging the furniture of my old life, create a new house bought by Your Son, furnished for Your pleasure, owned by You, and always open to Your guests. Come and stay, not as a guest but as Head of the house. As You form Your nature in me through Christ, the old passes away, and all things become new. Recreate me after Your will. Bring me to the place You have designed, not made with human hands. Lord of Life, fill me and those around me with Your light until no darkness remains and the world sees only You. In Jesus' name, amen.

Jesus answered, "Most assuredly, I say to you, unless one is born of water and the Spirit, he cannot enter the kingdom of God. That which is born of the flesh is flesh, and that which is born of the Spirit is spirit. Do not marvel that I said to you, 'You must be born again.'"

John 3:5-7

Eph. 4:1-24

~~~~~~

REST OF OBEDIENCE

June 9

"Come to Me, all you who labor and are heavy laden, and I will give you rest."

Matt. 11:28

Through rest and obedience, the priorities of God enter our lives. Obedience is a form of rest, laying down our ways and surrendering to God's ways, to give Him room to work. If we don't obey, we will not be able to rest, and if we don't rest, we will not be able to obey. Both operate together in His will to bring us to refreshing life. Rest is a form of trust. In that trust, obedience tries to make a step, a start in His direction, even if only a small step, and then leaves it to Him to bring us all the way. We take that step of faith so His power can carry us, deliver us, adopt us, and renew us one day at a time. In faith, the momentum increases. Out of rest and obedience comes peace, real life-changing peace that trusts God alone, and this peace allows the burning of His holiness to bring us home. In His power, eternal life is activated in us now through the one complete peace offering, the sacrifice of Christ, the burnt offering for all time.

The light burning in the love of Christ's sacrifice is the living light of our destination in which we already walk while here in this world (1 John 1:7). It illumines the inside of hearts and melts the outer reaches of human will. Once we experience rest, obedience, and peace, then out of peace grows unity. Peace and unity work together. In His Son, we are melted together by God's pure fire (Col. 1:19-22; Matt. 3:11).

The fire of His holiness burns surrendered hearts into unity with Christ as our wills melt in His love. The fire of this holy love melts everything into unity with Christ's sacrifice, which still lives in the operation of the cross daily in our lives. True peace is accepting Christ's blood today, not only in theory but also in living reality, as we realize it's not our actions but the power of His sacrifice working through us that produces results. Unity is letting that blood and fire do its complete work of healing and forgiveness.

We are born to walk in the holy light of a new creation in Christ through rest, obedience, and unity in Him, all vibrating together in the harmony of His light, each part of the harmony needing the other—and the sound is joy. We must let Him tune us together to His pure music. Rest is laying down our own works and songs to join the one song of heaven and earth whose infinite harmony originates in God. Resting in Him, will you sing now in work as well as in words?

Father, I rest in Your love. Melt me into the obedience of the cross of Christ so my life will sing of Your love. In Jesus' name, amen.

Heb. 4:9-16   Matt. 26:27-30   Ps. 40:1-8

June 10

RUNNING ON EMPTY

Lord, I thought if I were empty of human strength, You would not receive me. I thought I had to be full of something good to come to You. But there was nothing good in me. When I tried to put something into my life to please You, it only ran out again. So I was running on empty, going faster, always trying harder, and hiding. Now, I'm no longer running. I'm turning, still empty, to You. Fill me with Your truth and holiness in Jesus Christ. Look on me in mercy and shine Your love through my heart completely, until I shine full face toward You in freedom. You are my Lord. I see now that I had to be empty in order to be filled at last with the joy that runs to You. Draw me and fill me with Your Son. In Your power, bring me to the place in Your kingdom where You plan for me to live daily, full of the life that never ends. In Jesus' name, amen.

Jesus answered and said to her, "Whoever drinks of this water will thirst again, but whoever drinks of the water that I shall give him will never thirst. But the water that I shall give him will become in him a fountain of water springing up into everlasting life."

John 4:13-14

Rom. 7:4-6

MULTIPLYING BREAD   June 11

And they said to Him, "We have here only five loaves and two fish." He said, "Bring them here to Me."

Matt. 14:17-18

If we try to keep Jesus for ourselves, He cannot multiply His bread through us. Sometimes, we want to be like the boy with the loaves and fishes, but we also may want Jesus to bless our lunch and let us keep it for ourselves, to distribute what's left after we're full. As our Bread of Life, Jesus asks us to give it all to Him, to let Him be broken for us and in us to feed many. While the disciples worried about logistics, Jesus was concerned mainly about the people. The disciples thought it would be more reasonable to send them away from Jesus to a human point of supply than to let the power of God feed them by blessing, breaking, and multiplying in divine power what little we humans could give Him (John 6:5-11).

Consider Peter after he had denied Christ. He was terribly hungry for that living bread, but he just wanted to go away, back to fishing in his old ways. Surely, there would be some food there that he could catch himself. At least, he understood what to do. But he and the others fished all night and caught nothing on their own. Then, by the shore, Jesus had bread and fish already cooking before they came with the catch He found for them (John 21:1-17). Multiplying what we cannot see is one way He feeds us even now.

After that breakfast and letting them eat their fill, did Jesus launch into a lengthy discourse on theology and criticize them for running away? No. He simply asked, "Do you love Me?" and He instructed Peter to feed His sheep. Notice He did not say they were Peter's sheep. Only the Shepherd can feed His flock. With that true Shepherd's love in him, Peter could be blessed, broken, and offered to the hungry by that living bread from above working in him. In that love is food for a multitude who see not only Peter but also their Shepherd broken for them and who see the same love with which He loved them working and multiplying in the church. How do we plan to feed the flock He has given us today? Will we send them away to a human source or some institution we control? Or will we surrender them and ourselves to Jesus?

The hungry are His sheep, not ours. The only One who satisfies is Jesus, who multiplies Himself now through the Holy Spirit as fresh bread for all who will come in obedience (Heb. 5:8-9).

Father, multiply the living bread of Christ in us in Your hands. In His name, amen.

John 6:33-35   1 Cor. 10:16-17   Heb. 13:20-21

June 12

SANDAL STRAP

O King who walks this dusty road, I am not worthy to unloose the strap of Your sandal. Yet I bow to do so. I touch the dust of my road that clings to Your steps. I feel the heat of the noonday sun still in the leather and the dried sweat of a long journey. I will never go as far as You did. I will never experience the humiliation of divinity tied down to earth with straps of skin. I will never know how it feels to go up that rocky road to the place where they drive spikes through these feet. How beautiful upon the mountains are the feet that bring good news to those who wait for You now! In welcome, I will go and get water to wash Your feet, knowing I am the one You will wash in each dusty trip through the world. Rather than water, better for me to do this with tears and love from one who has been forgiven much. First, I will let go of everything else I was carrying, even this towel, and lay it down. Now with hands free, still unworthy, I bow and loosen the strap of Your sandal. You are watching, leaning forward, ready to loose all in me that holds me back. I take off the strap and bow lower still to remove the sandals completely, beginning to pour out pure praise at Your feet, for You have released me, clean, into freedom and fullness of joy. All praise to the Father, whose love in the Son meets and conquers my dust. In Jesus' name, amen.

"It is He who, coming after me, is preferred before me, whose sandal strap I am not worthy to loose."

John 1:27

Luke 7:36-50

HIS LOVE WORKS

June 13

"Ask, and it will be given to you."

Matt. 7:7

Try one thing: Ask for God's love to work in you. There are many who know God loves them, but they cannot receive divine love on His terms. They are willing to love with their love, but not His. From eternity, God loved us and created us able to ask and receive His kind of love in His Son. It is so high and fine, totally other than human love, and it rolls down upon us like a liquid flame of pure joy. Only the cross could kindle this fire. When Jesus asked Peter, "Do you love Me?" Peter was still looking within himself. He responded yes, but only in human terms. But Jesus asked in divine terms, "Do you love Me?" He asked if Peter loved Him with that flame of God flowing through him in full forgiveness. Peter couldn't come up with that love on his own, and neither can we. Without the divine love of God burning within him, Peter could know Christ very well but still deny Him anytime in the future. Jesus didn't ask Peter, "Do you know Me?" or "Will you serve Me?" He asked Peter if he loved Him with God's love.

God's flock can only be fed with that divine, *agape* love. Anything else leaves us hungry. Human love always falls short, locked in self-interest. Remembering his denial of Jesus, Peter could only respond in the human *phileo* of brotherly love. But when God's love through the Holy Spirit was poured out on Peter at Pentecost (after asking), then he could freely proclaim the Christ he had previously denied. He fed the lambs of God's flock after he had feasted on the Lamb of God's love. Then Peter poured out what was pouring through him, not what came from within him or his knowledge.

Divine love does two things human love cannot do: It casts out fear completely to free us, and it holds full sway in our hearts, pointing our eyes beyond ourselves (1 John 4:18-19). Peter's heart was fully changed, and he had no more fear of human loss or gain.

In the case of the rich young ruler, what Jesus really asked for was this kind of whole-hearted love (Mark 10:17-27). Even the best human love is always divided among various people and needs. God's love is united in His creative power that does not change. His love covers every need and enlarges every heart. To ask for God's love is to ask Him to pour out His unchangeable presence through you. It will not come from within you but from Him. Asking opens the door. So does waiting, which makes you realize that what you are waiting for is more real than your time. God has waited for us far longer than we will ever have to wait for Him. Ask. Through the Holy Spirit, the edges of a love that is bigger than the ocean will touch your spirit, confront your sin and wash it away, soak your life, and soften your will to conform to His beauty. It's real.

Father, feed me with Your love so I can feed Your sheep. In Jesus' name, amen.

Luke 12:32-34   1 John 3:17   1 John 4:12-16

June 14

ON THE RAILING

Lord, I am sitting here on the railing between two worlds: Your will and mine. Once, I thought it was a fence between two equal pastures, but it is a railing separating light from darkness with stairs that go up or down. In my own strength, I have been sliding down, away from You. Now please bring me up into Your light. If I continue to just sit here, gradually, I will slide down farther because the pull of sin is in that direction. Lift me in Your power to come on up in faith. I want to live in You on higher ground. Help me to get off the railing and take the next clear step up into Your kingdom. Please give me grace to take a step of faith beyond the place of my own doubts. I can't sit on the edge anymore. In Your truth, Lord, in Your arms, I know I'm going the right direction. Help me take the next step up. In Jesus' name, amen.

Now we have received, not the spirit of the world, but the Spirit who is from God, that we might know the things that have been freely given to us by God.

Cor. 2:12

Mark 9:27

LOOK ON THROUGH TO JOY June 15

The voice of my beloved! Behold, he comes leaping upon the mountains, skipping upon the hills. . . . He is looking through the windows, gazing through the lattice. My beloved spoke, and said to me: "Rise up, my love, my fair one, and come away. For lo, the winter is past, the rain is over and gone."

Song of Sol. 2:8-11

In any situation set before you, look on through to your beloved Savior until you see His strength and joy as He looks through to you now. Seek the One who went to the cross for the joy set before Him. See your struggle in the full truth of God's kingdom unfolding all around you. Each day it comes closer to completion, although invisible to the world. Old blindfolds of sin and fear can make us stumble around, still depending on our abilities and memories for direction. Instead, ask God to remove the blindfolds to reveal His way, a new creation that begins in the middle of our mess.

Can you see what God is doing even when others are in despair, or when your mind sees no escape? Ultimately, God in His Son will take you through safely. Look through to where He will carry you. He comes where we are now through the Holy Spirit so that we can come forward in faith and see what He has promised (John 16:13-15).

Through the Spirit, our beloved Savior gazes through the lattice in the shape of the cross into our lives so that we can look back to Him through that same window of sacrifice and love. He communicates through the cross, and we respond through the active opening it makes in our lives. How? Look for Him; seek His face. Let the power of His cross work in your heart to make room for an answer.

As the blind man asked to receive his sight, we can ask to receive spiritual sight (Mark 10:50-51). By faith, we receive what God has planned through the unstoppable power of His Son's love in action, as surely as winter turns to spring. He wants that love to pass through the cross to you. You can be blind to it, but you can't stop it. That love is coming through the lattice, the opening the cross has already made in your world. Don't wait for others to fix things or tell you what to do. Look on through to Jesus and what He can do. Follow His love now.

Lord, thank You for seeing me and loving me just the way I am. Restore my sight so I can see Your joy in what You will do here today. In the name of Jesus who comes, amen.

Heb. 12:1-2   Isa. 61:1-3   John 1:47-51

WHICH ROBE?   June 16

"Because you say, 'I am rich, have become wealthy, and have need of nothing'—and do not know that you are wretched, miserable, poor, blind, and naked—I counsel you to buy from Me gold refined in the fire, that you may be rich; and white garments, that you may be clothed, that the shame of your nakedness may not be revealed; and anoint your eyes with eye salve, that you may see."

Rev. 3:17-18

Which one, which of these many robes, shall I wear? That's the question I asked the Lord when considering choices of churches and denominations, where to attend and what to do. Which one is right? What kind of work did the Lord want me to do in His kingdom? Each possibility had something woven in that seemed good, but there were flaws also. I wasn't sure any of them would fit me. The Lord's answer was direct. He wanted me to consider how they fit Him.

The same question applies to choosing a job or a house or even a mate. Various choices present themselves, so we try them on, perhaps look at ourselves in the mirror of our own desires or others' opinions, and then try to make a decision. Which robe do we wear? But would it fit our Savior's life? Instead of trying on the various robes of the world, even the beautiful robes of work in His kingdom, to see if they fit my plans, I need first to let His truth try my heart and turn my eyes to the beauty of Christ alone. As His beauty changes me, then I can change robes. It's not really a question of which one fits me but of how I fit into God's purpose. In His power, the fit is perfect. Change the heart; then choose a robe.

Father, clothe me in the purity and power of Jesus Christ. I lay aside my old garments for the new creation You bring in Him. In Jesus' name, amen.

Mark 10:46-52   James 4:4-6   Luke 15:11-22

PEACE AND JUSTICE   June 17

"Knock, and it will be opened to you."

Matt. 7:7

In God's eyes, peace is linked to justice. To go through the door of peace, you first will have to knock on the wood of the cross of Christ's sacrifice. Justice is often thought of as a social issue, but it begins as a personal issue on the threshing floor of our hearts. In Christ's cross and resurrection, God has assured peace forever, if we will just knock on the door and go through the cross. Many of the things we seek on our own—comfort and stability and peace—actually become the causes of unhappiness, restlessness, and war within ourselves and with others. Peace without comes first within.

If we seek peace in other people, they will often disappoint us. If we seek peace in money or a better job, it can become a demanding god. If we seek peace in withdrawal from the world, our inner world can torment us more than the evils of society. So where is peace? It is in the cross of God's Son. It is not at the cross, for there are many people and causes standing at the cross, some mocking it. Only a few live in the cross. They knock on the door of sacrifice in daily life and go through the cross into the resurrection power of Christ's living peace. These are the ones who can truly help others find justice.

Anything I personally could do for peace would be an imperfect sacrifice. I cannot balance the scales of justice, but I can participate in God's balancing them for eternity. To participate, I must confess my sin flat out—everything, no excuses. There must be complete surrender. The scales of justice rest squarely on a flat threshing floor, illuminated now by the Holy Spirit within our hearts. The chaff is blown away, and the threshing floor is swept clean and purged with fire (Matt. 3:1-2, 11-12).

Peace grows from justice, and justice from true confession, and confession from knowing the love that went to the cross for all. Without tasting that love, my mouth will not open in confession and receive the healing stream of peace. By Christ's stripes, by His wounds, I am healed. Never mind how unfair others are or how evil; if I do not acknowledge my own sin, what is within me, then the love that died for me and for them will never be put into action in my life. True justice is not my sacrifice or anyone else's sacrifice, but Christ's. If I give Him my sin, He will make it right, starting with me and reaching out to others. In His cross, the scales are balanced, the debts all paid. Knock on that door of peace, and it will be opened in perfect justice.

Father, I confess my sin and Your solution. I hold nothing back. Cleanse me in the blood of Your Son, and lead me in Your peace in the justice of the cross. In Jesus' name, amen.

Col. 1:19-20   John 14:27   1 John 1:7-9

June 18

~~~~~~

MAKE ME SEE WHAT YOU SEE

O Lord God, make me see what You see and work as You work to glorify Your name in this place. So much more is going on than what my mind can know or my hands direct. Great are You, O King, working wonders and salvation in the earth. Reveal the truth of Your Son's cross and resurrection power in my situation today. Show me the difference between my plans and Yours, and give me the grace to follow Yours. In Jesus' name, amen.

Then Jesus spoke to them again, saying, "I am the light of the world. He who follows Me shall not walk in darkness, but have the light of life."

John 8:12

Ps. 119:105-144

~~~~~~

LIVING FLAME June 19

So he looked, and behold, the bush was burning with fire, but the bush was not consumed.

Exod. 3:2

God's love is a living flame in us. More than just seeing that light and studying it or feeling its heat occasionally, we must let it live in us, consuming everything that is not of God. This holy flame does not just burn; it lives! Through eternity, its light carries the very being of God, who is a consuming fire (Heb. 12:29). This fire brings life and light as it destroys darkness by the power of the very nature of God.

Scripture says to "walk in the light as He is in the light" (1 John 1:7), but we must know how He is in the light. Our Lord is not separate from the light but is that light burning from the core of His eternal being. So the idea of walking in the light as we walk in sunlight is not complete, because we are separate from natural light. As we move through sunlight or artificial light, our hearts can be full of darkness and sin, but in God's kingdom, we must be full of living light, burning within, in order to move with Him. Through the blood of Jesus, we can become truly one with God's holy light so that it is fully inside as well as outside, moving through us while we move through it, ever closer to the Source. This light comes from God, not from us or any other source.

The burning bush drew Moses' attention. But that was not all. When he turned aside and came near, he could hear God's voice and receive His life-giving Word. Then he received that spiritual fire burning in him to deliver God's people. Moving through the desert, the fire that guided and protected them was also burning on the inside of Moses as he communed with God. To walk in the light, you must turn aside, seeking God and hearing His Word, and allowing the light to come into a surrendered heart.

When His living flame of love shines in and through you, the way will open up before you in His glory. This light of the gospel is not something you can hold in your hand and carry like a flashlight. It is a gift from God that holds you, carries you, and draws you into the Son through the Holy Spirit. Turn aside now. In the cross, let the living God burn His life in you.

O Lord, Creator, create in me a clean heart and burn in me forever through the sacrifice of Your Son and the power of His resurrection. I turn to receive Him now. In Jesus' name, amen.

Luke 11:34-36   2 Cor. 3:15—4:7   Isa. 9:2, 6-7

SINGLE SPARROW

June 20

"Are not two sparrows sold for a copper coin? And not one of them falls to the ground apart from your Father's will."

Matt. 10:29

Have you ever felt like a sparrow, hardly worth the trouble of a single coin? One sparrow worth only half a coin would be too much bother to be considered much of a profit. In the world, we can be bought and sold rather cheaply, perhaps considered too insignificant to be worth much notice, but before God's eyes, we are worth watching. Sun or rain, wind or snow, the sparrows sit out there and reply to Him in the quick notes of bright, unrehearsed little songs. In the fragile humility of these sparrows, we see that what the world considers almost worthless, God can use for beauty and the completion of His creative plan.

He sent His Son, not just for the people who are busy buying and selling His creation, but also for the poor ones, the unnoticed, for all of His creation who are often mute to our ears but speak to His heart. Their humility has great value in the Father's eyes. If we will acknowledge how small we are, even when we think we have important business, we too can be poor enough to be held in the Father's hand. The payment He offers is priceless. He gave His only Son for us.

Jesus mentioned the sparrows when He was teaching about the cost of discipleship. He cautioned the disciples not to fear the power of a human society that does not measure its values on God's infinite scale. "Do not fear therefore; you are of more value than many sparrows" (Matt. 10:31). It is precisely when we are also fragile and seemingly useless to the world that God can reveal His strength in us. If you find yourself alone today, perched on a barren rooftop somewhere, keep singing. He sees you right where you are. Nothing will fall to the ground outside His will.

To become productive disciples, we may have to join our Lord and be sold for a few coins or persecuted by people who do not know their own value, let alone ours. The tragedy is not only that many do not realize their value to God and to His Son, as the bride to the Bridegroom, but also that they never see the value of others and their potential in God's plan, created for His glory alone. He still hears the sparrows sing.

Father, I know You see me here and keep me calmly in Your care because Your eye is on the sparrow and on me. Thank You for the life of Your Son, who went from the highest to the lowest and then returned to You. May His life in me be my song to You. In Jesus' name, amen.

Ps. 102:1-2, 7   Ps. 84:3-12   Matt. 19:13-15

June 21

~~~~~~

SAVIOR, FIND ME

My God and Savior, find me where I am lost in myself. Rescue me! Make me the person You designed me to be in You, not the crippled ruler of my own dead world, no matter how I might appear on the surface. You are the only One who rescues the lost with life and mercy. Help me receive Your grace and rise up in the power of Your Son, the Lord of all, who takes my hand. Through the Holy Spirit, bring me forward in the clear light of Your truth. In Jesus' name, amen.

"And I will pray the Father, and He will give you another Helper, that He may abide with you forever—the Spirit of truth, whom the world cannot receive, because it neither sees Him nor knows Him; but you know Him, for He dwells with you and will be in you. I will not leave you orphans; I will come to you. A little while longer and the world will see Me no more, but you will see Me. Because I live, you will live also. At that day you will know that I am in My Father, and you in Me, and I in you. He who has My commandments and keeps them, it is he who loves Me. And he who loves Me will be loved by My Father, and I will love him and manifest Myself to him."

John 14:16-21

Isa. 40:3-31

~~~~~~

NO OTHER NAME   June 22

"Nor is there salvation in any other, for there is no other name under heaven given among men by which we must be saved."

Acts 4:12

Our hope rests in the name of Jesus. His very name means God saves. His name becomes more than a word or a series of letters on a page but the reality of a relationship that is eternal. There is no other name that reaches into eternity. Our minds and our lives are full of other names on a daily basis, but when we turn toward heaven, there is no other name that will open the gates. Imagine standing before the gates of heaven and offering some other name for your salvation, perhaps a powerful one from the Bible: Pharaoh! Moses! Samson! Caesar! Peter! Paul! Nothing will happen. These names are silent, but there is One that still speaks: Jesus, the firstborn of the Living God.

There is no other name, even though we may try others. By our actions we are crying out other names daily, showing where our trust lies. Today, we may have our own caesars and put our trust in them, or in self-reform or human power, but none of these names will open the gates of heaven. There is no institution to which heaven will respond or any human plan of action that will move the heart of God. The Father responds to His Son, who shares His life with us.

Some turn to the idea of Christianity, to a system of religion, and try everything else in the Bible but Jesus Himself. God sent us His Son, not a system. He wants us to call on Him by name, not on our idea of Him by concept. Some are reluctant to call on him personally because they are more comfortable with human ideas rather than with the Son of God on a daily basis. Whose name are you calling today? By your lifestyle and actions, you are calling and living in some name today. Families, companies, churches, jobs, sports, and countries are names openly displayed in our lives. All these will fall short. No other name but Jesus will get us where we need to go, changing us on the way.

When we live in His name, His life is expressed through us, just as saying the name of someone you know expresses your understanding of that person. When you say the name of a close loved one, it carries an expression of that relationship, something of the love you feel, the memories you share, and the trust you keep. Think how you respond when someone you love says your name. The very sound communicates more than words. How do you say Jesus' name? Will He know your love when He hears you? Today, let the Holy Spirit speak Jesus' name in you, both in word and in action.

Father, help me pray and live in the beautiful name of Jesus. In His name, amen.

Acts 3:11-16   John 16:23-33   John 1:12-13

THE POINT OF HIS PRESENCE
June 23

Let this mind be in you which was also in Christ Jesus, who, being in the form of God, did not consider it robbery to be equal with God, but made Himself of no reputation, taking the form of a bondservant, and coming in the likeness of men.

Phil. 2:5-7

The flow of God's presence is so much bigger than our lives that it has to squeeze into a form we can see. At that point of contact, we see Christ in a form we can begin to understand. Into this small human dimension, He comes to write His love on our hearts and transform our lives. Christ, who is God, took our human form and still remained God. In a dimension we can see today, His power is compressed into human form, filling us only to overflow our boundaries and explode in resurrection possibilities through the work of the Holy Spirit in His imperfect people.

Consider for a moment a huge, billowing form of light representing God's presence and power. It is larger than a galaxy, but in order to become visible even in our small things, it funnels down into this world at a certain point, like a huge feather pen balanced on the point of a quill. The top of the pen is much larger than the point touching the paper, but it is perfectly balanced to write what we understand. The tip is shining with the liquid intent of the Author touching the paper. That is the point where we live in Him. All we see is where He touches us and writes visibly in our lives. Only that point of contact is seen, but above it and beyond it in every direction is the giant dimension of God's power that shelters and hovers over the world in glory.

His wing of love that extends into infinity has focused down into one shining point to write liquid hope in our lives now, a tiny point of contact, condensed into this time, this day. The point of the quill pen is touching the paper in your life today. Above you, invisibly and beyond you in every direction, is the huge, unseen dimension of His majesty and loving care. Where your life is yielded, His presence will flow out in a form we can understand. God's hand holds both the unseen and the visible tip of His power. What is He writing in you today?

Lord God, thank You for coming right here, right now in Your Spirit. At this point in my life, I give You full reign to reveal Your truth and beauty as You will. In the name of Jesus, amen.

2 Cor. 3:3-6   John 14:22-26   Heb. 10:12-17

June 24

~~~~~~

NOW

O Father, only You can save us now, as You have saved us from the beginning. We didn't know it until now. At this moment, we begin to see what You see through all time: how much we need Your grace poured out on our dry ground—now! We can't wait until tomorrow or next year. We will dry up forever on our own. Today, we will come and drink of You. Today, we will hear and not harden our hearts. Today, we will see what You have opened our eyes to see. Today we will be Yours, instead of trying to make You ours. Now, already, the fields are white for Your harvest, and today salvation will come to this house. Now we will come and dine at the table You have prepared for the children of the King, even those who are forgiven much. Now we will wash Your feet with our tears and love You according to the love with which You first loved us. Now, out of our hearts we say, "Abba, Father." You have made us Yours. Now we are ready to go through the door that You open. Now we receive Your life as You live it in us one day at a time, not looking back but pressing on in the upward call of Your love in Jesus Christ. In His name, amen.

"Now I will praise the Lord" (Gen. 29:35).
"I have heard of You by the hearing of the ear, but now my eye sees You"(Job 42:5).
"And now, Lord, what do I wait for? My hope is in You" (Ps. 39:7).
Save now, I pray, O Lord (Ps. 118:25).
"I will rise now," I said, "And go about the city; in the streets and in the squares I will seek the one I love." (Song of Sol. 3:2).
"'Repent now everyone of his evil way and his evil doings, and dwell in the land that the Lord has given to you'" (Jer. 25:5).
"'Come, for all things are now ready'" (Luke 14:17).
"You have kept the good wine until now!" (John 2:10).
Jesus answered them, "Do you now believe?" (John 16:31).

Behold, now is the accepted time; behold, now is the day of salvation.

2 Cor. 6:2

~~~~~~

SECRET OF SIMPLICITY   June 25

For our boasting is this: the testimony of our conscience that we conducted ourselves in the world in simplicity and godly sincerity, not with fleshly wisdom but by the grace of God, and more abundantly toward you.

                                                              2 Cor. 1:12

The secret of simplicity is your heart's desire. If you desire worldly things, you won't have simplicity in the one Seed of eternal life. Since your life follows your heart, wherever your heart goes determines where each day's schedule goes. Pursuing many paths at once results in exhaustion and a fractured life. It's been said that a man once got on his horse quickly and rode off in all directions. Where did he go? The result is no lasting fruit anywhere.

My life can become a blur of conflicting personal desires and goals instead of giving myself completely to the One who simply moves me in love. The simplicity of Christ's love shows a depth and purity beyond the surface. If someone loves you with complication, something else is going on besides love, perhaps a need for attention and control, a fear of rejection, or guilt in disguise. True love moves forward in simplicity, not manipulation. When deep calls unto deep in Christ, it is a pure call and brings peace.

Busyness can be a mask for impurity. It's possible to accumulate and polish lots of empty cups but never go to the source of water and risk a simple commitment. A busy life of cups does no good without the water of life. We can drink deeply only one cup, one swallow at a time. Deep things are profoundly simple.

Working below the surface, God changes everything from the root. Even complicated, nasty situations, like pesky weeds become simple when the tap root is located. Don't waste time trying to clip off all the leaves on the surface day after day. In prayer, go directly to the root, and let God pull it up in one deep motion. He can turn a weedy, stony field into a fruitful place once the land is cleared of all distractions and given to Him. Our heart's desire must let Him be Creator in us now. In trying to impose our image on creation, we blur the holy beauty that reflects His pure power.

In your heart, let the heat of His divine purity melt everything in love until all you want to see is the glory of God shining in the face of Jesus Christ. He became simple and laid down all for you. The light of that purity will transform all who simply turn to Him.

Father, forgive me for trying to serve You with complications when what You want first is for me to love You in simplicity. In Jesus' name, amen.

2 Cor. 4:5-10   Matt. 18:1-4   Mark 10:17-27

THE PRESENT CHRIST
June 26

"And lo, I am with you always, even to the end of the age."

Matt. 28:20

Where is the Christ you know? If He is only in heaven, waiting the coming day of glory, or in the past, recorded in stories, you can miss His active power now. For each of us, there is an active "today" in our salvation, as we live each day to the fullest. "Jesus Christ is the same yesterday, today, and forever" (Heb. 13:8). It's possible to focus on yesterday or tomorrow and miss walking with Jesus today through the Holy Spirit. Many of us focus on the historical Jesus and say, "Yes, I believe He died for me and rose again." But what is He doing now in your life?

We can only receive a gift in the present, today. It is not possible to open a gift in the past or the future. For it to be truly ours, we must open it now while it is in our hands. Jesus didn't go through the cross and rise in power just so we can sit here until it's time to go to heaven, leaving His beautiful gift on the shelf until then. Some prefer this wait zone, pondering the past and looking forward to the future, leaving the present under their own management and control. They think that as long as they get things straightened out before He comes, they'll be all right. But our Savior is in charge now, as interested in you today as He was when He died on the cross and rose again.

It is the same love that led Christ to the cross that He wants to live out in us now. With the same resurrection power He will bring to the earth to make all things new, He comes now into our lives through the Holy Spirit to make us new where we are today (Eph. 1:19-23; John 14:15-18). Don't shut the door on today by gazing far into the past or waiting for the future. He wants to live in you now as much as He wanted to save you then, and He has the same power available to help you now as the life-giving stream that brought Him up from the grave. Through the Holy Spirit, you can walk with Christ today, right where you are. If you aren't sure, ask Him to reveal Himself to you. Live now, pray with the present Christ, and follow Him one day at a time.

Father, I pray to You in the name of Your Son Jesus Christ. By Your Holy Spirit, please reveal Your Son to me, living in me each day, walking with me all the way, not just waiting until the end. Thank You for sending Your love to us today. In Jesus' name, amen.

Rev. 3:18-20   Phil. 1:3-6   John 14:21

June 27

LORD OF NOW

When I live daily in Your future, Lord God, You will change the present and redeem the past. Since the kingdom of heaven is at hand, I can receive Your reality now as I repent and change in the resurrection power of Christ working in me through the Holy Spirit. Father, do a new thing here as I surrender to you. Let Your living water flow in my life, refreshing my heart and melting my will to walk in love. In the name of Jesus Christ, amen.

"Do not remember the former things, nor consider the things of old. Behold, I will do a new thing, now it shall spring forth; shall you not know it? I will even make a road in the wilderness and rivers in the desert."

Isa. 43:18-19

2 Cor. 5:14—6:2

SHARPER EDGE
June 28

"Every branch in Me that does not bear fruit He takes away; and every branch that bears fruit He prunes, that it may bear more fruit."

John 15:2

Something must be cut away to make a sharper edge in our lives so that we can move freely in God's Word. If we have what we want and stay comfortable, we'll be too dull to move through the world's walls and bondages. Only God can cut away what blocks our walk with Him. When we're washed clean, the old deadwood is gone. Pruning is removing what seems good but blocks the way. Sometimes what is missing from our lives can speak a louder witness to others than many shallow activities we think are for the Lord.

Holiness grows where the lust of the world has been taken away, and power in prayer rises up after the old carnal voice dies. As we are sharpened, we experience resistance, but as we move on, that resistance only increases our ability to penetrate what used to hold us back from the truth of God. Don't be afraid to let Him sharpen you where you are right now. His Living Word will move you into active truth and the unseen fullness of His power. You can't go any farther without that sharper edge. Let Him remove whatever hinders His love and polish the fine lifeline of truth in your heart.

Father, sharpen me to live clean in Your word. Make me free to be the person You are creating now in the power of Jesus Christ. Make me true to You. In Jesus' name, amen.

Ps. 1   Matt. 5:21-30, 43-48   2 Cor. 4:8-18

MORE THAN A PHARISEE   June 29

"For I say to you, that unless your righteousness exceeds the righteousness of the scribes and Pharisees, you will by no means enter the kingdom of heaven."

Matt. 5:20

It is possible to know about the kingdom of heaven and not enter it. The scribes and Pharisees were experts in religion who busily tried to obey every detail of the law. On the outside, they looked good. What was missing? To enter the kingdom of heaven, Jesus said we must go farther in obedience than keeping surface rules and the outward appearance of loving God. We must actually love Him deeply with all of our heart, mind, soul, and strength. Then we can begin to love our neighbors as ourselves and fulfill the law. But this requires more than human effort. It requires a new birth in the Holy Spirit that takes us past religion into direct relationship with the One we worship (John 3:3-6). As we live in Him, He lives in us, giving us the love to activate His life in us today. We become sons instead of scribes or soldiers or hired servants.

Surely, the Pharisees thought they were more religious than Jesus. They carefully kept the rules, or changed them so they could. In the eyes of the world, they were successful, correct in their teaching, and upright, moral supporters of their culture; but they did not really love or care for orphans and widows or go out of their way to help anyone else, especially those not as respectable as they were. Apparently, their heads worked, but their hearts did not.

In becoming experts, the scribes and Pharisees chose to use religion for their own advantage with a twist here, a new rule there, or a reward for what they could accomplish. They wanted control. Do we? Have we studied about the Messiah in order to know and control Him rather than to love Him and to simply live in that love? Our minds alone cannot grasp Jesus. The Holy Spirit comes to lead us into all truth through a new birth in the depths of our hearts. Going through the motions on the surface will not get us there. Simple honesty will. To qualify for heaven, we must be disqualified as Pharisees.

Do we consider ourselves outcasts and sinners before a holy God or experts in saying what others should do? Like the Pharisees, we can be full of religion but have our hearts empty of anything but ourselves and our own world. These blind guides couldn't see the kingdom of God and His Son standing right in front of them. Can we?

Father, create in me a clean heart, conformed to the love of Your Son, Jesus. Take away my pride and focus on the world. Make me alive in Your Son so I can truly know Him and You through the Holy Spirit. In Jesus' name, amen.

Rom. 8:2-11   Matt. 9:9-17   Luke 18:9-14

~~~~~~

STRAIGHT GATE

Father, I know my sin cannot squeeze through Your straight gate. In trying to enter on my own, my crooked ways are bumped, bruised, and finally stuck. Wash me in the blood of the Lamb Jesus, and take away my sin. Please take the selfish things away. Straighten me out, Father, and remove all the rough edges, the crooked desires, and self-concern. Create in me a clean heart, and renew a right spirit within me so that when I come into Your gates with thanksgiving and into Your courts with praise, it will be with the sacrifice of a broken and contrite heart. The straightness of Your gate has made me suddenly aware of all the crooked things I try to bring with me, conformed to the shape of this world. Conform me now to the shape of Your way in Your Son so when I come to the straight gate, like the eye of a needle, Your sacrificial love will bring me through by grace. May I turn from any other love that does not follow You. I seek Your face and come, accepted in the Beloved, returning to the Father who runs to embrace me. Bring me through the beautiful gate to Your feast that lasts forever. In Jesus' name, amen.

"Enter ye in at the straight gate: for wide is the gate, and broad is the way, that leadeth to destruction, and many there be which go in thereat: because straight is the gate, and narrow is the way, which leadeth unto life, and few there be that find it."

Matt. 7:13 (KJV)

Ezek. 33:2-20

~~~~~~

THE LIVING DOOR   July 1

Therefore, brethren, having boldness to enter the Holiest by the blood of Jesus, by a new and living way which He consecrated for us, through the veil, that is, His flesh, and having a High Priest over the house of God, let us draw near with a true heart in full assurance of faith.

Heb. 10:19-22

Christ offers us a living, open door. It is more than an entrance; it is a way of life that leads to more than human life. In this world, many doors are available to us that are neither living nor open. Most of them look good on the outside but are really empty shells of human effort. Even some religious doors try to swing on human ability to reach for divine power. In Jesus Christ, the divine love of God reaches for us and brings us through to walk in His life and light. If you're looking at a dead door now, even an attractive one, don't expect to find life on the other side. If you prefer a door of human reason, ajar with power that you can lean on to please yourself, it will soon harden into a mirror of death. All the "easy" doors are actually difficult and will lock behind you.

The door of Christ is not difficult in Him, and it overflows with amazing life. When you're living in His life, you will move right through into deep truth and peace. In simplicity, this living door swings open as you approach with the key of faith in Christ crucified and risen for you personally. No other key will open it. Going through, you become one with the life of the Son of God, who changes you and carries you in His power where the best human effort cannot go. His cross opened the door, and His resurrection makes it alive for you now, to work through whatever faces you and conquer anything that holds you back from knowing God. Even the best the world has to offer looks dim to those who pass through in the shining life of God's risen Son.

Before He created you, He created this living way into a new creation. You can come through only carrying a cross and wearing the clothes of a servant. Any other shape is not alive enough with love to fit through that door. Unless you are carrying a cross today, your pattern of life will not match the only opening to eternity. The only place to find and carry such a cross is in the world right where you are (Mark 8:34). Each servant becomes a child of God as our Creator opens that door through this world and into the next. There is no limit to where you can go in Christ, who Himself is the door and more, the Alpha and the Omega, in whom all things consist and are made new (Col. 1:12-20). Look around. Many doors are available today. Choose the living One!

Father, bring me through the living door of Jesus Christ. Thank You for opening it for me and giving me the faith to come through, changed for You. In Jesus' name, amen.

John 14:1-6   John 10:7-10   Ps. 118:17-29

July 2

~~~~~~

SHAPED BY HIS WILL

Out of the house of bondage You have brought me, O Lord. Let me be shaped by Your will alone. Make me depend on You alone, not on the approval of others or their strength, or my own strength, or life in the world, or family, or material resources, or mental ability so that I am not shaped by these but by Your will. Otherwise, they will shape me into their images, which may seem good for a time but are only dead images of ourselves. These can become gods ruling over the hearth of life. Help me not to trust in the abundance of things or in the poverty of things. Let me not glory in my own life-style, good or bad. Let me not worship what I can do or follow what is made in my own image. Free me in the blood of the Lamb Jesus. Form me in the fire of Your holiness. Shape me after the will of the Son, only begotten of the Father, dwelling among people with hearts of stone and rolling away the stone. Now may Your Living Word come with resurrection power into my heart and mold me into Your image with no human boundaries, no carved corners, and no heavy pedestals that fall into death. Before You, Lord God almighty, I lay down my other gods and release them from my will. I give myself to You completely and surrender to Your purpose. Shape me into Your life in Jesus Christ. In Jesus' name, amen.

"You shall have no other gods before Me."

Exod. 20:3

Matt. 6:21

~~~~~~

REST TO RUN   July 3

Therefore we also, since we are surrounded by so great a cloud of witnesses, let us lay aside every weight, and the sin which so easily ensnares us, and let us run with endurance the race that is set before us.

Heb. 12:1

To run well, we must lay aside not only what keeps us from running but also what keeps us from resting. Rest is twofold: spiritual and physical. Many concentrate on physical rest and forget the spiritual turmoil that keeps them constantly exhausted. Only the Prince of Peace gives the rest that truly refreshes for the long run and sustains us all the way across the finish line. In the race of life, most of our energy goes into running well, but how we finish is determined by how we rest as well as by how we run. The pace is important. Regular rest is as important as a steady stride.

To those still growing up, rest is important to digest what they are learning. Keeping children constantly busy in organized activities is like eating constantly and stuffing in food without restraint. It will produce heartburn and sickness. Many of our youth now have an inner heartburn that won't go away, and they express it in violence. Unstructured time allows children who are already fed God's Word to digest the deeper lessons of life and experience spiritual joy independent of things and physical power (John 6:48). To young adults, rest is important because they have more to do than anyone else. Physical strength and spiritual peace go together, bringing them vision to choose the right path revealed to them only in time apart with God (Matt. 11:27-30).

For older people who naturally begin to rest more physically, their spiritual rest becomes all the more important as their outer package and natural ability weakens (2 Cor. 4:16-18). Spiritual rest works inside us to strengthen the contents and also helps the outside package be more resilient. Rest restores what activity cannot replace.

Deep rest is the only thing we really must make time for, even though it's often invisible on our calendars. If we don't rest, we can't run. Since we run well only in Christ's power active in our weakness, we must lay aside even the weight of some good activities in order to run in Him (1 Cor. 1:27—2:5).

Father, You have taught us how to pray and how to run. Now teach us how to rest so that we can know Your amazing grace and run the distance in Jesus Christ. In His name, amen.

Isa. 40:28-31   2 Cor. 12:9-10   Luke 10:38-42

BE SILENT BEFORE THE LORD July 4

Be silent, all flesh, before the Lord, for He is aroused from His holy habitation!

Zech. 2:13

When the Lord comes to us, our flesh will be silent in awe. This deep silence acknowledges His presence more truly than words. If we want to praise Him later with our whole hearts, our flesh must first bow in silence. Jesus said the Father was seeking those who would worship Him in spirit and in truth. He did not say in flesh and in truth, but it seems many try to impress Him mainly with loudness or energy or elaborate ritual. However, the entrance comes quietly in spirit and in truth. The sacrifice God seeks is a broken spirit, a broken and a contrite heart, that allows us to come first with nothing in our hands but His mercy (Ps. 51). Our silence before God begins at the cross of Christ.

Simply to His cross we cling. Have you come quietly with nothing in your hands or voice or mind but what His Spirit puts there through His Word? Seek Him quietly. Then He will release you into the words and music He chooses. You will begin to hear it coming from His Word through His Spirit into and through you, but not from you. There is a place for the flesh in worship, but spirit and truth go through the gates first. Then the flesh follows humbly, led by the Spirit, singing and moving in a heavenly design.

When someone says to "spend some time in silence," we may think, "Oh no, the silence of my own mind, plus its little distractions." When I try to enter the silence of my own mind, it's like trying to stand still while a motor is racing. It's a strain. But our Father calls us to enter His silence, not ours. Nothing hidden or dark remains when we are exposed to the light of Christ and His cross. Go with God there. It is not within us but in His presence that we worship. When I enter God's silence, it's like entering the intimacy of His wings over me, and the huge wings lift steadily into the life of His Son. We are lifted in His peace into worship. The movement may create a little air noise, as some quiet song of praise. The silence of God's life is full of riches that spill over into songs of peace and joy that may later grow or become louder in a group but still are never as big as the original silence of His holiness, which is beyond us. Our words and songs will never be bigger than that silence but will spring out of it. Have you met Him there?

Father, I want to sing Your praises in the love that flows from Your heart. Let me meet You where joy grows in the truth of Your presence rising in Your Son. In Jesus' name, amen.

Ps. 46:10 John 4:14-24 Isa. 57:15

July 5

~~~~~~

LOVE'S DEEP SIGHT

Father, Your light makes day and night both visible in love's deep sight. Shine on us, change us in Your mercy to live in Your heart today. By Your grace, make our lives to be as worship acceptable in Your sight. Forgive us when we fall short, wash us, and fill us with living water shining in the light of Your Son, who leads us on to glory. In Jesus' name, amen.

When Jesus had raised Himself up and saw no one but the woman, He said to her, "Woman, where are those accusers of yours? Has no one condemned you?" She said, "No one, Lord." And Jesus said to her, "Neither do I condemn you; go and sin no more." Then Jesus spoke to them again, saying, "I am the light of the world. He who follows Me shall not walk in darkness, but have the light of life."

John 8:10-12

Ps. 80

~~~~~~

RUNNING TO HEAVEN   July 6

Let us lay aside every weight, and the sin which so easily ensnares us, and let us run with endurance the race that is set before us, looking unto Jesus.

Heb. 12:1-2

We are running to heaven from the first moment of our salvation. Life itself is a gift, and the breath of God moving into us returns to Him through His Living Word as a stream of life carrying us forward in faith. It is the stream from Christ's side on the cross. Our life here is to move in that stream that is born of heaven and returns there. The river of God is running to heaven, and we are in it, saved by Christ's blood and washed by living waters. Love draws us to the heart of that unseen river, and our steps in obedience move us toward the Source. As our Creator covers us, we are changed in His liquid light.

"And do this, knowing the time, that now it is high time to awake out of sleep; for now our salvation is nearer than when we first believed. The night is far spent, the day is at hand. Therefore let us cast off the works of darkness, and let us put on the armor of light" (Rom. 13:11-12). When our wills are liquid in the light of God's love, they will flow into His will. Then we can run, covered with His armor of light. It is not heavy. It does not bind and limit. The helmet of salvation allows us to see clearly. Worldly armor is heavy, binding us in cold, blind weight. To run is to believe in, to hope in, and to enjoy the presence of God. In His light armor, we move with new strength, as He carries us.

Daily, we move not against His stream but with the flow, having bowed prostrate before Him. In this attitude, our feet propel us forward. Humbly moving in that stream of living water, we will easily go in the right direction. When our strength and hope fail, that holy stream of new life in Christ carries us in God's Word and the Holy Spirit.

Running is different in rhythm, breathing, and concentration than walking. A runner must be focused on the way ahead, avoiding any distraction. A walker can pause and talk along the way, even rest in the shade and look at his feet. A distance runner paces himself for the goal ahead and runs straight to it, resting in the knowledge of that goal. He divides the air in a way the others do not. He moves forward and does not look back. Everything the runner does is for the motion forward. When we live running to heaven, everything we do must fit into the flow of that motion forward. Some thoughts and desires cannot run to heaven. Some projects are dead weight. Everything in our days and within us has to be one with what flows from God and returns to Him. Run well!

Father, I run to You in Your mercy. Bring me through in the power of Jesus Christ. In His name, amen.

Phil. 3:12-14   Luke 9:20-26   Ps. 119:28-40

July 7

~~~~~~

THE BLOOD OF THE LAMB APPLIED

Father, please apply the blood of the Lamb Jesus Christ to my life for healing, cleansing, and power to witness through Your Holy Spirit. Not just in talk or thought but in the full reality of Jesus' new life in me, change my heart to follow Yours. Bring me forward in faith to the place in Your kingdom You want me to live for You. In the name of Jesus, amen.

Then He took the cup, and gave thanks, and gave it to them, saying, "Drink from it, all of you. For this is My blood of the new covenant, which is shed for many for the remission of sins."

<div align="right">Matt. 26:27-28</div>

Rev. 12:10-11

~~~~~~

FROM START TO FINISH   July 8

. . . being confident of this very thing, that He who has begun a good work in you will
complete it until the day of Jesus Christ;

Phil. 1:6

Only God can finish and complete the creation of new life in us now. Everything He has for
us to do fits within the context of His ongoing creation, not our specific project. We have only
a little piece of what He is doing, and it must fit into His overall design or it will not produce
life beyond itself. Sometimes we want Him to start, to provide us the opportunity, and then let
us finish it according to our desires, our needs, our "perfect" plan.

At other times, what we have started in human strength, we want Him to finish to make us
look good or to correct our mistakes. After all, we think we know exactly what God should do.
The branches are sure they know how to produce fruit that will never be messed up by someone
wanting to eat it or plant its seeds. The very rudeness of the pruning and the harvest, the pain
of separation, and the loss that seems unbearable all are part of the plan of true life. For fruit
that endures, the life must come through the Vine, and the seed must reproduce the image of
the Vine that gave it life to multiply true life into the future (John 15:1-5).

Perhaps this is the secret of answered prayer. Our Father is waiting to give us what we will
release to Him to control, what will return to Him because He is the source of all. In Him we
live and move and have our being, whether we know it or not. The cycle of eternal life, turning
on the axis of divine truth, always turns toward the Creator and seeks His face, working steadily
into His purpose. It does not revolve around us. Through the Vine and the branches, real life
moves in holy light, not in the artificial illumination that humans turn on and off with a switch.
Anything outside of God's complete, eternal circle is operating toward death. Even though it
shines with momentary pleasure, it is artificial and eventually moves us into darkness.

Our lives may not produce fruit because we take the seed for ourselves and try to make it
produce our stony image, or we leave it on the shelf and ignore its potential. Perhaps we see a
true sprout, but then try to transplant it onto our own dry stump, into a human context or institution instead of the Vine of eternal life. Are our lives rooted and nourished in the life-giving
flow from God who alone finishes what He begins?

Creator, make me clean to receive the life that You will create in me for Your glory.
I give up trying to do it for myself and release my whole life to You. In Jesus' name,
amen.

John 15:1-4   Matt. 7:15-20   Rev. 21:3-8

A SMALL ROOM

July 9

For who has despised the day of small things?

Zech. 4:10

A small room presents limitations that seem to block God's purpose until we see that the small room is built to His design as part of His house. Our limitations of suffering and testing can squeeze us into a seemingly impossible corner, from which we think we will never escape. Sometimes we get ourselves into a corner, and God will keep us there until freedom's lesson is learned. Once when I stayed in a very small motel room that did not seem cramped, I looked around to see the secret of the architect's design, which made me feel comfortable in a small space. I noticed that the ceiling was unusually high, with far more space above than in a normal room. So in Christ, we are raised from sin to live with Him here and later to dwell in heavenly places (Eph. 2:4-7). With the realization of this, there is enough space above to make it tolerable, even comfortable below.

Also, this particular room had a window seat to encourage some time spent looking outside. God designs our small lives with a window seat built in so that we will spend some time resting and gazing outward rather than inward (Ps. 37:3-11). If we look out and care for the needs of others, allowing time to be refreshed by His beauty, our room will not seem so small.

In addition, one entire wall of this small room was covered with a mirror, extending the view as if into another dimension. As we gaze into the mirror of God's love and His Word, He gives us not just an extension of our boundaries, but another dimension as we partake of His divine nature (2 Pet. 1:2-4; James 1:22-25). Then a small room not only seems larger, but it is larger, having been multiplied in grace received.

In this little room, most of the furniture was built into the walls or the floor. So in our lives, if the furniture we use is attached securely to God's walls and His foundation, no thief will steal it and no other plan will rearrange it—it will not be moved. To live in a small room with these blessings is better than to live in a wide mansion of low ceilings, self-focus, and fluctuating furniture. The dimensions of our lives are planned by the Architect who knows the end from the beginning. If you're living in a small room today, let it become His design, and you will have room to grow.

Father, make the room of my life open to Your dimensions. In Jesus' name, amen.

Luke 1:37-38   Phil. 4:11-13, 19   Ps. 119:45-58

July 10

~~~~~~

PURE TREASURE

Father, help me let go of worldly things so that I can take hold of Your treasure in Jesus Christ. On the cross, Your Son purchased pure life for me so that I can live now in the riches of His righteousness in resurrection power active in this world. Gladly, I surrender my filthy rags and attitudes so I can receive pure garments of praise to match Your treasure shining in me now. All this time, I've been running away. Now I come to find my heart's desire in You. In Jesus' name, amen.

"Again, the kingdom of heaven is like treasure hidden in a field, which a man found and hid; and for joy over it he goes and sells all that he has and buys that field."

Matt. 13:44

Eph. 1:3 — 2:8

~~~~~~

SETTING THE TABLE   July 11

"'Tell those who are invited, "See, I have prepared my dinner; my oxen and fatted cattle are killed, and all things are ready."'"

Matt. 22:4

Every feast begins with an invitation and a time of preparation. Invitations are exciting, but before that, there is detailed preparation. Sometimes the process of getting ready seems longer than the feast itself, but the delight is worth it. Before God calls you to completion, He will submit you to preparation. In prayer, we often make plans and rush to set the table for the feast we want to receive, forgetting what must happen first.

When we invite guests to eat with us, we plan ahead for a time and place. Then we set aside whatever else we could do at that time and get ready for the feast. Supplies and food are purchased in advance. We clean the house. We start cooking in stages in order to have it hot. Then we set the table. At the appointed time (and hopefully not too much earlier), the doorbell rings, the people arrive, and we are ready to eat. If we just set the table without other preparations, we'll be eating cold food, if any, in the middle of a mess. Yet in prayer, we often expect God's blessing without His timing and preparation.

Have you ever wondered where the food and the people are in your life, or why things are in such a mess, when you tried your best to set the table for God? Did you let Him clean the house first? Prepare the food? Plan the time? He alone knows the date, time, and place of everything we are supposed to do, having prepared it all through His Son (Eph. 2:10). For our completion in love, God has already planned a feast beyond what we can purchase or design. Any work we do is only part of getting ready for the feast He prepares, both in heaven and in our lives now.

To receive what God has planned, we are to set aside the time for Him to cleanse us and prepare with quiet days just to store up supplies. Everything has already been purchased. Even now, the supplies are gathered each day. Before the cooking begins, God will straighten us up and remove anything that keeps us from the table. He lines up the table and chairs according to His will and then spreads out a clean tablecloth and smoothes the wrinkles out of it. Finally, He turns on the fire to cook and sets the table.

When the guests arrive, it is because the Lord brings them in His grace into our lives. At the right time, the doorbell rings. The people who enter may not be the ones we were expecting but the ones of His choice. The feast will begin after we have released our lives to His timing, His cleansing and preparation, His beautiful table, and His guests. Only then can we truly welcome them, and only then will the food be satisfying.

Father, I open the house of my life to Your power. Please prepare it for Your feast with You as the Host. Let it be Your way and in Your timing. In Jesus' name, amen.

1 Cor. 2:9-12   Ps. 23:5   Matt. 22:1-9

BE PRAISE
July 12

. . . that we who first trusted in Christ should be to the praise of His glory.

Eph. 1:12

Even when times are difficult, we can simply "be to the praise of God's glory." We often think of doing something for God's glory, but in this verse we are reminded that in His will, we can "be to the praise of His glory." Many try to learn how to offer God praise. How about *being* the praise? Being is harder than saying or doing, yet it is the source of all other activities in a life pleasing to God, no matter what the outward action. If all the surface were removed from your daily life, all words and actions, leaving only the quietness of your being, would that in itself glorify God?

Only through the gift of Christ on the cross can we be cleansed in His blood to be to the praise of God's glory. Try to focus on being in God through the life of Christ, and notice its effect on the words and actions that come out of that union. If we simply try to *be* to His glory in the depths of our hearts, as Christ makes us new through the Holy Spirit, then words and actions that truly are to His glory and not ours or just something done to please others will flow from us.

Of course, we will soon discover it is impossible to *be* to God's glory without repentance, new birth in Christ, and surrender to the washing and regeneration of the Holy Spirit (Titus 3:4-7). If you're wondering what to do for God, ask Him first to form your heart simply to be to the praise of His glory. Let the Holy Spirit change your inner being and fill you with the light of Christ. In that light, you will be who He created you to be in any situation.

Father, make me new in Your Son so I can live as He did to the praise of Your glory. Thank You for Your love in His sacrifice on the cross, which takes away my sin. Cleanse me so I can be the person You have created me to be here today. In Jesus' name, amen.

Col. 2:6-10   Ps. 84   John 3:3-7

July 13

REALITY OF THE CROSS

Father, please work the reality of the cross of Christ in my life to produce fruit for Your kingdom. Wash me in His blood, His life given to take away my sin and sickness. The medicine we don't want to take is what saves us, not good intentions, beautiful music, or expert knowledge and technology. Touch us and wash us in the reality of the cross and the power of the blood of Jesus Christ received to change us for Your glory. In Jesus' name, amen.

For by Him all things were created that are in heaven and that are on earth, visible and invisible, whether thrones or dominions or principalities or powers. All things were created through Him and for Him. And He is before all things, and in Him all things consist. And He is the head of the body, the church, who is the beginning, the firstborn from the dead, that in all things He may have the preeminence. For it pleased the Father that in Him all the fullness should dwell, and by Him to reconcile all things to Himself, by Him, whether things on earth or things in heaven, having made peace through the blood of His cross.

Col. 1:16-20

Heb. 9:14-22

THE SIEVE   July 14

We are hard-pressed on every side, yet not crushed; we are perplexed, but not in despair; persecuted, but not forsaken; struck down, but not destroyed—always carrying about in the body the dying of the Lord Jesus, that the life of Jesus also may be manifested in our body.

2 Cor. 4:8-10

Our life on earth is like a sieve through which God's glory can press and pass as it returns to Him again, having changed the sieve in the process. With connecting pieces and openings, the sieve's pattern forms a cross. This is the point of contact where we are pressed into new life in Christ, as the flesh is separated from the juice. Without the sieve, fruit could not be washed or processed. By taking on human flesh, Christ passed through life, death, and resurrection to translate us into His kingdom of light. He makes a way through our difficulties. It is the light of His life that flows through the cross, as water and the blood of grapes pass through the sieve. Pressure must be applied. When we bow down or are pressured, the sweet juice of heaven is pressed into and through us, coming out the other side as a sacrifice pleasing to God through His Son.

In Christ, God calls us to let our lives become daily, living sacrifices that will let His glory pour through into this world. He wants to move through the open sieve of your life surrendered in love to Christ. Without the cross, most of God's glory is stuck in heaven. It cannot move through our flesh or through this world without the cross working in everything and causing a flow of praise back to the Father in resurrection light. Daily we are pressed down, or we bow down voluntarily, so that the free flow of His glory can come through here. New wine is pressed out of surrendered grapes, pressed through the sieve of His will. Have you come to that point of pressure yet? Does God's glory find a place in you to press through and spill out in holy light and new wine? This is preparation for the marriage supper of the Lamb. Come pressed through the cross.

"Have this mind among yourselves, which you have in Christ Jesus, who, though He was in the form of God, did not count equality with God a thing to be grasped, but emptied Himself, taking the form of a servant, being born in the likeness of men. And being found in human form He humbled Himself and became obedient unto death, even death on a cross. Therefore God has highly exalted Him and bestowed on Him the name which is above every name" (Phil. 2:5-9 RSV).

Father, let Your life in Christ press through and change me. Let Your glory pour through my life in the cross and bring me into Your kingdom. In Jesus' name, amen.

Rev. 19:7   Eph. 5:2   Matt. 10:38-42

SAME LOVE ANY HOUR   July 15

"Let your light so shine before men, that they may see your good works and glorify your Father in heaven."

Matt. 5:16

God cares as much for you in your next hour on earth as He will care for you the first hour you are in heaven. From His perspective, the value of those hours is the same in His mercy and love. His infinite light shines the same. We may think He will love us more or approve of us more when we get to heaven, but He approves of us now in His Son and loves us now as much as He will then, even as He loved us in Christ before the foundation of the world. It is the same love in any hour to Him. The intensity of His gaze and the desire of His heart toward us is the same in our next minute, hour, and day as for all eternity.

There is power in that love shining through our lives now on earth. Think for a minute about what you plan to do in the hour or day ahead. How will God's love shine through you? He cares for you and protects and loves you the same whether you are just going to sleep, or preparing to do some great work, or coming before Him in heaven.

All days are the same now in His love. It is our love that flickers, and our hours, days, and plans seem different to us, but His love burns with equal intensity for eternity. Sometimes we feel loving and effective in our work and sometimes not, but each hour, any hour, is the same in God's merciful measure. He does not change. So your next hour, whatever it is, has the same value in His love today as when you move into eternity.

Let that love light shine the same in you now as it will then, and it will make a difference. Even here, spiritual fruit grows in the light of heaven. Don't wait for any other hour. Don't depend on some man-made light that flickers and changes. Let God's love shine through you now in the power of Christ, who is the same yesterday, today, and forever. Your forever is also now.

Father, send the light of Your Son into my heart now, so I can begin to shine for You here. Produce in me the fruit that tastes like heaven on earth. In Jesus' name, amen.

John 12:28-36   2 Cor. 5:1-11   Col. 3:9-15

July 16

I SEEK YOU

Lord God, I seek You with a thirst that is beyond this world. My heart is still incomplete and searches for Your completeness. My soul thirsts for You as for life beyond itself, a thirst for Your righteousness and grace, a clean flow all the way into eternity. Your light is alive. Searching on my own, I would turn to the right or the left, but You have called me to come straight ahead into the narrow gate, through the living way, into fullness of joy that never ends in Your presence. I seek You for You, not any longer for me, because You alone are holy and You alone are life. I have sought You for myself, to change me or to make things right, and although this will happen, that is not the main thing. I must see You in Christ before I can see anything else. Otherwise, I am blind to the reality of eternity. In the perfect fire of Your love, I begin to see, and then in Your pure radiance everything melts into truth. Let the fire of that love bring me to worship You in spirit and in truth. All along this road, one dusty step at a time, You have shown me Yourself in Jesus. Now in Him, You have brought me to His cross and then to my own cross, where I see the light of the resurrection power of Jesus shining through all that happens. His sacrifice is on fire now with Your love. In the cross, one day at a time, I see His love burning with complete joy on Your altar. Bring me where I cannot come. Burning with that love, Father, I seek You more each day. In Jesus' name, amen.

But from there you will seek the Lord your God, and you will find Him if you seek Him with all your heart and with all your soul.

Deut. 4:29

Deut. 30:11-20   John 14:4-12

THE PREFERRED LIFE   July 17

But as many as received Him, to them He gave the right to become children of God, to those who believe in His name: who were born, not of blood, nor of the will of the flesh, nor of the will of man, but of God.

John 1:12-13

In reality, most of us prefer our own lives to Christ's life. His life involves humility, sacrifice, transformation, and power beyond our control. Usually, we choose to control a lesser quality of life than to be immersed in the overwhelming beauty of the river of life from above. Our actions show which life we prefer. I've often preferred my own little life to Christ's creative life, but slowly He is changing me. I simply wanted a humanly manageable life, not realizing that it is a slow death.

To live as He did seems impossibly hard and impossibly good at the same time. So we may choose to stay where we are, never trying to get close enough to Christ to experience the real power of His life in our world today. Even though He is King of eternity, we prefer a lesser assignment that we can control; we prefer being rulers of our own imperfections.

To prefer His life is to prefer a perfection that is possible only by surrendering our earthly crowns, real or imagined, and our weapons as well as our weaknesses. To prefer the life of Christ is to prefer the cross to any crown and the resurrection to any rest in the status quo. Once we receive Christ, His death becomes our only life, and His new life is the only death to our self-will that can lead us safely through this world into life everlasting.

He doesn't expect us to carry any cross without His life there to guide us and lift the load through the Holy Spirit. Since He preferred us and offered Himself for us, can't we at least prefer Him by accepting what He can do through us once we are emptied of self-will? The results of the life we choose are revealed long-term in the fruit our lives produce or the barrenness of the ground we call our own. Is there anything you do today that counts for eternity with God? If so, that is where your life truly touches the life of Christ. It could be simple, unnoticed by the world: giving a drink of cold water to the thirsty or spending "extra" time to worship and thank God for who He is above all. Whose life do you really prefer? Each day, your answer grows in action.

Father, breathe on me so I will choose the life of Christ that brings me to You instead of preferring my own dead ends. Let my preference be clearly seen today. In the name of Jesus Christ who loved me and gave Himself for me, amen.

Gal. 2:20   Matt. 11:27-30   Matt. 25:31-40

SABBATH FRUIT

July 18

Remember the Sabbath day, to keep it holy.

Exod. 20:8

To produce fruit that remains, both physical and spiritual, we need deep roots in God's creative pattern. Sabbath rest is really a rest from ourselves. It's not just shutting away the world and its business for a day but hiding in the bosom of the Father to escape the relentless surge of human will and worry. Only then can we visibly let go of our projects and openly acknowledge that we are part of His. As Owner, God is the Builder, and we can live in His house only as children, not as landlords (Lev. 26:2). Some of us are addicted to the gods of our own work and our need to perform to define our worth in the world. Our roots are tied to superficial human patterns.

The fruit from such bondage is sour and soon wastes away. For fruit that lasts, we need to be plugged into the outlet of eternity, and it's not of human design. Six days is enough for the spirit to struggle with the shallow work and whims of the flesh. On the seventh, our spirits need to rest deep in the Father's Spirit and receive His energy, which makes all things new. It's a divinely guaranteed design, not something we dreamed up, and it produces in us a kind of life that is impossible on our own (John 15:4-5). Christ connects us to eternity now if we will take time to know Him.

Sometimes truly resting is harder for us than working. But batteries can't recharge themselves simply by becoming better batteries. They need to be inserted into a higher, running current to replenish what was lost. By our own choice, we often unplug ourselves from that full charge of life. Yet our Savior was broken and opened to give that life to us daily, even in difficult places. Have you laid aside your own work and come to rest completely in His creative power, not for a day here and there, but on a regular basis? The Sabbath will plug you into that higher current, straight from the Source. To miss it, is to miss everything we were created for—living fully charged in God, joined to His Vine. Rest in Him, and the invisible roots will grow deeper and the visible fruit sweeter.

Father, I thought doing my own thing would refresh me, but it hasn't. Now, I come to drink in Your river of life flowing freely through Your Son. I am thirsty. Bring me completely into Your creative pattern, and fill me up with new life. In Jesus' name, amen.

Isa. 56:1-8   Matt. 5:17-20   Isa. 58:13-14

July 19

~~~~~~

RIPEN THE FRUIT

Father, shine on us. Ripen in Your people the fruit of Your presence. Where we are stiff and immature, soften our hearts to do Your will, and open us through the Holy Spirit to new life and the perfection of Your timing. Let there be a sweet aroma of the sacrificial love of Your Son growing in us each day, even in difficult situations. The fruit belongs to You. In Jesus' name, amen.

For with You is the fountain of life; in Your light we see light. Oh, continue Your lovingkindness to those who know You, and Your righteousness to the upright in heart. Let not the foot of pride come against me, and let not the hand of the wicked drive me away.

Ps. 36:9-11

Heb. 12:11-24

~~~~~~

THE SMELL OF SACRIFICE   July 20

Now thanks be to God who always leads us in triumph in Christ, and through us diffuses the fragrance of His knowledge in every place.

2 Cor. 2:14

A sacrifice that pleases God releases a certain aroma of purity. You can see the sacrifice offered, hear the right words, and smell the wood burning, but when the sacrifice is actually consumed, then a deep spiritual aroma ascends to heaven. In the Spirit, we can carry that scent of sacrificial love in our daily lives to quietly remind people of Christ's offering of Himself. It is not an entirely pleasant aroma to human nostrils. There is something about it that smells of suffering, smoke, fading flesh, and ashes. There is also a hint of tender beauty, like the smell of lilies, damp earth, palm branches, cool stone, and fresh water.

We can ready the sacrifice, say the words, and stack the wood, but there is no sweet fragrance until the sacrifice is consumed. To some, it is the aroma of old life transformed into new life. To others, it is only the aroma of old life fading away. They haven't yet smelled the lilies for themselves or met the risen Lord in a new garden of prayer. Without the aroma of Christ's life active in us now, our work for Him will produce nothing. What fragrance permeates your life today? Does whatever you do carry the life of Christ, or does it carry the smell of self-concern?

Think for a moment about recent situations and the people involved. What aroma do they release? Without realizing it, we can sense the spiritual content of a situation and say, "Something just doesn't smell right here," or even, "That really stinks," even when there is no physical scent involved. Whatever the aroma is, we are living in it daily. Even our clothes and our work continue to carry the aroma after we have gone on to other things. Where there is no hint of sacrifice, our work will produce no lasting fruit.

Remember the woman who anointed Jesus? The aroma she released that filled the house came not only from the ointment but also from her sacrifice and commitment to who He was. When Jesus hung on the cross, He carried the same aroma that had touched all those who dined with him that night. The fragrance permeated them. When we live with Him, and He dines with us, we will also carry the same aroma. The works of God are complete only in the fragrance of Christ's sacrifice. Along the way, you may smell some work "for God" without the pure aroma of His Son's humility. Consider the leaders you follow and the work you do for the Lord today. What aroma do you carry?

Father, please fill me with the aroma of Your Son and His sacrifice on the cross. In resurrection power, let it spread freely through my life to draw others to You. In Jesus' name, amen.

Eph. 5:1-2   John 12:3, 24-26   Rom. 12:1-5

ALL FOR GOD'S GLORY

July 21

Therefore, whether you eat or drink, or whatever you do, do all to the glory of God.

1 Cor. 10:31

What would our lives be like if only those things that give God glory became our daily priority? The results might be surprising. If we actually do all for His glory, what would have to be eliminated? To this picture, we can then add those things we haven't had time for yet but we know He wants us to do: visit the sick or lonely; listen patiently instead of speak; acknowledge His beauty revealed even in unlikely places; finish, not just start, the assignments He gives us; stand clearly with the poor; bring our thoughts as well as our actions into line with His truth; go deep in love and worship to God. Surely the list could go on as long as eternity, and it will. If we are willing to begin in faith, He will finish what He has begun in us. In His Son, we are complete (Col. 2:6-10).

For now, as we come fully into alignment with God's will in joy, with no hesitation and wandering, straight into the path of His glory one day at a time, we know the rest will be beautiful as our Lord is revealed all in all. In Him, through Him, and to Him, our daily lives will say, "Glory!"

Father, forgive me for seeking to work for anything but Your glory. Keep me from wandering. Create in me what pleases You and follows Your heart so that all I do magnifies Your name in this place. In Jesus' name, amen.

Isa. 42:5-9   John 17:20-24   1 Pet. 4:7-16

COME AHEAD   July 22

But if we walk in the light as He is in the light, we have fellowship with one another, and the blood of Jesus Christ His Son cleanses us from all sin.

1 John 1:7

Even when we fall behind in the world's eyes, we are coming ahead in Christ. He has already walked where we walk and won the victory for all time. Since Christ has perfectly covered our imperfect ground in His blood, each step we take has already touched this victory and entered the light of God's Son. That is why we do not look back but look to Him and live in Him. To come ahead, we must look forward in faith and think forward (2 Cor. 5:7). How can we walk in His light if our minds dwell in darkness?

When we look at our circumstances, any hope of victory may seem impossible and elusive. It was the same with Jesus Christ, but He counted on what God was doing, not on what a carpenter from Nazareth could do. He saw how God, His Father, was working. So even while Christ was walking in the dust of this earth, He was already in a position of power with His Father in heaven. Following Christ, we also, even though we are still behind in struggles, are coming ahead of our present location in the power of His cross and resurrection. In this sense, we are already seated with Him in heaven, even while we still walk here in our earthly days. Move on. Come ahead in the life He has for you now!

When you stumble—not if, but when—get up and try again, because already Christ has won the victory and brought you to a new spiritual place of safety and rest, even in a storm. Christ has prepared an eternal way and a destination of power for us in His love now. No matter where you are, come ahead in Him by faith. Put the past behind you and the present under your feet, which are under the feet of Jesus Christ. Match His pace, follow His mercy, and share His strength. Look to Him, stand up, and come ahead!

Father, please move me forward in faith, so I can walk in the light of Your Son, Jesus Christ, and not look back. Change me in Your power and mercy. In Jesus' name, amen.

Eph. 2:1-10   Prov. 4:20-27   Mark 9:23-32

July 23

FOR THE FIRST TIME

Father, I come for the first time separated to You alone. I know I've come other times for other reasons; but now for the first time, I come for You and not for me. Take first place in my life, and have Your way for Your glory alone. Make me new in Christ so that I don't even recognize myself or my old familiar ways. Lead me in the new, living way in Your Son to complete in me what You have begun. For the first time, let my old chains fall off completely, and let me not drag them along to the new place You have created. For the first time, let me not look backward but forward into the eyes of My Savior, who keeps me close to His heart. For the first time, let a new song overcome my mourning for the things of the world that are left behind, which cannot satisfy. For the first time, help me see and receive beauty for the ashes I used to sift and hold. Now, I let them go to make room in my heart for Your love. Thank You for restoring my life in Yours. With my whole heart, I will seek and find You in the beauty of holiness. You are more than enough, more than all! In Jesus' name, amen.

He chose us in Him before the foundation of the world, that we should be holy and without blame before Him in love.

Eph. 1:4

Matt. 9:16-38

ALREADY WON
July 24

But this Man, after He had offered one sacrifice for sins forever, sat down at the right hand of God, from that time waiting till His enemies are made His footstool. For by one offering He has perfected forever those who are being sanctified.

Heb. 10:12-14

We cannot gain by human effort what Christ has won by His blood. Knowing He has finished the work, we can receive and cooperate with His plan. Already, it is sealed for those who believe and obey (Heb. 5:8-9). Do not refuse what He has already gained and given to you. Why run from the battle or fear the pain, when the ultimate victory is already won? Walk in that victory now, right where you are, or you will slide gradually into a defeat of your own by not receiving all Christ has won. Think on His victory even in the middle of struggle, as you live in the Holy Spirit each day (John 14:15-17). Any wounds that come to you now as you follow the Son of God are not death, because He has already conquered death, and you are sealed in His life (2 Cor. 1:19-22).

Victory comes in faith that sees our daily war already won through Jesus Christ by focusing on Him instead of the struggle. He has been there, done that, and risen above anything that would bring you down now. Instead of you, let Him do everything in confidence now as then, knowing that in God's will even today's battle has a purpose already set in victory. It's all about Him.

When the stakes are high and the fighting is fierce, still the outcome is set in your new life in Christ from this day forward. Move ahead in what He has already won. Something bigger is going on here than the mess of the moment. As you see the victory, He will give it to you as you walk right through the battle with your eyes on Him. If you look the other way to defeat, or dread chaos, or run away, He cannot give it to you because your heart is still focused on yourself, and your mind is full of fear. Trust Him. Stand and let Him fight clear through the gates into the city to reign completely. In the past, you knew Christ gave Himself for you. Now let Him give Himself to you in the middle of the struggle. Begin to see what He has already won where you are right now.

Father, I accept Your gift of life through Jesus' cross and His victory now through resurrection power working in me. By Your Holy Spirit, help me to walk in His life today. In Jesus' name, amen.

1 Cor. 15:57-58   Rom. 5:1-10   John 10:31-39

ANOINTED AND FREE   July 25

It shall come to pass in that day that his burden will be taken away from your shoulder, and his yoke from your neck, and the yoke will be destroyed because of the anointing oil.

Isa. 10:27

In Christ, the Anointed One, we are covered and made free. When kings received anointing, it was a symbol that they received a higher anointing and authority as the oil poured down upon them. When we are anointed in Christ by receiving His life in the cross, we are under a higher authority and saturated with God's power, which destroys the yoke of the world. The anointing that destroys the yoke of the oppressor is the anointing that breaks the yoke of death so that we are joined to the yoke of life in Jesus Christ. We are tied to either one or the other for eternity.

God is the only One who gives us free will, even with the yoke of Christ, which carries us in the true rest of grace (Matt. 11:27-30). A deliverer will call people to freedom and break their chains. An oppressor may talk of freedom but never takes off the chains, never allows his people free will. Instead, he keeps them chained with fear or the illusion of their control while he manipulates their self-centered desires. Other people and the ways of the world do not give us a completely free choice. Often, they give us choices with chains attached, offering plans for us based on what is best for them. Even in a democracy, we are subject to the rule of the majority, which can be misled. The only yoke that is not slavery is the yoke of the cross, where divine love finds a way out of self-serving slavery into the life of God, which moves us beyond ourselves.

No one goes through life without ties to something. Even the most independent person is chained to himself, perhaps a slave to his self-interest or fear of commitment to anything else. An ardent atheist often ends up imitating and serving the intellectual gods of this world. In Jesus, we are offered an open door beyond ourselves. To pass through, we receive the life of the Anointed One, covering us, moving in us, drawing us out of our old ways into His new life through the cross.

We can tell whether we have received this anointing by observing whether we run backward, stumbling in our old ways and clinging to them for support, or press forward into the high calling of Christ. Some prefer to keep their old chains rather than to bow before the only One who can anoint them with life. To receive the anointing of freedom that lasts forever, lay aside all else, bow before your Creator, and let truth open the door.

Father, let the pure oil of Your life in Jesus pour over me and into me so that I will run freely in Your strength and live forever in Your power. In Jesus' name, amen.

Luke 4:18-21   John 8:28-36   Rom. 8:1-2

THE AUTHOR'S AUTHORITY

July 26

The earth is the Lord's, and all its fullness, the world and those who dwell therein. For He has founded it upon the seas, and established it upon the waters.

Ps. 24:1-2

Authority, as the word implies, comes from the author. If you were the author of your life, if you generated it and wrote all its mysteries and loves and challenges, then you would have the originator's authority. Since God through Christ is our Author and Finisher, we acknowledge His full authority to complete the story. You still have a few chapters to go, and only He knows the ending (2 Cor. 3:3-5; Heb. 12:2).

Let the Author of the universe create in you what conforms to the total pattern of His plan, so that your life here matches up with the farthest galaxy and turns in His love, joining each part of the day He has created from the smallest detail to the highest beauty. If even the sparrows receive His care, you can know His eye is on you, and the Author's authority will keep you and protect you for whatever He calls you to do. Let Him write His love in your heart, His forgiveness in your will, and the rest will be easy. Only in following what God has written, do we have the light of life. Let the One who has full authority complete His work in you. He has signed the book Himself.

Father, form me in the creation You have planned in Your Son. In Your love, finish what only You can do in my life now. In Jesus' name, amen.

Matt 6:24-26   Heb. 10:15-23   Ps. 19

~~~~~~

REVEAL WHAT IS HIDDEN

Creator, only You can put all the pieces of our lives together and restore in Your power even what is hidden and unknown to us. In mercy, fix what You see and show us how to release all the pieces to You to fit with Your plan, including what we cannot see. Through Your Son's cross and resurrection, bring us out of darkness into Your glorious light. Shine Your pure truth into our brokenness and wash us, bringing everything together to match Your will. By the blood of Jesus applied to every part, release us into Your whole truth, and make us new forever in Him, made whole and complete in Your power. In Jesus' name, amen.

But the woman, fearing and trembling, knowing what had happened to her, came and fell down before Him and told Him the whole truth. And He said to her, "Daughter, your faith has made you well. Go in peace, and be healed of your affliction." While He was still speaking, some came from the ruler of the synagogue's house who said, "Your daughter is dead. Why trouble the Teacher any further?" As soon as Jesus heard the word that was spoken, He said to the ruler of the synagogue, "Do not be afraid; only believe."

Mark 5:33-36

Isa. 64:4-9

~~~~~~

BEAUTY OF GOD   July 28

Your eyes will see the King in His beauty; they will see the land that is very far off.

Isa. 33:17

There is nothing more stunning than the beauty of God's purity, the beauty of His glory, the beauty of His power, and His mercy that endures forever. The earthly version we usually want is only a small reflection of the Source, who creates in us a clean heart and renews a right spirit in us to reflect His eternal beauty that changes lives. To see God's beauty and to really look into it brings change, because in beholding Him we become open to His nature and moldable to His will. Only in God's will, do we receive healing, grace, and strength. When His face shines on us, we receive the warmth of peace in all dimensions, a peace that passes understanding (Num. 6:22-27).

No matter where you are, His beauty works and shines through all dimensions of life. Today, when the world around you may look difficult, even ugly, take a moment to search for God's beauty, both visible and invisible. Look with your spiritual eyes all around you for signs of mercy, grace, and power that the world cannot see. Even in the worst possible place, He shines. If you miss God's beauty and see only this world, you are missing most of reality. Since the Creator's reality is much more than we can see, and His beauty far greater than anything on earth, we are missing most of what's real if we look only at our mistakes and the situation around us.

In the greater reality of His beauty, we can live and move in truth. Lift your eyes to God's sacrifice in Jesus Christ and the power of His resurrection. It's for you. This beauty works physically as well as spiritually, because the power of God filled a human body with unsurpassable beauty to transform those who will see and receive all that Christ can be and do in them. His beauty can walk here, right through your life, because Jesus walked here and leads us now through the Holy Spirit.

In a very practical way, divine beauty transforms earthly things into a heavenly pattern that works new life in us. Transforming us into the image of Christ, our Creator fills us, day by day, with purifying fire and living water. Thinking about it is not enough. We must truly look to God with open hearts. As we look to Him, He will draw us further into His life and truth. Look, and let His beauty become your reality.

Father, help me look to You in Your Son today to know the truth of Your beauty that transforms my life. Make my heart ready for eternal reality. In Jesus' name, amen.

John 12:32-46   Ps. 80:7   Ps. 27:4-8

CALLED AND CHOSEN   July 29

"For many are called, but few are chosen."

Matt. 22:14

"God has chosen the foolish things of the world to put to shame the wise, and God has chosen the weak things of the world to put to shame the things which are mighty" so "that no flesh should glory in His presence." He has chosen "the things which are not, to bring to nothing the things that are" (1 Cor. 1:27,29). Even if you subtly think you are wise or well able to handle things in this world, you cannot be chosen by God. You may be called, but it is impossible to be chosen until you dwell in Christ's humility and simplicity. In the cross, Jesus became as One who is nothing in order to conquer everything that exalts itself against God. Following Him, we too must be willing to be as nothing in this world in order to reveal the life that endures forever (James 4:4-10).

You may be called—many are called and invited—but few are chosen. Few are willing to be weak, to confess their foolishness or their need, and to put on the armor, the shining garment that comes only from God, who alone wins the battle. At the wedding feast of Matthew 22, only the host could provide the wedding garment for each guest. One could not come in his own clothes, even his best robes. If we are too full of ourselves, we cannot enjoy God's banquet. Only He can give us the covering of His Son's righteousness, and by the Holy Spirit, our Creator completes His calling in our lives.

Our calling, our ministry, is His design and moves to fruition only in His power. Many are called, but few are chosen because they prefer not to follow directions, wear the humble clothes handed to them, or carry a cross. They are reluctant to qualify as poor in spirit or to identify with the unseen riches of the needy. On the other hand, if you are willing to be a fool for Christ and to acknowledge His strength, to surrender your best ability as mere foolishness in comparison to the magnificent riches of Christ, then you can be chosen for His victory. Many are called, but the only ones chosen for the team are those who recognize and humbly follow the Captain (Heb. 2:9-12).

Father, thank You for calling me to Yourself in Jesus Christ, who covers me and fills my life with amazing grace. May I be empty enough to receive Him. In Jesus' name, amen.

Matt. 22:1-14   John 15:16-19   James 3:13-18

July 30

~~~~~~

SEPARATE TRUE FROM FALSE

Lord of the harvest, only the pure seed You have separated and planted can produce good fruit. Separate the true from the false in me, and plant what You want to grow through the power of the Holy Spirit. In Jesus' name, amen.

"I indeed baptize you with water unto repentance, but He who is coming after me is mightier than I, whose sandals I am not worthy to carry. He will baptize you with the Holy Spirit and fire. His winnowing fan is in His hand, and He will thoroughly clean out His threshing floor, and gather His wheat into the barn; but He will burn up the chaff with unquenchable fire."

Matt. 3:11-12

Col. 2:8—3:4

~~~~~~

ALL THE TIME IS NOW   July 31

God is our refuge and strength, a very present help in trouble.

Ps. 46:1

God is good all the time! Because all is in His hand, all the time is now. By His power the heavens were made and the earth filled with life. Since the beginning of creation, God has not changed, nor has His power changed with time, for He creates time. A day with Him is as a thousand years, and a thousand years as a day (2 Pet. 3:8). We know what He has done in the past and what we hope for the future, but in this very hour He is fully in charge in the same magnitude of comprehensive creativity.

By His power, we are alive today and able to work, talk, and move in His life, given to us in Christ moment by moment. Even quietly by prayer, we can move mountains, whether physical or spiritual, because Jesus Christ came both physically and spiritually to walk with us (Col. 1:17; Mark 10:18-20; 1 John 3:22-24; Acts 16:25-26).

Every molecule moves by God's will, and the cycles of time fulfill their assignments according to His plan. All the time is now. What if you knew you had only one prayer left, and these moments were your last on earth? The first priority in that case should be the first priority now. What are you doing today that fits His pattern for eternity? Why worry about tomorrow and analyze yesterday? Let Him work His good purpose where you are today, as you move freely in His love. It will be far better than anything you could plan or promote. Eternity is not far off; it begins right here. In Christ, we are one with it, moving through one day at a time, carried by grace.

Father, open my heart to receive who You are now in my life. Create in me a clean heart to follow Your way today. Help me not to miss it. In Jesus' name, amen.

Matt. 4:17   2 Cor. 6:1-18   Rev. 1:7-8

PILLARS AT THE DOOR   August 1

Then he set up the pillars by the vestibule of the temple; he set up the pillar on the right and called its name Jachin, and he set up the pillar on the left and called its name Boaz. The tops of the pillars were in the shape of lilies. So the work of the pillars was finished.

1 Kings 7:21-22

At the doorway to Solomon's temple, two huge pillars were set so that all who entered would pass between them. One was named Jachin, meaning "He shall establish," and the other was Boaz, which means "in Him is strength." Even today, when we go through the open door of Christ into God's presence, we are entering in the strength He has established, not in our own strength or knowledge. Our entrance into God's kingdom comes in Christ's strength and sacrificial love in the way He has established through the cross. In obedience, we pass through it, letting Him change us.

Are we coming in His way, or do we set up pillars of our own strength in what we have established? Anyone can step into the outer court in his own strength, but entering the holy place requires not only sacrifice and cleansing but also a complete surrender to the will of God in Christ. It is His creative pattern in His Son that we follow. We can enter only by walking right through the middle of His power, right into the middle of His will, which makes all things new. What He establishes must direct us and surround us completely. There is no other entrance.

The tops of the two pillars at the temple entrance were decorated with lilies. How beautiful to decorate the height of strength with lilies that have grown in the valley! Now we can enter and pass through in the power of the risen Christ, who decorates our hearts with His beauty, even passing through the valley of the shadow of death. As we come in that beauty and strength, the Lord creates the temple of His design in us. To enter new life, we must not only look up to God but also go through in the strength of Christ's blood and resurrection power. Look up to the lilies. In God's established design, Christ is the way. Walk through in His strength.

Father, set up the pillars of Your strength in my heart so that my life becomes Your temple through the power of the Holy Spirit. Breathe in me the beauty of the lilies. Establish Your will and way at the door, and bring me through in Jesus Christ. In Jesus' name, amen.

Heb. 10:19-25   1 Cor. 3:16-23   Acts. 1:4-11

CLOSEST TO HEAVEN   August 2

But whoever keeps His word, truly the love of God is perfected in him. By this we know that we are in Him. He who says he abides in Him ought himself also to walk just as He walked.

1 John 2:5-6

The closest we can get to heaven on earth is to do God's will right now. It can't be put off, because the journey has already begun, and there's a destination approaching sooner than we think. Imagine the very best possible life here in this world, with every luxury and success on human terms. No matter how good, it falls short of what God has planned for you on His terms. To walk a little closer to heaven today, move into the center of His will.

Each step we take in this world, even the little steps, moves us either closer to our Creator or away from His plan. For those who are unsure, the journey becomes a mixed-up shuffle. Progress comes when we quit trying to straddle the difficult choices and step out clearly into His grace. One day at a time, walk confidently in the hidden beauty and the fullness of His power. Don't try to see around the corners, because in choosing Him you already have everything. Though difficult, in walking His way, you will go far beyond where your own strength could take you even if you knew the future.

In love, take a step closer to God. Come closer to heaven on earth than you have ever been before. Walk into the center of His will as best you can know it today, even one small step at a time, and He will show you the rest and the future path that keeps shining and moving on, even through a dark night. The way to heaven starts right here where you are living. Each step moves you either a little closer to paradise or farther down the dark stairs of self-focus, where the Son doesn't shine. Turn to walk with Him, and one day you'll walk into heaven.

Father, direct my steps into the love of Your Son and move me into Your plan for my life. Help me to leave my sins behind and come home free. In Jesus' name, amen.

Prov. 4:18-23   Matt. 10:7-8   James 2:10-18

CREATE IN ME   August 3

Create in me a clean heart, O God, and renew a steadfast spirit within me.

Ps. 51:10

When we ask God to change us, He will generate new life, not simply improve the old one. The old is not redirected but actually passes away. All things, not just some, become new. When the Potter takes us in His hands, He touches and shapes every part, making each side turn together on the wheel of His will, until the clay is no longer its own but the image of what lives in the Potter's mind and heart. What the Potter sees is what gradually takes shape in the clay. Often, we say we want change, but we're really just talking about a little adjustment here and there in what we see, according to our image, leaving the rest of what we're doing intact. Sometimes, we don't want to see what God sees in us, but He can change what we cannot and make us completely new.

Our Creator is calling for a new creation in Jesus Christ. When we pray, are we trying to remodel certain areas of our lives and substitute one thing for another we can do better; or will we open our souls to the new creation that only God can finish? Consider how your Creator can completely remake, not just readjust, your life today to reveal His Son in you. Give Him some time with no limitations. Let Him have total access to every area, and you will be surprised by the fresh power of a surrendered life that truly follows the Lamb of God.

Living that life is a creative process, full of the light of heaven. Even now, it transforms us into what we will become: children of God through His Son (John 1:12-13). Still in clay vessels, we begin to move and walk in His light, even through the dirt of this world. From above, the light creates fruit in good ground with the help of the Spirit's wind and the rain of the Living Word. By itself, our good ground, even rearranged, would produce nothing more than sophisticated dirt. In His hands, with the incorruptible seed of the Lamb of God, this earth yields a new crop, a beautiful harvest, and a vessel full of praise. Today, let the Lord create in you a clean heart, full of the fruit of heaven.

Father, forgive me for telling You how to change my life. Create in me what pleases You. Wash me, and make me new. My heart's desire is for Your will to be done. In Jesus' name, amen.

John 3:3-5   2 Cor. 5:14-21   Rev. 14:4-5

August 4

LAY ASIDE

Lord of all, today I lay aside all my cares to say I love You above all. My problems and gains are nothing compared to Your beauty and compassion. Your majesty and holiness far outshine anything I can do or think today, even if everything went perfectly. I seek Your presence and come with my whole heart to worship You in spirit and in truth. My greatest accomplishment any day—past, present, or future—is simply to live another day in Your love, which swallows up all creation in eternal victory. Take these things that worry me and do with them whatever You will in Your time. Your reign is my only gain, Your cross my only hope, and Your new life more than any loss. In loving You, I will truly grow, expanding even in pain, climbing even through dirt into the beautiful fruit of Your nature living in me. Lord of all, I now lay aside whatever keeps me from loving You more, and in doing so, I find everything. In Jesus' name, amen.

Let us lay aside every weight, and the sin which so easily ensnares us, and let us run with endurance the race that is set before us.

Heb. 12:1

Luke 5:3-32

229

DISCERN TO LIVE   August 5

Then you shall again discern between the righteous and the wicked, between one who serves God and one who does not serve Him.

Mal. 3:18

Many of us think of discernment as an extra, an added ability that will improve our spiritual lives, but it is essential to the main root of our spiritual lives (Mal. 3:16—4:3). Without it, we are left with neither root nor branch, having chosen seeds of disobedience and subtle falsehood. Even seemingly good things that grow tall with interesting fruit will be uprooted if the Father did not plant them (Matt. 15:13).

Do not become attached to the false plants or allow them to grow unseen in your life, for whatever is clinging to them will be destroyed. Through prayer, discern to live true to the Lord of life. Come out and be separate. Death follows the enemy who sowed tares in the Master's field. Don't become entangled with the weeds or accept their fruit, which leads to unity with them.

Whatever questions arise must be lined up against the eternal answer of God's Son. Whatever confronts you now, place it on the cross of Christ. If it doesn't accept Christ's cross or fit that pattern of sacrificial love from above, it is leading you astray into a selfish end. What may look good on the surface may be covering up poison underneath. Root out whatever is trying to take hold in your life that is not one with the cross and the resurrection life of Christ and is quietly producing His fruit. God has given you eyes to see and a heart to know Him personally. To be one with the true Vine, you can't be united to the fruit of anything else. Take time to ask for clear vision and a clean heart. Discern to live in the Son.

Father, cleanse my heart and open my eyes to see Your truth now in my life. Take away what is not pleasing to You, and put in what produces fruit for Your glory alone. In Jesus' name, amen.

Isa. 5:18-24   Heb. 4:12-13   John 7:16-18, 24

WHOSE AUTHORITY?   August 6

And Jesus came and spoke to them, saying, "All authority has been given to Me in heaven and on earth."

Matt. 28:18

Our lives operate according to someone's authority. When God is in charge, our lives are open to His power and provision. When we're in charge, our scope of possibilities is narrowed to what only we can produce. Much of contemporary culture wants us to believe that we are the source of authority and power. This is like trying to power the lights of a house on a tiny, expiring AA battery. Our frustration increases as needs exceed our natural ability, but we keep believing the lie that we are our own authority and say we'll have to change the house, downgrade its wiring and fixtures, and plan to use only one small light at a time. That way we're in charge, even though the results are dim, far below the capacity of the original design.

Since the houses of our lives are fully wired for power from a huge generator provided by the original Creator who runs all lights everywhere, not to mention central air and heat for the universe, it is clear that hooking up to our Creator will bring us much brighter results. Only when we submit to God's authority do all the lights come on in our lives and those around us. Obedience flips the switch.

Our Creator has much more in mind for us than we could ever design for ourselves. Christ paid the price for all we will need, and the connections are complete in our lives now through the Holy Spirit. The only condition is that we repent and let Him turn the switch that He has given us. In other words, we must give up our own power and lay our will aside. Our consent to the Creator also recognizes the price He, not we, paid to connect us to His power. When the original connection was broken for everyone, only the One who designed the whole system could fix it.

The question of authority is key when Satan tempts us, as we see in his temptation of Christ in the wilderness (Luke 4:1-13). The enemy's first suggestion is to use God's power to meet our fleshly needs: turn the stones to bread. This would alter reality according to our desires, making our flesh the final authority. The second temptation is to gain earthly power by worshipping Satan. This denies the reality of God's authority and the worship of God alone. Finally, just as the enemy suggested Christ force God to save Him and so make people believe, he may tempt us to try to manipulate God's authority to impress others for what seems good yet makes human approval our god. We fall when we do not accept God's authority over all. Only He can turn on the lights forever.

Father, I accept Your authority in all of my life. Please turn on the lights now. Neither my flesh, nor the world, nor the devil has the final authority. You do. In Jesus' name, amen.

Heb. 5:8-9   Matt. 26:39   Phil. 2:8-13

August 7

~~~~~~

THE FACE OF THE SON

Father, shine in the face of Your Son revealed in us so that others can see Him working here today. Live out Your "Yes" and "Amen" in Christ in us, as we say "Yes" to You even in these difficult places. What is impossible for us is possible for You. Help us to not hesitate but to see clearly and to walk in the light of Your Son and the truth of Your covenant into the future You have already completed for Your glory. In the name of Jesus Christ, amen.

For it is the God who commanded light to shine out of darkness, who has shone in our hearts to give the light of the knowledge of the glory of God in the face of Jesus Christ. But we have this treasure in earthen vessels, that the excellence of the power may be of God and not of us.

2 Cor. 4:6-7

2 Cor. 1:3-12, 17-22

~~~~~~

EVEN UP

For it pleased the Father that in Him [Christ] all the fullness should dwell, and by Him to reconcile all things to Himself, by Him, whether things on earth or things in heaven, having made peace through the blood of His cross. And you, who once were alienated and enemies in your mind by wicked works, yet now He has reconciled in the body of His flesh through death, to present you holy, and blameless, and above reproach in His sight—if indeed you continue in the faith.

Col. 1:19-23

To even up whatever has gone crooked requires a look up, a look to a higher standard than looking down provides. When our lives are out of balance, tilted into darkness, only the light from above can even things up. We cannot push them up from below or ask others to even our load with some of their darkness. There is nothing anyone else can do to help straighten out what human hearts mess up. The problem will be evened up and balanced only when it evens up in God's truth coming from a higher source, a higher love (Luke 22:20). In prayer, we are connected to that love, and as we obey what He tells us in prayer, crooked things begin to melt into the shape of His will, not ours, so that a lasting solution, deep reconciliation, and true peace are possible.

We've wasted a lot of time trying to even things up by looking down, working down, and pulling down in our own strength. It's time to look up and ask up. Christ comes to even us up and break the gravity of our sin, straightening out what is crooked with the same power that created the universe. God is drawing everything up through our Savior, as He lifts us. We can't straighten it out on our own slant until we let go of what pulls us down and take hold of His hand. Let go. Take hold of Christ. Let Him raise you up with Him in faith even now.

Father, I let go of the weight pulling me down in my own strength, and I take hold of Your love and mercy in Jesus Christ. Even it all up in Your power. In Jesus' name, amen.

Phil. 3:12-14   John 6:37   Ps. 37:1-11, 23-24

COPIES

August 9

Then God said, "Let Us make man in Our image, according to Our likeness."

Gen. 1:26

Created in the image of God, we are like flat copies of the original full life of heaven. Though made to be like Him, we often choose instead to be full of ourselves, as Adam and Eve chose their own way over His. Without God, we are like a photograph or a paper drawing of a three-dimensional, living, breathing person. The copy is similar but lifeless. You see hints of the original, but it is not the same. The secret of eternal life is that the copies here can be made more like the original through Jesus Christ (John 6:47-57). The Son of God became human to bring us into God's fullness.

Although we are lifeless in ourselves, we can be filled with the original in multidimensional grace. We are made complete in Him so that we can move from our dead mirage into the living reality of God's family. Of course, we are free to choose less life and remain flat copies. What we see in this world is a shadowy reflection, a perishable version, and a temporary drawing of the original eternity of God's plan for our lives. To be filled with God's life by adoption, we must become one with God through Christ in His fullness.

In Christ's cross and resurrection, God's plan is alive in a way that carries us beyond earthly dimensions. Otherwise, we throw our existence into disposable copies, working busily for a short time but ending up in the trash bin of sin. He lifts us out in His Son. Sometimes we see a little hint of the original here and there, but we never find a clear opening into it until we accept God's way of transformation. That way is the cross.

When Christ is lifted up, we can become one with His life. Unified with God's mercy in the cross and Christ's resurrection, we live in union with Him, not just in heaven but beginning here. Even now, our copies can be transformed in this world by laying down their old existence and choosing to be changed in His light. Through the Holy Spirit, Christ's power brings us into the full pattern of our Creator.

Through adoption, as we cry out, "Abba, Father," He will take us where we cannot go on our own—if we allow Him. Sometimes we try to become dead copies of the world instead of children of His divine nature, regenerated and accepted in His Son. Whose copy are you? Lay down your old life, that faint copy, and receive the Master who makes you one with Him forever.

Father, make me one with You through Your Son, born again in the power of His cross and resurrection working in me now. In Jesus' name, amen.

John 1:1-5   Col. 1:26-29   1 Cor. 15:22, 47-49

EVERYTHING WORKING

August 10

"Without Me you can do nothing."

John 15:5

According to how much we let God do to solve our problems, He is either all in all, or He's a part in a part. As long as we hang onto and control some part of our lives or the problem before us, it's not all in His hand. To have everything working in the direction of God's will, there's not one inch of it that can be subject to our will until our will is perfectly lost in His will. In His kingdom, total release is not partial. Our relationship is complete, not compartmentalized.

That's where I strayed. In my eagerness to solve everything, I handed God only a part of it. I wanted to see how well He would do with that part before risking the whole thing to Him, or as some say, the whole enchilada complete with sauce. Hungry and hurried to solve it all myself, I've still got enchilada sauce all over my hands and a piece of the thing on my fork. An embarrassing mess! This life is His plate, His meal, His table, and His house. How is He all in all if I don't let Him have all of me and wash me?

When we seek Him, He will feed us with the living bread of heaven (John 6:48-58). He will also multiply what is given to Him in this world to feed others (Luke 9:12-17). The only way to have everything working is for God to be everything in us. Wait on Him, serve Him with love, and everything else will follow.

Father, forgive me for hanging onto what is forever Yours. Take it all, and make it new. Change me, according to Your purpose. In Jesus' name, amen.

Ps. 81:8-16   Mark 14:35-38   Luke 9:18-20

August 11

~~~~~~

GENTLE SHEPHERD

O Father, bring me to the place in You where I have no want because I am satisfied in You, where my paths are full of Your righteousness and my will ready to rest in Yours. Make me able to yield, to lie down in the green pastures of Your presence and not wander off into my own desert. Refresh me with the still waters of Your peace. Restore my soul. May the strength of Your living water flow quietly through me, carrying me through the valley of the shadow of death. With each step, I depend on the strength of Your rod and Your staff to destroy the enemy, to guide and to discipline me here, to keep me whole and perfect for Your purpose so that I dwell in the Father's house, forgiven, all the days of my life. Even in the presence of my enemies, may I see the table prepared before me and eat of Your life in the bread and wine of the new covenant, in the new creation of the God of Abraham, Isaac, and Jacob. In Your gift of salvation, I receive the blood and the broken body of the Lamb of God, the Son of God, the Son of Man, who died for me and rose again. In You, my earthen cup runs over with the power of resurrection. Anoint my head with the oil of gladness and wisdom in You, O God my Savior. Each day, as You call me by name, I will come in the strength of Your joy. O Father, trusting in Your Son, I will walk in Him to You. In Jesus' name, amen.

The Lord is my shepherd; I shall not want. He makes me to lie down in green pastures; He leads me beside the still waters. He restores my soul; He leads me in the paths of righteousness for His name's sake.

Ps. 23:1-3

Isa. 53

~~~~~~

THE CREATOR WHO COMES
August 12

You are all sons of God through faith in Christ Jesus. . . . And because you are sons, God has sent forth the Spirit of His Son into your hearts, crying out, "Abba, Father!"

Gal. 3:26; 4:6

As God's children, we are created to call out for an answer. Call out to your Father, who will answer you with true life. He is the only One with that answer! The Creator of everything cares about everyone individually and knows each one intimately, even each memory, each dream. Remember that He made them and you out of nothing by His power alone. He will answer the voice He has made and the cry of your heart in Christ. Something new still comes, and you are being created as His child to walk in what God has already designed. Trust for today that this is true forever. Live open to what is first true in God's plan, instead of what others do or want from you.

Hope when all hope is lost in the One who comes here and comes again. Start looking for Him even in the darkness that gives way to dawn. Find the Son who touched you and made a way to follow Him, the Bright and Morning Star. His truth keeps you in His love through the darkness and brings you out on the other side into something new. Ask, seek, and knock, and you will receive and find, and the door will be opened that no man can shut. Then you will have come all the way in God's power and love, as He comes for you. Meet Him there in prayer, and be ready to move from prayer into action. That is what He does when He comes.

Father, thank You for coming in Your Son so I can come to You. Create in me a clean heart, and open my eyes to see what I have never seen before. In Jesus' name, amen.

Matt. 7:7-12   Matt. 1:20-23   Rom. 8:15-20

JUST A LITTLE   August 13

"And he said to him, 'Well done, good servant; because you were faithful in a very little, have authority over ten cities.'"

Luke 19:17

Just a little trust goes a long way. Don't wait for a lot of faith or understanding. Don't wait for the situation to improve. Just a little faith now, even as small as a mustard seed, can produce astounding results when it is planted and simply given to the Creator. The less we depend on ourselves, the more we will depend on Him to accomplish what only His divine nature can create in us.

If we keep our seeds in a comfortable jar to study or to contemplate each Sunday, nothing much will happen. If we say we need more faith and so keep putting more seeds into the jar, still nothing will grow. If one day, we take out one small seed and plant it, more can be produced than any jar will hold. When we are willing to let go, the harvest increases. In His direction, one step of faith multiplies into what He can do, where He can go, what His touch can accomplish.

One step can begin the process and make a turn into His unlimited potential. Don't hold back because you have just a little faith, just a little love, or just a little hope. The key is to let our Savior multiply what you do have. Then you will receive more as you let Him do more. Much happens when we are less in charge. Yes, it pays to be organized, but the first step in organization in His kingdom is to let Him move first and organize you according to His plan. We cannot organize God. He can do more with just a little given completely to Him than we can do with a lot on our own. Become small in your own eyes, and let God be as big as He really is. In that reality, He begins to multiply what is released to Him. It's already His field. Just a little trust releases the harvest.

Father, make me small enough to let You be as big as You really are. Make me faithful in the little things that lead to more than I can know or do. Multiply Your truth in me. In Jesus' name, amen.

John 5:6-8   Matt. 17:18-21   John 3:30-36

DIRECT CONTACT   August 14

"But the hour is coming, and now is, when the true worshipers will worship the Father in spirit and truth; for the Father is seeking such to worship Him."

John 4:23

Fellowship with our Creator comes only through direct contact. Are we so wired electronically, that we cannot hear God's still, small voice directly? Has our work for Him become a goal in itself? Some want to do things for God so much they have no time for even one hour resting in His presence in prayer. It's impossible to make direct contact with God through Christ when we constantly depend on other things to bring us closer to Him. Programs and gadgets, music, the beauty of art and nature, uplifting words from others, and detailed study of Scripture all have their place, but they must come after the Creator Himself. Unless we first spend time with the Lord alone, quietly, humbly, not distracted by any other good things, even church activities, our spiritual life will have no real foundation for growth. Yes, we can find God in church, in serving others, or even outdoors, but unless there is a private place for Him to dwell inside us, those outside encounters become shallow and have no root to produce fruit that lasts.

The root of your relationship with God is not in other things but in His love for you poured out through Christ directly into your heart. This relationship gives meaning to all the other "spiritual" things you do. It is the only source of true worship. The light of His presence shines in those who have allowed Him to touch them with His Spirit as they invite Him into the center of their lives. God has created us with all the equipment we need to receive Him. In the Holy Spirit, we can wait on God, commune with Him alone, and dine with Him, enjoying the beauty of His presence (Rev. 3:20). Then we are ready to invite any others He calls and to share His life with them at the table. Filled to overflowing, we are also ready to obey and move in His kingdom.

As the inner love God has given us is expressed outwardly, everything else begins to shine. The lights come on only when the switch makes contact. Studying the switch or singing to it does no good unless there is direct contact. Through the blood of His Son, Jesus Christ, God has made contact and opened a way for us to come directly into His presence. In repentance and surrender to His will, we can receive His touch of grace directly. Since the fall of Adam and Eve, the Lord has been looking for people who will not hide from His presence. Are you open to His touch today?

Father, open me to Your presence in Jesus Christ so I can know You directly, not through my efforts and gadgets, but through Your grace. In Jesus' name, amen.

Ps. 51:7-17   John 5:39-40   Matt. 9:18-29

~~~~~~

THIS SWORD CUTS FREE

Father, let the sharp sword of Your Living Word cut me free from fear, free from the bondage of this world, free from pride, and free from all diseases of body and soul. Penetrate to the core of my idea of myself and my seeking to please others, and free me to please You above all. Work in me the complete separation of light from darkness, clean from unclean, and holy from unholy, so that my heart will be pure for you and ready for Your purpose. With Your sword, come now and live in me. Make my body Your temple, and drive out the money changers and whatever is in me that would barter or compromise Your holiness. Let me worship You in spirit and in truth. May Your sword, sharp and shining with truth, cut me free from all the lies that entangle and hinder my running the race already won in Your grace. This sword that You have first worked in me is the same one You will use to defeat my enemies within and without. Firm in Your Word, I will watch as You slay them before my eyes, and I will shout with the victory You have won. This is a sword not just to be studied, but also to be worked in and through each day's problems so that Your power is released in us now. To those who submit to the fine edges of its truth, this sword releases Your life and brings every rough desire into alignment with Your will. Probe my excuses. Pierce my facade and rule my life. Open the veil that has covered the bride for Your Son. In Jesus' name, amen.

For the word of God is living and powerful, and sharper than any two-edged sword, piercing even to the division of soul and spirit, and of joints and marrow, and is a discerner of the thoughts and intents of the heart.

Heb. 4:12

Acts 2:32-39

~~~~~~

FIRST

August 16

"Do not be afraid; I am the First and the Last."

Rev. 1:17

Since Christ is the Shepherd and we are the sheep, we must let Him go first. Some of His flock expect the Shepherd to follow them. They stumble over each other, bleating loudly, as their Shepherd is relegated to a lesser role and told to keep in the background. In fact, they are going nowhere fast. In Christ, we can go much farther and faster by following His directions, because our Shepherd not only knows the way, but He also is the way, the truth, and the life. And He was there first. If we go first, asking Him to please us and give us what we want, we have no direction and will blindly fall into the ditch of our own irrelevance.

From the beginning, Christ takes us exactly where He has already been, where we can live with Him and in Him. At the last, when we arrive, He closes the gate and circles us in His protection. All things are complete in Him, our all in all, our Alpha and Omega. Our Savior first loves us before we learn to walk in His love. Our Master first serves us before He calls us to serve others. His sacrifice precedes and heals all of our suffering through His finished work on the cross. Through the power of His resurrection, Jesus Christ is the same yesterday, today, and forever; so wherever we are, He is first.

The Prince of Peace can calm our storms whether in the past, present, or future because He was there before the beginning, before the water, winds, and clouds that confront us now were created. Long after they are gone, He will still be Lord. Is there anywhere you are trying to go today without Him first? Consider your options. In which direction would Jesus take the lead? If He cannot be first in the way you take, then that path will lead you nowhere. It simply doesn't exist in the reality of eternity. Go where He is always first.

O Lord God, guide me into the center of Your will first, as You lead all the way. I let go of my own plans and directions. I'm going where You're going, Your way. In the name of Jesus, the Bright and Morning Star, amen.

John 10:1-4, 30   Matt. 6:31-33   Mark 12:28-30

THE BATTLE   August 17

"Then all this assembly shall know that the Lord does not save with sword and spear; for the battle is the Lord's, and He will give you into our hands."

1 Sam. 17:47

Who's in charge of our daily battle? If we're wondering why nothing is improving, take a look at who is giving the commands. If the battle is the Lord's, it's not ours to direct and own. The one to whom the battle belongs is the one to whom the victory belongs. If the battle depends on us, then the victory belongs to us and the real victory of God's righteousness is set aside. But in our battle today, God owns the victory, and we share in it by surrendering to Him, waiting on Him, and praising and following Him, even as He conquers the enemy all around us and within us. The battle is the Lord's because the victory is His alone, and we are hidden with Christ in God (Col. 3:1-4). We share in the victory because we are His, and He has conquered our sin within as well as our enemies without.

If we are claiming the battle and trying to fight in our own strength, we will miss what only He can do. The battle is won according to His rules, not human effort and ingenuity. Therefore, position yourself humbly in line with His will and follow His commands. Remove whatever stands in the way of His pure light and power. Get out of the way, and let Him fight freely in your life.

When God is acknowledged for who He really is, when He is fully in charge in your life, then the battle is turned, and victory is in sight. You will be surprised at what starts to move and change in your life. Instead of complaining, there will be a shout of victory even before you see it, because you know He is in charge. Live each day, your whole life, ready for the winner's crown that you will lay at His feet. The battle belongs to the Lord now! When your life shows you know this, the battle is already won, and you will taste the victory of His new creation.

Father, I step aside and acknowledge Your power to win the battle here. The victory is already Yours. Take my situation in Your hands, and unlock Your purpose and Your peace in my life. In Jesus' name, amen.

2 Chron. 20:12-22   Ps. 46:4-11   John 5:19-20

A FRESH LOOK   August 18

"While the earth remains, seedtime and harvest, cold and heat, winter and summer, and day and night shall not cease."

Gen. 8:22

What works to produce life in one season does not always work for the next season. Summer's warmth in the middle of winter would ruin the next crop and stunt its growth. Following God's creative pattern, each life unfolds in a unique, unrepeatable beauty for its time. For good fruit, something new must be allowed to happen within the Creator's order. Leaves will not be the same size in the same position on all the branches where they were last year. Nor do they choose the time of their own unfolding. Some of us are stuck in problems because we think of them in old terms based on old seasons instead of in terms of the new season that only God can produce.

This year's grapes don't plan their location, their ripening, or their flavor. In fact, they don't want to go through winter at all, but they hold on and stay united to the Vine, concentrating more on that connection than on their own plans. Often, we see some problem and think about what to do based on what we've done before. God's solution may require something entirely new, something beyond our ability.

It's not so much what you can or should do or what other people should do, but what God can do in the long run. He always does a new thing, sometimes waiting to do a new thing until we let go of our old things and seasons.

Is your life a treadmill of human control? If you're constantly thinking of what you must do to fix everything, perhaps God is waiting for you to get out of the way so He can fix it and bring you forward in His power. Get off the treadmill of your own will. Then He will have something for you to do, but it will be entirely new. Our lives are moving toward a goal, and our minds cannot grasp it. Circumstances, seasons, and opportunities will change beyond what we can see, producing new life according to God's purpose (1 Pet. 1:18-25).

Take a fresh look at your current situation and let Him do all He has in mind. Resting in the peace of His fruitful pattern, focus more on your connection to Jesus Christ than on your ability to make things happen. Get off the treadmill, and get into the Vine. New fruit is coming.

Father, gently I place my life in Your hands to unfold in the beauty of Jesus Christ. Forgive me for trying to fix things that only You can make new in Him. In Jesus' name, amen.

Matt. 9:16-17   Jer. 17:5-10   John 15:4

August 19

LISTEN AND KNOW

Father, help me to be still and know that You are God before I speak. May I be more interested in Your love than in saying what I need. My prayers are often lists, sometimes pleas, sometimes praise, and sometimes worry wheels of self-concern. Forgive me for doing most of the talking. Now I will listen before speaking. When I take in Your Word, I will open my heart to hear. When others come to me with their needs, I will listen before helping. Sometimes the greatest gift I can give them is not what I have to say but letting them say what is in their hearts. When I see Your beauty in unexpected places, I will listen for Your still, small voice. When trouble comes, I will hope in what You say, not in what I can say. My past approach was to study, to serve, and to strive to know, but now, finally, I am ready to listen and simply be to the praise of Your glory. Only in listening will I be able to truly know You and follow Your revelation not only of the path ahead but also of Your presence with me, walking here each day. My listening is for more than information; it is also to draw near to You, and then I will know all the rest. In quiet obedience, I will hear You and know Your heart. My best answer is Your will; my best knowledge, Your love. In Jesus' name, amen.

"It is the Spirit who gives life; the flesh profits nothing. The words that I speak to you are spirit, and they are life."

John 6:63

Luke 10:38-42   Eccl. 5:1-7

DYING TO LIVE   August 20

He has delivered us from the power of darkness and conveyed us into the kingdom of the Son of His love, in whom we have redemption through His blood, the forgiveness of sins. He is the image of the invisible God, the firstborn over all creation.

Col. 1:13-15

In our natural world, we usually think of life preceding death, but in a spiritual sense, death must precede life. The same occurs as a seed falls into the ground (John 12:24-26). On the cross, Christ died to conquer our sin, to erase it, and then He rose again to bring us into His life. For us to live spiritually, the old nature must completely die so that we can be born again of water and the Spirit. The flesh profits nothing in the long run unless it gives way to the power of the Holy Spirit (John 3:5-8). Better sooner than later. Each day, we die to our own wills so that we can live in God's will, which brings us into the power of His eternal life even now (Eph. 1:17-21).

There is no other way. By our own wills we cannot drag our fleshly life into God's kingdom. However, through the cross, His grace can subdue our carnal will, bless our flesh and our spirits, renewing them after the image of His Son now, and refresh us and all creation with resurrection power in His way, in His time. That time is after accepting the cross of Christ and after a death to self has occurred and our human wills have been set aside so that new wine can flow into us from the Vine, the Son of God.

In the depth of night, He appears as the Bright and Morning Star (Rev. 22:16). Emptiness is the beginning of fullness. As we bow down in humility before the King of Kings, He can raise us up in His power. To repent is to turn from our power to His, to let go completely of our own strength so that God can graft us into the Vine of His choosing, rooted in the light of divine truth and reaching to heaven. Each day, something in our lives should speak of our death to this world and our life eternal in Christ, beginning now. If there is no worldly death, neither the cross nor Jesus' life is visible to others.

Father, I accept the cross of Christ and the power of His resurrection. May both be clearly seen in my life. In Jesus' name, amen.

Luke 9:18-26   Gal. 5:16-26   Gal. 6:14-15

FERTILE TEARS   August 21

Those who sow in tears shall reap in joy. He who continually goes forth weeping, bearing seed for sowing, shall doubtless come again with rejoicing, bringing his sheaves with him.

Ps. 126:5-6

If you're working for God, your tears are fertile. The tears you sow now, if you plant them in the Lord and give them to Him, will bring a harvest much more than could grow without the tears. While you go forth weeping, the key is to bear God's seed for sowing. Notice the harvest does not come from weeping alone, but to those who continue sowing while they are weeping. Sorrow and bitterness alone produce nothing. But turned toward heaven's purpose, sorrow produces more than worldly happiness which is turned toward selfish ends. When the tears are for repentance, prayer, release from old bonds, and from suffering and laboring long in His will, they are fertile tears.

What is sown in weeping produces more growth than seed planted in some dry soil that has never known suffering or regret. Without tears, the ground becomes hard under the print of human accomplishment, encrusted with self-satisfaction. Often we prefer things to stay dry and comfortable, rather than risk the richer crop that trouble brings and tears moisten. If we never cry the first tears, will we ever find the deep joy of the fruit those tears would water?

With much turmoil, hard ground is broken up and deep places exposed. Forgiveness breaks up the old clods and stony places of self-will. Then when the sky darkens and the rain comes, the hope of life hidden deep in the earth rejoices at the spiritual light in that water of suffering carried clear to the depths in God's will. Tears soak in much farther than we can see, making once dry ground amazingly fruitful. Even now, our repentance, our release of all into God's hands, and our quiet tears are changing the inner landscape of what will later become fields for His harvest. What are you watering today? And what seed are you sowing?

Father, You have seen my tears. Let them water what is planted for Your purpose to produce a good harvest in Your kingdom. In Jesus' name, amen.

Gal. 6:7-9   2 Kings 20:5   John 11:32-37

August 22

YOURS NOW

Father, make us Yours now. Bring us out of the shadows. Forgive us for wanting to belong to ourselves or anyone else but You. Grow us up into Christ, into the fullness of His stature through the cross and the resurrection so that His light will shine through us now and produce fruit for You. We belong to You first. Any other way will not produce life. From the sacrifice of Christ working in us today, generate Your life in the very center of our lives. Let the fire of Your love burn here and turn us from the past and our fear of the future so that Your Spirit can live in us fully today, with the bright fruits of righteousness in Jesus Christ. He is the firstfruits of Your kingdom, and He brings us with Him, unified and grafted into the Vine. In the past, we've been partially Yours as we walked in our old ways and worried about the future with divided hearts. Remove our partiality and make us whole, mature, settled, and pure, established on the Cornerstone, whom the builders of the partial have rejected. Set us fully with Him in Your will, all of one accord with You. Father, You know whose we have been in the past. We are fully Yours now. Fill us with the life of Your Son. In Jesus' name, amen.

"By this My Father is glorified, that you bear much fruit; so you will be My disciples. As the Father loved Me, I also have loved you; abide in my love."

John 15:8-9

John 17:10-21

PARTAKERS   August 23

Grace and peace be multiplied to you in the knowledge of God and of Jesus our Lord, as His divine power has given to us all things that pertain to life and godliness, through the knowledge of Him who called us by glory and virtue, by which have been given to us exceedingly great and precious promises, that through these you may be partakers of the divine nature, having escaped the corruption that is in the world through lust.

2 Pet. 1:2-4

To partake of Christ's divine nature, we must receive Him personally by faith, receiving His life and surrendering to God's way. We cannot partake through a human design, our good intentions, accumulated knowledge, improved technology and media, or through someone else's experience. He is not offering information or a technique, but Himself—not instructions so we can work, but His presence working through us.

God's Word says we are partakers, not studiers, or explainers, or organizers of Christ's divine nature revealed to us. It is easier to study than to actually partake. Participating in His life indicates we are one with Him, with His love, with both His power and His suffering. Obedience to His Word is the key to receiving His life now. Then He will do the explaining and organize our efforts according to the divine design that matches His nature.

When reading God's Word, partake to the point of change. Apply all of its fresh truth to your life. If we partake, then He can use us in His design. We do not participate in His power by trying to use Him according to our design. This is the danger in being a member of a human organization instead of a member of Christ. We cannot partake of an institution or a well-designed project and receive the life that comes only through the person of Jesus Christ. To participate in His life, we must receive His divine nature. Otherwise, we partake of human ability and information instead of who He is now.

A project, a ministry, a community, or a plan is empty without the person whose life empowers it and directs everything according to His will. As the Vine, His presence alone gives us new wine. The life in the seed of the gospel depends on the life in the person of Christ living in the members of His body, the church. He changes them from the inside out; thus, He can do more in them than they can ever do alone. Only the divine life in the seed can produce both the strong branches and the full harvest.

Father, forgive me for merely studying You and thinking about You instead of receiving Your life in Christ. Help me to partake of His divine nature and to live in Your full power. In Jesus' name, amen.

John 15:1-7   Col. 1:27-29   John 6:57

DAVID WAS READY   August 24

O God, You are my God; early will I seek You; my soul thirsts for You; my flesh longs for You in a dry and thirsty land where there is no water. So I have looked for you in the sanctuary, to see Your power and Your glory. Because Your lovingkindness is better than life, my lips shall praise You.

Ps. 63:1-3

David was ready. As he watched the sheep, he carried a staff, a sling, some food, and an instrument of praise to God. He was always alert to the needs of his flock but also always alert to the presence of his Lord, who was his Shepherd, guiding him through the pastures, hills, and valleys. David was ready. He was called a man after God's own heart. In what way was that true? He was as ready to sing to God and to commune with God, as he was to ask help from God and to work for Him.

On a daily basis, he was as ready to praise as he was to fight, as ready to follow God's directions for his own life as he was to lead his little flock to the next pasture or, later, his armies to the next battle. David was ready to confront danger because he was strengthened and refreshed by God's presence in the green pastures, and he drank deeply of the still waters of God's Holy Spirit.

Sometimes David the shepherd had to discipline his sheep and get them back in line, but because he was after God's heart, he also was ready to let God discipline him and bring him back when he strayed. David was ready. He was a mighty warrior and a magnificently successful king because he learned first to worship God, to magnify God's majesty and to seek His face. He was after God's heart more than His power.

David wanted a relationship with God more than he wanted a reward from God. Therefore, God rewarded him with majesty. David was ready to be used by the Lord because David knew intimately the only source of his blessing and strength. He was more interested in dwelling in God's house forever than in enjoying an earthly kingdom. In his own imperfection, David was all the more aware of God's perfection and beauty. David was ready for the coming Savior, who later said, "My sheep hear My voice, and I know them, and they follow Me" (John 10:27). Daily, he listened for God's voice and followed. David was ready. Are you?

Father, make me ready to praise You and to seek Your face so that I will know Your voice and follow You. Make me able both to sing to Your glory and to conquer a giant. In Jesus' name, amen.

Ps. 27   Ps. 23   Ps. 24

FULLY DESIGNED
August 25

Then Jesus called a little child to Him, set him in the midst of them, and said, "Assuredly, I say to you, unless you are converted and become as little children, you will by no means enter the kingdom of heaven. Therefore whoever humbles himself as this little child is the greatest in the kingdom of heaven."

Matt. 18:2-4

Even small and weak, we are already fully designed to worship God and to do what He plans for us to accomplish. Our part is to live out the design that our Creator has already set in motion for all time. By our own means, if we try to add or subtract something from the original design, we'll miss eternity. A child of God does not have or control what only the Father can give him. Eve's problem was that she wanted to add something God did not plan, especially the knowledge of evil. Our problem today is that we want to add something of our own to the mix that God is already cooking up with the sweet savor of Jesus Christ. With our additions or subtractions, it won't smell like the Savior's life, and it will lack the nourishment of His sacrifice (Eph. 5:1-2, 18-21).

Without God's design we are lost, no matter how complex our technology or how well meaning our intentions. Already, we are designed to worship our Creator in spirit and in truth without extra gadgets or constant electronic stimulation. A quiet and humble spirit and a heart broken and submissive to God are all the equipment needed to please Him. Some would neglect these simple things and seek to add technology or theatrics to worship, but there is no real value in these, no deep amplification of worship beyond the purity of a contrite heart that worships God humbly in spirit and in truth (John 4:23-24).

If we come seeking Him in His way and not our own way, we are fully designed to know God. If we depend on some external equipment, habit, or display to aid us in worship, we are merely adding to our own pleasure and not to His. The biggest video screen in the world cannot show anything more than the innermost chamber of your heart purified in His love, and it really cannot show that. God does not want a show but a surrender of your heart to His. This may be unnoticed by the world, but to the Creator it is the recognition of His new creation in Christ fully designed to worship Him.

In His presence, we walk in the love that flows through repentance, obedience, and joy in the One who gave Himself for us. In simplicity, you are fully designed to please God now. Put aside everything else, and come to Him in truth, as He created you completely for Himself.

Father, I come to you as a child, by no other means than having Your life in me, and I ask that You lead me to grow up in faith into the fullness of my Savior's love so I can worship You in spirit and in truth. In Jesus' name, amen.

2 Cor. 11:3-4   John 1:10-13   Ps. 51:10-17

August 26

TEACH US TO PRAY

Father, teach us to pray in Your heart, not in our minds alone, but reaching into Your love, which reaches out to us in Jesus Christ. Send Your Holy Spirit to pray in us what Your heart desires for this moment. Before asking anything, may our desires be formed in the movement of Your heart for Your kingdom. Then let our words follow the intent of Your will to save us and heal us in the same power that You used to raise Jesus from the dead. For surely, we are dead without You. As You lead, we come in Your power to whatever situation is now before us and speak life, the life of forgiveness and truth that reaches into eternity. Your heart is bigger than ours, and Your mercy endures forever. Your ways are higher than ours, and Your thoughts produce more than any prayer or human effort. Whatever Your plan is, we trust it. In praise, it all belongs to You and returns to You. Make of this life what is beautiful in Your sight, cleansed in the blood of Jesus. Do what only You can do. How we pray determines how we will live. Teach us to pray as You live in Jesus Christ in us. In Jesus' name, amen.

Now it came to pass, as He was praying in a certain place, when He ceased, that one of His disciples said to Him, "Lord, teach us to pray, as John also taught his disciples." So He said to them, "When you pray, say: Our Father in heaven, hallowed be Your name. Your kingdom come. Your will be done on earth as it is in heaven."

Luke 11:1-2

Rom. 8:5-11, 26-32

FAITH THAT WORKS
August 27

Thus also faith by itself, if it does not have works, is dead. But someone will say, "You have faith, and I have works." Show me your faith without your works, and I will show you my faith by my works.

James 2:17-18

Our lives depend on grace received through faith. As a by-product of grace, faith becomes visible in works. Crying out to God in repentance and seeking Him will bring us to faith, and faith to works, which in turn increase our faith. God made the first move by coming to us. Our response is to know our need and to receive by faith what only He can do. He even gives us the faith!

Then why do we focus on the work? Our first goal is really not to do things for the Lord but to receive what He can do through us and in us. When we receive Him by faith, then everything else will follow. Yes, we must be obedient to complete through visible works the invisible work of faith God already has planted in our hearts, but we are able to believe and work only as He works in us first through the grace of His Son's sacrifice (Gal. 2:20-21).

Christianity is not about us but all about Christ, who makes us new as part of who He already is. As new creations in Him, we can become part of what He is doing right where we are, even in impossible situations (Eph. 2:8-10). Faith will move us to work with Christ, looking at Him and loving Him more than all. If we gaze upon His face to know His heart as well as His hands, then we will know the power of His faith working through us and producing visible fruit. Both faith and works are necessary. One is dead without the other in a living relationship with God's Son.

Only in close contact with Christ can we receive the grace and faith to truly serve those around us (Gal. 5:1, 5-6). Through grace, faith produces work, but work without a living relationship with the Source, has no grace or faith. It falls flat and produces no fruit that remains. The living seed of God's Word depends on good ground open to a relationship with the Creator and free of footholds for the enemy, hindering stones, or thorny relationships with the world.

Grace comes in the mercy and power of God. He buys the field, clears the ground, and plants the seed. Then the works will grow by active faith in His love. Together, both invisible faith and visible works reveal His harvest where you are now.

Lord God, let Your truth work in me. Thank You for buying the field. Increase my faith and produce good fruit for Your kingdom by Your love and grace moving through me here in Jesus Christ. In His name, amen.

Matt. 13:18-23   Phil. 1:6-11   Luke 18:35—19:10

August 28

THE GIFT

Father, help me today to do what pleases You above all. Something little or something big, whatever Your heart desires, I want to give you what You will enjoy. Make my life Your delight, even in the middle of difficulties. Forgive me for considering each day in the pale light of my own desires, when it is Your delight that fuels eternity. Take Your pleasure today in what You have given me to offer back to You. Ignite in me the fire of Your pure love, and let it burn through my stubbornness and fear. Move me in Your direction, because I want to please You more than anyone else and offer You part of Your own harvest of love. Make my life full and fruitful in Your will because I delight to offer You sacrifices of joy that fill Your tabernacle with praise. Hear Your child, O Lord, singing to you with more than words. In Jesus' name, amen.

And He said to them, "Render therefore to Caesar the things that are Caesar's, and to God the things that are God's."

Matt. 22:21

Luke 17:11-21

THE LAST, FIRST   August 29

"They will come from the east and the west, from the north and the south, and sit down in the kingdom of God. And indeed there are last who will be first, and there are first who will be last."

Luke 13:29-30

Look around your world today at those who appear to be last on the scale of earthly success. Consider these candidates for first place in the kingdom of God, as they depend on Him alone and not on human ability or approval. In the world's eyes, those who are already first don't need any help from God. They think they are doing quite well on their own. How could anyone, even God, improve on their position if they are indeed first or at least pretending to arrive there soon?

The truth is that none of us is first or ever will be. Consider the Milky Way galaxy, just to put our little worldly agenda in perspective. One is first, and that is the Lord God, Creator of heaven and earth (Mark 12:28-34). To make ourselves first or to insist on the top position is to make ourselves gods in a world we would control. To depend on human ability and approval and to ridicule those who seek God's ways is to elevate human will to divine status. Only those whom the world labels last can escape the idolatry of trying to be first in the worship of human pride.

Those who are last, because they are free from this shackle of pride, can run the race swiftly and win the prize of God's peace. By acknowledging their dependence on Him, they become independent of worldly cares and the deceitfulness of riches that drag others down. The last are good runners. They arrived at first place before the race began. Since they have their eyes on the One who is first, they become like Him, living in Him as He lives in them. First place is not only within their reach; it is growing inside them. Since the Lord is first, they are first in Him. Do we avoid the royalty of His kingdom?

Father, help me keep my eyes on Jesus, the First and the Last, who carries us to victory as the race is completed in His power alone. In Jesus' name, amen.

Mark 10:13-16   Matt. 11:25-30   1 Cor. 1:22-31

THE FIRST, LAST

August 30

So the last will be first, and the first last. For many are called, but few chosen.

Matt. 20:16

On the cross, He who was first became last. The firstborn of all creation became as the very least of us in order to bring us into the fullness of God's family. Crucified as an accused criminal, the Son of God bought our freedom. Even if we think we're something, we can do nothing without Him. The things we cling to in an effort to be first will make us last in the kingdom of God. If our Master was willing to become a lowly servant (Phil. 2:5-9), losing through death and destruction all on earth that was dear to Him, can't we let go of the worldly treasures we hold so closely?

If we're right and even deserving of some benefits and honor, so was He. On the other hand, if we're mistreated unjustly by the world, so was He. If we're dying, so was He. If we're living for the right cause, so was He. If we are falsely flattered by those who would destroy us, so was He. If even our friends have left and we are alone, so was He. If our usual worldly support is gone, and we are without a place to call our own, so was He (Luke 9:57-58). This is the true position of the first. The last place on earth we would want to be turns out to be our doorway to heaven.

Those who willingly give up what is first in the world, taking Christ's place as last in line, will find themselves at the beginning of a royal banquet for all time. Those who now stand first in line, having placed themselves expertly at the head, will be last. Where do you stand today?

Father, help me see my position in Jesus and take His place with the least, the last, and the lost to serve You. By the riches of grace, bring us together to Your banquet table as we choose the way of Your Son. In Jesus' name, amen.

Matt. 25:37-40   Mark 10:23-27, 35-45   Mark 8:35-36

August 31

TO THE ROOT

Father, forgive me for clipping leaves off the weeds in my life with surface gestures of repentance while letting the roots remain to grow again. With Your truth, reach down to the source of my sin and cut it off; blot it out in the blood of Your Son, Jesus Christ. Go to the root of my iniquities, hidden from others and even from myself. Take away my bent to sinning and proud rationalizing that allows old habits to remain and sprout up in other directions. Pull out the deepest entanglements of fear and guilt, disguising themselves as something necessary or helpful; take them clear out so the true seeds of fruitful life have room to grow. Where my selfish desires have nestled in the corners, hard to reach and intermingled with seemingly good things, pull them out so they no longer choke off any new growth in You. When the weeds are gone, let my open ground please You. Plant the good seed deep, and tend it well. My heart is open to Your harvest now. In Jesus' name, amen.

But He answered and said, "Every plant which My heavenly Father has not planted will be uprooted."

Matt. 15:13

Heb. 4:12-16

TABERNACLES—ATONEMENT, RECONCILIATION

Come through repentance to the feast of receiving God's forgiveness by grace in Jesus Christ, who is our atonement, our peace, our dwelling place, and the reconciliation of all things in the Father's will. In Him, we become a new creation through the power of God, who made heaven and earth and who will send his Son again at the sound of the trumpet.

Lev. 23:23-43

John 7:1-2, 37-39

Matt. 26:26-29

1 Cor. 15:20-23, 50-58

2 Cor. 5:17-21

Eph. 1:7-10

Heb. 9:11-15

Rev. 1:7-8

THE TRUE MIRROR   September 1

"And I, if I am lifted up from the earth, will draw all peoples to Myself."

John 12:32

When you look into the mirror of the world, you'll see a distorted image of what God has created. When you look into the mirror of your hidden desires, you also get a false version of the original plan designed in God's love. He calls us to look into His Son. His love came in the flesh to offer the true mirror of life and the window into eternity. The mirrors of the world and the mirror of your mind carry you back into a dark maze of selfish interests and complicated detours. In the purity of God's Living Word, you see the only reflection of His true creation in you. Turn and look.

What do you see today? How does your lifestyle appear in that mirror? Let the purity of Christ cleanse any stains and iron out anything crooked that is not of God's plan. See what the Creator can do in you and those around you when you gaze on the face of His mercy in Jesus Christ. The other mirrors will not show you that peace or that power. Keep your eyes on the prize, the upward call of life in Jesus, where He's already walked and lived God's Word each day. You'll never be able to walk through the door of life until you look into the true mirror and see yourself as you really are. It's the only way to go forward. Even a few minutes a day makes a difference, as you begin to see what is true.

Take time to absorb God's Word, and the direction it gives will be worth more than all else on your calendar. In the end, you'll come out farther ahead than if that time were spent in other things. If you look into Jesus' eyes, His life, cross, and resurrection power, He will draw you forward beyond anything of this world. The reality of His presence and the clarity of God's Word will reveal truth you've never seen, right where you are now. Turn and look. Go through the door He opens. In faith, He will bring you forward, alive in His image.

Father, shine on me through Your Word so I can live in the image of Your Son. In Your mercy, may I see clearly and understand who I am in Your design. In Jesus' name, amen.

Luke 2:30-35   John 1:1-9   James 1:12-27

PROOF OF LOVE
September 2

"Greater love has no one than this, than to lay down one's life for his friends."

John 15:13

In seeking proof of God, we are talking not only about cold facts but also about a growing relationship that confirms those facts. Facts alone are never enough, although there are plenty of them—the expanse of the universe, or the probability of 1 in 10 to the 157th power of Jesus Christ fulfilling hundreds of prophecies; the radical changes in lives of believers; good works, miracles, signs, and wonders in God's presence for thousands of years; and the success of nations who follow His ways. Something must be going on! However, **logic alone won't move us when love in action is missing** (Luke 24:13-35).

For belief to be confirmed in action now, the heart must also engage. The most convincing proof of God is love in action, revealing its eternal Source. There is creative power in this love, as glimpsed in the physical world but perfected in the Holy Spirit. The world knows Jesus' disciples by their love coming from Him, not from their own knowledge or human love. The one thing children have in capacity equal to that of an adult is love, and God calls us His children if we live in the love of His Son. Out of that love, new knowledge grows in His creative care for us, and hearts are deeply changed.

But how could He actually love us? Consider the facts of creation, the prophecies fulfilled, the gift of His Son, and the quiet healing of broken lives. Consider the love He can place now within your own heart. Well, you say, "I just don't feel it, and if I did, why should such a subjective, fluffy thing as love be the basis for my recognition of God?" It is because love's apparent fluffiness is stronger than steel, hiding a stream of pure passion that shines into the core of your being, indeed into the creation of the cosmos. Even hidden, it will last longer than life, carrying you where you cannot go alone. This is impossible for us to produce. If we're looking only to ourselves or others for proof, forget it. Our Creator offers much more.

Our version of love is just a hint of the love that spins the galaxies. Most of us think our hint is all there is. We're so stuck on ourselves that we're missing the bigger picture and the larger love. To those who ask, seek, and knock, there is more. Even the hardest heart will melt in the presence of the Creator who moves everything, both seen and unseen. But there is a question to be asked first. If you are not sure of God's love, ask Him. Ask your Creator, if He is there, to please show you His love and to reveal the truth to you. Give Him some time. He does not respond well to snapped fingers, but He will answer a humble heart. That answer is your proof.

Father, reveal Your love to me, and open my heart to know You. I am willing to accept the action, not just the fact, of Your love in my life now. In Jesus' name, amen.

John 13:6-7, 34-35   John 1:10-16   Matt. 5:43-48

September 3

TAKE MY OWN SIN OUT

Father, apply the blood of Your Son's life, and wash me in the Holy Spirit to take my own sin out. Remove whatever blinds me, so I can see clearly to behold Your beauty and also see the needs of others. Cleanse me completely in Your mercy and power. As far as the east is from the west, take away any known or unknown sin that keeps me from reaching out freely to do Your will. In Jesus' name, amen.

"And why do you look at the speck in your brother's eye, but do not consider the plank in your own eye? Or how can you say to your brother, 'Let me remove the speck from your eye'; and look, a plank is in your own eye? Hypocrite! First remove the plank from your own eye, and then you will see clearly to remove the speck from your brother's eye."

Matt. 7:3-5

Ps. 51   Ps. 103:11-18

THE SLANT OF SIN   September 4

I press toward the goal for the prize of the upward call of God in Christ Jesus.

Phil. 3:14

We are born into the slant of sin. If we press forward in our own strength, the slope is too steep, and we slip down. Each one of us is conformed to the slope of Adam, a precarious leaning that slides away from the perfection of eternal creation. Every step we take has conformed to that slope, as one who struggles uphill but slides down. By self-will, we have tilted ourselves into the weight of death. In Christ, God comes to set us right and tilt the scales toward life. In Christ, we can lift up our heads, open our eyes, and walk where He has walked. When we see ourselves on an uneven slope that slides steeply down, He calls us to look up and see the cross of Calvary above us, the cross that lifted up Christ, who lifts us. In pain, He walked that upward path for each one of us, rising above the slant, straining against the impossibly heavy pull of our sin. He broke free and rose again. In surrendering to Him, we are lifted up where only He can bring us.

If we prefer our slant of sin and look to ourselves or others, we will slide down. If we stand on that slant of sin and do nothing but just try to be nice, we're still sliding down because our hearts are a mixture containing the deep weight of sin. It is a heavy yoke. It is Adam's choice built into us. He certainly knew God and how to obey, but he wanted to please someone else more. In Adam and in us is a willingness to choose against God and for us that leads us down that slippery slope—unless Christ pulls us up!

Until the Spirit of Christ raises our eyes to His life, we are sliding the way of Adam every day, even while professing to be Christians. Only in surrender to the cross does upward momentum come, as smoke rises from a sacrifice in the fire of His love. In the cross we can make real progress, as Christ takes the load and brings us in resurrection power where our human will cannot go. His yoke is easy, and His burden is light as He carries it with us in the Holy Spirit. This is not a matter of our deciding to do it but of our deciding to let Christ do it—to let Him live in us the life that goes up (Eph. 4:21—5:2).

In His anointing, our old yoke is broken, and in His life we are lifted off the slippery slope and into a sacrifice of holy fire that rises from the rock of Calvary. Christ's power breaks the power of Adam's sin as the purity of Christ's obedient will breaks the power of Adam's self-will. To verbally claim salvation but then not take up the cross in action in our lives allows the full weight of the flesh to pull us back down. We slide unless we release our wills and allow His Spirit to work in us, lifting us in Christ's blood applied now. It's the only way up. Step out of sin, and grow up in the cross.

Father, bring me in the blood of Christ, as a sacrifice rising to You. In His name, amen.

Matt. 26:39-41   1 Cor. 15:22   James 4:10

FOR GOD'S GLORY ALONE   September 5

"I am the Lord, that is My name; and My glory I will not give to another, nor My praise to carved images."

Isa. 42:8

Sometime, somewhere, set a regular day aside just to please God as best you know, a day that is wholeheartedly in line with His will above all else. Maybe you already do this in addition to the Sabbath, but often the "else" gets in our way of seeing God as more than just one of many priorities during the week. He is all in all. This is true on a regular workday as well as a Sabbath. All in all expands beyond Sunday. Joy grows when He is the focus even in the middle of turmoil and deadlines. Other things may happen in a day set aside for Him, but they are clearly subordinate and molded into the pleasure of His will.

Amazingly, if we please God, we will also be pleased with new freedom and a deeper grasp of His all-encompassing love for us. We are so easily sidetracked into the dead ends of our own desires that it is helpful to designate some particular day to startle us into the reality of His sovereignty and bring us right into the middle of His highway to eternity. Hopefully, the other days will begin to follow that pattern as we acknowledge who He really is now, living among us through the Holy Spirit.

What would a workday that is set aside just to please God and to meet His requirements for success look like on your calendar? How would that day be different from any other? Perhaps it's a matter of attitude in serving others, finishing what's promised, or spending time in communion with the Lord, taking in His word, and feeding on Him. Maybe it's all of the above. Do whatever He suggests. Ask the Lord what a day pleasing to Him would actually look like, given your work and living requirements. The answer is the direction your life can now take to walk in His peace and His power all year. Have more than a nice day. Have a life for God's glory alone.

Father, teach me how to live for You and not for myself. Bring me through Jesus Christ into the peace of seeking Your glory alone each day. In Jesus' name, amen.

Isa. 43:7-13   Matt. 10:27-33   Eph. 5:1-21

FRUIT CHECK

September 6

"You did not choose Me, but I chose you and appointed you that you should go and bear fruit, and that your fruit should remain, that whatever you ask the Father in My name He may give you."

John 15:16

It's time for a fruit check for yourself and those on whom you depend. Your future depends not only on producing fruit but also on discerning fruit that is rotten at the core, even though appearing good on the outside (Phil. 1:9-11). When poked, good fruit doesn't take on the imprint of man but firmly keeps the shape of God's Word, whose seed gave it new growth. Unspotted from the world, good fruit shows the even glow, the consistent beauty of living separate from the dirt and destructive pests that swarm around it. Good fruit doesn't smell too strongly of itself but smells of the tree that bears it, the sunlight and fresh air of the Holy Spirit that nourishes it, and the unique life that flows through it for others. Good fruit results from receiving Christ, and it belongs only to Him.

Good fruit opens easily, divides correctly according to God's sharp word of truth, and is not mushy or wishy-washy, lost in weak flesh. Good fruit is not misshapen or extended in bulges of other designs but follows exactly the turn of its Creator's hand. When opened for others, it clearly reveals viable seeds, still distinct and not tarnished with corruption. Good fruit is willing to die to itself so that others can live. Good fruit carries the aroma of the joy of its Creator and not the dark scent of deception and destruction. Good fruit draws others to the tree of obedience and humility and does not send anyone away empty from the truth of new life in the cross of Christ. Our hope continues only through Him, our Lord, the firstfruits of all creation. Check the fruit in and around you. Does it carry the aroma of God's life?

Father, through the tree of the cross, produce in me the fruit of Jesus Christ. Make me alive with His power and purity. In Jesus' name, amen.

Matt. 12:33-37   Gal. 5:16-26   1 Peter 2:21-25

September 7

SIMPLICITY OF THE VINE

Father, forgive me for wanting the false fabrications of the foolish instead of the true simplicity of the Vine that grows into eternity. Prune away whatever limits Your fruit in me. Deepen my roots to reach Your living water. Open my heart to Your Son and breathe on me through the Holy Spirit as I rest in humility and grow in the life of Jesus Christ. I have no other source but You. In Jesus' name, amen.

"But he who is greatest among you shall be your servant. And whoever exalts himself will be humbled, and he who humbles himself will be exalted. But woe to you, scribes and Pharisees, hypocrites! For you shut up the kingdom of heaven against men; for you neither go in yourselves, nor do you allow those who are entering to go in."

Matt. 23:11-13

Gen. 49:8-11   Matt. 21:1-16

EIGHTH DAY   September 8

"At that day you will know that I am in My Father, and you in Me, and I in you."

John 14:20

Whatever your calendar holds, each day points to the fruit of the eighth day of God's promise of new life (Luke 2:21; John 20:19-23; 1 Cor. 15:20-23). With regular cycles in time and eternity, the first day of the week also becomes the eighth day, following the rest of day seven in God's original weekly pattern. The seventh day follows the sixth day, when the work of the flesh is completed. Just as God rested on the Sabbath of the seventh day after He created this world, we rest from our work in the flesh. Then He sets everything in order for the new world on the eighth day. The purpose of the first seven days is to arrive at that eighth day. In God's eternal plan, we're all going somewhere new right now. We move steadily toward that eighth day when He renews all things through His Son.

The main purpose of days one and two is to reach three; and the purpose of three, four, five, and six is to reach the blessed rest of day seven; and the purpose of resting on day seven is to reach the renewal of all creation on day eight, when time blends into infinity. In the Jewish Feast of Tabernacles, the eighth day is a solemn assembly after seven days of feasting in temporary leafy booths. On the eighth day, the people are led out of the temporary booths into a permanent place of new life, just as God led them into the Promised Land, a permanent dwelling place where He would live with them in the beauty of His temple (Neh. 8:5-18; 2 Chron.7:1-14).

As we follow Christ out of our wilderness, our lives become His temple. The entire life of Christ pointed toward the cross, but also toward what happened after the cross when He arose on the eighth day. So should our lives. Without the resurrection active in us now, there is no power in the cross, no reason to be redeemed. The works and rest of man and the Son of Man are completed on that eighth day when Jesus rose from the dead. By the works of the flesh and to pay for the sin of carnal man, He had died on a day of work, a day of the flesh. By His stripes we are healed. On that sixth day, the work of the flesh was finished. On the seventh day, Jesus rested in the tomb. On the eighth day, He rose again to bring us to new life even now. Our Savior, Alpha and Omega, covers both the old and the new with grace. Plan everything you do today, your whole calendar, in the light of that eighth day. It is coming! Walk new now.

Father God, Creator of all, make me a new creation in Your Son, a place for Your Spirit to dwell to reveal Your eternal beauty in this day. In Jesus' name, amen.

Gen. 2:1-7   Rev. 21:1-6; 22:1-5   John 7:1-2, 37-39

THE ONLY EXPLANATION
September 9

"As the Father loved Me, I also have loved you; abide in My love."

John 15:9

We've all heard the questions. What in the world are we doing here, and does it really have any meaning? There is one explanation that surpasses all others. This answer encompasses human knowledge but exceeds it and reaches to the farthest ends of the universe without neglecting the smallest sparrow. Even the inner workings of atoms move in its power, and galaxies unfold to bloom with its hidden beauty. Its logic is based on more than reason; in fact, the answer is based on loving sacrifice that transcends reason. This explanation is still being spoken today in actions and words where the love of God shines clearly. Often our most violent problem, our worst scenario, really hinges on two questions: Does anyone love me? Why am I here?

Our Creator's love, though not seen or heard by some, is trying to move us into eternity through the gift of His only Son. The reason we were created is to love God and to be loved by Him. Any other answer falls short. Since we fell away, He picks us up through His Son's cross and lifts us to His heart. Those who have ears to hear and eyes to see will receive His love and pass it on, even when it seems unreasonable. Mercy is unreasonable. For the Son of God, who did not have to die, dying is unreasonable, and dying for sinners is impossible without supernatural love flowing freely.

What is there in your life today that can be explained only by the love of God at work in you? For what He has rescued you from and what He calls you to do now, no other explanation is possible. If His work could be accomplished with the world's methods, through money or human talent, it would not point to God as the source. There would have been no need to send His Son as our Savior. But there was, and He did. Through the Holy Spirit, He confirms that answer today.

The world will look for a human explanation. But when it is something totally impossible without God, the witness is clear and rings true. His love is the only explanation. Sacrificial, pure, and steadfast love is what people are looking for today, a clear demonstration of the reality of God's amazing love at work in your life. In the coming days, they will be even more desperate to see it. Show them the only explanation in action, His living truth.

Lord God, fill me with Your love to the point that it becomes visible in action and overflows to others seeking mercy and true life. Make me impossibly new in Your Son. In Jesus' name, amen.

Matt. 5:14-20   Matt. 19:16-26   1 John 3:16-24

~~~~~~

USE ME

Father, please use me today. All the things I've been talking about and complaining about are changed only when I act in Your will. Move me closer to You, and open me to the fruit You want to bring out of this situation. Join me to the Vine as I yield to Your life. Forgive me for trying to use You. Use me, change me, and shape me to Your will right here. No more sitting back and studying things in my own way, no more whining and crying over whatever was not done, and no more finding reasons for my old ways and rationalizing my own comfort. It's time for action. Father, cover me with the armor of Your light inside and out. Wash me in the blood of Jesus, which cleanses and heals. Today, use me for Your glory alone. Let my actions speak louder than all the words I have said while doing nothing. In Jesus' name, amen.

"You are My friends if you do whatever I command you."

John 15:14

Ps. 111

~~~~~~

PAIN'S PERFUME   September 11

I am the rose of Sharon, and the lily of the valleys. Like a lily among thorns, so is my love among the daughters.

Song of Sol. 2:1-2

No one is immune to pain's perfume. When we suffer pain, there are three ways to deal with it. Each method produces its own fragrance. For the perfume there is no difference whether the pain is deserved or undeserved, our mistake or someone else's, avoidable or unavoidable. Everything around us is soaked with the perfume of how we deal with pain, and the aroma lingers long after we are gone. We have these choices:

1. Keep the pain inside. There it slowly eats away at our lives, while we pretend everything is all right until only a thin shell is left, a facade easily broken. And then there is the additional pain and effort of maintaining the continuous lie of the facade. Within us, the pressure of the pain slowly produces a compressed fragrance that smells falsely flowery, like thick deodorizer in a room with no fresh air—stagnant and subtly bitter.
2. Place the pain on others through criticism and blame as a sort of anesthetic for our own wounds. In other words, get so angry at people they will stay away and not see our weakness. Eventually the anesthetic wears off, and we awake to see our wounds multiplied in the lives of others. The odor is so sour it repels all those around us, as if something spoiled is rotting away. This is the aggressive stench of the will of the flesh.
3. Give the pain to Jesus. This sounds too simple and very abstract, but it works in unexpected ways. Try it and see. Jesus is not a dead abstraction. He is more alive than we are. On the cross, He has already felt our wounds and still loves us anyway. To lay everything down and give it to Jesus means that we will finally lose control of our pain. Sometimes we hate the pain, but we love to control it and others; so we would rather stay in our pain than give up that control. Those who say the cross will not work have not surrendered all to it. They ask God to work as they control their own lives.

Which is really productive, our control or His? His fragrance is sweeter and more beautiful in multiple dimensions. Our Lord alone is worthy because His purity has conquered pain, and His wounds heal ours directly by His blood and the power of His resurrection. If you don't believe it, try it anyway. At least you'll smell something different along the way: a fragrance of release and deep beauty—not icky sweet, overly spiritual abstractions, but the deep-down surrender of a fragile lily growing in a real valley. Here is a fragrance of life that has known death and the God-given beauty that conquers it. Why have any pain at all? It's the only way to get the best perfume and that clear aroma of peace the lilies know.

Father, I want to neither toil nor spin but to breathe Your beauty. In Jesus' name, amen.

Matt. 6:28-34   John 16:33   Eph. 5:1-2

LISTENING BRINGS RESULTS   September 12

So then, my beloved brethren, let every man be swift to hear, slow to speak, slow to wrath; for the wrath of man does not produce the righteousness of God.

James 1:19-20

What are the results of your listening recently? Daily, I'm learning that more fruit can be produced for the kingdom of God by listening than talking. Problems can be solved more by listening for what is being said between the lines than by trying to say more lines myself to get my point across to others (Matt. 5:5). Results come from listening first to God in prayer, then to others, and then to yourself. When you can hear God clearly, you can then hear others clearly and also know the condition of your own heart. Often, I've been surprised to hear what I was actually saying in my tone of voice, my haste, or my shortsighted anger.

Have you listened to your own thoughts and desires lately? They are propelling the words that get you into trouble. Try listening to the deepest desires of your heart. Line them up with God's will, and let Him do the talking. When He speaks creatively, action will result, walls will fall, new life springs up, and you will suddenly find yourself listening to the first sounds of a new creation. You can only go where you have first listened.

Father, cleanse my lips to speak only in the love that I have first heard from You. Teach me to listen to the Holy Spirit and to the truth deep in others' hearts. In Jesus' name, amen.

James 1:17-26   Ps. 19:7-14   Matt. 12:33-37

SWEET HOUR OF PRAYER   September 13

"To him the doorkeeper opens, and the sheep hear his voice; and he calls his own sheep by name and leads them out. And when he brings out his own sheep, he goes before them; and the sheep follow him, for they know his voice."

John 10:3-4

If Jesus often spent all night in prayer, where is our one hour of prayer? It may seem like an interruption in our schedules, but the sweetness of that hour will permeate everything else we do. An hour of prayer alone with God is essential to knowing His voice and following Him. If we study God's Word without time alone with the Author to speak to us and apply it to our lives, His truth will be lifeless in us. The seed will have no deep root and bear no fruit. If we spend several hours a week in church or doing things for God but no time alone with Him, the one-on-one intimacy that allows us to really know Him and recognize His call is missing. Focusing on God alone while we are alone allows us to hear His still, small voice revealing wisdom, love, and power.

We want to spend time alone with those we love, not with a crowd. We'll never get to know them otherwise. In time alone with God, we become immersed in His love and the joy of His presence so that we can truly know the desires of His heart. In this relationship, His Word comes alive and finds room in our lives to operate. Nothing else will satisfy or seem right. If we're saturated in the life of His Son with the truth of His Word ringing inside us, then that sound of His truth in us will either match or reject those other voices and suggestions that come. In His Word, the vibrations of His love within us and other vibrations coming from outside will either agree or disagree. The difference is clear, allowing the door to close or open in recognition of the Shepherd.

Many voices call for our attention. Some sound good and even quote God's Word and use the Lord's name. But the witness of the Spirit within us will ring true only in harmony with another voice that carries God's truth. There is a sweet spiritual taste and the sound of His life that rings true inside and outside. God's Word in us harmonizes only with His Word active in the world and in the work He has already prepared for us to do (Eph. 2:10). God is not the author of confusion, and His Word living in you can find the right path, the one option out of many that leads to maximum fruit. Are you abiding in the Lord, or just studying Him occasionally? To begin abiding, taste the sweetness and power of an hour of prayer.

Father, help me to spend time with You to know the Shepherd's voice so that I will not follow the voice of a stranger or a thief. I want to know You more than I want to know what to do. Lead me, and I will follow Your love. In Jesus' name, amen.

Luke 6:12   John 10:1-30   Rev. 3:20

~~~~~~

WASHED IN THE LIGHT

I want to walk in Your light, Lord, every day, not only to see what is ahead but to be washed and made clean entirely for Your purpose. Let Your light change me, as Your Word lives in me. Let Your presence in the Holy Spirit make me clean in the blood of Christ, the Living Word, so I can know which way to go. Your Word is a lamp to my feet. Illumine my soul to run after You, in Your strength and peace that passes understanding. Christ said we are made clean through His Word in our hearts (John 15:3). So let that Word come and take root in my heart to bear fruit that pleases You and fruit that remains. Make me clean on both the inside and the outside. Let me walk, breathing in Your air, the breath of the Holy Spirit, that holy air both within me and all around, so I live and move and have my being in You. O Light of the world, make ready a people clean for Your covenant with hearts bathed in Your Word. Wash us in Your light like newborn babes, like disciples with dusty feet, like those who are blind and need to see. We want to walk in the power of Your holiness, able to see what is revealed by pure light in the sacrificial love of Christ. Bring us completely into Your will. In the name of Jesus, amen.

But when the kindness and the love of God our Savior toward man appeared, not by works of righteousness which we have done, but according to His mercy He saved us, through the washing of regeneration and renewing of the Holy Spirit, whom He poured out on us abundantly through Jesus Christ our Savior,

Titus 3:4-6

John 13:3-8

~~~~~~

HOLD ONTO GOD

September 15

Truly my soul silently waits for God; from Him comes my salvation. He only is my rock and my salvation; He is my defense; I shall not be greatly moved.

Ps. 62:1-2

Days are coming, are even here, when our only hope is to hold onto our Lord, "who is and who was and who is to come, the Almighty" (Rev. 1:8). Now everyone is busy holding onto something or someone for some reason even unknown to them. Those independent hearts who claim they need no such anchor are merely holding onto themselves, a dangerous delusion that ends at the cemetery. Where is your anchor? If you toss aside everything in your life that does not give you life, what is left? At the last moment of existence, nothing will be there but God holding you forever through His Son (Heb. 6:19-20; John 10:27-30).

Already our Creator is holding onto you. In the center of your heart, He has offered to give you His Son's life and make you new as you receive Him (John 1:12-13). Through Jesus Christ He has given you life here and beyond this earth. Cast off those things that have gotten in the way. Brush them aside, and look straight into His face and His mercy for you today. Enter the reflection of the glory of Jesus Christ looking at you and those around you. In the freedom of His sacrifice, leave behind the bondage of old sin and its guilt that weighs you down.

No matter where you are now, He is calling you to take hold of that one anchor that will hold through any storm. From before the foundation of the world, you were His. Now, our Lord is asking you to make Him yours, your only anchor today. Quit grasping at the false ones, the illusions and lies that leave you drifting, tossed, and beaten by the winds of life. Hold onto God as He holds onto you. Quietly, His truth will root you to the foundation that precedes all else, that creates more than we can see, and transcends all time and trouble with grace. Take hold. Hold onto the only One who will never let go of you!

My Father, forgive me for holding onto everything else but You. I release those things and relationships that have stood in the way and take hold of Your truth now in Jesus Christ. Hold me as I hold onto You. In Jesus' name, amen.

Matt. 6:24   Matt. 7:21-29   Ps. 61:1-4

GREATER LOVE

September 16

"I in them, and You in Me; that they may be made perfect in one, and that the world may know that You have sent Me, and have loved them as You have loved Me."

John 17:23

There were people who wanted me to dance for the world, but I said, "No, a greater love, the Lover of my soul, dances with me."

There were those who begged me, "Bow down and worship what we worship: our names and our high banners." I said, "No, I belong to an eternal family, obedient in humility and the power of Jesus Christ."

There were some who said I could serve their masters of the moment and mine at the same time, but I said, "No, there is only one Master, and He rules through all time."

Others came, asking me to turn their stones of contempt into bread for their cause, and I replied, "No, I feed on the Bread of Life, who has mercy for all who receive Him."

Some then drew me to the fountain of knowledge and success, saying, "Drink this and live well, way above the others!" But I said, "No, I'm already satisfied in the simple life of a child growing in God's grace, free in His Son."

Others who ran out of wine said, "Please don't ask God to change this old need we understand into new wine we can't control," but I answered, "No, it's too late; I'll ask for new wine, having already tasted the life of the Vine, a sweet stream flowing into a new creation."

This greater love of the One who gave Himself, His life for me, still comes in the Holy Spirit, saying now, "Drink, and be filled to overflowing." And I say, "Yes, today I will put aside all else, take up the cup of salvation, and walk in Your love!"

Father, help me to taste the greater love You offer to those who seek You. Nothing in this world will ever taste the same. Fill me with the life of Your only Son, offered for all who will come to Him. In Jesus' name, amen.

John 2:1-10   Ps. 116:12-14   John 7:37-39

THIS DAY
September 17

This is the day the Lord has made; we will rejoice and be glad in it.

Ps. 118:24

Although we may plan our calendars, God is creating the time that our calendars try to measure. This day is new in the Lord because He has made it to please Himself. Each day, we see only a tiny fraction of what God unfolds all around us to match the stream of creation He is guiding even to the farthest galaxy. When we hear, "Have a nice day," the usual thought is to please ourselves. However, the best we can accomplish, the most creative thing we can do today, is to please our Maker, to match that larger stream of creation, even if the specific job He assigns us seems little.

On His timetable, that little thing may be very big. More is going on here—more seeds growing, more hearts turning to truth, more buds unfolding, myriads of atoms spinning, wounds healing, and unknown beauty arriving—than we can measure with any calendar. In this river of divine power, following our own plans is like trying to hold rushing water in a paper bag. If we try to control it, our system will spring major leaks, leaving us dry and lifeless, until we begin to move as one with God's design.

One day at a time, we grow into the kingdom that is timeless and draws us beyond time, as the fruit of that journey develops according to our obedience. We cannot add to or take away from yesterday's fruit or tomorrow's. We can only smell the aroma of what God is doing right now and yield to His life flowing in us for each season.

There are stages of growth, but the most creative part we have is to yield to the Vine of God's life in Jesus Christ. If we look at this day in the light of God's fruit, what can we do to move with the life-giving flow of His Vine? With joy, our surrender to Him joins us to that sweet fruit, a good aroma, and seeds that last for the next generation. Those who struggle after selfish desires will slowly turn sour and lifeless. Today, good fruit is ripening in and around us, some as yet invisible. Are we ready to let go of the old so that the new can come? This is the day that the Lord has made. Let Him finish it His way.

Father, today I yield my will to You because I want to become part of what You're doing instead of what I'm doing. Bring me into life that lasts. All my times are in Your hands. All my days are Yours. In Jesus' name, amen.

Ps. 90   John 15:1-2, 16-17   Ps. 31:14-16

JOY IN THE MORNING   September 18

For His anger is but for a moment, His favor is for life; weeping may endure for a night, but joy comes in the morning.

Ps. 30:5

Joy comes in the morning because Jesus Christ is our light that overcomes all darkness. Morning comes when Jesus finds us just as we are and delivers us from the darkness of our old ways to bring us into the light of His love. In His power, we can go in faith from night into the dawn of a new creation, even now. He didn't shine on us just to leave us in our shadows! There is nothing so astounding as the bright purity of His presence penetrating our darkness as it touches our old wounds and melts away fear, removing sin as far as the east is from the west.

When Jesus shines into our hearts, the deepest shadows flee. We cannot send them away on our own or ask others to pour their lives into us to fill our darkness with human effort. We need the Morning Star Himself to clean us out and fill us up with the brightness of resurrection power moving over the horizon of our lives now. Otherwise there is no day and no real future (2 Pet. 1:19, Rev. 22:16).

The night ends only when morning comes, and the Son breaks through everything that was there before. Dawn is not partial or optional, occurring here and there; it is whole and complete, steady and dependable, saturating every part of our world with a new day. There is no stopping it, no holding back the advancement of the light because even though a few shadows remain, everything that is hidden from the light will one day be revealed in the completeness of Christ's coming.

We see this lesson repeated for us every twenty-four hours, but there is a day coming that will never end (Rev. 21:22-25). In fact, in Christ, it's already started as we move forward in faith and obedience (Prov. 4:18-27). The Morning Star has come to release us from sin in the darkest hour. The Son has risen to reveal victory, and now in perfect rhythm the day is steadily advancing in joy until that perfect day in which there will be no night left. Why live weeping in a night that is passing away? The Light of the world has already come and is staying forever. As you welcome Him, true life shines!

My Lord and My God, bring me into Your light and out of my shadows. Forgive my sin, and wash me in the light of Your power on the cross that removes the depths of darkness. Restore to me the joy of Your salvation, and create in me a clean heart for a new day. In my Savior's name, Jesus, amen.

John 8:10-12   Luke 1:76-79   1 John 1:5-7

September 19

~~~~~~

THE LIVING PATH

Today, Father, guide my steps Your way in Christ's life, a living path of pure light even here. When my eyes are on Your Son, I will know where to go and how to walk as You lead me through Him one step at a time. Nothing is too hard for You. Open my heart to receive Your Living Word to not only show me the way but to change me to become one with Your Son who is the way, the truth, and the life here where shadows flee before His name. In the name of Jesus Christ, amen.

Then Jesus said to them, "A little while longer the light is with you. Walk while you have the light, lest darkness overtake you; he who walks in darkness does not know where he is going. While you have the light, believe in the light, that you may become sons of light." . . . Nevertheless even among the rulers many believed in Him, but because of the Pharisees they did not confess Him, lest they should be put out of the synagogue; for they loved the praise of men more than the praise of God. Then Jesus cried out and said, "He who believes in Me, believes not in Me but in Him who sent Me. And he who sees Me sees Him who sent Me. I have come as a light into the world, that whoever believes in Me should not abide in darkness."

John 12:35-36, 42-46

John 14:3-17   Ps. 119:101-112

~~~~~~

JESUS, LIKE NO OTHER

September 20

And a great windstorm arose, and the waves beat into the boat, so that it was already filling. But He was in the stern, asleep on a pillow. And they awoke Him and said to Him, "Teacher, do you not care that we are perishing?" Then He arose and rebuked the wind, and said to the sea, "Peace, be still!" And the wind ceased and there was a great calm. But He said to them, "Why are you so fearful? How is it that you have no faith?" And they feared exceedingly, and said to one another, "Who can this be, that even the wind and the sea obey Him!"

Mark 4:37-41

Jesus is like no other teacher, no other leader, no other person, because God sent Him as His only begotten Son, not created. Carrying the Father's spiritual nature, He joined us in our humanity as Immanuel, God with us. In the willing vessel of Mary, God made Himself present in human flesh. No religious theory can explain the mystery of God coming to us and living in us. Many teachers have come as strong leaders, but none has claimed to be "God with us." Even two thousand years later, Jesus is like no other. His divine and human natures live together to reveal God's new creation here.

Jesus Christ, the Carpenter, in His sacrifice and resurrection, made of the wood of the cross a way for us to become one with God. People were looking for a prophet, a priest, or a king, not a carpenter, and yet Jesus fulfilled all these functions. Like no other prophet, Jesus was Himself the Living Word that He proclaimed, by which God created all things in the beginning and by which He makes them new even now.

Like no other priest, Jesus presented His own blood, full of divine life, to the Father, covering our human loss with payment for the penalty of sin for all people who will receive His sacrifice. Even now through the Holy Spirit, that blood overcomes the power of sin in our world. Total redemption, revealed in His resurrection, cleanses all of creation in preparation for the fullness of God's glory on earth as well as in heaven. Like no other king, Jesus entered the lowest rank of humility to reign above all kings.

Each function of prophet, priest, and king works in our lives today as we let Jesus come like no other. He can calm any storm. Is there a part of your life where He has not been welcomed in full power? Perhaps you've let Him come as prophet, but not as king and priest. Accept His presence actively in all three ways. He is with you as the Living Word, the complete Sacrifice, and the only reigning King, touching your world directly with the power of God. By the Holy Spirit, let Him come as He really is—like no other.

Father, I open my life to Your Son and keep no part back from His power working in me. If there is anything I have not let Him do, I ask now, "Please change me completely, heal me, and let the Prince of Peace reign in every area of my life." In Jesus' name, amen.

John 3:16-21   Heb. 1:1-9   1 Tim. 2:5-6

HEALING WOUNDS   September 21

"So he went to him and bandaged his wounds, pouring on oil and wine; and he set him on his own animal, brought him to an inn, and took care of him."

Luke 10:34

Wounds resting in the Savior's wounds will receive His healing. Through the Holy Spirit, our Savior comes alongside and comforts us, then strengthens us with the new wine and oil of His covenant in resurrection power. Our Lord wraps up our gaping wounds with the pure linen of His righteousness and lifts us onto His own donkey, like the one that carried Him through praise into the city of God, a foretaste of the New Jerusalem. First arriving humbly but coming again royally, our King pays the price for our healing with His own wounds. He climbed the hill to Calvary so that He could carry others to salvation and wholeness in Him.

Even if we have been strangers to Christ, if we call out and ask Him now to see our need, He will stop and come to us through the Holy Spirit when the rest of the world passes us by. Without a lengthy lecture or any condemnation, He bathes our wounds in the same way He washed the disciples feet, letting love speak for itself. And once we are cleansed and covered, He brings us to a safe place. He pays the full price for our continued recovery, our complete renewal, indeed a new life (Luke 10:25-37). No broken and bleeding person who has been picked up from the side of the road and washed clean, covered, and carried to a new place will ever be the same again—especially knowing the price is paid in full. We can serve others only with what He has done in us.

He comes today for those ambushed on their way through life, ready to heal and carry us forward, resting in faith. Through the power of His Spirit, God can touch the point of our greatest pain with Christ's healing wounds. When opened to the light of His gaze, our wounds are healed by His stripes (Isa. 53:5). As we open up to the washing, the clean covering, and the powerful lift of His presence, He takes us where we cannot go on our own. May the One who suffered and then rose to heal all who receive Him now lead us to a new place, as we accept the application of His wounds to ours.

Father God, I accept Your touch even where it hurts. Complete the cleansing process and heal me with Your Son's wounds. I release my wounds to You. Uncover my hidden sin. Wash me in my Savior's blood. In resurrection power, pick me up and cover me in His anointing of grace and mercy, and carry me to a new place to serve You. In Jesus' name, amen.

Matt. 26:26-29   Luke 4:16-21   1 Pet. 1:18-23

ONLY HIS POWER   September 22

For we are His workmanship, created in Christ Jesus for good works, which God prepared beforehand that we should walk in them.

Eph. 2:10

Our Lord has created us to do what can be accomplished only in His power operating in love. Only His life can accomplish what we have to do in our lifetimes. To really do His will, all must be done in love, surrendered to the One who planned it. Good intentions and human initiative will not be able to complete the tasks prepared in heaven and anointed with the oil of His Son. When we try to finish them in our own power, He lets us fail until we realize that only He can make everything beautiful in its time. Sometimes the biggest roadblock we face each day is our own will. When we can set that aside, things begin to move in our Creator's power. Otherwise, we are like toddlers given a plane, unable to get off the ground and wondering why we're going nowhere. We need the Pilot who can take off, navigate, and land safely.

We are His workmanship for a reason beyond ourselves. Even with maximum effort, we cannot complete and make perfect our own lives any more than we can complete the mission He has sent us to do. There's nothing too small or too big for God to handle and to work into line with His will, which makes us complete in the process. To let God graft us into His fruitful Vine, rooted in eternity, we must let go of old ways and selfish loves (1 John 2:15-17). Step back and take your will off of whatever He is trying to do through you now, whatever assignment faces you, whatever relationship seems impossible. Let the Creator of the universe be fully in charge of what He already does well. Do not despise the day of small things when they are in the Lord's hands. The result will make both you and whatever happens beautiful.

Father, make both me and what You are doing through me beautiful in Your sight, according to Your design. Expectantly, I surrender to Your creative power. In Jesus' name, amen.

Phil. 2:13-15   Zech. 4:6-10   Prov. 3:5-15

KNOW HIS WILL
September 23

Thomas said to Him, "Lord, we do not know where You are going, and how can we know the way?" Jesus said to him, "I am the way, the truth, and the life. No one comes to the Father except through Me. If you had known Me, you would have known My Father also; and from now on you know Him and have seen Him."

John 14:5-7

The only way to know God's will is to know Him in Person through Christ. Then He will reveal His will to us step by step, as we walk with Him in the transforming power of His Son. We're not going to get a hold of His will without Him first being in the center of our lives holding us. Some say, "If God would just show me His will, then I would do it." Yet His will is more than what we can see or do. We could not know it all even if He told us, and if He told us, we certainly couldn't do it without Him. Instead of asking for information so we can do it, we need to ask for refining so that He can do it and move us forward through His life.

We will know more of what our Lord knows when we live as He would live. Otherwise, we're trying to fit a divine river into a tiny teacup of human design. No matter how pretty to the world, our individual skills and wills will not hold the power of God. However, we can learn to swim in what He is creating all around us and in us. To really know His will, ask Him to reveal Himself to you, and be willing to spend more time with Him than with the information you want.

The next step will then become obvious, because you know the One who creates it and moves you forward in His love. As a light moves through a dark night, you can see farther ahead when you stay directly in touch with the source. Your next steps will become clear as they are illuminated and soaked in the light of His presence with you and your increasing nearness to Him. As you know Him, you will know what to do.

Father, reveal Your life to me, and lead me personally so that each step I take is in Your will and in tune with Your heart. Complete Your purpose in my life by Your power in Jesus Christ working in me, bringing my heart to Yours. In Jesus' name, amen.

John 17:3   2 Pet. 1:17-21   Rom. 11:33—12:5

September 24

~~~~~~

THIS PERSON IN YOUR HANDS

Father, only You know who I am. You know me better than I do, in all the ins and outs of my thinking and trying, even my running away from You. Forgive the thoughts and desires that have carried me far away. Now I come to You with an open heart. Cleanse me and make me complete in Christ. Implant Your Word in me. All the things I know about myself are only partial. My Creator, in Your hands the vessel of my life is complete. Smooth out the faults and the scars. Make me a vessel of Your love in humble clay. Let the old be gone and the new come. I realize there are several options for this clay. I can be the vessel of Your choice, the vessel others choose, or the vessel I choose. Please make me the vessel of Your choice, where Your light dwells in truth. Help me to refuse all lies spoken over me or in me and to receive Your victory in Jesus Christ. Break whatever in me hides Your light, and I will be free. This person in Your hands has no plans but Yours. Wash me in the blood of the Lamb on the inside and the outside. Form me in Your discipline. This person in Your hands needs nothing more than to feel Your life-giving touch. In Your hands, I rejoice when You use me to pour out a cool drink to others. This person in Your hands delights in Your taking hold of an imperfect vessel to fill it with the perfect joy of Your feast. At Your table, I will taste and see that You have saved the best wine until now. In Jesus' name, amen.

"O house of Israel, can I not do with you as this potter?" says the Lord. "Look, as the clay is in the potter's hand, so are you in My hand, O house of Israel!"

Jer. 18:6

Col. 2:6-15

~~~~~~

JOY IN OBSTACLES   September 25

looking unto Jesus, the author and finisher of our faith, who for the joy that was set before Him endured the cross, despising the shame, and has sat down at the right hand of the throne of God.

Heb.12:2

Beyond the cross, Jesus saw the joy that awaited Him, the oil of gladness in His Father's will; but He also saw the oil of that joy upon the cross itself, transforming the obstacle set before Him, as He laid down His own will. The oil of that joy is poured out for us now in Christ, the Anointed One. Most of us in looking at the cross or in looking at our own obstacles do not see any joy. After it is over maybe, but not now. We see hardship, pain, and even death. A sour aroma of hopelessness hangs over our heads. Indeed, we think joy would come only from removing the obstacle, solving the problem, or changing the situation. In Christ, the situation will change, but first we must see His joy upon our obstacles, as our Father's will works through them.

When the oil of His Spirit is upon our difficulties, God will cause us to see Himself with us in the midst of them. Through them, our Creator will transform us from self-sufficiency to His sufficiency, from limited abilities we control to divine energy only He can direct. Joy grows in His purpose and withers in our control. Our comfort zones are really barren ground for God's kingdom. There is little joy in the battles we can win for ourselves by pushing the right buttons and having the result drop out like a cold item from some machine of human will.

Joy grows in the knowledge of the glory of God in the face of His Son, the Living Lord, who still walks with us even in prison, or poverty, or powerlessness. The One who suffered and conquered the grave brings us the victory over the deadness of our empty self-concern. In the Lord's presence alone is fullness of joy. So a road of obstacles with Him is better than an empty, smooth path without Him. Any victory is empty that does not include the victory of Christ over death, the world, the flesh, and the devil. Only God can conquer these.

The obstacles that force us to rely on God, to call out to Him and draw closer to Him (name some of yours) will bring the immense joy of His presence. Our Creator answers to reveal His glory, covering us with the oil of gladness that covered Christ, that aroma of divine love, as when the woman broke her alabaster box to anoint Him. What really broke open that day was the joy of the Lord. Once we see that joy, we'll go forward in the aroma of broken obstacles, even while they are still standing before us.

Father, pour on me the oil of gladness that was in Jesus Christ so I can know the fellowship of His suffering and the power of His resurrection. In Jesus' name, amen.

John 12:1-13   Matt. 5:2-17   1 John 2:20—3:2

ONLY THIS

September 26

"But when he came to himself, he said, 'How many of my father's hired servants have bread enough and to spare, and I perish with hunger! I will arise and go to my father, and will say to him, "Father, I have sinned against heaven and before you, and I am no longer worthy to be called your son. Make me like one of your hired servants."' And he arose and came to his father. But when he was still a great way off, his father saw him and had compassion, and ran and fell on his neck and kissed him. And the son said to him, 'Father, I have sinned against heaven and in your sight, and am no longer worthy to be called your son.' But the father said to his servants, 'Bring out the best robe and put it on him, and put a ring on his hand and sandals on his feet. And bring the fatted calf here and kill it, and let us eat and be merry; for this my son was dead and is alive again; he was lost and is found.' And they began to be merry."

Luke 15:17-24

If you did only this one thing today, it would be a successful day, a fruitful day, and a profitable day in the kingdom of God, plus it would bring joy and healing to your life and those around you: Simply love God more than yesterday, enough to come completely to Him now, and enough to receive those He sends to you. In humility, forgiveness received leads to forgiveness given and sets many prisoners free. This becomes possible when you receive God's Son by believing on His name, resting in His grace and the power of the Holy Spirit to produce the real fruit of mercy in your life. No matter the circumstances or the years that have passed, love calls you home in the heart of God. Only your answer to this call will ring true to all around you and to generations yet to come.

Father, I love You more than my life. I turn from my own things and come into the fullness of Your life, walking in Your forgiveness. Thank You for waiting for me for so long. As I dwell in Your house, help me also to welcome those you call home. In Jesus' name, amen.

Matt. 5:6-9   Rom. 5:1-11   Isa. 58:6-12

FINER, HIGHER
September 27

"For My thoughts are not your thoughts, nor are your ways My ways," says the Lord. "For as the heavens are higher than the earth, so are My ways higher than your ways, and My thoughts than your thoughts."

Isa. 55:8-9

Just as God's strength and creative ability are finer and higher than ours, so is His love. God loves more than any human can love. I think this is what Jesus meant when He said we must love Him more than our families or anything in this world. He speaks of a higher form of love that makes our family love and brotherly love of this world pale by comparison. Not to negate our human love but to lift it higher into the realm of His divine love, He asks us to love Him first, more than these. Then we will have more than human love to give to others, including those closest to us.

To struggle to love God with our human love more than our family and friends is not the point; it's not even close. Instead, we are to love in His love as He first loved us, as revealed in Christ. This becomes easy when He shines through us, as light passes through a thin curtain that stops everything else. Christ's love penetrates where human love cannot go and moves beyond it.

Our love of God is not only first in order of beginning, but also first in magnitude and essence. He calls us to enter into His love, putting Him first, and shifting into His will, shifting gears to let this love pour out of us to others, lifting all up into a finer, higher relationship that leads to new life. His love, *agape* in Greek, is sacrificial (Gal. 2:20). We have a hint of this in human love, but it can be short-lived and self-geared.

To love us, God surrendered Himself to us in His Son before we loved Him. His wooing of us is selfless, perfect, eternal, and unstoppable. Consider those you love for a moment, and then consider God's love for you. There is a similarity but also a huge difference in quantity and quality. God sent His Son to reveal directly to us and then to bring us into that finer love, higher and deeper all at once, outdistancing in every direction anything that ever entered our hearts. Living in that stream as a child with a humble heart, we can then place our human relationships into that same stream of truth, grace, trust, deep intimacy, beauty, and power that we have simply labeled "God's love." If we are standing in that river, loving others from that heavenly stream, all those around us will taste the difference, finer and higher.

Father, I open my heart to You. Fill me with Your love and power in Jesus Christ, who gave Himself for me. Help me to taste the difference and drink deeply of His life so I can love others with Your love. In Jesus' name, amen.

John 3:12-17   1 John 4:2-14   Matt. 18:21-22

PRESS TOWARD THE MARK September 28

Brethren, I count not myself to have apprehended: but this one thing I do, forgetting those things which are behind, and reaching forth unto those things which are before, I press toward the mark for the prize of the high calling of God in Christ Jesus.

Phil. 3:13-14 KJV

Only God can bring you forward to the goal, the mark, of His high calling in Christ, who lives forever to bring you to Himself. Notice the steps necessary to go forward, to move into the fullness of Christ. First, Paul said he counted not himself. In prayer, do you count yourself first or count on others to do what only God can do? Paul was not depending on himself to apprehend or take hold of the life of Christ. He knew he could not grasp it or carry God in a box. Instead, he focused on forgetting what was behind him and reaching out to what God had planned for the future.

To forget is to lay down some heavy things. In Christ, it is possible to forgive and also to forget old things that still hold your attention. Letting go of what draws back also lets you reach out to what is new. This reaching is not a grasp for control but an openhanded reach, an empty, submissive reach for what only God can give.

Only in no longer counting on yourself or the ability of others, in forgetting as well as forgiving, and in reaching forward to receive and not control can you begin to press toward the mark. Pressing indicates there will be resistance. This life is not a passive journey. Yes, there is surrender to God, but you also must press forward through difficulties and the thorny thickets of compromise that infect our world. The key is to focus on the one thing that God calls you to do. The truth and power of that one thing will cut through all knots of distress and distraction (Matt. 13:22).

This one thing that you do in God's power takes the place of many other, lesser things that the world is calling you to do in your own power. The prize of living in Christ is well worth it. Paul could have left out "prize" and said simply "I press toward the mark of the high calling of God in Christ Jesus." The mark is the goal of your salvation, union with God in Christ, which also brings a treasure, a prize: the riches of divine love, the creative power that moves the universe, dwelling in your heart and you dwelling in God's heart by sharing Christ's life. This is a prize worth lining up and aiming for—to hit the target, to press toward the mark, as He helps you move forward one step at a time. Sin is described as falling short of the mark (Rom. 3:23). Line up! Press forward!

Father, bring me into the fullness of Jesus Christ through the grace of this one thing: knowing You and loving You in receiving Your Son's life. In Jesus' name, amen.

Luke 10:41 — 11:4 Deut. 8:1-11 2 Tim. 4:2-8

September 29

WHATEVER COMES

Lord of all, give me strength to do Your will. In Your purpose, You leave nothing out and You make all things new for Your glory, so I agree with Your ways and count it all joy to receive whatever comes according to Your plan. Make me ready. Make me fruitful in the aroma of Your love and forgiveness. Make me one with You. Bring me forward in faith, whatever comes. In Jesus' name, amen.

Where can I go from Your Spirit? Or where can I flee from Your presence? If I ascend into heaven, You are there; if I make my bed in hell, behold, You are there. If I take the wings of the morning, and dwell in the uttermost parts of the sea, even there Your hand shall lead me, and Your right hand shall hold me.

Ps. 139:7-10

Rom. 8:26-39

WHEN? September 30

"Then you will call upon Me and go and pray to Me, and I will listen to you. And you will seek Me and find Me, when you search for Me with all your heart."

Jer. 29:12-13

When will you find God? When will your load be lighter? When will you experience the reality of His presence in your life? It will be when you call upon Him, when your heart is completely His, unified in His love. When Jesus said to the fishermen, "Follow Me," they left all they were doing, their business connections, houses, families, friends, and whatever else had to be done that day, and followed Him. In your heart this is what you can do, even though you may not change location. In the middle of business, family, and friends, you can follow the Master first, when your heart turns fully to Him.

It's the same level of commitment that makes a fisherman leave his boat and nets behind. When your heart turns to follow the Master, then nothing else of this world holds your attention as does His gaze and His voice. In serving Him first, you are able to serve others as He would. You watch how He moves, and you break bread with Him. Then there is bread for a multitude. You go where He leads, following His steps and directions, not human opinions.

Perhaps there were many then who believed that Jesus might be the Son of God, but they did not have time to leave what they were doing to go to Him or follow His ways. They turned back to their work. Perhaps another time, they thought, but since the timing was in their hearts, it never happened. The real answer to the question of when is in the heart. It's not about scheduling time but turning the heart, which opens the time.

How do you answer the Lord today? When will you love Him with all your heart, soul, mind, and strength if not now? He is calling you now, and "now" to Him has the weight of eternity. Can you answer with nothing holding you back? Whatever may hinder you from coming now is the very thing that will hinder you forever. The call simply identifies it.

That question of when shines right into the corners of desire and free will. Ask the Lord to cleanse you and turn your life in His mercy and light. Responding to His love, make one step today in His direction that you have never made before. Make it in His power, and all the rest will follow. When? Now, in your heart, eternity is arriving with or without Him.

Let me come to You now, Lord, as I never have before. Father, turn me in Your mercy and grace so I can follow Your love and fully receive Your Son's life. In Jesus' name, amen.

Jer. 31:3 2 Cor. 5:21—6:2 Matt. 4:12-22

SET BEFORE YOU   October 1

"I know your works. See, I have set before you an open door, and no one can shut it; for you have a little strength, have kept My word, and have not denied My name."

Rev. 3:8

Christ is the One who is the door and has opened the door of His purpose in our lives that no one can shut. Perhaps we have not been able to see it, but now, as to the blind, He calls us to see the door He has already opened. He calls us to move through in the power of His cross and resurrection, even in the works we are called to do in a little strength. Since we are God's workmanship (Eph. 2:10), He will finish all the work, including the part we are too weak to accomplish, which only He can complete in the light of eternity. We cannot break through the door of our calling in our own strength or open doors He has closed in His infinite wisdom and purpose. The door God has opened is now set before you. The choice is clear: go through, or miss your future in Him.

To study the door, the lock, the keys, and the principles of action and reaction will not be enough. We must go through the door. Four steps are given in the Scripture: to see the door (which no one can shut), to have a little strength, to keep His word, and to not deny His name. Where is the door the Lord has opened in your life today? Do you see His light anywhere? Ask Him to renew you so you can see it more clearly and receive His strength and faith. Then move through in the power of the Holy Spirit. Only our Lord can set before us an open door. Only He can bring us through in grace and truth.

O Lord, touch me and heal me so I can see the door You have opened and set before me.
By Your grace, bring me through in Your power and purpose. In Jesus' name, amen.

John 9:30-39   Josh. 24:14-18   Luke 23:33-43

THE VEIL OPENED   October 2

"God is Spirit, and those who worship Him must worship in spirit and truth."

John 4:24

In His heavenly pattern of Christ's cross and resurrection, God can remove the veil of death and line us up in obedience with His eternal life. He calls us to follow Christ, not to aimlessly forge our own path. Our desires of the flesh blind us as we walk toward death, content with our games instead of the real life of God. Playing at life, we rush ahead to do it all ourselves and then want God to play along with us. We can fish hard all night and have nothing without His direction. In seeking that direction, I tried to find it on my own, saying, "Yes, Lord, I want to follow You, so here is what I plan to do." Like searching earth to find heaven, it simply doesn't work. Often the flesh invents religious games we can win through control of ceremonies and elaborate constructions, but instead the Holy Spirit simply brings us to Christ's cross and complete surrender each day so that we become children of life instead of experts in tombs.

The Son of Man comes to us with in-depth experience in both heaven and earth. He has been there, done both, conquered it all, and now invites us to His banquet as we surrender daily. Just as a husband lifts a bride's veil, so we can come only in Christ's name, moving beyond ourselves. We look up and let go of everything but His hand.

A nail-scarred hand leads us, and that makes us uncomfortable. Yet the heavenly way, uncomfortable now, is the true life of the flesh. It denies not the flesh but the control of life by the flesh, and so brings us ultimately to new life in a new body as well as in spirit. As I prayed, God asked me something like "Do you want the pattern of yourself or the pattern of heaven?" I was too dumb to answer. I wanted heaven, but I didn't want to die, and that's the catch. Jesus shows us clearly that if we don't give up our flesh, we will die, and if we do choose to live now with Him by the Spirit, we will truly live, even in our flesh. He became incarnate so we can become like Him now in His resurrection power.

In Jesus Christ we inherit a fuller life beyond the veil of what the flesh can see. Denying self, Christ followed the way of the Spirit, who took Him all through the world, through the veil, and into amazing life. Now look at my life. Look at your life. Is our lifestyle here set up to make our flesh comfortable? Do we welcome Jesus with a cross—or without a cross? Many prefer Him without a cross and hang onto their veils, as a blind bride never willing to open up to new life. Yet if only a little corner of our veil is lifted and occupied by a cross, His light enters now.

Father, I put aside my old ways to ask for Your new way in Christ's cross. Lead me out of the darkness of my flesh into Your living light and joy. In Jesus' name, amen.

Luke 9:23-39   Heb. 9:14   Matt. 27:45-54

ONE CHOICE FOR ALL TIME   October 3

"I call heaven and earth as witnesses today against you, that I have set before you life and death, blessing and cursing; therefore choose life, that both you and your descendants may live; that you may love the Lord your God, that you may obey His voice, and that you may cling to Him, for He is your life."

Deut. 30:19-20

Our free will is a gift from the Creator, whom we can choose to reject. He gave us the ability to ignore Him and His love. Choose well. This choice has consequences. It is made not on a linear scale of personal history but on an unlimited scale of eternal potential. Our future life is a mystery, but we do know the One who is both the Beginning and the End, the Alpha and the Omega, the Firstborn of all creation, the Bright and Morning Star still shining in our darkness today. He chose you. He wants you to let Him do more through you than you can do for yourself. Although some play with molecules as toys and think they are creating something, we cannot create ourselves, nor can we create something out of nothing. Someone gave us the toys. Many people think God gave us the beginning, and then we determine our own end; but in fact the end is already set in motion, and our choice merely focuses on one of two eternal alternatives.

Even those as yet unaware of the gift of life in Jesus Christ were included in the cross and the love He offered (Luke 23:34). Not only is our free will a gift from the One we can choose to reject, but He is also the source of our freedom and our will to act. His creation includes our beginning and our end. Those who would try to create their own salvation on a human scale forget that even the minds they use to do this were given by the Creator who loves them more than they can know. Not wanting to give their minds or their choices to someone they cannot control, many simply shrink their options to include only what human minds can manipulate.

The freedom found in Jesus Christ offers more. Making one choice for all time to live in God through Christ is not a narrow choice but a specific acknowledgment of the widest of all possibilities: to participate in His divine nature that loves enough to die for us and bring us new life right where we are. Choose well. Do not let anyone else or any political or cultural agenda make the choice for you. Use the gift of free choice to know the Giver. One step can change the journey.

Father, I come Your way and choose Your life through Christ. All other roads are ultimately lifeless. I want to follow Christ through His blood, which cleanses me, and the power of Your life in Him, which raises me to stay forever with You. In Jesus' name, amen.

John 6:27-35, 57   Luke 12:25-34   1 Tim. 2:3-6

October 4

~~~~~~

REMOVE THE VEIL

Father, please remove the veil from our hearts and minds so we can see the Bridegroom now through Your Holy Spirit. Open us to recognize the signs of His presence and to receive His gifts already here in the Spirit, molding us into the shape of Your kingdom, making us one with Your will. In Jesus' name, amen.

Nevertheless when one turns to the Lord, the veil is taken away. Now the Lord is the Spirit; and where the Spirit of the Lord is, there is liberty. But we all, with unveiled face, beholding as in a mirror the glory of the Lord, are being transformed into the same image from glory to glory, just as by the Spirit of the Lord.

2 Cor. 3:16-18

2 Cor. 4:1-18

~~~~~~

TURN TO SEE

October 5

Jesus said to her, "Mary!" She turned and said to Him, "Rabboni!" (which is to say, Teacher).

John 20:16

Like Mary, one day I turned from my own expectations and saw the Lord's reality opening before me like nothing I had ever considered before. Even though Mary loved the Lord and followed Him, at first she could see only the empty tomb and Jesus as its caretaker (John 20:11-15). She stood facing a problem and wondered what people could do. Then He called her name, and she turned completely to see Him as He really was, standing before her in resurrection power. As she worshiped Him, Christ told her what He could do. Many of us have seen the empty tomb and turned slightly, still thinking in human terms and solutions, but not turning our hearts to see Jesus as He really is today.

In resurrection power, He calls us here, not as we expect or as our intellect will grasp, but as the Living Lord who cares for His people through the Holy Spirit. It is one thing for us to witness to the empty tomb and talk about what people can do. Many churches have this witness. It is quite another to turn completely to witness what only the Living Christ can do in our lives now (John 14:10-17; 1 Cor. 6:17-20).

Few have seen Him in the full power of His death and resurrection because they have not fully turned from the world. Still focused on human effort, the world is blind to resurrection power. No wonder so many are weeping. Turn and open your eyes now through the Holy Spirit to the Living Christ. Listen for His call and His direction. When you have turned completely to that call, you will see more than you do now.

For some, this is a major change in lifestyle and attitude. For others, it's a slight turn, the completion of a long process. Most of the body already may be in the right position, but the mind and will are still pointed away from full resurrection life. In our heads, we rehearse the problem and what is humanly possible. We go through the motions, think about the past, and wonder why the circumstances have crucified our Lord and our best hopes. We call Him "Lord" but presume that His work is over and ask whoever appears, "Where have you carried Him?" Our minds are prepared to work with a dead body when a living One stands ready to help us. We think we have to carry Him, when by grace He will carry us. Turn now to recognize Christ with you, as He really is today through the Holy Spirit. No problem or power can take our Living Lord away from us. He is our answer and our only solution. In your heart, turn to see Him.

Father, by Your Holy Spirit, help me see the light of Your risen Son and to answer His call. Turn me fully to recognize You working today through Him. In Jesus' name, amen.

John 14:15-23   Eph. 1:17—2:5   Rom. 6:4-14

WHERE HE GOES   October 6

As Jesus passed on from there, He saw a man named Matthew sitting at the tax office.
And He said to him, "Follow Me." So he arose and followed Him.

                                                                    Matt. 9:9

There is a place Christ calls us to go that only He can go. We can't go there on our own. He
calls, and we answer, saying we will follow. Then once we get up and come, we discover that
He is leading us where we cannot go humanly—into the depths of divine love. This is a place
beyond human dimensions. Even with the best intentions and great strength, no person can
enter into the complete spiritual victory that Christ has won. His blood transforms us into His
likeness. He is calling us, not to do what we can do, but to do what only He can do, far beyond
human action or human love, although these are wonderful by-products of the hope of His
calling. Christ is calling us to enter and live out the victory He has won. His divine love blows
our minds and wills entirely out of the human boat and onto the uncontrollable sea, which only
He can overcome.

If our eyes are on Jesus Christ, His love will draw us to where He is. But if our eyes are
distracted from the depth of His gaze, as they will be eventually, we are lost until He takes hold
and lifts us up. To truly answer His call is to be willing to depend totally on His strength. We
must decrease so that He can increase beyond our limitations. He will use our human ability for
His calling, but we will not use it for Him. Wherever Christ calls us, we cannot go there until
we let Him become fully Himself in us, fully revealed.

Most of us are willing to let God use us as His temple, according to our design and limitations, according to our idea of who He is or should be for us and others. But we don't know
His design and are unable to complete it. Only the Spirit of God in Christ can bring our lives
to completion. Getting out of the boat is one step. Arriving depends on our willingness to let
Him lift us up and bring us there. His purpose is not that we should walk on water, or become a
beautiful temple of human design, but that He might become fully Himself in us. Then we will
walk on the waters of a new creation and live in His light here and in the world to come. Christ
will call you to a place you cannot go on your own. Will you follow?

*O Lord, bring me where You want to go. My first step is to You. In repentance, I bow
before You. Lift me up in Your love and bring me all the way in Your power and purity.
In Jesus' name, amen.*

Matt. 14:22-36   James 4:10   Col. 4:2-6, 17

THE DAY FOR WASHING

October 7

"Though your sins are like scarlet, they shall be as white as snow."

Isa. 1:18

This is the day for washing. Sometimes dirty things pile up, and we pick through the stack of soiled clothes taking one or two, leaving the others to wait. This is the day for washing everything. Whatever you have brought to the Lord to wash in the past, that was good, but now He asks you to also bring whatever has been left behind, covered over, and left unseen at the bottom of the pile. Bring everything. There is something much deeper that He will wash in you as His love uncovers it. The Lord will not take it from you forcefully but waits patiently for you to bring it of your own free will.

This is the day to lay it all before Him and plunge it into His healing stream. Bring Him the deepest part of your life, perhaps still unknown to you, not just the surface things needing to be changed, but also the twisted roots that have grown in darkness. Through the power of the cross, Jesus will pull up and stretch out, search through, and wash clean everything so that His cleanliness becomes bright hope in you, pure joy, your deepest source of strength and fruit. Hold nothing back. It only becomes sour as the stains grow deeper. This is the day for washing and releasing the sweet fragrance of forgiveness. This is the day to come clean in Jesus.

Father, wash all of me in Your mercy and love. I hold nothing back. I want to be clean in the blood of Your Son, the Lamb Jesus Christ. In His name, amen.

Rom. 13:8-14   Ps. 51   Rev. 1:5

TAKE A DRINK
October 8

On the last day, that great day of the feast, Jesus stood and cried out, saying, "If anyone thirsts, let him come to Me and drink. He who believes in Me, as the Scripture has said, out of his heart will flow rivers of living water."

John 7:37-38

You have to come near to take a drink. Room service is not available. Drive through will not do. No one else can get you there. To drink of Christ requires more than just coming near physically. It involves a change of heart and humility of mind that turns your focus completely to God's power and His answer. How many of us wander, thirsty for spiritual life, but we're still too busy drinking the sand of our own desires to realize there is eternal water available? Take a drink of the One who lives forever and truly satisfies.

Jesus said we will not thirst when we are close enough to drink of Him through the Holy Spirit, not just observe Him, or sit next to Him, but to take in His life so that we flow as one with the Living Word, sharing His purity and power (John 6:57). The supply is inexhaustible. There is no end to the water that flows from this Rock in a weary land. Physical water gives us a hint of what Jesus was talking about when He said to drink of Him. Water is necessary for life, but it cannot be captured and held with our fingers or our minds. A clean vessel is needed. Even then, we can't just hold this water and study it; we must receive it deeply so life will enter every cell of our bodies (Rev. 21:5).

If we keep the water on the outside, even washing the surface with it, we will die. A real drink is taken in completely to become one with us, working in every area and producing action. The water that saves a life has come into that life and lives in and through each action. No section of our bodies can be blocked off from absorbing the drink. It moves throughout, soaks in, and produces more than what we can see. Take a drink of Jesus' life today by opening your will, your heart to Him in prayer and repentance, by absorbing God's Word and receiving His cup of the new covenant. It's not just for you to taste but for you to act on and overflow to others (Matt. 10:42). They are thirsty too. What do you have to offer them?

Father, fill me with Your living water in Jesus Christ. I have been drinking things that do not satisfy. Now with all my hope in You, I open my life to You. I'm thirsty. Fill me with the life of Your Son, who makes all things new. In Jesus' name, amen.

Rev. 22:13-17   Ps. 42   John 4:10-14, 23-26

October 9

~~~~~~

TABERNACLE WITH US

Father, come and dwell with the people You have cleansed and healed in the blood of Your Son Jesus. Let Your power protect us and Your light purify us to live as children whom You can welcome through Your Son. Please tabernacle with us, even now through the Holy Spirit, and as Jesus came with new life, let Your life dwell in us and reach to others wandering in the desert, those whom You call to come home. In Jesus' name, amen.

Then He took the cup, and gave thanks, and gave it to them, saying, "Drink from it, all of you. For this is My blood of the new covenant, which is shed for many for the remission of sins. But I say to you, I will not drink of this fruit of the vine from now on until that day when I drink it new with you in My Father's kingdom."

Matt. 26:27-29

Ps. 91   Rev. 21:1-8

~~~~~~

REST AND REPENTANCE
October 10

And Jesus said to him, "I will come and heal him."

Matt. 8:7

Sometimes in our rushing after Jesus, we need to stop for a moment to rest in the trust that He will come in the Holy Spirit to us. Others are praying and pleading for us, as even Jesus our High Priest is, so it's not necessary to depend on our own strength to bring Jesus our way or to run fast enough to catch Him to capture His attention on our terms. Once we have asked, we can rest in all that He offers, which is already given for those who receive Him humbly as a child. As we trust and obey, Christ comes to save us because it is His desire to come, not because we plead well enough to make Him come.

Of course, we should pray and seek Him, but when we knock as He leads, we can trust the door will open in God's will. If we try to break the door open with our own efforts, even with good intentions, we are not in His will, after His heart. Only when we cease from doing our works, can He fully do His work in us. To repent is to turn from our power to His, leaving our baggage behind. As we rest in God's mercy, we can forgive others. As we lay down our weapons, peace comes in like a river that washes us into the amazing power of His kingdom.

It's impossible to truly rest without repentance and to really repent without resting from our own agenda. In a dynamic way, both lead us into deep freedom, a kind of active rest in which God's energy and love flow through us, changing both spirit and body.

The purpose of the Sabbath is to turn us to God, to open us to His creative power and the gift of His Son. In taking time out from our own routine, we turn to His creative pattern of life. In this way, rest and turning not only heal the past and restore what energy was lost, but they also prepare us for more action in the week ahead. Rest gives us insight as well as energy. God is preparing us now for His new creation. If we keep going with no rest, we will die and miss it. If we keep going with no repentance, full speed ahead on our agenda, we will also die and miss it. Only His rest leads to full life.

Our Savior calls us to come a new way, to turn aside from the controlling pull of the world and the desires of the flesh and the mind. To say, "I surrender *all* to God" means *all*. With that weight gone, we are free to come to quiet waters, green pastures, true paths, strength and comfort in the valley, and a banquet even in a battle zone. Rest is His peace in you now.

Lord God, forgive me for being too busy running on my own to follow Your directions for rest. Bring me home Your way. Create in me a clean heart to follow You and allow You to complete Your purpose in the peace that passes understanding. In Jesus' name, amen.

Heb. 3:18—4:16   Ps. 23   Phil 4:5-8

NEW MERCIES   October 11

Through the Lord's mercies we are not consumed, because His compassions fail not. They are new every morning; great is Your faithfulness. "The Lord is my portion," says my soul, "Therefore I hope in Him!" The Lord is good to those who wait for Him, to the soul who seeks Him.

Lam. 3:22-25

Since God's mercies are forever new, they are more powerful than our old problems. When you wake up spiritually, you see that the problems that follow you from the past are no match for the power of God's mercy, which shines now, renewing His creation in magnificent love that overcomes every shadow. As the day progresses, the light becomes brighter. As our faith increases, we can see more clearly how the shadows flee away as the Son rises. As we watch, we see a rhythm, a progression, a judgment, and a balance of light and shadow in our lives, but the reality of the light remains the same.

When evening comes, it is not a sign of defeat but a signal of rest before dawn. The light has not vanished but disappears, as in our flesh we turn away from it. If we turned with the sun, we would always walk in the light. As the sun is much stronger and brighter than any earthly shadow, so God's Son is stronger and bigger than any earthly sin.

If you see the shadows lengthening and the time of your trouble increasing, know that God's mercies are steadily renewing, even while you are in the darkness. For a time, the light will not be visible, but it is there all the while. The reality of God's creative presence never ends. While we sleep, turned away in the deepest night, the Morning Star announces what is already coming.

No one who sees only the shadows will be prepared to welcome the dawn, the whole reality of God's light. Those who think their night is permanent will not be ready for the new day that is advancing even during their darkest hour. In the power of our Creator, the sequence ends in light. God's creation, in which we dwell, began in light (Gen. 1:3) and ends in the full light of Revelation (Rev. 21:1-3, 22-25; 22:5). In the power of your Creator, your personal sequence of trials and victories, failure and faith, will all culminate in the light of His presence. Walk now in the reality of that light, even through the temporary shadows of this day.

Father of lights, bring me into the center of Your will and the fullness of Your life in Jesus Christ that overcomes all darkness. Shine in me forever. In Jesus' name, amen.

James 1:17-18   Gen. 1:1-5   John 1:1-13

REJOICE ALWAYS   October 12

Rejoice in the Lord always. Again I will say, rejoice!

Phil. 4:4

To rejoice always is to let the Morning Star shine in your heart always, day or night. He is the same yesterday, today, and forever. When the situation is darker, joy shines even brighter. To rejoice always is to lay aside every weight that drags your spirit down and to run by the Spirit, even when you're too weak to get up, letting Jesus carry you through every difficulty in the race that He already has finished for you. When the Morning Star is shining through you and His promises ring true in your life, nothing can stop the movement of joy that strengthens you even in sickness or struggle. Rejoice always, and the Creator's joy becomes your strength (Neh. 8:10). Why should He give His strength to someone who will not rejoice in it?

Keep running so your spiritual muscles do not become weak in clinging to some earthly satisfaction. Don't study the sidelines or look back to that comfortable bench where you were sitting. Even in disaster, the Lord calls you to move forward in His strength. Move forward now, even in weakness, and enjoy His presence in the middle of what you're doing right here, the place where your steps will go next. Keep praising God so that your eyes are taken off your own feet and lifted to the goal that awaits those who rise on eagles' wings. Rejoice always in God, who rejoices always in your living in His Son (Zeph. 3:17). In the long run, your joy will end unless it is in Him, and He is in you. The "always" depends on Him, and it starts now. Run straight into the Son, rejoicing always.

Father, lift my eyes to who You are, moving in power, so that I can run freely to be the person You created me to be. Forgive me for trying to go anywhere else or have anything else. Fill me with Your joy in Jesus Christ. Today, I will rejoice in Your mercy and Your presence with me always. In Jesus' name, amen.

Rev. 22:16-21   Heb. 12:1-11   John 16:33

ONE IN JESUS

October 13

". . . that they all may be one, as You, Father, are in Me, and I in You; that they also may be one in Us, that the world may believe that You sent Me."

John 17:21

To be one in Jesus is to be one in the Father and to live in His life. It is possible to talk about Jesus' life and learn all about it, but unless we are one with Him, we are dead (John 1:11-13; 3:36). Many of us say we know the President of the United States. We can name him, read about him, and even guess what he might do in a certain situation, but most of us never meet him personally. Some are that way with Jesus. We've read about Him, but we don't know Him intimately through the Holy Spirit.

We can go through this world doing wonderful work and attending church every Sunday, but unless we are one with the Living Word, we do not truly know Him. Jesus points this out in Matthew 7:21: "Not everyone who says to Me, 'Lord, Lord,' shall enter the kingdom of heaven, but he who does the will of My Father in heaven."

It's impossible to do God's will unless we live in Him through His Spirit by receiving the life of His Son active in us now. To do good works out of our own effort instead of letting them grow out of the Master's life in us produces no lasting fruit with the taste of deep joy flowing from an intimate relationship with Him. Unless we lay down our weapons and surrender to His love within us as streams of living water, our work will not produce the long-term sweet fruit of His life.

Jesus says those who truly know Him are those who do the will of the Father. Since only the life of Jesus can fulfill the Father's will, we must first become one with Jesus in order to become one with God's will. Otherwise, our eager work with the name of Jesus stamped on it will head in the wrong direction. He is patient to let us run around doing "Jesus" things until we finally realize we can't do it, that our own fruit tastes dry and lifeless, and we fall at His feet in full surrender. Then the Father can graft us into the Vine by faith to produce His real fruit through us. Others will taste the difference.

First, we need His life, not more programs or complicated study, just the Lamb slain before the foundation of the world. He asked that we become one in Him so the world will believe. If all that they ever see of Jesus is what we do on our own for Him, they will not believe. If all they hear is what we say about what Jesus does, they will not believe. They want to see how He lives in us now. If they find His fruitful life made visible here, even in an imperfect container, they will reach out for Him. When they eat that fruit, they must taste the Vine. Then they will believe, not in our work, but in Him.

Father, make me new in Your Son so Your life can flow to those around me, bringing the fruit of His life to those who are hungry. In Jesus' name, amen.

John 5:26, 39-40   John 17:22-23   Titus 3:4-7

REALITY OF HUMILITY   October 14

But He gives more grace. Therefore He says: "God resists the proud, but gives grace to the humble."

James 4:6

Humility is a reflection of eternal reality. We can receive Christ only when we see Him as He truly is and therefore recognize ourselves as less, as poor in spirit and needing forgiveness. When we are aware of our poverty, then we can accept His riches. Otherwise, we are full of everything else, both good and bad, with no room to receive eternal life. When we recognize our humble position in the universe, then we are in alignment to see His full majesty and to share in His power, even in small things. Christ was born to show us reality, which is both beyond us and intimately in us at the same time.

Our pride is a false mirror and very flat. In looking into God's Word, we can fully see the perfect law and love of God revealing our position as forgiven sinners, made whole as children of God through His gift of Himself in Jesus Christ. Let it not be said that we are so rich in the emptiness of this world there is no room for the treasure of His sacrifice bringing us into the reality of God's love. He came to make us truly complete.

Is there room for Christ now in the inn of each of our days? If we're not so busy with the bigwigs and our "important" projects that we have no time for His little ones, He will come in and bring new life. What else could we be doing that would be more real? New birth comes to those who are very small in their own eyes because the gate is narrow, but it opens forever to a wider life. Humility is the reality of eternity changing us now as God's new creation.

Father, forgive me for thinking too much of myself and the world and too little of You, who created it all for Your glory. Lead me into the humility of Jesus, who died for me and rose again to bring me to You as a child of Your kingdom. In His name, amen.

James 1:9-27   Matt. 5:1-12   Ps. 25:4-15

WHERE TO MEET
October 15

"And he arose and came to his father. But when he was still a great way off, his father saw him and had compassion, and ran and fell on his neck and kissed him."

Luke 15:20

God will meet us on the way home, well before we get all the way there. We can still have the grime of the pigpen on us and the smell of it all over us, but if we have left it behind, He will meet us as we are headed home in repentance. We don't have to reach some worthy position or attitude or have all the riches we wasted repaid and made up. Because we are His children in Christ, He will save us and clothe us and bring us to a feast. Where is the turning point? The Father does not come to the pigpen. He might hear our complaining and know what a wasted mess we are in, but nothing happens. Complaining is not coming to Him. Describing the situation is not coming. If our prayers are only describing the mess and begging for relief, we're stuck. He is waiting to see us repent, to turn around and come home.

He longs for us to say, "I will arise and go to my father, and will say to him, 'Father, I have sinned against heaven and before you, and I am no longer worthy to be called your son. Make me like one of your hired servants'" (Luke 15:18-19). In our prayers, the Father is not waiting to hear us say over and over how bad things are but to say who we are.

The facts of the situation are well known to Him. He wants to know if now we know who we really are in the middle of it and how much we need Him. He wants to hear our heart and see us coming now. A request in action is a request He can answer. The Father waits for our recognition, not of the circumstances, but of our inability to help ourselves. Faith is that recognition of Him as the One whose Holy Spirit reveals the truth and shows us the road home. Love means the gate is always open in Christ who is our mercy seat (Ex. 25:21-22; John 20:1, 11-14).

If our Father loves us, why doesn't He just come to the pigpen and drag us out or make us come home? Doesn't He already know what we need? Yes, but He knows that more than just food what we need is a full realization of who we are that leads to repentance, turning toward the love that can make us whole forever. Food without faith might as well be pods for the pigs. Food with faith is a banquet of joy in the Father's forgiveness. It's a long road home, but He will meet us there.

Father, I need You more than anything or anyone. What once looked so good to me is now a stinking mess, and I am hungry. I will get up and leave the past behind and come to the house of Your will and Your love. Please meet me on the road. I'm coming. In Jesus' name, amen.

Luke 15:11-32   Luke 14:15-24   Matt. 6:9-13

~~~~~~

WIDE MERCY

Thank you, Father, for Your wide mercy that moves through and beyond us into eternity. Help me to forgive others and myself as You forgive us. No one deserves the gift You have already given, but You want us to receive now what only You can do. In Your grace, I will let You do it all. In Jesus' name, amen.

"And whenever you stand praying, if you have anything against anyone, forgive him, that your Father in heaven may also forgive you your trespasses. But if you do not forgive, neither will your Father in heaven forgive your trespasses."

Mark 11:25-26

Eph. 4:17—5:2

~~~~~~

SWEEP CLEAN   October 17

Or do you not know that your body is the temple of the Holy Spirit who is in you, whom you have from God, and you are not your own?

1 Cor. 6:19

For us to be swept clean, we must be willing to work and pray on the floor. This can be humbling—to bow down and come near the foundation. Perhaps we would rather dust the pictures or the tops of lamps, but no one has ever swept a house clean by merely waving a broom in the air. There may be other cleaning to be done, but all of that dirt eventually comes right down to the floor, and when the floor is finally clean, the room is clean. Look at the floor of your life all around you. What are you standing on? Is it littered with things that will trip you up, or is there a clear path, a smooth surface for the work that brings life into your world?

Some of us spend a lot of time clearing one area, only to move the same things to another area, where they eventually have to be dealt with again. Getting it all out is not rearranging it or making it look more attractive. To sweep clean means getting down to rock bottom in prayer on the foundation of Jesus Christ and letting the sword of His Word dig out the dirt between the cracks or wherever things have piled up in the corners. In Him, you can carry out the big things. Then little things are swept from crevices, lifted from almost invisible places on the familiar surface of life. His sharp Word digs them out.

Sweeping brings up unseen particles we didn't even know were there until we see the pile of dirt growing before our eyes with the momentum of each stroke. Move it on out the door! Don't leave it on your threshold or even the front step, but put it clear out and away, far enough that the wind can take it and blow it away. If you blame it on another person, putting the dirt in a human trashcan, someone else still has to bear that burden. Don't dump your dirt on someone else. Let the King of the temple clean out your house, exposing everything to the wind of the Holy Spirit.

In that cleansing holy wind, the dirt will be carried away, far beyond your knowledge or ability. Let go of the little pieces, and the big things will fall into place. It does no good to rearrange the furniture unless you sweep the floor under it. Otherwise every step you take will carry the imprint of that old dirt. Sweep clean. Open your heart. The King is coming to your house for dinner, and He wants to stay forever.

Father, I open my life to Jesus Christ to sweep me clean. Move everything and help me to let go of the big and little things that make my life a mess. No more bargaining and selling in this temple. Take everything out that does not please You. Make my life a clean house of prayer, washed in the blood of Jesus. In His name, amen.

Matt. 21:12-17   Mal. 3:1-3   Eph. 5:25-27

PASS THE TEST October 18

Then Jesus, being filled with the Holy Spirit, returned from the Jordan and was led by the Spirit into the wilderness, being tempted for forty days by the devil. And in those days He ate nothing, and afterward, when they had ended, He was hungry.

Luke 4:1-2

Jesus Christ passed the test because He was filled with the Holy Spirit and because He fed on the Word of God and worshiped and served God alone. In this way, God could work in Jesus according to divine plan, not human will. Are we ready to do the same? The first test for Christ was to try to manipulate divine power to meet human needs. Instead of seeking what satisfies the flesh, Jesus knew that only God's Word can truly satisfy. He knew that with God alone as His source, every need would be met.

The next test offered worldly glory through worshiping the devil instead of worshiping and serving God alone. Again, Jesus repeated what He had been feeding on all His life: His Father's Word, alive and sharper than any two-edged sword. He offered no other argument or debate, knowing that God's Word alone was enough.

The next test was subtler. Satan tempted Jesus to force God to act and so prove His divine identity. But the Son of God knew that He could not lead God to act but that God would lead Him as He stayed in intimate fellowship with His Father through His Word and worship. God would confirm His faith and identity at the right time. All three tests were passed through the power of God's Word and waiting on Him alone by faith.

It is the same for us today. If you feed on the Word and depend on God, you will pass test number 1. If you pass number 1, then you will be able to pass test number 2, because true worship and service flow out of God's Word. Through knowing the Father, you will then discern how He wants to move in you and confirm your faith and identity in action. With His Word first, every other answer follows. God gives us Himself in the Living Word; we feed on Christ, receive His nature, and then return by faith that Word to God in love. As Christ passed the ultimate test, He helps us pass our tests (Heb. 2:10-12, 17-18).

If you live in His Word and worship the Father alone, He can work through you in whatever comes. Don't expect to pass the test of discernment until you have first walked in His Word and truly worshiped God with obedience. Too many try to make full proof of their ministry before passing the first test or the second. Feed on His Word, worship and obey Him above all, and you will be ready to pass any test.

Father, I depend on You alone to meet every need. Strengthen me in Your Word and in the cross of Christ so I can worship and serve You alone. Make me ready for any test. In Jesus' name, amen.

Luke 4:3-21 Heb. 4:14-16 John 4:34

WHOSE DAY IS IT?   October 19

This was the Lord's doing; it is marvelous in our eyes. This is the day the Lord has made; we will rejoice and be glad in it.

Ps. 118:23-24

Have you ever had your day ruined or said, "This just isn't my day"? Of course, we all have. Yet in reality, on our own, "our day" is internally ruined to start with; in fact, it never is our day. This is the day the Lord has made, and we are created to rejoice in it. It is the Lord's doing! We are the creatures, the created ones, responding to what our Creator has already done as we complete in miniature the plans He makes possible. Our true day is not formed by our plans and effort but by God on an eternal scale.

Hopefully, we are walking through it, completing surface details to fit with the deep purpose already woven into His eternal pattern. If not, we become sick in body, soul, and spirit. Anything we can accomplish happens because the Creator who made everything in the beginning allows it, even paves the way for us to have the molecules at hand and the wits to do something with them.

It is like a parent watching a toddler shakily stack some blocks the parent purchased with the strength the parent has passed on to him. On his own, the toddler can move things around, but he knocks over more than he builds. With the parent's hand guiding, something new begins to take shape to the delight of both.

As clay vessels, we shouldn't imagine we are potters and expect to turn the wheel. Since we're made in the Potter's image, He helps us to create on a smaller scale in harmony with His work. God's hand alone turns the wheel to complete everything, most of which we cannot see (Jer. 18:1-6; Isa. 43:7). None of us has yet learned to make the earth turn or the sun shine. Our Lord alone makes all things new, and He made us to rejoice in what He is creating, including ourselves. Most problems arise when we try to remake ourselves, others, and the world in our image. How incomplete! Only the Lord's doing is marvelous! Whose day is it on your calendar?

Father, make me and this day something beautiful in Your creation. Forgive me for being more interested in getting things done than in rejoicing in Your power. In Jesus' name, amen.

Phil. 2:12-18   Isa. 44:6-8   John 5:17-23, 30

October 20

~~~~~~

WISDOM PRAYER

Father, to ask for wisdom is to ask for You. Come, in the grace of Your Son, and renew my mind, body, soul, and spirit in the wisdom from above so I will live and love completely in You. Help me to listen as a child and grow, not just in the accumulation of facts and things, but in the understanding that love brings. Open me to the experience of Your grace right here where things are most difficult. On the inside, turn me to receive the light of Your Son, and let that light melt my will into His as You heal my wounds in His. From this healing, make me wise and clean and gentle. Let grace grow in me and build a temple for Your Holy Spirit. Let it be a clean temple. May Your light bring fruit to my life and others, as You plow and sow in me what pleases You and what brings blessing to future generations. Make me into the likeness of Your Son, my King, for He is life now and in the future. He is my wisdom. It is not that I am wise, but I am in Him, and His wisdom grows in Your perfect design. When He comes into my life in fullness, reigning supreme, then there will be no room for self-effort and worry because He will cleanse every corner, all in all. I accept the wisdom of the cross. In its commitment, make me wise in deep simplicity and the power of the resurrection. May the Living Word rise up in me and produce new life. Then the fragrance of Your wisdom will fill this garden, and there will be life, even through death, for this season and the next. In Jesus' name, amen.

How much better to get wisdom than gold! And to get understanding is to be chosen rather than silver.

Prov. 16:16

Luke 21:1-19

~~~~~~

WHAT CHRIST SEES
October 21

So when Jesus had received the sour wine, He said, "It is finished!" And bowing His head, He gave up His spirit.

John 19:30

As Christ on the cross, with arms outstretched and nailed for us, looked up to His Father, He saw what He still sees today: our sin and God's love for His children. At the intersection of God's divine power and human need, He still reaches out toward us and washes us with His blood. The nails of our sin had driven Him and affixed Him to this intersection of the vertical power of God and the horizontal cry of human need. As the Son looked out at the people, He offered forgiveness, even to His enemies. Have we?

In the church, we see first the vertical focus of worship toward God and then the horizontal direction to meet human needs. They are not separate but one and the same, depending on God's power (John 12:32). The upward call of the Father and the outward call to others meet in the heart of Christ. He sees both and still lives both directions now through the Holy Spirit working in those who will allow themselves to take up a similar cross, giving themselves wholly upward to God and outward to others, out of the love that still flows from Christ's wounds.

In the resurrection, the two directions, upward to God and outward to man, became one, so that our lives here are infused with power from above, and His life as the Son of Man intercedes and reigns over all principalities and powers for our redemption, working one day at a time, even in our dust. He already sees us made one with Him, living in the Father's house. Have you seen what Christ sees where you are today?

Father, seeing how Your love comes down here, I can see outward to others as Jesus does. But I can't carry a cross; I can't make it to that intersection where both become one until I let You carry me into the heart of Jesus. Carry me now. In His name, amen.

Luke 15:4-10   Luke 23:33-49   John 13:20

YES TO GOD   October 22

For the Son of God, Jesus Christ, who was preached among you by us . . . was not Yes and No, but in Him was Yes. For all the promises of God in Him are Yes, and in Him Amen, to the glory of God through us.

2 Cor. 1:19-20

Our yes to God is an echo of His yes to us in Jesus Christ. Saying yes to God is more than a one-time affirmation; it's a continuous yielding to a relationship that lasts for eternity. Our yes to God is more than words. It includes actions that break free and supersede a self-focused routine. When did you last consciously say yes to God without any conditions? When did you last say yes to God by quietly giving up something you wanted or spontaneously stepping in to help someone else? Even if the world never hears the yes in our hearts, God hears it when we step fully into His will. Our delight in Him alone is part of the unspoken yes that He loves. Our growth in surrender to His ways reveals the amen to what He is already creating in us, even when our flesh would prefer to say no (Gal. 5:16).

There's an amen after the yes; there is nothing after the no. The Holy Spirit's yes is stronger than the flesh's no, but we have to move in the Spirit to hear that yes. If we're choosing surface pleasure and living all day in a big no or a string of little no's, how will we hear God's deep yes? In whatever is confronting us, the answer to the bottom line is yes and amen to what God has planned, even if we can't understand it fully. To agree with the blessing that's coming to us in Christ, we must say what the Giver is saying, and He says yes and amen!

Our yes to God, spoken or unspoken, also involves a clear no to something or someone else. We must let go to take hold of God's promises and then let go of even more to bring the amen and fully receive it all. Otherwise, our hearts are divided and our commitment too weak to produce good fruit. The branch that's connected to the Vine is not drawing nourishment from anything else. I've tried saying yes both to God and to the world, and it doesn't work. A divided heart becomes dry and deceptive. With enough illusion and rationalization, it may appear to work for a while, but a withering reality soon sets in, forcing a clear choice. Yes to God is no to the world. Most of us will shout yes to God and mumble no to the world, but He wants to hear both equally clearly. To say yes to God is to become holy, more and more separated to Him, and separated completely from what is not of Him. What does your life say yes to today? Amen?

Father, I say yes to You because You have said yes and amen to me in Jesus Christ. Change me so all of my life will reflect that eternal yes. In Jesus' name, amen.

1 John 2:3-6, 15-17   Matt. 26:38-42   Luke 5:4-11

TAME THAT HORSE
October 23

For we all stumble in many things. If anyone does not stumble in word, he is a perfect man, able also to bridle the whole body. Indeed, we put bits in horses' mouths that they may obey us, and we turn their whole body.

James 3:2-3

To become mature in Christ, we must allow ourselves to be tamed and guided home. Otherwise, we wander in the wilderness of our own wills. To tame a horse requires much patience and the skill of a master. The horse cannot tame itself. It certainly would not insert a bit of cold metal into its own mouth. Yet it is this small bit that truly leads to obedience because once it is in the mouth, the whole head can be turned, and then the whole body guided. A horse is in no way capable of doing this even if it wanted to. The horse cannot put the bit in its own mouth and then gently bring the bridle over its head. The master must do it.

It's more difficult when the horse rears up and tries to keep control of its mouth. The more the horse resists, the more energy is wasted before any real journey with the master can begin. Eventually, the horse comes to trust the master's touch and voice enough to wait quietly, head ready, mouth willing to receive. Within the church, accepting the bit of obedience in the mouth first can lead to the whole body turning at the Master's direction. More than the tongue comes under control as we submit to One greater than we are and to a language of love greater than ours, as He guides us.

To do this, we must allow that cold, hard bit to come against our tongues. The bit is about the same size and shape as one of those Roman nails that pierced the body of Christ. The power of His sacrifice is the only love that can completely tame us in trust. Would you let one of those nails touch your tongue and control it, then allow the Master to bring over your head, mind, and will the bonds of a love so great it will lead you home? The straight way to the Master's house comes with His sacrificial bit in your mouth and the bridle of His love over your head.

Master, I accept Your will in my life, in my mouth, in my work, in my every movement, so You and I may move together in one love. In Jesus' name, amen.

Matt. 12:35-37   Prov. 15:1-5, 23-33   John 8:28-32

October 24

THE MANAGER

Father, in the fullness of Your power, lead us where we cannot go on our own. Help us to quit trying to manage You and instead let You manage us in every detail of our lives. In Your love from above, teach us which pastures are green and which waters are peaceful and pure, full of Your life. Breathe in us and release us from our dead ways to walk in the living way of Your Son here, according to Your creative power. In Jesus' name, amen.

"I am the door of the sheep. All who ever came before Me are thieves and robbers, but the sheep did not hear them. I am the door. If anyone enters by Me, he will be saved, and will go in and out and find pasture. The thief does not come except to steal, and to kill, and to destroy. I have come that they may have life, and that they may have it more abundantly."

John 10:7-10

Rom. 11:33-12:21

MY LORD JESUS CHRIST   October 25

Then He said to Thomas, "Reach your finger here, and look at My hands; and reach your hand here, and put it into My side. Do not be unbelieving, but believing." And Thomas answered and said to Him, "My Lord and my God!" Jesus said to him, "Thomas, because you have seen Me, you have believed. Blessed are those who have not seen and yet have believed."

John 20:27-29

What is the difference between someone saying that Christ is the Lord, our Lord, or my Lord, as Thomas did? We should know Him as all three, the last being most direct, and perhaps the only One you would die for, just as He died for you. Who do you say He is? He is fully human but more than human, fully God but also living fully in human dimensions. Our Lord Jesus Christ is unlike any other teacher, prophet, priest, or king. If we see Him only as a good teacher, a social reformer, or a spiritual leader, we miss His true identity, which is inextricably linked to our identity. We will never truly know who we are until we know who He is in living reality today. It's not who you or others say He *was,* but who *you* say He *is.* Would this be obvious from your life today?

As the Son of God, Christ shares God's nature and applies it to us. As the Son of Man, He shares our nature and offers it to God, covered in His blood. The two natures meet in Him as in no other person. As Lord, He carries the authority, power, and love of God to reconcile these two in eternal peace. As Jesus, He comes where we are now, born to live with us and in us to save us from our sins. As Christ, He carries the anointing of spiritual riches and divine grace to transform us now through the Holy Spirit and also to prepare us for the life to come. Many Scriptures* show Christ to be the Savior who changes us and our world. There are other witnesses to Him right now where you live. Can you think of any other teacher or leader who carries this identity and a divine love that gives all of Himself, all that God has for you? In light of this gift, who are you?

Father, let my actions show that I am Your child made new through the living power of Your Son, Jesus Christ. Send Your Holy Spirit to lead me now. In Jesus' name, amen.

Eph. 1:3-10   1 John 2:20-27   Matt. 16:13-17

(* Some examples: John 8:23-24; 1 Cor. 15:22-28; 2 Cor. 5:17-21; Gal. 4:4-9; Col. 1:12-20; Gen. 3:15; Gen. 22:7-8; Job 19:25-27; Ps. 22; Isa. 7:14; Isa. 9:1-2; Isa. 53; Zech. 9:9; Mic. 5:2-4; Matt. 1:21; Luke 2:11, 25-33; Phil. 2:5-11; Heb. 10:11-14; John 1:29-34; John 3:1-17; John 4:25-26; John 6:46-54; Mark 14:60-64; Luke 24:1-11; Matt. 28:16-20; Rev. 1:4-8.)

ONLY YOU

One thing I have desired of the Lord, that will I seek: that I may dwell in the house of the Lord all the days of my life, to behold the beauty of the Lord, and to inquire in His temple.

Ps. 27:4

This is the day—there may not be another one—for us to come to the Lord, to draw near in our own way, to get as close as possible, and then to say simply, "Lord, I want only You." What is there in our lives today that would keep us from saying that? Consider for a moment anything that stands between you and your Lord, and then ask Him to remove it, so all that is seen of your life is His life in you.

Nothing you can do today on your own would be more beautiful or more outstanding or more successful or a brighter treasure than to have the fire of the Lord Jesus Christ burning so brightly in you that any others watching could say, "I see You there, Lord, in that life, only You." That is your true work. Lay aside the old garment of blind self-interest and rise up to meet your Lord, the Son of David, the Bright and Morning Star, who shines brightest in those who say, even in darkness, what we say now to Him, "Only You, Lord, only You!" When your life and actions also say that you want only Him, then He will cause you to see His beauty and become like Him.

Lord of all, You know my heart and its many divisions and desires. I now lay them at Your feet and ask You to make me whole on the inside and the outside so that my life says "Only You." In Jesus' name, amen.

Matt. 5:8   Mark 10:46-52   Luke 9:20-26

TRUST AND OBEY   October 27

So He said, "Come." And when Peter had come down out of the boat, he walked on the water to go to Jesus.

                                                              Matt. 14:29

To taste joy, we trust and obey the One who calls us wherever He leads, even on stormy seas. Somehow we prefer to trust ourselves and follow directions to some beach with an easy taste of self-focus. Notice it's not trust and try on our own, or trust and think, or trust and talk, but trust and obey. One builds on the other and takes us farther than either one alone. It's impossible to obey without trust and impossible to trust in the long term without obedience. Without some experience on which to build our trust, we wait in paralysis by analysis, self-serving, and halfhearted.

Peter's relationship with Jesus Christ included enough experience of his Lord's true power to make Peter get out of the boat. Perhaps the others trusted Jesus somewhat, but not more than themselves, not enough to step out on a risky sea. Their relationship with Him was not strong enough to ask for or answer His call. Peter got out and moved toward Jesus. With divine love working in him, Peter's love for the Lord exceeded his human fear. Even though he later had to be rescued, Peter also had a beautiful walk back to the boat with Jesus. Imagine that walk of rescued faith! The last part of Peter's walk with Jesus far surpassed his initial leap in getting out of the boat.

It's the same for those who seek healing; they must go to the Source and reach out in obedience to touch Him. Action is required. Every round goes higher as we climb up Jacob's ladder to an encounter with God in Christ. He will meet us in the most unexpected places and call us to do unusual things, one step at a time. When you trust, you place your foot over the side of your own boat. Then obedience takes you farther. If you slip on the way, the Lord is there to catch you and bring you to the destination He has planned. Have you just thought about it, or are you willing to step out in action and trust Him more than yourself? Stormy water, with Jesus, is safer than the boat without Him.

Father, increase my faith so I can trust and obey You completely, no matter how rough the water around me or what others will do. I trust You to bring me to the place in Your kingdom where You want me to be. In Jesus' name, amen.

Matt. 4:19   Matt. 14:22-36   Luke 5:4-5

October 28

~~~~~~

WHERE WE ARE

Father, anoint us today in Your Son to bring the gospel to the poor where we are, to heal broken hearts, to speak deliverance to the captives and recovery of sight to the blind, to set at liberty those who are oppressed, and to proclaim the acceptable year of the Lord. The time is now. They are here with us. So are You in the person of the Holy Spirit. Open our eyes to see Your harvest here and now. In the name of Jesus, amen.

"Do you not say, 'There are still four months and then comes the harvest'? Behold, I say to you, lift up your eyes and look at the fields, for they are already white for harvest!"

John 4:35

Luke 4:16-21, 31-40

~~~~~~

IGNORANT OF GOD'S RIGHTEOUSNESS   October 29

For they being ignorant of God's righteousness, . . .

Rom. 10:3

To be ignorant of God's righteousness is to miss the point of being, to miss your own identity and the source of life. By the essence of who He is, the essence of the Creator, the universe moves. It's not just a matter of mechanics. All creation depends on the nature and character of the One who is who He is, whose pure being is the basis for everything else. Creation is not just a matter of reactions but of the essence of the One who caused the actions and reactions in the first place. Who we are prompts what we do, and so who God is prompted all of creation. It existed first in His being and then was revealed in action. When He spoke, His thoughts were formed in a visible fertility beyond any human capacity for purity or production.

Take a look at the universe, and you will see a glimpse of who God is. Take a look at yourself, and you will also see a glimpse of who He is, for we are made in His image. But we are not all that He intended us to be, since that original image was marred in disobedience, rejecting His truth. To be ignorant of God's eternal righteousness is to miss your own potential. He sent His Son to restore all of it.

If we are ignorant of God's righteousness, we may try to measure the universe on a human scale, which eventually falls short. It isn't enough. Some of us try to do the same thing with our lives, to measure them on a human scale, but we're missing the wider scope of God's reality and our true potential. To be ignorant of God's righteousness is to believe we alone are in charge of everything. One quick look at the smallest galaxy will tell you that we're not. So why should we run our lives as though we are?

I asked the Lord to show me some of the ways, practically speaking, that I've been ignorant of His righteousness. Your list may be different, but here are some symptoms of my ignorance: wasting time on trivial projects/pleasures for myself; trusting God for the possible but not for the impossible; measuring my life on a worldly scale; looking at the future based on what I can do instead of what God can do; making up my own rules as I go along to justify what I already know is wrong. The list goes on. What would your list include? How would our lives change if we loved God according to His creative purity? Following His commandments, obedience from the heart, and worship in spirit and in truth all come after we begin to know Him and His righteousness personally.

Father, reveal Your righteousness in the life of Jesus Christ active in me now by the Holy Spirit. I want to know You more than anything or anyone else and to live my life in the reality of who You are revealed in Your creation and Your Living Word. In Jesus' name, amen.

Jer. 9:23-24   Matt. 6:3-15   Ps. 97

OUR OWN RIGHTEOUSNESS   October 30

For they being ignorant of God's righteousness, and seeking to establish their own righteousness, . . .

Rom. 10:3

In considering our own righteousness, the key word is "own." This is what we have in our possession, under our control, and on display to advertise ourselves. Our righteousness operates under our name and for our benefit. God's righteousness operates under His name and for the benefit of His kingdom, which includes us and many others, blessing us more than anything we could do. Human systems of righteousness are described in the Bible as filthy rags (Isa. 64:6). They are full of the infection of sin. No matter what party we attend dressed in them, we are asking to receive our own death.

Our own righteousness keeps us from the banquet God provides through His Son and the fuller benefits of divine creation and eternal life. God's gift to us is the purity of Christ's sacrificial love, creating spotless garments for His wedding feast in His kingdom. The fruit in that feast is eternal life. But some don't want to be invited. They prefer their own parties, costumes, and rules where the prize is death.

1. **Our own righteousness is a righteousness we can master on our own by acquiring more knowledge and skill, often at a price (Gen. 3:6). We think it is ours because we have bought it and mastered it. Bible study becomes an intellectual exercise.** In contrast, spiritual life in Christ depends on Him alone and our acceptance of a relationship in which His life is implanted in us, growing as a seed, unfolding by His grace. The fruit of this relationship belongs to the Lord, who bought us in love by giving Himself for us. Our part is to let His life grow in us to produce fruit that remains (John 15:16).

2. **Our own righteousness is a righteousness we can control religiously by trying to manipulate or placate God with human effort in the institutions and rituals of our own design.** In Christ, we acknowledge that only He can please our Father, that only Christ's sacrifice takes away sin, and that only the Creator of the universe can make us wholly human. We give up our control to the God who comes, who makes us whole in true worship and who gives us more than our own efforts could provide (Mark 7:6-7).

3. **Our own righteousness is a righteousness that makes us look good and elevates human ability.** In Christ, we see Him elevated on a cross to die for all people and rising to give life to all who will humbly receive it. Nothing we can ever do will match that elevation or that love (John 12:32).

Father, forgive us for trying to set up our own righteousness. Fill us with the truth of Your love and mercy in Jesus Christ and help us to receive His pure life. In Jesus' name, amen.

John 3:3-8, 27-36   2 Cor. 11:3   John 12:32-50

SUBMITTED TO GOD
October 31

For they being ignorant of God's righteousness, and seeking to establish their own righteousness, have not submitted to the righteousness of God.

Rom. 10:3

Would you consider preparing a resume for a job application and then not submitting it? How about putting food in a pan and not turning on the heat? Either way, the process is incomplete, and something good is missed. There is little risk, but there is also less accomplished. Unless we are submitted to God, His righteousness will not change us. Risk avoidance is a major cause of fruitless Christians off course in their own world of self-justification. To be saved and sanctified by God through Christ, we will have to let go of our projects, release them into God's hands for the future, and accept the heat that changes us into the image of His Son. Otherwise, we are incomplete.

In trying to establish our own righteousness, in trying to stay comfortable, we cut our development short and never grasp the full potential our Creator planned and purchased for us. Submission is usually seen as a limiting factor, but it is actually an expanding factor, breaking us out of our old safety zone into something new. Ask the applicant whose letter is in the mail. Ask the meat sizzling in the pan. Something different is going to happen, and change is coming, even with the outcome still unseen.

Of course, loss is possible. But in submitting to God, we know the end result will be more, because we are trusting and giving ourselves to our Creator, not to the manipulations of man or the fear of human failure. The creative righteousness of God never fails. His power and love are everlasting. You can send the letter. Turn on the heat. Eventually, you'll receive some good news and a full meal. Even today, He is cooking up the future you have submitted to Him.

Lord, free me from the slavery of trying to be my own master and release me into the power that comes only in following You. In my Savior's name, Jesus, amen.

John 13:3-17   Rom. 8:28-37   James 4:4-10

REVIVAL
November 1

From that time Jesus began to preach and to say, "Repent, for the kingdom of heaven is at hand."

Matt. 4:17

Revival is exciting, not because of shouting and singing or big crowds or the numbers of people added to membership rolls. The excitement of revival is in the turning of hearts to the Lord. Drawn by the Holy Spirit, a deep turning by faith produces a small surface noise like the squeaking of a huge door opening. The door is much larger than the squeaking. In coming to Jesus and leaving behind our old ways, there is a momentum of hearts turning, breaking free as we begin to move through the door He has opened. Signs of revival are only the sound of that giant door of faith and salvation opening by His power alone. The depth of repentance is unheard or unseen, but the surface reaction of that work of the Holy Spirit is as if a heavy door groans on its hinges and opens in the light of Christ. You can't hear or see the depth of the change, even within yourself, but you know the door is open in His faith working in you.

Before that door opened, the Master knocked on many hearts. Oil was poured on the hinges. Then we could get up from where we were sitting and move toward Him, wanting Jesus more than the safety of our closed room. The door is unlocked in the cross, as He gives Himself to us, and opens completely as we are drawn to welcome Him by faith. In the Holy Spirit, Jesus Christ comes through to us and now asks us to be one with Him. When we invite Him into our lives, then He can bring us to His Father's house. The faith to let Christ come through to us and then to go through the door of salvation in Christ is a gift of God (John 6:37-45; Eph. 2:8; Rom. 10:17; John 1:12-13). He is the way, as we humbly repent in turning the will, mind, and heart toward God. When "the kingdom of heaven is at hand," then you can put your hand to the door. Jesus said we can turn now, because there is something to take hold of in His power, a real spiritual door opening right where you are by the faith He gives you. It's that close.

When you take hold of that door, you will feel the rough wood of a cross, which Jesus felt when He carried His for you. With a deep groan of repentance, the hinges turn, and a high cry of the heart recognizes our Lord! Some will think those hinges turning and the heavy door opening are too noisy. They prefer to keep the door quietly locked and talk to Him through it, while staying comfortably where they are. Will you turn now from what you're doing and get up to go to the door? Let the hinges creak. Bring more oil! Enter what Christ has opened for you. He is Lord of all, and He is near at hand!

Father, turn me in the power of Your love in Christ so the oil of His anointing will lead me deeper into His sacrifice. In Him, bring me through to You. In Jesus' name, amen.

Heb. 13:8   Rom. 8:22-27   Rev. 3:19-22

~~~~~~

SING AS THE LILIES SING

Father, draw me now to the garden of the empty tomb. Call my name, and I will sing as the lilies sing in resurrection power, even in the place where I am today, knowing You are making all things new in Your Son. In Jesus' name, amen.

Jesus said to her, "Woman, why are you weeping? Whom are you seeking?" She, supposing Him to be the gardener, said to Him, "Sir, if You have carried Him away, tell me where You have laid Him, and I will take Him away." Jesus said to her, "Mary!" She turned and said to Him, "Rabboni!" (which is to say, Teacher). Jesus said to her, "Do not cling to Me, for I have not yet ascended to My Father; but go to My brethren and say to them, 'I am ascending to My Father and your Father, and to My God and your God.'"

John 20:15-17

Song of Sol. 2:1-2, 16

~~~~~~

IN TUNE WITH GOD
November 3

Praise the Lord! Praise God in His sanctuary; praise Him in His mighty firmament! Praise Him for His mighty acts; praise Him according to His excellent greatness! Praise Him with the sound of the trumpet; praise Him with the lute and harp! Praise Him with the timbrel and dance; praise Him with stringed instruments and flutes! Praise Him with loud cymbals; praise Him with clashing cymbals! Let everything that has breath praise the Lord. Praise the Lord!

Ps. 150

To be in tune with God, our actions must praise Him. Not just "music," but all of life is tuned, adjusted, stretched, or wound tighter, just as musical instruments are tuned into perfect harmony with the pitch set by the concert master. Before beginning, an orchestra conductor will watch while the concertmaster leads the players to tune their instruments to his. The perfect pitch for life comes through One with an instrument like ours. He starts the process with a perfect, sure pitch that all the others must match. For us, the Son of Man came in human flesh with an instrument like ours to offer the perfect life so that we can follow Him, adjusting our lives to match that sound, vibrating in His love.

In the tuning process, we are transformed until the sound is the same as His. At first, the tuning sounds like chaos, but without tuning, even if the instruments carefully followed the same music, each would make a slightly different sound, off-key, not harmonious, not that sweet unity that lifts us beyond ourselves. The music of our lives rises like an offering to heaven. We need to be in tune with God in order to rise in that new song that only He can give (Ps. 40:1-3). Through testing, the actual singing and playing of it are adjusted to come out sweet and true, exactly on key with the Master. We can read all the music we want and play very loudly, but unless it's produced in tune with the humility of Jesus and His power as the Son of God, the song is not beautiful.

The right notes and the right instruments and a lot of air are not enough. Our Conductor may interrupt the performance and nod to the Concertmaster to bring us into tune before going any farther. He wants the sweet music of heaven to echo, however faintly, here in the world where His Son walked. Let Him tune you up. Soon, it will make you out of tune with the world. We simply can't play with the world and be in tune with God. Our Master uses a cross to tune us and the gentle breath of the Holy Spirit to move through us until we sound like Him. How does your life sound? Living praise is the most beautiful music in this world, revealing a hint of the next.

Father, make my whole life praise to You in tune with Your Son. Give me a new song from a clean heart. In Jesus' name, amen.

Acts 16:23-26   John 17:20-21   Rev. 5:8-13

SIMPLE POWER   November 4

"Consider the lilies of the field, how they grow: they neither toil nor spin; and yet I say to you that even Solomon in all his glory was not arrayed like one of these."

Matt. 6:28-29

In an information-saturated culture, pure simplicity speaks louder than a multitude of rational debates. Simplicity is startling. The simple truth can bang you right between the eyes and settle down deep, where it stays long after reports and statistics and sophisticated debates have faded into the crowd. Our path ahead becomes clear when there is enough simplicity in our lives for Jesus to shine through and room enough for Him to walk, leading us in purity where only He can go.

The Lord knows more than we do and encourages us to study and investigate—but in His light and following His example. Some of our dark problems would be quickly solved if we laid down our complicated debates and simply let the light of our Lord's teaching shine in without delay. Apply the simplicity test to your worst problem of the moment. Fit the template of Christ's simplicity and sacrificial love right on top of it, and see what sticks out, what doesn't fit His pattern. Let His purity burn it up.

Simplicity avoids delays and doubts. Our conflicted excuses quickly evaporate in the pure glare of our Savior's presence, and truth bubbles up when our clutter of intricate backtracking is removed. Follow Christ straight through the distractions. Trust Him today enough to be simple. Then you will receive His power where there is plenty of room for truth to stand and love to speak and faith to act. Trusting the truth is more powerful than whatever else you can think of doing.

Father, make my life simple enough to receive the fullness of Your new creation through Jesus Christ. My mind cannot grasp it, but You give freely to all who trust You. Change me now. When my cup is clean and open, it will overflow. In Jesus' name, amen.

2 Cor. 11:3-4   Matt. 5:3-16   Ps. 19:7-14

PULL OVER

November 5

There remains therefore a rest for the people of God. For he who has entered His rest has himself also ceased from his works as God did from His.

Heb. 4:9-10

Pull over. Rest a while and check the map. You may be traveling fast but in the wrong direction or missing some beauty along the road. Let the engine cool from the heat of your hurry and worry so it can take you the full distance. Shut down the noise, and listen for the creative voice of love in those who are with you or to the music of sparrows along the road and the song of the wind. To complete a symphony or a journey, the rests are essential to the rhythm and development of each movement, the personality of any melody, and to understand your journey so far. In a Sabbath rest, you allow God to realign what has shaken loose from His will or obscured the revelation of His love.

Let the place where you pull over be one of His choosing and timing, since there may be something the Creator helps you hear or see only in the place of refreshing He has designed. On His day for rest and renewal, allow God to pull you over, cleanse your heart, and open your ears. In the long run, you will travel much farther and discover more than human maps reveal.

Let Him show you how and when to rest in the freedom of His plan and the power of His presence. On the seventh day of creation, God rested. On the eighth day, He began a new creation through resurrection and a pattern of rest in the finished work of Jesus Christ. With a grateful heart, a pause along the way will acknowledge His creative power instead of yours. In the aroma of Christ's sacrifice and new life, in the beauty of our Creator's house, our rest unfolds as a kind of release into His will and a fast from selfish effort.

Imagine entering your Father's house but continuing to work and talk on the phone instead of sitting down with Him to enjoy His presence. Acknowledging the Sabbath is our admission that we need Him more than whatever else we wanted to do to create a world according to our desires. Pull over for a day. Hear and see what only rest reveals in His design.

Father, help me to rest in Your finished work on the cross and in the power of Your Son's resurrection. Waiting on You, serving You, is more powerful than working on my own. Silent before You, I hear the whispers of eternity and see the way. In Jesus' name, amen.

Matt. 11:27-30   Ezek. 20:12-16   Luke 23:52—24:7

TWO MASTERS   November 6

"No one can serve two masters; for either he will hate the one and love the other, or else he will be loyal to the one and despise the other. You cannot serve God and mammon."

Matt. 6:24

Serving two masters is exhausting. Can you imagine having two simultaneous full-time jobs? On Monday morning, you're supposed to be at two different places at 8:00 a.m. So you hurry to one and do a little there before sneaking out and spending an hour at the other place. Then it's back to the first spot with no time for lunch. Besides exhaustion, the result is that neither job is done to your satisfaction or the employers' satisfaction, so you are restless, nervous, and just waiting for the ax to fall, never knowing any joy. This is how many of us live our spiritual lives, constantly running back and forth between serving the world and serving God. Is He pleased that we at least show up for an hour or two here and there? Not as much as we like to think. He has requested a wholehearted decision to give our lives to Him completely. We can't repair ourselves with more work in the world.

Jesus said the greatest commandment is to love the Lord our God with all of our heart, soul, mind, and strength. Then we can love our neighbors as ourselves (Mark 12:28-31). Isn't that humanly impossible? Yes, but God's love working in us changes hearts to love Him more with His love, see ourselves as He does, and overflow to others.

We receive from God the gift He offers us in His Son so that we can give it back to Him with our whole heart attached. His Son died and rose again, freeing us from sin and making us ready to love. On our own, we can't let go of the self-worship that goes with serving the master of lies. That master offers to make us look good, as he offered to Jesus (Luke 4:5-8) with one huge chain attached: Satan wants us to worship him, and he uses our desire for control to control us to reach that end. That cancels our love for God. The other master makes no mention of love. Only our Creator offers us new life free of deception so that we can love Him, ourselves, and others fully, as He loves us forever.

The enemy claims to heal our wounds by creating other wounds in us and those around us. Our Creator heals our wounds with His own wounds. Do you want to know whom you are serving? Is your work done freely in love, leading to eternal life, or is it done in fear and a thirst for control, leading you and others to a dead end of self-interest? Is there anything you couldn't walk away from if God asked you to leave it? This is the chain that holds you to the other master. Christ has broken that chain in love. Walk free.

Father, I choose life in Your Son Jesus Christ, who sets me free from sin and death. Teach me to walk in that freedom so I live entirely in Your love. In Jesus' name, amen.

Rom. 7:22—8:6   Luke 9:23-26   John 15:9-20

SPEAK LIFE IN US

Touch us, Lord God, with Your holy fire, like a tongue of flame. We will never be the same. Speak life in us and through us in resurrection power. As our lives become a living sacrifice, let the fire of Your altar never go out, let our faith increase to receive what You have promised, and let us live and speak as a witness to Your truth in Jesus Christ. In Jesus' name, amen.

And suddenly there came a sound from heaven, as of a rushing mighty wind, and it filled the whole house where they were sitting. Then there appeared to them divided tongues, as of fire, and one sat upon each of them. And they were all filled with the Holy Spirit and began to speak with other tongues, as the Spirit gave them utterance. And there were dwelling in Jerusalem Jews, devout men, from every nation under heaven. And when this sound occurred, the multitude came together, . . . Then they were all amazed and marveled, saying to one another, "Look, are not all these who speak Galileans? And how is it that we hear, each in our own language in which we were born? Parthians and Medes . . . Cretans and Arabs—we hear them speaking in our own tongues the wonderful works of God."

Acts 2:2-9, 11

Lev. 6:8-13   Rom. 12:1-9

POWER IN PERSECUTION   November 8

. . . that I may know Him and the power of His resurrection, and the fellowship of His sufferings, being conformed to His death, if, by any means, I may attain to the resurrection from the dead.

Phil. 3:10-11

You can escape persecution by playing it safe in the world and still be in real danger spiritually. A healthy, wealthy, worldly person who ignores God's call is in more danger of death than a persecuted Christian in terrible circumstances, resting in the life of Christ. Better to be with Him now in temporary suffering than to be in temporary comfort and apart from Him forever. Even those who escape physical death in persecution will die one day. It is just a minor delay on the scale of eternity. The life of Christ in us is our only hope, and the power of His resurrection is our power in persecution. There is no other defense against death that will work.

God's witness is strongest in persecution, when the focus zooms in on this truth of life and death. Whether or not we suffer to the point of death, the power of Christ's sacrifice and resurrection enlivens our witness and increases our faith to overcome impossible odds and unknown trials. As He died for us and rose again, so we will live. At the right moment, God gives us the power to do the impossible and to speak the truth of His Word, which is quick and sharp to pierce the enemy's armor at just the point where it reaches the heart. No battle, no victory.

Run to where the victory is. Run into the Lord! He alone is our strong tower. Self would try to preserve physical life at the cost of spiritual life, unwittingly killing the true life that goes on forever. Self would open the door to the enemy who comes in with flattering words and promises of worldly success. Persecution may appear to come from other people, but it is really the work of the enemy attempting to deceive God's children by scaring them into choosing safety instead of God. Satan tries to lure us into his camp with deceptive promises of success only to kill us there. We die spiritually at the point we receive his lie. If, in order to escape persecution, we choose anything less than God, the end is death. Choose the Creator's life. Do not run, rebel, or hide from heaven's gate.

Stand in the power of God. He may ask you to stay, fight, and die, or to go to another place to wait until the storm is past, or to speak out now, depending on the work you are called to do. Finish it. Live hidden with Christ in God.

Father, make me ready to do Your will to bear fruit for You. Help me to move at the right time in the life You have planned forever. In Jesus' name, amen.

Luke 22:39-51   Phil. 2:8-18   Col. 3:1-13

TAMBOURINES IN THE WILDERNESS November 9

Then Miriam the prophetess, the sister of Aaron, took the timbrel in her hand; and all the women went out after her with timbrels and with dances. And Miriam answered them: "Sing to the Lord, for He has triumphed gloriously! The horse and its rider He has thrown into the sea!"

Exod. 15:20-21

God's people had timbrels, or tambourines, as they crossed over on solid ground between the waters of the Red Sea, delivered from their enemies. Trusting in God, they passed through safely where their enemies later sank. On the other side, Miriam and the others praised God for His power to deliver His people. Those tambourines of praise and joy also went with them all through the wilderness ahead, jingling clear to the Promised Land, where they would once again celebrate victory. During their wilderness time, the tambourines made music at weddings, at the breakthrough points of new life. All along the journey, the sound of the tambourines packed for the trip could be heard jingling as they moved along, even through barren and difficult places.

The joy of the tambourine is not in what we can do but in what God can do in us, His instruments. When you come to your place of deliverance, the breakthrough point of new life, come with joy and praise in what only His hand can accomplish. Carry a treasure of joy in your heart all through the wilderness and then across the Jordan. Know that other victories are coming, where God will win the battle against overwhelming odds. Then there is yet a great wedding and feast awaiting you!

Hold on to your tambourines in the wilderness. Even when a desert surrounds you, keep your joy and praise ready. Let the delicate bells of your laughter rise in a still, dark night. Practice the song of your next victory, and offer it to God when everything seems uncertain. He loves the sweet sound of tambourines in the wilderness, already rejoicing in the high sound of His victory!

Father, I offer to you the sound of praise You are longing for in my heart. Thank you for Your victories of long ago and Your victory beginning in me now. I will praise you as we go through whatever is ahead. In Jesus' name, amen.

Heb. 13:12-16 Ps. 149 John 16:32-33

TRIPLE PROTECTION   November 10

When He had been baptized, Jesus came up immediately from the water; and behold, the heavens were opened to Him, and He saw the Spirit of God descending like a dove and alighting upon Him. And suddenly a voice came from heaven, saying, "This is My beloved Son, in whom I am well pleased."

Matt. 3:16-17

In troubled times, we have a threefold protection in God. Let Him keep you in all three, make you aware of all three, and guide you to move forward in all three. As we understand God's nature in the Trinity as Father, Son, and Holy Spirit, we can also understand His triple protection as He makes us a new creation. First, we are protected by who God is. Before He delivered Israel from Egypt, He announced His identity as "I AM WHO I AM" (Exod. 3:14). God is nothing else besides Himself, and there is nothing beside or equal to Him. All the weight of glory of eternity resides in who He is, and He is on your side when you give yourself to Him. Nothing in this world or the next can stand against the source of everything. He is all in all, even right where you are now.

The second aspect of God's protection is the gift of His Son, whose life, death, and resurrection purchased your new birth as a child of God. How will this protect you today? Christ's blood cleanses from all sin and erases the power of darkness for those who will receive Him. There is no more amazing protection available to anyone today than the blood of Jesus Christ. It was the blood of lambs upon their doorposts that saved Israel from the death of the firstborn, and it is the blood of God's Firstborn upon our lives that saves us from the power of death and destruction. We may have to go through death, as Jesus did, but its power to hold us is broken so that we rise, as on eagle's wings, even in the face of suffering. We are already on our way to a new creation one day at a time.

Third, you are protected in God by what He does through the Holy Spirit. The Creator of the universe can do anything, anytime, anywhere. Since the beginning of the world, His creative power has not changed or failed to touch us. The light of the Creator still shines in the darkness, and the darkness has not overcome it. Through the Holy Spirit, He shines into our hearts, our prisons, our problems, and our prayers even now. Let Him speak His life in you and those around you. Let all the walls come down that we have built, expecting God to do nothing. He is ready to do whatever it takes to make you His new creation in Christ (John 1:12-13). Will you accept His full protection?

Father, cover me in the protection of who You are, the gift of Your Son, and the power of the Holy Spirit. Change me to fit into the covering of Your truth. In Jesus' name, amen.

Ps. 46   Matt. 1:20-23   Acts 1:4-8

November 11

WHO YOU ARE

Lord God, the beauty of who You are far exceeds anything I can know or ask today. Let me rest in the presence of Your mercy and truth that go on forever. The full assurance of Your love makes everything else bow down and rejoice. Nothing that is happening anywhere today comes close to Your power and the excellency of Your work. So have Your way completely. I know it will be beautiful even in difficulties. Lead me into Your will. Shine on me and melt away my fear. It's not more comfort or more information that I seek, but more of Your life in Your Son. Let Your beauty transform my actions into Your pattern of holiness, always seeking more of who You are. In Jesus' name, amen.

One thing I have desired of the Lord, that will I seek: that I may dwell in the house of the Lord all the days of my life, to behold the beauty of the Lord, and to inquire in His temple. For in the time of trouble He shall hide me in His pavilion; in the secret place of His tabernacle He shall hide me; He shall set me high upon a rock.

Ps. 27:4-5

Heb. 1:1—2:18

IN THE RIGHT PLACE   November 12

There is one body and one Spirit, just as you were called in one hope of your calling; one Lord, one faith, one baptism; one God and Father of all, who is above all, and through all, and in you all.

Eph. 4:4-6

The place we are spiritually determines our fruit-bearing capacity. As the Vine, Christ never changes, but the point at which we, the branches, connect to that life-giving source, and how we surrender to the Vine, varies from person to person. You can have great faith but insist on inserting it into the wrong place and produce no lasting fruit. On the other hand, you can be a person of little faith, but because you allow God to graft you in where He chooses, fruit results far beyond your ability (John 15:4). If you are in the right place, God can use you, according to His plan and His strength. In the right place, He gives you energy and opens doors that no one can shut.

Spiritual location has much to do with maturity and the coming harvest. To labor in His fields, we must be in the place He assigns, doing what the Master has already planned. There is a divine plan of creativity that far exceeds our plans and desires. More than geographic location, the spiritual place you live now includes your openness to the presence of God, those friends who labor with you, submission to God's will and His order of discipline, the power of the cross active in your life, cooperation with God's timing, the impact of your testimony, and above all the calling God has prepared for you. Find your location through prayer and His Word. Here are some locators.

1. Holy Spirit—Live in God's presence no matter what chaos swirls around you.
2. Friends—Share your heart in the body of Christ, working together in His love.
3. Order—Follow God's order in how He would arrange each day for His glory.
4. Cross—Each place you go should have the cross as its anchor. If not, don't go.
5. Timing—God makes appointments only He can keep; follow Him. Don't lead.
6. Testimony—If no words were allowed, what priorities does your life speak?
7. Calling—The fruit of your position in the Vine is produced by God's infinite power in the finite place where He has called you. You truly live only there.

With a sweet aroma, all of the above flow together to produce fruit tasting exactly like the Vine. After checking the pattern of your life, what changes could bring you to the right place with God? Let Him help you make them. All of the above are read daily by others watching your actions. Go forward in God's power to the place He calls you.

Father, line me up with Your plan for us in Christ. Make me fruitful in the right place at the right time to bring life to others. Your love is my testimony. In Jesus' name, amen.

John 16:1, 13-15   Prov. 16:2-9, 17-20, 25   Matt. 19:16-21

LOVE DISCERNS

November 13

And this I pray, that your love may abound still more and more in knowledge and all discernment, that you may approve the things that are excellent, that you may be sincere and without offense till the day of Christ, being filled with the fruits of righteousness which are by Jesus Christ, to the glory and praise of God.

Phil. 1:9-11

God's love discerns better than knowledge, anger, or self-focus. Even the best minds, without His love, offer a narrow view of the world around us. In anger, we are locked into our own prisons of fear and reprisal. Selfishness shackles us even further in our own limitations. Only love comprehends the whole picture of what is before us.

Our view is wider from fields of mercy that are ripe with God's love and the fragrance of His wisdom in the mind of Jesus Christ "who, being in the form of God, did not consider it robbery to be equal with God, but made Himself of no reputation, taking the form of a bondservant, and coming in the likeness of men. And being found in appearance as a man, He humbled Himself and became obedient to the point of death, even the death of the cross. Therefore God also has highly exalted Him and given Him the name which is above every name, that at the name of Jesus every knee should bow, of those in heaven, and of those on earth, and of those under the earth, and that every tongue should confess that Jesus Christ is Lord, to the glory of God the Father (Phil. 2:6-11). Since Jesus offered Himself for us in love, the order of our world and all true knowledge revolves around that amazing grace. Anything else is off balance and blind.

If we wonder how our situation fits with God's plan, love will discern how our decisions must match the sacrificial love of Christ. When our actions and words follow His pattern of humble servanthood, then our decisions will also lead to the power of His exaltation to the glory of God. There is a clear pattern to follow. What is lacking is the will to follow, and the will is only changed by love. He gave us that love when He gave us His life. In humility, let love discern the way into His power. Whatever doesn't match that love has to be removed. Then we go forward with more than knowledge.

Father, free me from serving myself so I can serve You and others and see clearly the path of new life leading me forward in the pure truth of Your love. In Jesus' name, amen.

Phil. 2:1-5   John 14:15-17   1 Cor. 13:1-6

WHICH VERSION?   November 14

"'These people draw near to Me with their mouth, and honor Me with their lips, but their heart is far from Me. And in vain they worship Me, teaching as doctrines the commandments of men.'"

Matt. 15:8-9

Which version of Christianity are we living? There are two versions: the human version and the one lived fully by Jesus. They present similar words but different fruit. One follows the patterns and ways of man, and the other follows the ways of God. "For My thoughts are not your thoughts, nor are your ways My ways," says the Lord. "For as the heavens are higher than the earth, so are My ways higher than your ways, and My thoughts than your thoughts" (Isa. 55:8-9). As the rain comes down and waters the earth, producing fruit, so God's ways produce in us what human ways can never generate, even though many of us try hard with good intentions. Our seed cannot produce His life.

Most of us prefer the human version of Christianity with its detailed lists of good things to do, because we think we can understand and perform them correctly. (We might even control them and take credit for the results.) Also, the human version can be changed to fit our perceptions. It draws mainly from within us to please human desires and culture with some mention of God. The divine version draws from the eternal Source, the Other, and moves through people, blessing them more by remaining focused on God alone. His ways are mysterious and out of our control, but they will bring more than we can know. The only way His life can rain down into ours and produce good fruit is when we yield to His version of Christianity and accept His seed. What version are you living? Ask yourself these questions.

1. Is the work I'm doing for God something I could do alone, or is it totally impossible without Him (John 15:4-5)?
2. How welcome is Jesus in the pattern of each day I have planned? Is He first?
3. Is my reward for this work the approval of others or the love of God? Would I do the very same thing if no one else knew that I was doing it but God?
4. Can I recommend my lifestyle without reservation to my children, both physical and spiritual? (You are recommending it each day you live it.)

Many of us live a mixture of the human and divine versions of Christianity. How do we enter God's way with an undivided heart? By surrendering completely to the only One who can live it. May God lead us fully into Christ's life today through His Holy Spirit to follow Him one step at a time. Then there will be a cross—and a resurrection.

O Father, make me whole and one with You through Jesus Christ, so that my heart will no longer be divided between two ways but united in Your love. In Jesus' name, amen.

John 1:12-18   Matt. 6:24   Ps. 81:8-16

November 15

TOUCH THIS CLAY, BREATHE LIFE

Creator, please touch this clay You have made from the beginning. Breathe into us, and speak Your word of life through vessels opened and turned in Your hands, shining with the baptism of Your Son, who washes us from all sin. Today, I submit to Your freedom and power, moving on the wheel of Your will. Breathe on us, O King. Under Your gaze, everyone who turns with Your touch comes alive to hold what You are planning to pour out at the right time. In Jesus' name, amen.

So Jesus said to them again, "Peace to you! As the Father has sent Me, I also send you." And when He had said this, He breathed on them, and said to them, "Receive the Holy Spirit."

John 20:21-22

Jer. 17:5-14; 18:1-6

A VESSEL FOR HONOR
November 16

But in a great house there are not only vessels of gold and silver, but also of wood and clay, some for honor and some for dishonor. Therefore if anyone cleanses himself from the latter, he will be a vessel for honor, sanctified and useful for the Master, prepared for every good work.

2 Tim. 2:20-21

The integrity of a vessel and how much light it reflects are obvious even before a feast begins. Vessels for holy purposes are separated from those for ordinary use. They are set aside for God to use in His house. In the temple in Jerusalem, the vessels served a function like no other in any other place. When we are set aside for the Lord to serve Him first, we do work that is unlike any other in any other place and of a nature and focus beyond the daily routines, although we're busy in humble tasks. Even in the middle of ordinary business, our nature is changed and our focus seeks a higher plane.

Some of the humblest vessels on earth are vessels for honor to the Lord because they are dedicated to Him. Even once as clay deep in the earth, they are changed to shine with holy light to honor a higher authority. The honor is not for the vessel itself but for the one to whom it comes. The light that shines within is for the owner. As we come to the Lord, He receives from us what He has placed inside us, so the honor is all His, both to create and to consume. In His holy ways, we are carried by power beyond ourselves to bring what satisfies God into His presence. Vessels do not come on their own power.

In a king's court, a vessel of honor is carried to the lips of the king, and he drinks what is inside of it. When we come in worship to the King of Kings, He accepts and drinks what He has already created in us. Vessels of honor do not create themselves or fill themselves. What fills them is of far finer substance than they are. The honor they carry is so much more than they can contain that they receive a value beyond their physical boundaries, a sense of authority and a bond of cherishing in belonging to the King that is far greater than the outer lines of appearance.

Their identity is in the one to whom they belong. Complete in serving Him, they move toward the King and His touch of joy, His eternal satisfaction. He will drink from them what pleases Him. A vessel for honor shines with the light that spills over the rim, full of His love within. A vessel for honor serves first the King but then at His direction also refreshes the other guests. A vessel for honor conveys a greater meaning and a deeper love than it can hold. Whether empty or full, may He make you a vessel of honor!

Father, make me a vessel of honor that pleases You, my King, and that serves those who have answered the invitation to Your table. Fill me up and pour me out with the light that comes from You alone. In Jesus' name, amen.

Ezra 6:5   Matt. 25:37-40   Rom. 9:20-26

YOUR HEART
November 17

The Lord has appeared of old to me, saying: "Yes, I have loved you with an everlasting love; therefore with lovingkindness I have drawn you."

Jer. 31:3

In fellowship with you, the Lord is mainly interested in your heart. Others will look at your outward appearance, how hard you work, the words you say, and what you can do. Foremost, the Lord searches your heart to see how much room there is in it for Him. If there is room, He can give you Himself and then His work. Even today, our Creator is sorting through all the other things in your heart, looking for a place where He can dwell in you in the Holy Spirit through His Son, Jesus Christ. Then from that relationship, not just rules of religion, He will draw you to live with Him. This relationship will include rules, but the relationship comes first.

Compared to giving Him your heart, all the other things you do are nothing, even the things you do for God. In all of creation, only your heart can give and receive the love for which He created you. If your heart does not receive Him, your hands never will. The soul, mind, and strength will follow your heart into His love.

If there were only work to be done, He could do it; if there were only doctrine to be taught, the Holy Spirit could teach it; if there were only sacrifices to offer, He could do it, and has already done it all in His Son. What He seeks from you today is your love. Give Him that first, generously, as He has given first to you, even before you were created. Take some time to do nothing but love Him today. Make sure it's clear He is first in your heart, not just one of many others. Then see what He has for you to do.

Father, I've said I would give you many things, but first I give You my heart, completely Yours forever. Fill me with the love You pour out through Jesus Christ for all people. Gladly, I receive it now. Let it overflow to You and others as freely as You have given it to us. In Jesus' name, amen.

Mark 12:28-34   Ezek. 36:25-27   Prov. 4:20-23

WARM WILL VARY   November 18

"I know your works, that you are neither cold nor hot. I could wish you were cold or hot. So then, because you are lukewarm, and neither cold nor hot, I will vomit you out of My mouth."

Rev. 3:15-16

Warm will vary. It cannot be counted on for anything. We know what hot can do. If we are hot with the Lord's living light, He shines and burns in us so many will see and come to Him. If we are cold and dead in a grave-type life, He can raise us up for a testimony for renewal. But if we are warm, we will vary, and the results are doubtful. Hot is hot enough to cook something. Cold is cold enough to keep it for the right time. But warm is room temperature, at which good food spoils.

The truth is that warm is a mixture. It has some cold in it, some death in disguise under the surface. On the other hand, you can tell the hot water by the steam, the beauty that rises from it. At which temperature are you living your life? Is God cooking up something good in you right now to purge out the impurities and leave only the pure gold of His righteousness within? Or does He have you in cold storage, waiting for another season? Even there, He knows where you are. At least, those who are cold know they need help and are ready for the fire when it comes.

The warm ones don't know they need help and won't ask. If you are warm, it may seem safe, but you are really not where He can use you effectively to shine out to others. Even those lost in doubts and sin, cold as they may be, can be converted for an amazing testimony. They can come out of the grave of the past as Lazarus did for a witness that draws others to the Lord. But in playing it safe, the lukewarm witnesses will convert no one. Worse yet, they give the illusion of some light, some life, but so weakly that nothing happens, nothing multiplies. That's when the good seed sits around too long and begins to spoil, rotting away in a comfortable place.

Since there is a pleasant appearance, nothing is done to change the situation. If someone is downright cold, others will try to warm him up; but those who are lukewarm will be passed by because they don't seem to need anything, even a wake-up call. You can sleep when it's warm. If it's really hot or cold, you will wake up. Are you awake? Let God light His holy fire in you, even if it makes you uncomfortable at first. It's time!

Father, bring me where I cannot go unless You carry me into the pure light of Your life. I see the flame, but my flesh draws away from it. Bring me safely through Your living light into the arms of my Savior, opened for me on the cross. In Jesus' name, amen.

Mal. 3:1-3   Matt. 3:11-12   Luke 24:30-32

~~~~~~

YOUR WHOLE WILL

Father, heal us to do Your will by letting You do all of Your will in us, not just a part of it on our terms. Both spiritually and physically, heal us and change our will to complete Your purpose in our lives as we give You full control. Help us not to stop halfway but to walk wholly into Your kingdom now. Whatever has held us back, we cast it aside as the blind man seeking healing cast aside his beggar's garment and rose up to follow Jesus. Help us to see You working here as never before. Uncover our old ways, cast them out, and replace them with Your new life. Cleanse us for Your purpose so we can worship You in spirit and in truth. Glorify Your name as we surrender to Your power and follow You, beginning here, beginning now. In Jesus' name, amen.

"If anyone wills to do His will, he shall know concerning the doctrine, whether it is from God or whether I speak on My own authority. He who speaks from himself seeks his own glory; but He who seeks the glory of the One who sent Him is true, and no unrighteousness is in Him."

John 7:17-18

Mark 10:42-52

~~~~~~

WITNESS

November 20

The Spirit Himself bears witness with our spirit that we are children of God.

Rom. 8:16

God says we are to be His witnesses (Isa. 43:10) who will know, believe, and understand who He is. Our witness now is to recognize God's love, confirmed in action. As in legal matters, a witness confirms facts, testifies to the truth, and always points, not to himself, but to another event or person. For us, that event is the life of Christ given on the cross and resurrected to bring us to glory. A witness does not occupy the stand to primarily describe his own life but the life of another.

A witness is not called to talk about himself but about key events that determine the outcome. In questioning us silently with hardened eyes, people in the world are now asking, "What can you tell me or show me that will determine the outcome of my life? What information do you have that can really change things and me?" How do you respond? A testimony does not have to be given in words.

A testimony implies a deep certainty for truth, as in matters of life and death, a meaning still reflected in our term "last will and testament." For our witness today, a death is required, the death of self so that the life of Another may be proclaimed. We cannot be witnesses to His majesty if we are still on the throne of our own lives, wanting others to serve us. Worse yet, how can we reflect the beauty of the King if we constantly check our own mental mirrors to see how we look to others?

In drawing up a contract or covenant, witnesses are required for the contract to go into effect. In God's plan for us, His Spirit bears witness to our spirit, and we are surrounded by a cloud of witnesses as we run the race into the future He has planned (Heb. 12:1). We are not the only witnesses. In the covenant God has given us, we become witnesses on earth of what has already been witnessed in us by the Holy Spirit and witnessed in heaven as God's plan of the ages.

"For there are three that bear witness in heaven: the Father, the Word, and the Holy Spirit; and these three are one. And there are three that bear witness on earth: the Spirit, the water, and the blood; and these three agree as one" (1 John 5:7-8). If we think we alone are responsible for our witness, we are missing the greater witness of heaven and the power of the Spirit with the water and blood of Christ's life active in us now. Is your witness today actively united with these eternal witnesses of His covenant?

Father, make me Your witness by the power of the Holy Spirit. Let Your Spirit confirm in me the testimony of Jesus Christ where I live, so that not only in words but also in action and love there will be more witnesses to Your glory. In Jesus' name, amen.

Acts 1:4-11   John 3:5-21   1 John 5:5-12

PROGRESS MOVES

November 21

"Do not remember the former things, nor consider the things of old. Behold, I will do a new thing, now it shall spring forth; shall you not know it? I will even make a road in the wilderness and rivers in the desert."

Isa. 43:18-19

Progress moves. Analyzing and complaining can't bring changes. Solutions come when you walk spiritually and physically in a new direction, as the physical grows out of the spiritual. First, faith moves your focus from the problem itself to God's power to solve the problem, which may involve changing you first. The answer comes as you receive the One who makes all things new. Progress moves, and the first step is within your heart. Ask God to show you the impossible. Look into God's Word, not at it; completely take it into your heart to see your whole situation in its light. Then give Him your life as He gives you His.

If God's Word is burning in you, you're going somewhere new even while you are waiting on Him in prayer. You're already on the way to the future when your spirit, soul, and body are burning with the life of His new covenant through Christ's blood. Although not obvious on the surface, through the eyes of faith, you will see a hint of what your Creator is preparing, just enough to take a step, then the next, then another, until more is revealed (John 13:17; 14:21).

Take some time to open your hands in prayer to receive what only God can create for the journey. Even if it's a small hint, be ready to move forward where your little faith is leading now. Don't get stuck in you or anyone else. Depend on God alone. Today let everything in your life line up forward with what He shows you to do. Take a step in that direction, even if it's small. As you move, thank God along the way because He is the One who makes the way. The more you let Him make it, the faster you will go.

Father, show me the path straight before me, and help me to walk in it as You make the way clear in Your love and power. In Jesus' name, amen.

Isa. 40:3-11   Matt. 9:5-6   Phil. 3:12-21

TAKEN AWAY   November 22

Then He said to them all, "If anyone desires to come after Me, let him deny himself, and take up his cross daily, and follow Me."

Luke 9:23

God reveals Himself through something that must be taken away. Often, this is not a pleasant process, but it becomes deeply beautiful. Our Creator removes roadblocks only He can see in order to move us forward in faith. Naturally, our flesh will protest this loss from our world, even if it leaves an opening to show us the beauty of the next. When the roadblock is taken away, the sacrifice produces more than before. It doesn't make sense to earthly minds, but we see powerful hints of this process in all of creation.

If your life today were measured only by your prayer life, how would you measure up? To make room for God's creative Spirit, something must be taken away from our worldly focus. To be truly made whole, some of the partial must be removed. To take away our sin, God experienced the loss of His Son, so we could gain eternal life as His children. Our losses can never match God's separation from His Son on the cross, but we do have losses that cut deep, that seem unexplainable, undeserved, and unresolved in our view. Usually, our first reaction is to try to replace what is missing with something else, often anger. However, God may heal us by first removing even more so that the space that remains, that gaping hole, can be filled only with what He has planned. Our loss, released to Him, will allow what He can bring to us, more than we had in the beginning.

If our prayers are unanswered, perhaps it is because, if answered, they would add to the flesh instead of increasing our capacity for His Spirit. Would you allow God to take something away in order to bring you something more, far beyond your current desire? We expect simple addition. He sometimes adds by subtraction, followed by multiplication (John 12:24).

Christ came to bring us life more abundantly than anything we could request or plan. How? Not by adding up a list of instructions and achievements, but by offering His life on the cross, subtracted for all people. It was the only way to resurrection. Three days later there was multiplication overflowing beyond anything we can understand. If we submit to subtraction, we will also experience multiplication in God's time. His answers work in dimensions beyond our grasp. Have you allowed Him to subtract as well as add? Is there anything other than Him you can't do without? He may remove it, and all the little things attached to it, until you are left with only enough room for Everything. Your loss has borders. God's love does not. In Him, Your empty cup will overflow.

Father, remove what keeps me from becoming complete in Christ. Multiply the fruit of Your love. I accept Your ways as You make room for Your Spirit to live in me. In Jesus' name, amen.

Job 42:1-10   Matt. 19:27-30   2 Cor. 1:3-12

November 23

VISION FOR LIFE

Lord God, please give me Your vision for life, not my own narrow view. Open my heart, my eyes, and my will to move into the living Branch, the Vine, and the firstfruits that are coming in Your kingdom. Calling out to You, I put my past behind me and step through Your door in the strength of Christ's life and resurrection power even now. As He appeared to the disciples shut behind their closed doors, come now and speak to my heart, penetrating its closed doors. Open me to follow You wherever Your new life leads, past all unbelief and fear, past all impossibility and the slow death of self-focus. Renew my mind, unlock my heart, and restore my soul so that I can see what You see as You walk here today. Forgive me for finding my blindness convenient at times. By the Holy Spirit, open my eyes not only to see but also to accept Your love gazing into me and through me to others. More than solutions or provisions or anything that answers to this world, help me to receive Your healing and power to rescue me now. Give me grace to be what I see in Your Son and then to do what He would do. In Jesus' name, amen.

Then Jesus cried out and said, "He who believes in Me, believes not in Me but in Him who sent Me. And he who sees Me sees Him who sent Me. I have come as a light into the world, that whoever believes in Me should not abide in darkness."

John 12:44-46

John 5:19-24

THE ORIGINATOR November 24

Then God said, "Let us make man in Our image, according to Our likeness; . . ." So God created man in His own image; in the image of God He created him; male and female He created them. Then God blessed them.

Gen. 1:26-28

Whatever plans we have for the future, how can we know they will definitely happen? In essence, we can't unless they match the original. God's original plan, in a sense, has already happened. When you make a copy, the original is already there, or no copies are possible. God's plan is the basis for all that follows and carries a blessing for the future (Eph. 2:8-10). Try as we may, we are not the source. We only work with copies. Our lives were freely given to us, not made or designed by us. Since God has the original plan for our lives, we can maneuver and manipulate all we want, but until we are in line with His plan, nothing will truly happen to impact future generations. With enough technology and self-focus, we may make copies of copies, according to our plans, but the results are lifeless and blurry. Only the original retains the clarity of eternal life.

Unless we are living in the Master, our lives are false copies. His life is left out. The original has existed from eternity and will continue long after the copies have faded. Since we are not the source, we have no control over the original design, even if we try to shape it to our pattern (Isa. 45:5-9; 55:6-11). Some people claim their copy is the original, but if you look closely, flaws begin to appear, and a change in quality reveals what is less than completely true. Only those familiar with the original can recognize the difference. Many of us are busy worrying and working in our lifetime to churn out as many copies as we can while altering them to fit our design. No matter how perfect they seem at first, over time, the false copies will fade away.

The original never changes. In the Originator's hands, it will produce beautiful results. Do your copies match up with the original plan, or has something else gotten in the way? Is what now seems crooked and meaningless just your own version? Go to the original. Let the Originator bring everything into line with His will and the beauty of His Son. When you place your life before God, releasing it completely into pure light, it will line up with Christ's cross and resurrection power active in you. When the Originator's light passes clear through you, it will make your life a clean copy of His original design.

O Father, shine Your light through me now in the power of Your love. Create Your pattern of life in me through Your Son offered on the cross and raised to glory. I receive His life in me now. In Jesus' name, amen.

Col. 1:12-20 John 5:25-30 Rom. 8:28-30

THE ONE THING THAT COUNTS   November 25

And Jesus answered and said to her, "Martha, Martha, you are worried and troubled about many things. But one thing is needed, and Mary has chosen that good part, which will not be taken away from her."

Luke 10:41-42

There is only one thing you can do today that counts for eternity. If you already knew what it was, would you sort the whole day out to be sure to do it first? The rest of the day would be easier, even satisfying, knowing that the one thing that counts is already complete. Whether we are prospering or persecuted, it is still the same. Nothing else matters but that one thing. Everything builds on it, or the whole day ultimately crumbles. I have had crumbly days, wondering where the one thing was and trying to do as much as possible just in case one of the many things I was doing might happen to be the one thing that counted. There was no need for all the hurry and worry that made me so blurry. Jesus has given it to us clearly. The one thing is to love the Lord with all we are and to enjoy His love for us, which spills over to others. That is the fuel burning at the core of our existence.

Without it, we are already dead, and everything we do—service, knowledge, even religious work—is dead (1 Cor. 13, Ps. 27:3-4). More than anything else, our Father wants our lives in Christ to move freely in His love, to dwell fully in its depths and heights. He saved us from sin so we could love Him and move in the power of that love far beyond human dimensions. Each day He longs for us to come as children who seek their Father more than anything they could do or want from Him. He would like for us to enjoy Him and what He is doing more than worry about what we are doing. Then He can do great things through us to reach others.

Created mainly to love God, we often run around all day trying to work for Him instead of letting Him work through us. Yet if we love Him first, the true work will follow, as He does more in our relationship with Him than we can do for Him on our own. Only love brings real obedience. Are you living there, in the one thing that counts?

Father, forgive me for seeking what to do instead of seeking who You are. In Your love, I will find all my answers. In the image of Your Son, create in my heart the love for You that counts for eternity and moves everything in Your direction. In Jesus' name, amen.

Mark 12:28-31   Luke 18:20-22   1 John 4:9-21

UNSHAKABLE

November 26

He has promised, saying, "Yet once more I shake not only the earth, but also heaven." Now this, "Yet once more," indicates the removal of those things that are being shaken, as of things that are made, that the things which cannot be shaken may remain.

Heb. 12:26-27

Shaking brings things to the point that their various components are revealed. Shaking produces separation so that the basic, true makeup of what is shaken is uncovered. Even in the structure of atoms, this shaking can accomplish drastic changes that reveal what was there all along. To be unshakable means that we have no add-ons or strange things mixed in that are separate from the original truth and love of our Creator. Patiently, through the gift of His Son, only God can remove hidden flaws or divided thoughts and refine us in the fire of His Holy Spirit to be truly His so that no separation from Him remains (Matt. 3:11-12; Rom. 8:26-39).

Unshakable means unified, solidified, so melted into one whole by the love of God, so molded together that each piece is one with Him and there are no seams to separate, no walls to divide. Only in God can we be unshakable in a pure nature born of the One who is who He is, completely holy. To be unshakable means to be one with Him and His people until we are unified in the very nature of God. He is our core original, not with add-ons that can be shaken off, but with every part surrendered and melted into His will. In your life, whatever is of God cannot be shaken. Everything else will fall away.

Let Him so fold you into Himself that your divisions and doubts disappear, your sin is washed clean in the blood of Jesus, and your mind is renewed to stay the course that leads straight into glory. His glory is unshakable, and He wants it to dwell in you, filling you with the light of life (John 17:3, 22-23). Whatever shaking comes, walk in the light of Jesus Christ. Although the ground below you may be moving, His light and love will bring you safely through it all, unshakable to stand whole in Him forever.

Father, in humility make me complete to do Your will through Your love and power. All my things are partial and shakable. Yours are not. Shine on me; mold my life into Yours so that Your grace alone makes me unshakable in faith. In Jesus' name, amen.

Matt. 5:3-10   John 16:33   Acts 2:22-28

November 27

SIMPLY PRAISE

Father, all praise is to You. I delight in simply praising You and the beauty of Your presence even in difficult times. In all things, may You receive the glory and honor due to Your name. Raise me up from my problems to praise You more, not just to have what I want. In complete wisdom, You know the end from the beginning, so now is the time, before I see the end, to thank You for the future in Your plan. The whole situation is under Your feet as You sit enthroned in the praises offered to You alone. Be welcomed here, be pleased, be glorified, and be honored in the praises of Your children, who cannot see the future but praise you now with all their hearts for the true liberty You give us and all creation in Your Son, Jesus Christ, the Firstborn, risen and alive in us now through the Holy Spirit. All praise to You, Most High, my Lord and my God. Blessed be Your name, O Lord who comes! Please dwell in our lives now as a house of prayer. In Jesus' name, amen.

But You are holy, enthroned in the praises of Israel. Our fathers trusted in You; they trusted, and You delivered them.

Ps. 22:3-4

Luke 19:29-40

WORK IN HIM   November 28

For we are His workmanship, created in Christ Jesus for good works, which God prepared beforehand that we should walk in them.

Eph. 2:10

Work in Christ, as He works in you. When we let the Lord do His work inside us, then we can work in Him. His light shines in and through our earth to produce fruit that is really His. Fruit lasts only as long as the one who generates it. Eternal fruit comes when we allow the Master Gardener to wield the tools, tend the garden, and work in us His way, as we stay connected to the Vine. Rootless, many of us have been running around with hoes and pruning shears, trying to make fruit. The Gardener is waiting for us to let our lives be completely fruitful in His Son alone. Our main work is to surrender to His work that has been going on for ages and will continue far beyond our lifetimes.

If we are doing our own work for ourselves, we become nervous and negative. If we let God have His way in us, it's all His work, the results belong to the King, and it will be finished in His energy and timeless calendar. Do God's life and joy run through our work, or is it full of human manipulation? Do we match the pattern of the cross? That is the tree of life. Since the Vine grows there, we must be there to grow.

For resurrection power to produce fruit in us, our work must flow with the humility of the cross. Quietly enduring affliction can be as much a success as producing some immediately visible result. The scale that weighs the fruit is eternal, and "our light affliction, which is but for a moment, is working for us a far more exceeding and eternal weight of glory" (2 Cor. 4:17). Patience is eternal work. So is cultivating grateful hearts. We usually think of work as service to produce a physical result. This is good, but not enough. Cain brought a sacrifice to the Lord that required much human effort (Gen. 4:3-5). Yet the Lord was pleased with the lamb brought by Abel, a creature not cultivated but born to foreshadow the perfect gift of God and our relationship through His Son.

While Cain sought God's approval through his own effort, Abel trusted in the blood of another, created solely by God, who provided the Lamb for the perfect sacrifice. There is nothing we can ever accomplish that will please God more than Christ's sacrifice. Hidden in Him, we are then able to offer God smaller sacrifices that please Him, such as broken and contrite hearts (Ps. 51:16-17), praise with service (Heb. 13:15-16), and feeding His sheep (John 21:17). How do we know our work is hidden in Christ? Test it on the altar of His love. Does it match the pattern of His cross and resurrection? Can you freely place your work in the fire of His sacrifice and watch it burn in love?

Father, work in me what pleases you in the power and love of Jesus. In His name, amen.

John 6:28-35   1 Cor. 3:11-17   2 Cor. 2:14—3:3

A VISITOR TODAY

November 29

"Behold, I stand at the door and knock. If anyone hears My voice and opens the door, I will come in to him and dine with him, and he with Me."

Rev. 3:20

You have a visitor here today. You have a visitor who comes to see you in person, not just to talk to you through a closed door. He is coming to see what He has created and what He has still to create. There is Someone knocking on the door of your heart, hoping you will open it to new life. He is waiting for you to open that door and not just take a quick look and recognize who is there with, "Yes, Jesus, You are Lord," and then slam it shut again. It may seem safer with Him out there, just telling Him through the door what is needed, but He is Lord only when He is inside. This Lord wants to come in and share your life, allowing you to share His.

If an out-of-town friend you often communicate with comes to visit, would you stay home on the day his flight arrives, quietly reading his letters or remembering his phone calls while he waits at the airport? No, you would pick up your friend, take him to your home, and share a meal, knowing it is one thing to read about someone and another to talk and live with him in person. Jesus is waiting. It is possible to read His teaching and talk about Him but never commit to bringing Him home.

Will you leave Jesus waiting outside your daily routine while you read about Him and talk to Him long distance? He prefers a personal visit through the Holy Spirit right in the middle of your life, at the head of your table. In the breaking of the bread of His sacrificial love, He will reveal Himself in a personal way to you. You can't share a meal with someone until you open the door. It is wonderful to read about Jesus, but the purpose of all this preparation is to welcome Him into the center of your life now, wherever you are. In obedience and love, the door opens.

He wants to communicate directly to your heart what is on His heart today. Do you have time? Through the Holy Spirit, our Lord wants to come in and stay a while, hopefully when you have time to listen as well as talk. This Visitor is really not a visitor because He has come to stay. He would like to share a covenant meal with you and live and walk with you, not just hand out some instructions for you to follow on your own. He will go through it all with you and speak to you in His Word by the Holy Spirit. With Jesus, you will see what you never saw before and experience a love unlike any other. Are you ready? Will you eat the bread that He has broken for you?

Father, come into my heart through the power of Your Holy Spirit, who can live the life of Christ in me. I welcome You to come, live here today, and stay. In Jesus' name, amen.

John 14:15-17, 23　　　　　John 6:48-57　　　　　Luke 24:15-35

November 30

~~~~~~

THE FEAST YESTERDAY, TODAY, AND FOREVER

Yesterday, today, and forever, Lord God, You come in Your Son to save us. Humbly, I repent and open my heart to You. Through the Holy Spirit, may Your Son come as He knocks on the door of my life to enter now, sit down, and eat with me. You are the head of my house. It is Your table, and I am fully refreshed with the feast of Your kingdom in Your Son. There is more than enough to cover the past. In the blood of Your new covenant poured out in Jesus Christ, the present and future are also purified. The table is spread, and all are invited as Your Son is lifted up. After we have dined together here, we will arise and follow Him to the feast in Your house forever. Thank You for coming in the One who is Alpha and Omega with us now. Thank You for feeding us the Bread of Life. In Jesus' name, amen.

The cup of blessing which we bless, is it not the communion of the blood of Christ? The bread which we break, is it not the communion of the body of Christ? For we, though many, are one bread and one body; for we all partake of that one bread.

1 Cor. 10:16-17

Hos. 14:1-9   1 Cor. 5:6-8

~~~~~~

ADVENT– EPIPHANY, REVELATION

See what God is doing here, even in the most unexpected places. He prepares our hearts today to receive His Son, who comes as a servant to save the lost, as the Scriptures say, to preach the gospel to the poor, to heal the brokenhearted, to proclaim liberty to the captives and recovery of sight to the blind, to set at liberty those who are oppressed; to proclaim the acceptable year of the Lord.* Through the Holy Spirit, will you see Him and welcome Him where you are now?

Isa. 9:2-7; 53:1-12

Luke 1:26-56; 2:1-32

Matt. 2:1-14

Matthew 3:1-3, 11-17

Luke 4:16-21*

Matt. 17:1-8

Matt. 25:31-40

Rom. 15:7-21

A COVENANT, NOT A CONCEPT December 1

Jesus said to him, "I am the way, the truth, and the life. No one comes to the Father except through Me."

John 14:6

In Christ, God offers us a relationship through a Person in a living covenant, not just a concept. His truth moves through a close relationship more than an intellectual formula, which can be changed. He does not change. In Christ, God came to look us in the eye. This is not a game or an intellectual gamble. It is a multidimensional relationship guaranteed by our Creator for eternity. Taking all the risk and loss upon Himself on the cross, Jesus Christ opened the door into eternity and invites us to come through in His power, not by our merit or effort. Our part is to let Him do His work in us and to come into intimate agreement with all of His life, participating directly in a love that has no end. Then in obedience we can look Him in the eye through the cross.

This is not a compartmentalized religious game we play, earning points to win. Our Lord has already won everything in every area and sealed the ultimate victory with His risen life. We enter a living relationship that cannot be broken because He has guaranteed it with His own blood. When we enter this covenant, we agree not just with our minds but also with His mind, not just with our lives but also with His life, so that each day we move in harmony with His nature and the power of His presence through the Holy Spirit.

If our relationship with God is merely a concept, then our mental grasp of it can be manipulated or negotiated with other concepts and religions; but if it is a personal covenant, then any manipulation or negotiation with another party is adultery or idolatry. This union with the Son of God is similar to a marriage between a man and a woman. It produces new life and continues for generations. In fact, the results of this union go on forever and include every area of our lives.

Imagine a marriage in which the partners merely studied one another from a distance but never knew one another intimately or lived out their daily lives together. In His Son, God wants to live with us through the Holy Spirit, to lead us into a relationship in which we can participate even now (John 14:16-23).

In the multiplying grace of God, we meet more than can be analyzed. It must be lived. The depth of the Person we are meeting in spiritual union far exceeds the ability of our hearts and minds to grasp. So we let Him grasp us as He took hold of the cross, leading us closer to the purity of His heart and the power of His new life. If you take one step into this new covenant, it changes your life forever.

Father, bring me into the new covenant in Jesus' blood that opens the way and reveals Your truth in His life in me now. In Jesus' name, amen.

Matt. 26:26-32   John 5:39-44   John 1:10-18

WALK IN THE LIGHT   December 2

But if we walk in the light as He is in the light, we have fellowship with one another, and the blood of Jesus Christ His Son cleanses us from all sin.

1 John 1:7

To walk in the light is to walk in the life of Christ in us and around us. Spiritual life grows in the eternal light of Christ, just as physical life grows in sunlight. Without the sun, no matter how busily we cultivate the soil or how many seeds we plant, nothing will come up. If the sun quit shining, no amount of work or the latest techniques of agriculture could produce enough crops. All knowledge of soil, seeds, and machinery would be useless. We need the sun. However, the created sun shines with only partial light to produce partial life that will eventually die. As Son of the Creator, Christ shines with full life for all who will receive Him (John 1:4). All else eventually produces death.

Through Jesus Christ, our Creator shines with uncreated, pure light to give new life to those who receive Him (John 1:12-13). Many try to produce spiritual life through some other means or the power of nature, but it is always partial and eventually ends. Only God is one, supernatural, undivided, truly whole, and full of divine light beyond nature and any created thing to produce the life that belongs to Him. When He shines on us, we take on that spiritual life as a plant soaks up sunlight and grows. By His power in Jesus Christ, we die to sin and live in Christ's life, which conquers sin, death, and all darkness, both physical and spiritual.

In the light of Christ, wet with the reality of His baptism, we are changed into His image, just as the Potter pours light-filled water onto wet clay. By grace, we become one with Christ. In His cross and resurrection, He produces in us the new creation of the light of His life. Our lamps are lit, and we can walk in that new life now into unity with Him and the body of Christ, the church, infused with light and cleansed by His blood. In the Holy Spirit, we move in resurrection light, even through dark places. Jesus said, "Let your light so shine before men, that they may see your good works and glorify your Father in heaven" (Matt. 5:16). If God's light lives in you, it will shine through you so that others can see His light and be drawn to new life in Christ.

If worship or work "for God" is done in human darkness, no matter how good the intentions, it can't be seen for God's glory, and no lasting fruit will grow. In darkness eventually we will stumble, even if we are saying the right things and going to the right places. As in the temple God designed, His lampstand must light up our hearts. If the light in you is darkness or anything but the whole light of God, then your works are in a sense not visible in the kingdom of God. Walk in His light, and you will see more of Him and less of you.

My Father, fill me with the life of Christ, and shine for Your glory. In His name, amen.

John 8:4-12   2 Cor. 3:17—4:7   Isa. 2:5

December 3

~~~~~~

THE FULLNESS OF YOUR COVENANT

Lord God, release us into the fullness of Your covenant, the firmness of Your foundation in Christ, and the fruit of Your Spirit. Shine on us now. Thank You for bringing us into Your kingdom through the Seed of Abraham, producing fruit among the nations. Make us one with the Vine to produce the fruit of Your life, given to us and moving through us for Your praise alone. In Your power, move us forward in faith in Your kingdom, where we are one with Your Son, washed in His blood, living clean in Your new covenant, walking in the light, and full of Your delight. In Jesus' name, amen.

"I am the true vine, and My Father is the vinedresser. Every branch in Me that does not bear fruit He takes away; and every branch that bears fruit He prunes, that it may bear more fruit. You are already clean because of the word which I have spoken to you. Abide in Me, and I in you. As the branch cannot bear fruit of itself, unless it abides in the vine, neither can you, unless you abide in Me."

John 15:1-4

Isa. 56:6-8   Isa. 25:1-9

~~~~~~

STAY CLOSE, STAY COVERED   December 4

But when He saw the multitudes, He was moved with compassion for them, because they were weary and scattered, like sheep having no shepherd.

Matt. 9:36

Sheep have no idea where to go, and if they do go somewhere on their own, they have no protection, no defense. God did not send us, His flock, just some information to follow; He sent us a Shepherd who has power and wisdom beyond the capacity of any flock or predator. This Shepherd is also the Lamb of God who gave His life to save the flock. He knows how it feels to be a sheep. Having lived in our world, He has already been everywhere we need to go. To go through dark days, we can follow the One who knows the way, moving where He goes, when He goes.

Straying off on our own, away from His life, attracts quick disaster and death. Under the guise of freedom and self-sufficiency, the enemy of our souls tries to entice us away from the covering of the One who loves us, just far enough away to kill us. While we're close to the Good Shepherd, the wolf cannot take us. Stay close and stay covered with your Shepherd's care. Whether the day is sunny or dark, the sheep need the same care. We just don't realize this when it's sunny. As the birds are singing, the sun is shining, and all seems safe, it's easier to wander than when evening draws near. As shadows grow, we instinctively draw near to our Savior, and that is one advantage of our weakness. Those who feel strong may not stay close, so their fall comes swifter and harder than for the weak ones, who allow themselves to be carried.

Another advantage of weakness as sheep is that we at least learn to stay together. We've seen how the stragglers and the wanderers are easily picked off. A lone sheep doing his own thing is an easy lunch for even a weak wolf. But a whole flock of sheep, especially if guarded by One stronger than the wolf, is more than a match for the predator. With us, we have the One who is stronger than any enemy, even our own fear.

Our Shepherd covers us with His righteousness as He leads and carries us where we cannot go on our own. Weak sheep who stay close know more than the sheep on the periphery. They hear more directly the Shepherd's voice, feel the touch of His hand, and listen to His songs. They also receive more discipline and grow stronger. Staying close, they're directly under the rod of His protection and correction, covered with holiness, and close enough to know the joy of the Shepherd's heart. Stay close, stay covered in Him.

Father, save me from my wanderings, and keep me alive in Your Son. In Jesus' name, amen.

Ezek. 34:11   John 10:1-18, 27-30   Heb. 13:20-21

SERVANTS TOGETHER   December 5

"If I then, your Lord and Teacher, have washed your feet, you also ought to wash one another's feet. For I have given you an example, that you should do as I have done to you."

John 13:14-15

Service is a two-way street. In reality, as we serve the Lord by helping others, He also serves us through one another, all for the glory of God. What the Lord calls us to do for Him, He does to increase our faith and to lead us on the path He has already cleared for us to travel in fellowship with Him. We are called to do only what Jesus has already done and more so, because He has gone to the Father and sent us the Holy Spirit as our Helper (John 14:12-17). As Jesus said He was following what He saw His Father do, our work is to follow Jesus in what God is doing now through the Holy Spirit (John 5:19-20).

With Him, we can participate in the foot washing of many people, the feeding of thousands, the opening of blind eyes, and the healing of sick bodies and minds. By the Holy Spirit, God is the One who does it all, and as we see what He has already planned to do, we can serve Him with what was prepared for us to do before we began (Eph. 2:10). When we help and feed those who cannot pay us back, we receive the Father's blessing and peace. Jesus said as we do it to one of the least of these His brethren, we do it unto Him, who has first served us (Matt. 25:34-40).

In His divine love, when we serve others, we can receive Jesus and serve Him as part of the same process (Matt. 10:8). When Christ is all in all, we are one in Him and one in the Father's love. Christ in us, working through the Holy Spirit, draws people to Himself by serving them in the love of the cross and the power of the resurrection. There is no higher service than the cross and no higher power for service than the resurrection of Jesus Christ. With Him through the Holy Spirit, come to the washbasin, the hungry faces, the sick bodies, and the blind eyes. See Him where you are now, serving you.

Father, teach me to serve You in Your own love and power, Your gift to me in Jesus Christ, working in Your kingdom today. In His name and by Your grace, amen.

Matt. 20:25-28   Rom. 12:9-21   Luke 6:38

SURPRISE! December 6

"If you then, being evil, know how to give good gifts to your children, how much more will your Father who is in heaven give good things to those who ask Him!"

Matt. 7:11

Are you willing to be surprised by what you ask of God? Unless you've already figured out everything He can do, you will be surprised. So why not open the door to it now by asking Him not only to answer your prayer but also to give you the faith to receive His surprising ways? Even in subtle reasoning, quit trying to limit how the Lord of the universe might solve your problem and arrange your world. Ask Him how He would like to do it, and then let Him do it. As intensely as you ask, as much as you pray for results, with that intensity and consistency let Him know you will let Him do it all. Say this clearly to God with heart and voice, and see what happens.

Perhaps the only thing delaying His response is your unwillingness to be surprised or moved in a new direction. The eternal answers God has for you will not fit into the tiny box of your own strength and will. When His response comes, the answer will surprise your socks off and leave you standing shoeless on holy ground. Shoes represent a human aid to reach a destination or to go your own way in your own power. Often, God must surprise us out of our old ways. When we turn to His ways, something of our old ways must be removed. When Moses turned to see the burning bush, the Lord had him remove his sandals before receiving divine direction (Exod. 3:1-10).

Turn aside now from your routine expectations, and come to the pure fire that burns through the world but doesn't consume a life that accepts God's holiness and continues to lift its heart in praise to Him. This is the life of the cross, the wood that held Christ's blood. This is holy ground for fertile results, a surprising harvest in the fire of His resurrection. Take off the shoes of your old ways, and let God's life burn through you in forgiveness and new life in Christ. You may lose your old ways, but you will gain new vision and strength to do God's will now. Get ready for the unexpected!

Father, You know the desires of my heart. Please remove my old ways and surprise me with Your answers, according to Your will and power. In Jesus' name, amen.

1 Cor. 2:9-12 Ps. 146 Heb. 11:1-8

December 7

WAIT AND SEE

Father, help me to wait and see what only You can do. When worry places my desires and fears on center stage, displace them with the power of Your Word. Waiting on You places my life in Your hands, where You can easily touch and heal, direct and transform more than I can see. Your Word lights up my path. I've wasted so much time waiting for the answer when I could have been waiting for You. When I wait on You and look for You, I begin to see and move in Your preparation for the answer to come. My Lord, Creator of all, teach me to desire only what You want and to love You enough to wait for You to make all things ready. Make me patient and focused like a waiter who watches the one he serves and looks for signals. Take away my worry so I can see who You are and what You are doing now in Your kingdom. Let my focus be on You and Your table. The feast I wait for is the feast I will see and receive, welcomed as Your child. Increase my faith to receive what only Your vision and strength can produce. In Jesus' name, amen.

But those who wait on the Lord shall renew their strength; they shall mount up with wings like eagles, they shall run and not be weary, they shall walk and not faint.

Isa. 40:31

Phil. 1:6—2:18

WITH WINGS AS EAGLES   December 8

"For where your treasure is, there your heart will be also."

Matt. 6:21

To mount up with wings as eagles, our hearts and our feet must no longer be stuck on clay. Following the wind of the Spirit, those who rise in the power of God are those who no longer depend on the earth and paths marked out by worldly desires. Exhaustion comes to anyone still relying on the feel of the ground, the patterns of this world, and the weighty approval of others. Flight comes only in stretching out our lives into the pattern of the cross, as Jesus opened His arms to give us life. To rise, we have to want His life more than ours. Then our true treasure is His love flowing from above, lifting us into the impossible.

There is a lot of flapping going on here on the ground by those who don't really want to leave and so have no power to lift off and let go of the anchors of their old ways. If a personal treasure keeps us earthbound, no amount of religious effort will make us rise up in spirit. Our earthly treasure could even be a wound we nourish. Where our treasure is, there our hearts and feet are also. Those Christians who keep flapping spiritually but also enjoy having their feet safely, solidly rooted in the world have no power. Their lives don't reveal the wide-open, upward pattern of the cross.

Some may think they can rise up for a moment and then return safely to earth and some old things, but the truth is that once we take off, the earth never feels the same again. The sharp ax of God's truth is laid to the root of every selfish and dark thing that kept us earthbound. We are free to move on the earth, living in the world to help others, but not of it, not rooted in the clay. The light above is different when we look into Christ's face. Once we have seen that view from above, earthly pleasures seem small and dusty. In God's truth, there is so much more to see, so much that is higher to explore. Your heart can soar only as high as your treasure already is, and when your heart rises, your mind and body will soon follow in action. Where is the treasure of your life? That is how high you can fly today.

Lord, forgive me for still clinging to the dirt I am trying to rise above. Lift me in Your power and love. I want to see my Savior's face. In Jesus' name, amen.

Isa. 40:25—41:4   2 Cor. 4:16-18   Matt. 6:19-26, 33

IN SPIRIT AND TRUTH December 9

"But the hour is coming, and now is, when the true worshipers will worship the Father in spirit and truth; for the Father is seeking such to worship Him."

John 4:23

To worship in spirit is to come in truth to the Father through His Spirit, who is already seeking us. Truth is what grows from the cross. Pilate asked, "What is truth?" and he was looking at it. In deepest terms, truth is the person of Jesus, who revealed God's sacrificial love for us in conquering our sin and bringing us through the curtain of death into our Creator's holy presence. That is where we are going in truth. I thought spiritual worship was the wonderful singing and focus on God that lifts our spirits above merely human design into the design of our Creator through the Holy Spirit. Yes, but there is more. Spiritual worship is also union with Christ in the obedience of the cross. It's singing in worship on Sunday and also singing in your heart to Him on Monday when problems are dumped on your head and you respond as He would. Truth opens veils.

Spiritual worship involves not only the activity of the Holy Spirit in us, but also the yielding of our spirits in joyful submission to His power daily. Truth makes beautiful music! I thought worship in truth was acknowledging the truth of God's power and majesty, the truth of Christ's atonement for our sin, the truth of His power active in our lives now. Yes, but there is more. It is also the truth that we can do nothing and must let Him do everything. It is the wide-open, flat-out truth that we are helpless without Him. We cannot truly worship God in the power of His majestic Spirit without first bowing our spirits humbly before Him in obedience. We are like worms before Him. Such a perspective is not meant to overdo our worthlessness but to acknowledge the huge reality of His greatness (Isa. 41:14). Until we come humbly in that truth, we have not worshiped (Ps. 51:15-17).

The woman who touched the hem of Jesus' garment moved in the truth that He could heal her and that it was impossible otherwise. She was an outcast, unclean, untouchable. It was the truth. She had to press in unnoticed, bowing and struggling between the others, bending low to reach that hem. Are we willing to bow that low to move into truth? She did, and Jesus felt her touch. It was a humble touch. She also told Him all the truth. True worship begins as we lay everything before Him. Even the disciples could not fully worship until they knew the truth about themselves. Didn't they say they would die for Him but they fled instead? Knowing us deeply, Christ died for us anyway and rose to bring us through the Spirit into the truth of God's love and mercy.

Father, breathe in me the power of the cross and resurrection so I can worship You in spirit and truth, bowing to reach the hem of Your glory. In Jesus' name, amen.

Luke 8:43-48 John 7:37-39 Jer. 29:11-13

December 10

UPON THE FLOOD

Father God, You sit in majesty over the flood of this world. Help me to come to Your Son upon these rough waters. When I step out of the boat, it is the first step to peace. Change me and bring me safely to You in His purity and power, as You reign over all. Through the storm, I look for Your truth and the power of Your hand. Increase my faith to trust You and to let Your Son lift me up as He is lifted up in truth now to bring hope, peace, and calm to many hearts here who will worship You. In Jesus' name, amen.

And Peter answered Him and said, "Lord, if it is You, command me to come to You on the water." So He said, "Come."

Matt. 14:28-29

Pss. 29—30

TUNE IN

December 11

"Why do you spend money for what is not bread, and your wages for what does not satisfy? Listen carefully to Me, and eat what is good, and let your soul delight itself in abundance. Incline your ear, and come to Me. Hear, and your soul shall live."

Isa. 55:2-3

When the static of life's chaos rages around us, it's time to tune into God's clear truth with power to get our bearings and find a way that works. Most of the static is not truth and lacks the power of God's living presence. It also lacks beauty. When our souls are tuned into divine beauty, then the way through our situation becomes clear. Mercy triumphs over judgment; what seems simple and weak suddenly overcomes the so-called knowledge of the world. If we listen only to static, we will be confused and discouraged. In the rush of our lives, God's channel is a narrow band to tune as we become lost in the maze of other choices launched at us. But the straight gate is worth finding. Moving through it, we come into a larger place, a wider mercy, and a higher love.

To find truth, we must be selective, tuning out everything else so that we can hear clearly what our heavenly Father is speaking into our lives. He speaks life, beauty, order, impossible grace, and power. What has to turn or change in your life to tune in clearly to Him? Sometimes it's only a small move away from the negative static. In other cases, we must go clear to the other end of the dial. Either way, there is more involved than a flip of the switch. Some think they can say yes to God once and never make any other adjustments in their lives. But when the slant of the world keeps tempting us off course, we must constantly turn, even if only slightly, to stay lined up with God's clear truth. Take some time today to tune into the real voice of life. What you hear is your future.

Lord, open my heart to Your truth, and line up my life with the direction of Your Word. Help me to hear Your voice clearly today. In Jesus' name, amen.

Amos 7:7-8   Ezek. 14:3   Matt. 7:13-29

WISDOM BUILDS   December 12

Through wisdom a house is built, and by understanding it is established; by knowledge the rooms are filled with all precious and pleasant riches.

Prov. 24:3-4

Listen as a child, and you will grow. Do not try to build until the Lord has built you, decorated you for His pleasure, and turned on the lights inside. Otherwise, you will be unable to build by yourself in the dark. Ask for His wisdom as you would ask for life (James 1:5; 2 Tim. 3:15; Ps. 127). Wait, open in wonder to God's creation and His Word. Let Him go first. His foundations are beautiful and last forever. You will need them. Even with liberty in salvation, don't think you can walk foolishly and not stumble. When we are little and afraid of the dark, we want all the lights on all the time. As teenagers no longer afraid of the dark, we say, "I'm not afraid of this dark. I can walk right through here with the lights off." Then we run into something hard and fall. It is better to grow up and have the lights on when needed, not because you are afraid of the dark but because you want to go through without stumbling.

Some of the "good" things you did before for the wrong motive, producing little fruit, God may now let you do for the right reason and in the right season, producing much fruit. Before you knew the right way, you may have scattered a few seeds, and some of them came up by God's grace! It was His sowing into you that spilled over into other lives. More of God's fruit will come as your life fully opens to all He can do. Since you can sow only what He has already worked through you, it is His harvest and His timing. Don't eagerly try to start digging in winter with less light. If you're no longer afraid and have the right seed to sow and are eager to do it, that's good; but it doesn't give you permission to beat against frozen ground. Know the season, and wait for the Son.

He is the Living Word, who gave His life to be sown in us at the right time, and His Father is the Gardener. Let Him shine first on where you will plant, and then let Him turn the earth. Submit to God's timing, and let Him build the life of Christ in you. His fruit is bigger than you, and its blossoms smell better than any of your best efforts. From Him alone, fruit will come to satisfy many who are hungry, and to leave seed for the future.

Father, plant Your life deep within me so there will be a harvest of Your design in the riches You have already given us in Jesus Christ. I release my life into the wisdom of Your love in Your Son. In Jesus' name, amen.

John 12:24-26   Gal. 6:7-9   James 3:13-18

TAKE INVENTORY
December 13

> . . . that their hearts may be encouraged, being knit together in love, and attaining to all riches of the full assurance of understanding, to the knowledge of the mystery of God, both of the Father and of Christ, in whom are hidden all the treasures of wisdom and knowledge.
>
> Col. 2:2-3

Check your stockpile. Check all files of information you have acquired about God and how to live for Him. If you never received another piece of information, would it be enough? When would you have accumulated all data necessary to really know Him? It is possible to have all the information in the world and still not be wise. Any description of God or what He wants you to do falls short of the living reality of His presence, guiding you through the Holy Spirit. The same could be said with your family or friends. When do you have enough information to figure them out? Probably never. It is better to just live with them and learn to love beyond your understanding. The living is the learning.

Take inventory of your current efforts to know God. Are they primarily accumulating more information about Him or simply living each day with Him at the center of your life? The living is learning by love (1 Cor. 8:1-3). Studying His Word is essential, but it is just as important to seek His face. In the long run, information alone will not be enough. Study is necessary, but there is more. The Living Word is hard to apply without His presence guiding you through the Holy Spirit. Seek the wisdom that comes from sharing fully in Christ's life, and you will have more than information. You will have the joy of His power and presence moving your heart, as well as your mind, and expanding your love beyond knowledge. From the beginning, His instructions are "follow," not just "study" (Matt. 9:9). Follow what you already know, and He will show you more along the road as you go. The purpose of taking inventory is to discard your old lists to make room for His new ways, letting God multiply His life in you each day.

Father, help me to follow You so I can participate in Your life in Christ, in action as well as in thought. Help me to know You and love You fully as You love me. In Jesus' name, amen.

Col. 2:6-15   John 1:35-39   John 13:6-12

December 14

~~~~~~

NOTHING WITHOUT YOU

We don't have anything, Lord God, without You, no matter what we do. It's not that we don't have, but that we are nothing without You. Only in You do we learn who we really are. Turn us to You, the true source of all, in whom we live and move and have our being for eternity. As we open our lives to more than ourselves, fill us with Your life in Jesus Christ for Your glory here, now, and forever. You are our life. In Jesus' name, amen.

". . . so that they should seek the Lord, in the hope that they might grope for Him and find Him, though he is not far from each one of us; for in Him we live and move and have our being."

Acts 17:27-28

John 5:21-27   Col. 2:16—3:4

~~~~~~

TODAY'S GARDEN December 15

So when the woman saw that the tree was good for food, that it was pleasant to the eyes, and a tree desirable to make one wise, she took of its fruit and ate. She also gave to her husband with her, and he ate.

Gen. 3:6

The menu for today in the garden where we live is a simple choice, an ancient choice: know God and everything else in His order, or know everything else without God, and slowly self-destruct. The best knowledge the world has to offer only makes the contents of our coffins more intelligent, the description of our demise more artistic. Lasting beauty and full life come only in relationship to our Creator, who wants us to be more than intelligently irrelevant. We can live fully in Him, where knowledge works life. Without Him, knowledge alone is sophisticated suicide (1 John 5:11-12).

Since the Garden of Eden, the enemy has tried to sidetrack us into selfish knowledge. It's an effective method because it appeals to our desire for control. We would rather be sophisticated and in control of our own stupidity than to be humble and submitted to God in His wisdom. His resources are a lot bigger than ours and can teach us more than several lifetimes of academic research, if we would let Him pour it into us His way. He wants us to use our brains on His power, which moves the universe, instead of on our individual sparks of self-interest. Our own accumulation of knowledge leads us down the deadly detour of trying to gain control of what belongs to God, much of which He would give us freely as we accept His love in Christ and return that love. Knowledge without love is as scary as a sexual relationship without love. It is the selling of a soul.

Led by human nature with its dark tendencies, science becomes a time bomb that will destroy both itself and those who carry it for their own ends. Knowledge is fruitful for us only when it is in relationship to God and plugged into the higher workings of His divine nature as seen in the creative order of the universe (Col. 1:16; 2:3). In the record of human history, we can see what happens when we try to set up our own universe. It crumbles. Our own efforts will collapse because we are finite and partial. Our best plans fold up like a broken chair under the weight of eternity. Neither can some electronic system bring us to perfection because we, designers and users, are imperfect at the core.

Knowledge is only a key to something bigger that God has planned. We can pick up the key of truth, but the door belongs to Him. Without Him, we have a key and no place to go. Eve took the apple and found a dead end. In Christ, the door will open.

Father, help me to love You with all of my heart, soul, mind, and strength. Live in me, and then I will truly know all that I need to know. In Jesus' name, amen.

Gen. 2:16-17 John 6:51-57 1 John 2:20-27

THE SEED OF HEAVEN   December 16

Since you have purified your souls in obeying the truth through the Spirit in sincere love of the brethren, love one another fervently with a pure heart, having been born again, not of corruptible seed but incorruptible, through the word of God which lives and abides forever,

1 Pet. 1:22-23

When a seed falls into the ground, it is invisible but still present. In time, it will reproduce visibly the inheritance it carries. In His children, God has planted the seed of His life in His Son, sown in the gift of His life on the cross, and raised visibly as the firstfruits of a new creation. In the same way, the seed of the kingdom of God, a foretaste of heaven, is present now in the Living Word of Jesus Christ implanted today in us, who are still vessels of clay but full of light within, as we receive Him (John 1:12-14).

The impression of the new creation, the signs of the new birth, are already seen in our clay, with the footprints and healing touch of Jesus moving through our lives now. Each day the seed of eternal truth is already forming in us the beginning of a new creation, the makings of perfection that only God can see and bring into final form. Even in the dirt, the seed is seeking, leaning toward new life, unless it is denied or carried away, but always there is a remnant of holy seed in good ground. Despite enemies or distractions, there will be a harvest (Matt. 13:16-23).

In a sense, heaven has already been planted here for the time when a new heaven and a new earth will appear, becoming one in God's plan through Jesus Christ (Eph. 1:10; Rev. 21:1-8). In the Potter's hands, as a wheel within a wheel, this world turns within the larger reality of eternal multiplication, just as a hidden seed turns into a bountiful crop.

Even if you see weeds and dirt today, live according to the incorruptible seed of God's Word, which grows the fruit of Jesus Christ in your heart. The weeds and the dirt and the waiting will one day come to an end, but the grain, much grain, will be carried into the Father's presence. Meanwhile, God's seed in you, though still in the clay, is already on the way to heaven. With the Living Word, the life of Jesus Christ crucified and risen again, growing within you, move ahead fruitful in His power.

Father, I surrender to Your plan. Make me conformed to Your will and ready for the fruit You will produce through me by the blood of Jesus Christ. In this world, even now still in the clay, make me ready for new life where I am today. In Jesus' name, amen.

John 12:20-26   John 3:3-8   1 Cor. 15:20-23, 42-49

WHERE ARE YOU?   December 17

And when they had come to the place called Calvary, there they crucified Him.

Luke 23:33

Where is your life today in regard to the cross? Do you stand near Jesus? It's the same now as when He gave Himself for us. There were several types of people involved at the cross: His followers who stayed and worshiped Him, those who scoffed and mocked, the disciples who loved Him but ran away, the soldiers who received worldly wages for crucifying Christ, the trusted disciple who betrayed Him, and the criminals on either side who were crucified with Him.

No matter where we stand, we have an advantage those people did not have because we see not only the cross before us, but also the power of the resurrection and the witness of the church for centuries. Yet how many of us draw near?

I want to stay with Jesus, but I've been living like those who love Him yet keep a safe distance. No longer. Out of love, I will come near and take hold of the cross. It is the only way to know Him and the fellowship of His sufferings, leading to the power of the resurrection even now in our hearts. Not wanting us to miss the full blessing of the resurrection, Jesus calls us to the most difficult place.

The followers who stayed were drawn there by a divine love that would not let them go, which was stronger than their human love for Jesus or their love for their own lives. His love moving in them enabled them to stay and later become the first witnesses of the resurrection. They saw power beyond fear.

Those who scoff and mock will also be found around the cross. If you carry a cross daily, they'll be there with you too. Then there are the followers who seem to love the Lord but deny Him and disappear when the going gets tough because they haven't received enough of His love to hold them near. God may hide them for a season to grow in faith until they produce fruit, as He did many disciples. After all, they were not running away from His cross so much as from their own crosses. Perhaps they could accept the fact that Jesus died for them, but they were running away from having to die themselves to their own wills. So do we.

There are those of us today who will betray or crucify our Lord for money and gamble for His robe, but now and then one of us awakens from our worldly slumber to recognize the Son of God. And of the thieves, what can we say? We are all sinners, deserving the punishment Jesus bore for us. Each day, we can turn and say, "Lord, remember me when You come into Your kingdom."

Father, thank You for Your mercy and power in the cross. In Jesus' name, amen.

Isa. 53:1-5   1 Peter 4:12-19   John 8:28-32

~~~~~~

YOUR SONG OF VICTORY

Lord God, sing in me Your song of victory. Lift me into higher harmony with Your will and Your freedom here. Even in what appears to be defeat, make me know the power of Your Son's cross and resurrection. The song of true victory rises from a humble heart worshiping You in spirit and in truth. In the name of Jesus, help me to sing Your song right where I am, so that the aroma of His sacrifice fills this place. In Jesus' name, amen.

I acknowledged my sin to You, and my iniquity I have not hidden. I said, "I will confess my transgressions to the Lord," and You forgave the iniquity of my sin. Selah. For this cause everyone who is godly shall pray to You in a time when You may be found; surely in a flood of great waters they shall not come near him. You are my hiding place; You shall preserve me from trouble; You shall surround me with songs of deliverance. Selah.

Ps. 32:5-7

Zeph. 3:8-17   Ps. 22:18-31

~~~~~~

THE POINT December 19

"Again, the kingdom of heaven is like treasure hidden in a field, which a man found and hid; and for joy over it he goes and sells all that he has and buys that field."

Matt. 13:44

Each of our lives points to something as the main focus for our existence. Even those not aware of our goals can see where our lives are pointing, as they watch us on a daily basis. Like a magnet pulling on a compass, the treasures of our hearts are pulling all the indicators of our lives in one direction. They point either to self or to God. All of the activities you are planning right now have some focus, even if it is hidden from direct view. All your activities and priorities are pulled toward the main desire of your heart. Where is your life pointing? Is it the same direction as your words?

For some, the goal is pleasing people or financial success or just staying comfortable enough not to open any old wounds. Some lives seem to have no focus, leaving the point of the compass to swirl wildly in search of meaning and direction. Our Creator has provided the ultimate point of direction in His love poured out for us in the cross of Christ and the open door of resurrection power. The cross becomes our compass.

Jesus Christ is the Bright and Morning Star who will never fade, because the light of the dawn of our redemption is unfolding all around us as we follow Him daily. Does the treasure of your heart line up with the riches of His grace? Even when nothing "spiritual" seems to be happening, many around you are watching to see where your actions and words are pointing (James 2:14-22). If I followed the direction of your life today, would I arrive in the arms of Christ?

Father, line up my innermost thoughts with Your treasure in Jesus Christ. Let my actions and attitudes point clearly to Him. In Jesus' name, amen.

Matt. 5:16 Prov. 21:2-3 Col. 3:8-17

RIVER OF GOD   December 20

The river of God is full of water.

Ps. 65:9

"There is a river whose streams shall make glad the city of God" (Ps. 46:4). The river of God is full. We can study it from the shore or design boats to float on it, but to live wet with its power, we must get in and swim. When our hands are covered with the river, our touch will always carry that living water to others. Our prayers will be full of the life of God. To only wade in the river, half in and half out, makes it possible to touch people, but with a dry hand. Those close to shore can dip and sip, but they're not covered with the water of life. In Ezekiel 47, the invitation is to come in deep enough to swim, to enter the river of God's power. When you bend to the flow of the water and let it carry you, all of your life moves in the life of God.

If you stay on the shore or in a boat, you can watch the river, but your life is not covered by the power of God's refreshing presence. Get clear in! Let go of what keeps you grounded in worldly things, and His waters will carry you where only He can go. Some prefer a boat, thinking they can direct it over the water. But a boat, even of religious design, is mainly for self-preservation and hauling what we can control. Instead, enter God's river through the cross, the blood of Jesus poured out to cover us. Resting in His power, we're carried into God's new creation (John 1:12-16; Matt. 26:26-29).

It is possible to ride all day in a big boat of your design and never get wet in the river that conveys you. Some think the boat is the river and miss direct contact with the deep movement of God's life and His refreshing presence. Eventually, the boat will be tied up to rot away, but the river flows on into the ocean of eternity in Christ. Where will you get in? Probably in a valley. In the mountains, the river is too swift and the bank too steep; but in a valley, there are low, humble places to enter. Don't just put in a toe—enter in complete obedience. Bend to the flow, and let it lift you off your feet.

Once in the river, you're hardly recognizable, covered in the shining garment of living water. Those who wade are still recognizable to the world, able to share in shore-side activities. But in swimming, your life is streamlined; your hands are empty to be filled only with the life of God. Immersed, you won't follow the world's conversation. When you reach out a hand to help others, it's covered with life-giving water, fresh from the source.

Those in boats may try to "rescue" you or run you down. On the surface they can reach you, but as a swimmer, you can go deep, and they will pass on. Go deep where the cross has already gone, and you will live in the stream that makes glad the city of God.

Father, bring me deep enough in Christ to swim fully in Your life. In His name, amen.

John 7:37-39   Matt. 3:11-17   Jer. 2:13

December 21

~~~~~~

YOU FIRST

Whenever I reach for people, O God, let it be only after I reach for You first in Your Son. Your are our Source and our Savior. Keep my eyes on You and bring me deeper into Your grace and power which flow into eternity. In Jesus' name, amen.

"Thus says the Lord who made it, the Lord who formed it to establish it (the Lord is His name): 'Call to Me, and I will answer you, and show you great and mighty things, which you do not know.'"

Jer. 33:2-3

1 Cor. 1:22—3:7

~~~~~~

DEFEATING DECEPTION December 22

"The truth shall make you free."

John 8:32

Deception, that old trap, is subtle enough to pass for good, yet it harbors evil. We can ask God to uncover and remove it and then work His truth and love firmly in us. Prayer will show what must be removed from our lives so that His Word can go in more deeply. Repentance is the first step, then action.

Consider that deception is not a concept we can fight with our minds but a tool of an enemy stronger than we are. Our minds alone will not be able to combat it. Only our Savior in His death and resurrection has conquered this enemy. Receive the sacrificial life of Christ living in you now! Be ready to lay aside anything He does not want and take up anything He calls you to do. If there is a hint of reluctance anywhere, look for deception in that area. It will not always come from outside; some deception comes from within us, but all of it lives to die in a self-centered nature that would be its own god.

Like a road map, God's Word leads us through the maze of deceptive images from our culture and personal sin. Filling our lives with Him is the best defense. If our lives are full of the presence of Jesus Christ, no lie can stay.

Focus on God first, then people. The love of God will never lead us astray. Worldly love of people will. "Love" by itself is not enough because human sentiment can be confused, manipulated, and substituted for the true sacrificial love of Christ that raises us beyond human dimensions into the love of God. Our truest love of people comes only through loving God first. The best gift we give to others is to love them for who they are to God, not just to us (Mark 12:28-31, John 17:23).

Walk in love and simplicity according to God's plan. Born in humility, true simplicity is a defense, giving God room to work and make changes we could never do on our own. It's not that our lives must be perfectly arranged, but we must let Him arrange them for His pleasure and occupy us fully with His love, His plans, and His ability. Too much of our busyness, often in good causes, takes the focus off our Lord's beauty shining here and robs us of the time to enjoy it (Matt. 5:6-8).

Make any situation an offering to Him. Would God accept your handling of your situation as it is now as an offering to Him? What must change in order for it to be an acceptable offering to God? Consider each area of your life, and offer all to Him. Make the changes and smell the sweet aroma of Christ's love on the altar now. The holy fire of His sacrifice will burn clean and true (Eph. 5:1-2).

Father, cleanse me of all deception so I can see Your face. In Jesus' name, amen.

Eph. 6:10-18, 23-24   John 17:11-21   Luke 4:1-12

A WEEK IN ROME
December 23

"We have no king but Caesar!"

John 19:15

The Rome of old is in ruins, yet many of its habits persist in today's world. How closely do our lives this week fit the pattern of first-century Rome? In the time of Christ, the Romans centered their lives on their famous elite, ruling dynasties, money, sports, success, entertainment, wealth, and dependency on the state's power, including emperor worship. Religion, for them, was designed to uphold the commercial and social engine of the state with a human leader as its head and human wisdom as its law.

Though we think we are more advanced, if many of our current interests were put into an early Roman format, the similarities would be striking. Bread and circuses are easily translated into pleasure, money, and entertainment to anesthetize the masses. Our lives today come very close to imitating Rome in terms of desiring expensive homes and hobbies, violent entertainment, marketing strategies to match every desire, and worship of human ability and pleasure. What pattern does your life follow? Do your actions this week make you culturally a citizen of ancient Rome?

Concerning the crucifixion of Christ, does the pattern of your priorities indicate you would be standing with the successful citizens of Rome and those who agreed with them, or with the fishermen of Galilee? What would have to change in terms of lifestyle to put you clearly on the (apparently losing) side of Christ? The religious leaders of Christ's day really wanted the approval of the Romans and the crowds more than they wanted the simple, eternal truth of God's resurrection power. That's why the Rome of old is gone, and Christ is alive today with followers all around the world (Heb. 13:12-14, 20-21).

Unable or unwilling to worship God alone in spirit and in truth, the religious elite preferred to honor and worship a human leader, perhaps one they could manipulate. The Roman governor Pontius Pilate was persuaded to eliminate anything that did not agree with the worship of Caesar, the exaltation of man. The city's elite sought to stabilize the local power structure of one who asked, "What is truth?" Each day, in actions and attitudes, our lives put us either clearly in the camp of Rome or clearly with Christ, crucified outside the camp of this world, on our way to the city not made with hands. Where do you stand today?

Father, I want to be a citizen of heaven and Your new creation, not a citizen of the fallen Rome of this world. Make my life line up with Your kingdom and its eternal power. In Jesus' name, amen.

Mark 12:41-44   John 18:36-40   John 20:13-18

December 24

SMALL ENOUGH

Lord, make me small enough to let You complete Your will in me. Under Your reign, forgive me for trying to make my problems bigger than You or my desires bigger than the pleasure of Your company, the balance of Your law, and the joy of Your salvation working in us. Turn me from the big things of this world to the small things of Your much greater kingdom. Make me Your humble servant so I can know the power of the King. Lead me to the little spring of simple work done in Your creative joy that flows into the river of eternity. Open me to the width and height of the love of Christ on the cross by making me small enough to go there with Him and not run away when the giants of this world begin to shout. In the little path of hidden beauty and hunger for righteousness, lead me to the gate of heaven for those who will come as a child. Form me small enough in Your hand to pass through the eye of a needle and follow Your purpose here, one stitch at a time. Let me see Your glory that is invisible to those who seek their own. In this place, make me small enough to sit beside Your manger quietly and not block the view of Your coming here. In Jesus' name, amen.

"He must increase, but I must decrease."

John 3:30

Matt. 5:3-10

TRUTH AS A PERSON   December 25

"For as the Father has life in Himself, so He has granted the Son to have life in Himself."

John 5:26

Truth is real and can be proven by experience because truth is a Person seeking a direct relationship with us. Truth lives in our Creator's very being, creative beyond our grasp, not just in words on paper. Continually, His existence is expressed in sacrificial love moving from before time through the creation we know to a new creation in the gift of life in His Son. Jesus Christ comes here to bring us to God, whom our sin has rejected. Even our existence depends on His, including the free will to choose or reject Him. Freely, God gives us the opportunity to reject or accept His life forever (John 14:5-6).

The truth of a person, what one's core reality is, can be evaluated completely only in a relationship. Information from a distance is not enough. Since this truth is a Person, evaluating His claim, rejecting or accepting His offer, can fairly be done only through knowing the Person firsthand in daily experience. Anything else is hearsay.

To really refuse Him, you must get to know Him first, and then you will be making an objective decision. Everything else is just guesswork, information about what someone else believes. Since all of creation is currently involved in His decision to give Himself for you, all of you, past, present, and future, is currently involved in your decision about that gift of life. To test whether it is true or not requires more than analysis of secondhand information. It requires opening your heart to make room for new birth. Honest hunger for new life will be answered (John 6:37-40).

To be directly objective, your decision must be based on a personal relationship with God through His Son, not just information about Him or what someone else has said or done. Try the Living Christ, not the ideas people have accumulated. Ask Him, not them. It will take some effort to find the core of reality discovered by those who walk with Him. Following His teaching for a while allows you to see for yourself whether truth multiplies along the way. Until you receive Him in daily life, you'll never know where that truth might lead or the clear face of amazing grace, the joy of returning to the root of forgiveness, or the power of stepping into eternity free.

Father, reveal Your truth to me in the way You choose and help me to walk wherever You lead. Open me to know Your Son's life directly. In Jesus' name, amen.

John 1:10-13   Luke 2:8-15   John 20:24-31

MYSTERY OF COMMUNION December 26

And as they were eating, Jesus took bread, blessed and broke it, and gave it to the disciples and said, "Take, eat; this is My body." Then He took the cup, and gave thanks, and gave it to them, saying, "Drink from it, all of you. For this is My blood of the new covenant, which is shed for many for the remission of sins."

Matt. 26:26-28

The mystery of communion is one we cannot explain but we can receive. In Christ, the spiritual becomes physical, and the physical becomes spiritual — not in two separate entities but one. That is the whole point of the incarnation, the whole motive of the cross, the whole miracle of the resurrection, and the mercy of our participation in Christ's divine nature in the Lord's Supper. We receive this mystery with thanks! I find it useless to argue whether the earthly bread becomes His body or the wine His blood when both are both in the Son of Man, who is the Son of God. Trying to separate flesh from spirit or analyze what is beyond our grasp reduces divine life to human knowledge alone. Communion, like the resurrection, is beyond us and takes us beyond ourselves.

Jesus has come to our feast to change our water into the wine of His new covenant, as we can receive it by faith. As Emmanuel, He comes here, living with us through the Holy Spirit, as we receive Him — with a meal (Rev. 3:20)! Whatever He says to do, we must do, as at the wedding at Cana (John 2:1-11). To taste His new wine, we cannot say it is still water and only a concept. What He shed on the cross was more. Christ is the real gift, and He is here now, however we can receive Him. Participating in communion by receiving Christ is a sign we believe He is who He says He is.

As real today as at the Last Supper, the power of His gift permeates every area of our lives. If we are thirsty enough to let Christ do what only He can do, new life will appear, and our lives are changed in union with His. In receiving His life, He Himself, not our understanding, satisfies our thirst. Our communion is with His gift on the cross and also with His resurrection, as through the Holy Spirit we partake of who Christ is now. He wants us to receive Him and worship God in spirit and in truth (John 4:24).

In His power, we become one with Him and His family. Then our earthly feast becomes a foretaste of the wedding supper of the Lamb, who was slain from the foundation of the world to open to us the life of His kingdom on His terms, not ours. In a covenant meal, let us enter even what we cannot understand and drink all of what He has given us.

Lord God, bring me into full communion with the life of Your Son Jesus Christ through His body and blood given for me. Make me a new creation in the new covenant You have planned and sealed by the Holy Spirit. In Jesus' name, amen.

Heb. 10:19-22　　　　　　　1 Cor. 11:23-27　　　　　　　John 6:47-57

December 27

REMEMBER

Father, forgive me for forgetting You when You have always remembered me, even before I knew You. Each day, I will remember who You are, not just what You can do. Help me to walk in obedience as my life grows in Yours through Jesus Christ who comes. No matter what I have done or how far I have strayed, thank You for remembering me in Your kingdom today through Your Son. In Jesus' name, amen.

And He took bread, gave thanks and broke it, and gave it to them, saying, "This is My body which is given for you; do this in remembrance of Me. . . . But he [Peter] said to Him, "Lord, I am ready to go with You, both to prison and to death." Then He said, "I tell you, Peter, the rooster shall not crow this day before you will deny three times that you know Me."

Luke 22:19, 33-34

Rev. 1:7—2:7

HE SHINES THROUGH   December 28

The people who walked in darkness have seen a great light; those who dwelt in the land of the shadow of death, upon them a light has shined.

Isa. 9:2

The light of God can shine through, penetrate, and change anything in this world. There is no wall, no idea, no sin that can stop it, because the Creator's power, even His very essence, moves in the light of His holy life. He shines through even the thickest problems, where words alone or human effort cannot penetrate. In a moment, God's presence can do more to heal, convict, and renew than all of our efforts over a period of years. Even after we analyze and rearrange it, our darkness is still incomplete. Darkness is the absence of light, not something that holds light back once it appears (John 1:4-5).

Once the light is seen, once the light enters a room, the darkness must flee before it, just as every evil thing retreats before the light of God's power. Often when we want Him to do something, we think our faults or the walls others have built will block the way. Ask His light to shine through them, just as they are now, penetrating and changing everything to match His will. In all of creation, there is nothing the Creator, the Father of Lights, cannot shine through, once the door is open in prayer.

If we ask, His light penetrates, even though some will run and hide from it. Eventually, the light will find them. This shining may be instant or slow and steady, but its advance and overcoming power is unstoppable. Like ice melting in the sun, old walls come down and cold hearts begin to change. Be sure He is shining in your life before you ask Him to shine into someone else's situation. It is crucial not only to know about God but also to let Him shine into your life through Christ, changing you in His Son so that you receive more of His presence and power than human knowledge alone can convey. Studying His Word is good. Shining with His presence completes it.

Receiving Him through the beauty of the light of His presence is similar to spending time with loved ones, looking at them face to face and listening, instead of merely studying photographs. When we pray for someone with our mind to change that person's mind, we work only on surface images. Instead, ask God to shine His presence directly into you and them deeply, changing both of you personally by the Holy Spirit to reveal our Lord, who comes to live in us today. Don't worry about what to say. When you get out of the way, He shines through.

Father, shine the power of Your presence into our hearts, and open us to what only You can do. Penetrate our darkness with the light of Jesus Christ. In Jesus' name, amen.

John 12:44-50   2 Cor. 4:6-10   Eph. 5:8-21

YOUR SON LIVES
December 29

Jesus said to him, "Go your way; your son lives." So the man believed the word that Jesus spoke to him, and he went his way.

John 4:50

At the point of greatest need, Jesus still speaks life to us today. Whatever the urgency or the difficulty, He will speak the truth with power to make His promise rise up in our lives, according to His will. Receiving that answer depends on belief and obedience. Before we can see an answer, we must turn toward it in our hearts and actions. This man believed the word of life and acted accordingly. He didn't stay for a third round of begging and pleading. He didn't scoff at the simplicity of Jesus' command or debate the details of Jesus' authority. He believed and went directly to receive His answer. Our actions also should be taking us to the place of the Lord's answer.

After you ask today for your answer, do you believe Jesus' word of life and follow His directions to receive it? "Go your way; your son lives," said the Master, and the willing servant turned toward home to receive the impossible. "Go your way; your son lives," says the Master today to those who will ask, obey, and turn toward what only He can do. If you will, He will.

Lord, I've done a lot of asking. Now help me to believe and obey Your will, turning my whole life toward what is impossible for me but possible for You. In Jesus' name, amen.

Matt. 19:26   John 5:5-9   Titus 2:13-14

December 30

YOUR WAY, IN YOUR TIME

Father God, everything that comes to pass is only temporary, while You, O Lord, live and reign forever. So my life is in Your hand. You are the only One who knows the whole plan of creation and completes it for eternity. Through the blood of Jesus, remove anything in me that prevents me from living in Your creative pattern. In Your mercy, move me Your way, in Your time. In Jesus' name, amen.

But as for me, I trust in You, O Lord; I say, "You are my God." My times are in Your hand; deliver me from the hand of my enemies, and from those who persecute me. Make Your face shine upon Your servant; save me for Your mercies' sake.

Ps. 31:14-16

Acts 1:1-11

THE CROSS OF CREATION   December 31

. . . knowing that you were not redeemed with corruptible things, like silver or gold, from your aimless conduct received by tradition from your fathers, but with the precious blood of Christ, as of a lamb without blemish and without spot. He indeed was foreordained before the foundation of the world, but was manifest in these last times for you who through Him believe in God, who raised Him from the dead and gave Him glory, so that your faith and hope are in God.

1 Pet. 1:18-21

Since the cross of Christ was planned from the foundation of the world, it affects every molecule of creation. It was not simply a human act of sacrifice but a divine reconciliation of all things in earth and heaven according to the Creator's plan. The cross is in effect now as much as on the day Jesus Christ was nailed to it, and its power will continue into the future (Ps. 90:4; Col. 1:12-20; Matt. 17:18-20; Rom. 8:16-25; Eph. 1:10; Rev. 1:7-8). That is why a mountain, spiritual or physical, will move in Christ's name.

The cross is in effect now as much as it was when Christ died, and its outpouring of sacrificial love will continue past all limits of history. Where do you live in relation to that cross, the active one? Many believe in the cross of two thousand years ago without considering its application to the next moment of their daily lives or its power to solve current problems. The cross of Christ not only paid the penalty for sin once but also conquered the daily grind of sin and so leads us out of selfish dead ends and into resurrection power at work even now.

Each step we take is not only a step out of sin, but also a step into the new life God has created for each one who will receive His Son alive through the Holy Spirit. He came then to give us freedom now. The Creator sends His Spirit to lead us through each day that He has designed. It's our part to actively receive what God has planned and walk through the door He has opened in Christ, serving others as our Savior did (Matt. 25:37-40). All creation hinges on that opening and waits to be renewed through Christ, the Living Word. It's the same Word by which God began creation and started the sequence of days that we busily fill on our calendars. Apply the cross of creation to your plans for today. Each molecule moves in God's power.

Father, teach me how to live in the power of Christ's cross and resurrection. Create in me a clean heart and a right spirit to do what You have planned today and forever. In Jesus' name, amen.

Gen. 1:26—2:7   John 1:1-14   Eph. 1:3-7, 17-23

INDEX

By Title of Devotion with Date and Main Scripture

(P) Prayer as main text of devotion
* Part of a series, each with same number of *

Open Door	January 1	John 14:23
Originator, The	November 24	Gen. 1:26-28
Our Own Righteousness	October 30	Rom. 10:3 ***
Over the Waters	May 23	Ps. 29:3 *

P

Pain's Perfume	September 11	Song of Sol. 2:1-2
Partakers	August 23	2 Peter 1:2-4
Pass the Test	October 18	Luke 4:1-2
Passover Door, The	March 1	Exod. 12:7
Passover Seasonal Page	Before March 1	
Peace and Justice	June 17	Matt. 7:7
Peace Now	May 19	John 14:27
Pentecost Seasonal Page	Before June 1	
Pillars at the Door	August 1	1 Kings 7:21-22
Point, The	December 19	Matt. 13:44
Point of His Presence, The	June 23	Phil. 2:5-7
Power in Persecution	November 8	Phil. 3:10-11
Powerful Voice, The	May 24	Ps. 29:4 *
Praise First	May 18	Ps. 50:23
Praise to Praise	June 5	John 7:38
Pray in Action	January 3	Matt. 21:28-31
Preferred Life, The	July 17	John 1:12-13
Present Christ, The	June 26	Matt. 28:20
Press Toward the Mark	September 28	Phil. 3:13-14
Pressed Down, Shaken Together	May 16	Luke 6:38
Progress Moves	November 21	Isa. 43:18-19
Proof of Love	September 2	John 15:13
Pull Over	November 5	Heb. 4:9-10
Pure Treasure (P)	July 10	Matt. 13:44

R

Reach Here	May 15	John 20:27
Reality of Humility	October 14	James 4:6
Reality of the Cross (P)	July 13	Col. 1:16-20
Recreate Me (P)	June 8	John 3:5-7
Rejoice Always	October 12	Phil. 4:4
Remember (P)	December 27	Luke 22:19 *****
Remove the Veil (P)	October 4	2 Cor. 3:16-18
Rest a While (P)	June 4	Mark 6:31
Rest and Repentance	October 10	Matt. 8:7
Rest and Revelation (P)	June 6	Song of Sol. 2:10-13
Rest from Above (P)	March 20	Ps. 131
Rest of Obedience	June 9	Matt. 11:28
Rest to Run	July 3	Heb. 12:1

NOTES

Now we exhort you, brethren, warn those who are unruly, comfort the fainthearted, uphold the weak, be patient with all. See that no one renders evil for evil to anyone, but always pursue what is good both for yourselves and for all.

Rejoice always, pray without ceasing, in everything give thanks; for this is the will of God in Christ Jesus for you. Do not quench the Spirit. Do not despise prophecies. Test all things; hold fast what is good. Abstain from every form of evil.

Now may the God of peace Himself sanctify you completely; and may your whole spirit, soul, and body be preserved blameless at the coming of our Lord Jesus Christ. He who calls you is faithful, who also will do it.

1 Thess. 5:14-24

ORDER INFORMATION

To order additional copies of this book, contact your local bookstore or the following:

Xulon Press   866-909-2665 book line or 866-381-2665 store orders
Suite 2140
2180 West State Rd. 434
Longwood, FL 32779

bookorder@xulonpress.com

Or Christianbook.com, Amazon.com, Borders.com,

Or send printed name, address, and check for price printed on back cover to:

Prairie Wind Communications
P.O. Box 764
Salina, KS 67402-0764

_____
_____
_____
_____
_____

Printed in the United States
144170LV00002BA/2/P

9 781606 478035